Kluwer Law International

Reverse Discrimination in EC Law

Alina Tryfonidou

Wolters Kluwer
Law & Business

AUSTIN BOSTON CHICAGO NEW YORK THE NETHERLANDS

Published by:
Kluwer Law International
PO Box 316
2400 AH Alphen aan den Rijn
The Netherlands
Website: www.kluwerlaw.com

Sold and distributed in North, Central and South America by:
Aspen Publishers, Inc.
7201 McKinney Circle
Frederick, MD 21704
United States of America
Email: customer.care@aspenpubl.com

Sold and distributed in all other countries by:
Turpin Distribution Services Ltd.
Stratton Business Park
Pegasus Drive, Biggleswade
Bedfordshire SG18 8TQ
United Kingdom
Email: kluwerlaw@turpin-distribution.com

Printed on acid-free paper.

ISBN 978-90-411-2751-8

Printed in Great Britain.

Reverse Discrimination in EC Law

EUROPEAN MONOGRAPHS

Editor-in-chief Professor David O'Keeffe

In this series *European Monographs* this book *Reverse Discrimination in EC Law* is the sixty-fourth title. *The titles published in this series are listed at the end of this volume.*

For my Family

Table of Contents

Chapter 3
The Court's New Approaches to a Link with EC Law: Responding to the Problems of the Traditional Approach 63

Acknowledgements

This work arises out of a doctoral thesis written at King's College London. This book would not have been possible without the support of a number of people. I would first of all like to express my deep gratitude to Professor David O'Keeffe, the editor of the Kluwer European Monographs series, for his continued encouragement and support. I would also like to thank two of my colleagues at the University of Leicester, Professor Robin White and Professor Erika Szyszczak, the former for his advice during the early stages of preparing this book, the latter for reading a previous draft of the book and offering incisive and constructive comments. A great debt is also owed to Mr Karel van der Linde, publishing manager at Kluwer, for being so patient and efficient in dealing with all my queries. Finally, but not least, I must express my heartfelt gratitude to my family, to whom I dedicate this book.

Alina Tryfonidou
Leicester, September 2008

List of Abbreviations

All E R	All England Law Reports
AJCL	American Journal of Comparative Law
ARIEL	Austrian Review of International and European Law
CEE(s)	Charge(s) having equivalent effect to customs duties
CEPS	Centre for European Policy Studies
CJEL	Columbia Journal of European Law
CLJ	Cambridge Law Journal
CLP	Common Legal Problems
CMLR	Common Market Law Reports
CMLRev	Common Market Law Review
CYELS	Cambridge Yearbook of European Legal Studies
EBLRev	European Business Law Review
EC	European Community
ECJ	European Court of Justice
ECR	European Court Reports
ECSC	European Coal and Steel Community
EEC	European *Economic* Community
EIPA	European Institute of Public Administration
EIoP	European Integration Online Papers
EJML	European Journal of Migration and Law
ELJ	European Law Journal
ELRev	European Law Review
EPL	European Public Law
ERPL	European Review of Private Law
EU	European Union
Fordham Int'l LJ	Fordham International Law Journal
GLJ	German Law Journal

ICEL	Irish Centre for European Law
ICLQ	International and Comparative Law Quarterly
IJCLLIR	International Journal of Comparative Labour Law and Industrial Relations
IJEL	Irish Journal of European Law
ILJ	Industrial Law Journal
IR	Irish Reports
JCMS	Journal of Common Market Studies
JEPP	Journal of European Public Policy
JSSL	Journal of Social Security Law
JSWFL	Journal of Social Welfare and Family Law
KCLJ	King's College Law Journal
LIEI	Legal Issues of European Integration/Legal Issues of Economic Integration
LS	Legal Studies
MEP	Member of the European Parliament
MEQR(s)	Measure(s) having equivalent effect to quantitative restrictions
MJ	Maastricht Journal of European and Comparative Law
MLR	Modern Law Review
OJ	Official Journal of the European Communities
OJLS	Oxford Journal of Legal Studies
OUP	Oxford University Press
Riv dir Internaz	Rivista di Diritto Internazionale
SEA	Single European Act
TEU	Treaty on European Union ('Maastricht Treaty')
TFEU	Treaty on the Functioning of the European Union
YEL	Yearbook of European Law

Chapter 1
Introduction

I INTRODUCTION

This work is a study of the problem of reverse discrimination in EC law. In particular, the question that this book aims to answer is whether reverse discrimination emerging in the context of the Community's internal market policy, is still a permissible form of differential treatment in the Community.

The term 'discrimination' always has a negative connotation. Discrimination is not, merely, differential treatment. It is differential treatment of similar situations that is not justified. It is the use of the term in the context of anti-discrimination law and, in particular, that of sex and racial equality, that is mostly known amongst laymen. In the twentieth century, as a result of the action of various political and human rights movements, it became generally acknowledged that it is inherently bad to differentiate between groups of persons, if the *only* ground on which the differential treatment is based is an immutable characteristic such as sex, colour or race. It is considered to be blatantly wrong to treat a group of persons more harshly than others, just because they possess a characteristic which cannot be changed and for which they cannot be held responsible. It is only if the differentiation is grounded on some other (acceptable) criterion and merely happens to disadvantage a particular group of persons who share a certain characteristic, that is considered to be justified and thus can escape the characterization of 'discrimination'.

Certain characteristics are the 'usual suspects' for turning instances of differential treatment into discrimination; in other words, persons who carry those characteristics usually form a group which is 'expected' to be discriminated against, even though this is totally wrong. In the context of EC anti-discrimination law, apart from sex which has, since the genesis of this Community policy, been considered to be a prohibited ground for differentiation,[1] recently-drafted pieces of secondary legislation enlist race,[2] religion or belief, age, disability and sexual orientation[3] as the grounds which turn differential treatment into discrimination prohibited by EC law.[4]

In the context of the Community's internal market policy, it is 'expected' that Member States will be inclined to favour their own nationals and products, as opposed to imported products and nationals of other Member States coming to their territory to work. This is problematic, not so much because it is unfair and unjust, but because it hinders the achievement of the Community's important aim of establishing an internal market among the Member States of the EU. Accordingly, it is not surprising that some of the fundamental freedoms provisions of the EC Treaty (1957) explicitly include within their wording a prohibition of discrimination on the grounds of nationality of persons or of the origin of goods and, where this is not provided expressly, the Court has read those provisions as including such a prohibition.

The fundamental freedoms, however, have not been interpreted only as prohibiting discrimination on the grounds of nationality of persons or the origin of products – in other words, Member States do not merely have to extend the treatment they afford to their own nationals/goods to nationals of other Member States and imported goods. In certain instances, EC law requires Member States to apply to goods or nationals of other Member States who enter their territory in the process of exercising an economic activity, a more beneficial treatment than the one they apply to their own nationals or goods. It seems that the rationale behind this has been the desire of the Community to achieve substantive equality – by granting some 'extra benefits' to migrant economic actors/imported goods, Community law merely wishes to bring them to the same position as nationals/goods of the host State so that they will be able to effectively compete in the market of that State. In this way, economic actors are not deterred from exercising an inter-state economic activity. Hence, and borrowing the term used in the context of anti-discrimination law, in certain instances, EC law requires a form of 'positive action' in favour of products/persons engaged in cross-border economic activities, in order to achieve

1. *See* Art. 141 EC (Art. 157 TFEU) which prohibits discrimination based on sex as regards pay. There is, also, a long list of secondary legislation instruments prohibiting discrimination on the grounds of sex in matters having to do with employment and social security linked to employment. Most aspects of sex discrimination in employment are now dealt with by 2006/54 (EC) Directive on the implementation of the principle of equal opportunities and equal treatment of men and women in matters of employment and occupation (recast), OJ L 204/23, 2006. Certain aspects of sex discrimination such as pregnancy and parental leave continue to be dealt with in other Directives.
2. 2000/43 (EC) Directive implementing the principle of equal treatment between persons irrespective of racial or ethnic origin, OJ L 180/22, 2000.
3. 2000/78 (EC) Directive establishing a general framework for equal treatment in employment and occupation, OJ L 303/16, 2000.
4. It should be noted that the EC is somewhat limited in the heads of discrimination that it prohibits. It is not concerned with complex multiple discrimination or difficult areas discussed in human rights law and at the national level, such as social or birth discrimination which can often be linked and be causative factors for the recognized heads of discrimination.

real, substantive, equality between them and the nationals/products of the host State and, thus, facilitate the exercise of cross-border economic activities.[5]

Discrimination is characterized as 'reverse', when an unexpected group of persons (or products) is treated less favourably than a group of persons (or products) that is normally treated less beneficially.[6] In instances where EC law requires a Member State to treat imported products or nationals of other Member States more beneficially than its own, reverse discrimination emerges, since an unexpected group of persons/products (i.e., nationals of that Member State and domestic products) is treated less favourably than a group of persons/products (nationals and products of other Member States) that is normally treated less beneficially.[7] Reverse discrimination has been considered to be a problem both by persons who have suffered as a result of its emergence and by some commentators and members of the Court of Justice. The question, therefore, has always been whether this form of differential treatment should be prohibited by EC law.

The aim of this chapter is to present the problem of reverse discrimination which arises as a result of the implementation of the Community's policy on the internal market. We will start by presenting the root-cause of reverse discrimination (i.e., the purely internal rule); and we will then move on to provide a further explanation of the notion of reverse discrimination and the problems arising from its emergence. The chapter will conclude with a presentation of the methodology used in conducting the research for this study, as well as the structure and methodology followed in writing the book.

II REVERSE DISCRIMINATION AND THE PURELY INTERNAL RULE

A The Origins of the Purely Internal Rule

The European *Economic* Community (EEC) was born in 1958, as the next logical step in the process of European integration after the creation of the European Coal

5. For an excellent analysis of the notion of 'positive action' and its implementation *see* N. Bamforth, M. Malik and C. O'Cinneide, *Discrimination Law: Theory and Context* (London, Sweet & Maxwell, 2008), Chs 6 and 7. Positive action has always been a central feature of the Community's anti-discrimination policy, this having been accepted both by the Court of Justice in its sex discrimination case-law and, more recently, by the Community legislature when promulgating pieces of secondary legislation. *See;* for example, *Kalanke v. Bremen*, Case No. C-450/93 [1995] ECR I-3051; *Marschall v. Land Nordrhein-Westfalen*, Case No. C-409/95 [1997] ECR I-6363; *Abrahamsson and Anderson v. Fogelqvist*, Case No. C-407/98 [2000] ECR I-5539. Art. 7 of Directive 2000/78, *supra* n. 3; Art. 5 of Directive 2000/43, *supra* n. 2; Art. 3 of Directive 2006/54, *supra* n. 1. *See*, also, Art. 141(4) EC (Art. 157(4) TFEU)); and Art. 23(2) of the (not yet binding) Charter of Fundamental Rights of the European Union, OJ C 303/1, 2007.
6. G. Davies, *Nationality Discrimination in the European Internal Market* (The Hague, Kluwer Law International, 2003), p. 19.
7. Staples has argued that reverse discrimination is discrimination caused by positive action in favour of EC free movers – *see* H. Staples, *The Legal Status of Third Country Nationals Resident in the European Union* (The Hague, Kluwer Law International, 1999), p. 15.

and Steel Community (ECSC) six years before. The latter formed the first model of supranational cooperation in Europe, following the devastation that the Second World War had left behind. The new, broader, form of supranational cooperation in Europe which was brought under the umbrella of the EEC had, as its main task, the creation of a single, common, market between the States that were the signatories to that Treaty. In other words,

> [T]o merge the national markets into a single market bringing about conditions as close as possible to those of a genuine internal market.[8]

For a single market to be built, freedom of movement of goods, services,[9] persons and capital between the States that form part of that market must be safeguarded. Labour must be free to move to the State where there is a surge in demand and thus is most valued, so that optimal allocation of resources is ensured; firms and traders established in a State that is part of that market, must be able to export their products to other States in order to expand their economic activities and, eventually, increase their profits by taking advantage of economies of scale; and there must be freedom to invest capital in the State which is more likely to allow investors to reap a substantial profit. Therefore, the drafters of the EEC Treaty included within it a number of provisions which, in effect, prohibited the

---

8. *Gaston Schul Douane-Expediteur BV v. Inspecteur der Invoerrechten en Accijnzen*, Case No. 15/81 [1982] ECR 1409, para. 33. The term 'internal market' has been predominantly used since the late 1980s as a result of the amendments made to the EEC Treaty by the Single European Act. According to Art. 14(2) EC (Art. 26(2) TFEU), the internal market is 'an area without internal frontiers in which the free movement of goods, persons, services and capital is ensured in accordance with the provisions of this Treaty'. A Treaty interpretation has not been provided for the terms 'single' and 'common' market. It should be noted that throughout the book, I will use the terms 'internal market', 'single market' and 'common market' interchangeably. For a brief explanation of these terms *see* K. Mortelmans, 'The Common Market, the Internal Market and the Single Market, What's in a market?' (1998) 35 *CMLRev* 101, 107-108. Some scholars differentiate between these terms. *See*, for instance, L. Gormley, 'Competition and Free Movement: Is the Internal Market the Same as a Common Market?' (2002) 13 *EBLRev* 517; P. Pescatore, 'Some critical remarks on the "Single European Act"' (1987) 24 *CMLRev* 11; L. Gormley, 'The internal market: history and evolution', in *Regulating the Internal Market*, N. Nic Shuibhne (ed.) (Cheltenham, Northampton, Edward Elgar, 2006), p. 14. Other scholars prefer to treat them as synonymous. *See*, for example, C. Barnard, *The Substantive Law of the EU: The Four Freedoms* (2nd edn, Oxford, OUP, 2007), p. 12; R. Barents, 'The Internal Market Unlimited: Some observations on the legal basis of Community legislation' (1993) 30 *CMLRev* 85, 102-105. The latter approach has also been adopted by the Court of Justice: *Polydor v. Harlequin*, Case No. 270/80 [1982] ECR 329, para. 16; *France v. Commission*, Case No. C-41/93 [1994] ECR I-1829, para. 19; *Commission v. UK (Indications of origin)*, Case No. 207/83 [1985] ECR 1201, para. 17. It should be noted that when the Lisbon Treaty (Treaty of Lisbon amending the Treaty on European Union and the Treaty establishing the European Community, OJ C 306/1, 2007) comes into force, all references to the 'common market' in the Treaties will be replaced by the words 'internal market'.
9. It should be noted that the term 'product(s)' can be used to refer collectively to goods; and services which can be provided without the need for the provider to move.

imposition of obstacles to the free (inter-state) movement of goods, services, workers and capital.

Towards the end of the 1980s and during the 1990s, the EC[10] had witnessed an unprecedented outburst of legislative activity and, more fundamentally, Treaty amendment. The Single European Act (1986) and the Treaties of Maastricht (1992) and Amsterdam (1997) have been the three main steps that led to the metamorphosis of the Community, from a EEC of limited, and purely economic, aims to a European Community with broader concerns and goals, which forms the central pillar of the newly-founded EU. However, even though a number of lofty aims and principles have been added to Article 2 of the EC Treaty,[11] and even though the list of the activities of the Community – as provided in Article 3 EC[12] – has been extraordinarily stretched as a result of the above constitutional amendments, the completion and maintenance of the single market continues to be one of the most important aims of the Community.

Therefore, the provisions of the EC Treaty still require that the free movement of goods (Articles 28 and 29),[13] self-employed persons (Article 43),[14] services (Article 49),[15] workers (Article 39)[16] and capital (Article 56)[17] is ensured between the Member States of the EU. Hence, in the European internal market, persons, products and capital can move freely between the Member States and these kinds of movement have been considered to be so important for the construction of this market that they have been termed the '*fundamental* freedoms'.[18] And, not only that but, more importantly, the fundamental freedoms provisions have been held to

10. It should be noted that, following the coming into force of the Treaty of Lisbon (*supra* n. 8), the European *Community* will be replaced by the European *Union* and, therefore, all references to the EC will have to be read as 'EU'.
11. Following the coming into force of the Lisbon Treaty, *supra* n. 8, this provision will be repealed and, in substance, replaced by the new Art. 3 TEU.
12. Following the coming into force of the Lisbon Treaty, *supra* n. 8, this provision will be repealed and, in substance, replaced by Arts 3 to 6 TFEU.
13. Articles 34 and 35 TFEU, respectively.
14. Article 39 TFEU.
15. Article 56 TFEU.
16. Article 45 TFEU.
17. Article 63 TFEU.
18. This phrase has been extensively used by the Court in its case-law. *See*, for instance, *Canal Satélite Digital SL v. Administracíon General del Estato*, Case No. C-390/99 [2002] ECR I-607, paras 28-30; *Criminal proceedings against Heinonen*, Case No. C-394/97 [1999] ECR I-3599, para. 38; *Criminal proceedings against Placanica, Palazzese and Sorricchio*, Joined Cases C-338/04, C-359/04 and C-360/04 [2007] ECR I-1891, para. 68. It should be noted that Arts 28 EC (Art. 34 TFEU), 29 EC (Art. 35 TFEU), 39 EC (Art. 45 TFEU), 43 EC (Art. 49 TFEU), 49 EC (Art. 56 TFEU) and 56 EC (Art. 63 TFEU) will throughout the whole of this book be collectively referred to as the 'fundamental freedoms provisions', unless specific mention needs to be made to one or more of those provisions. It should, also, be noted that in this book, contrary to the Court's practice and for reasons of clarity, the right provided in Art. 18 EC (Art. 21 TFEU) will not be referred to as one of the fundamental freedoms, but rather merely as one of the citizenship provisions.

be directly effective and thus Member State nationals can rely on them before their national courts in order to challenge any impediment to free movement that is imposed by a Member State or even, sometimes, by a private person.[19]

However, the internal market is the construct of a supranational organization, and not that of a nation-state. Therefore, the Community's competence in this area is not as broad and unlimited, as would have been if this was one of the policies of a nation-state.

When States come together to form international/supranational organizations, they are vigilant in guarding their sovereignty, by giving away as few of their competences as possible, whilst the international/supranational organizations, on their part, need to be given sufficient competence to be able to achieve the common goal(s) for which their States-parties have come together in the first place. Therefore, boundaries always need to be placed between the scope of application of the international/supranational legal system and the scope of application of the legal systems of the States that form part of that organization.

This, of course, applies to the EC which is a supranational organization. The relationship between the EC and its Member States has always been characterized by the need to respect the autonomy of the national legal systems whilst ensuring adequate enforcement and effectiveness of EC law. As a response to the above, the EC has adopted a system of multi-level governance: some competences have traditionally been considered to be central to the sovereignty of the Member States and thus fall within their exclusive competence; other competences have been considered to fall within the exclusive realm of the Community; whereas in other areas, the EC and the Member States have a shared competence. Accordingly, the EC is not a State with unlimited powers in all fields, but a supranational organization with defined boundaries in its competence.

The restricted competence of the EC finds its expression in Article 5 of the EC Treaty,[20] according to which the Community shall act within the limits of the powers conferred upon it by the Treaty and of the objectives assigned to it therein. Although in the EC, as in other supranational organizations, the need to accurately define the boundaries of the scope of each level of governance exists, a definite line has never been drawn between the two levels of governance (i.e., national and supranational). Rather, there has always been a loose division between EC and Member State competence, and the pendulum of powers constantly swings back and forth between Member State and supranational level. Moreover, it has been left to the Court of Justice to draw the boundaries between the scope of application of EC law and national law. The Court has laid down a guiding principle for that purpose, according to which the provisions of the EC Treaty include within their

19. Article 39 EC (Art. 45 TFEU) has been held by the Court to be *both* horizontally and vertically directly effective, and thus can be relied on *both* against the State and against private persons (*see Angonese v. Cassa di Risparmio di Bolzano Spa*, Case No. C-281/98 [2000] ECR I-4139, paras 30-36).
20. Following the coming into force of the Lisbon Treaty (*supra* n. 8), this provision will be replaced, in substance, by the new Art. 5 TEU.

scope any situations that are connected with one or more of their aims, this, most often, being satisfied when a situation involves an impediment to the achievement of those aims.[21]

Following the above principle, the fundamental freedoms provisions should only be held applicable in situations which present a sufficient link with their aim. Therefore, and as will seen, it is not surprising that the Court has held that those provisions only apply to products and factors of production that have moved between Member States in the process of establishing a single European market and, more specifically, that they only prohibit the creation of an obstacle to the *inter-state* movement of products and factors of production. Yet, the application of this (limiting) principle in specific situations has not proved a very simple and straightforward exercise and questions as to the exact scope of application of the fundamental freedoms provisions have, quite frequently, arisen. In fact, this has increasingly been so in the last few decades as a result of the fact that the dividing line between inter-state economic activities and economic activities the effects of which are confined within one and the same Member State has become perilously thin. Therefore, as a response to the need to provide a clearer delimitation of the scope of application of the fundamental freedoms provisions, the Court of Justice has concocted, through its case-law from the 1970s onwards, a number of principles that were to be used when drawing the boundaries between the scope of application of EC law and Member State laws. The purely internal rule has been one such principle.

B THE PURELY INTERNAL RULE

The Court has made it clear through its rulings that all the fundamental freedoms provisions are directly effective and thus can be relied on by individuals before their national courts.[22] This has proved immensely important for the success of the Community's aim of establishing an internal market, since it is largely through cases brought by individuals before their national courts and referred

21. It should be noted that the term 'scope' of the Treaty has a broader meaning than the term 'competence'. *See*, for example, *Forcheri v. Belgium*, Case No. 152/82 [1983] ECR 2323, para. 17. In other words, even though the Community may not have competence in an area such as criminal law, nevertheless, a situation which involves an impediment to the achievement of the aims of the Treaty may fall within the scope of EC law even if it relates to that area. *See*, for example, *Criminal proceedings against Bickel and Franz*, Case No. C-274/96 [1998] ECR I-7637, para. 17.
22. *Union Royal Belge des Société de Football Association ASBL & others v. Bosman*, Case No. C-415/93 [1995] ECR I-4921 (workers); *Ianelli & Volpi v. Meroni*, Case No. 74/76 [1977] 2 CMLR 688 (goods); *Van Binsbergen v. Bestuur van de Bedrijfsvereniging voor de Metaalnijverheid*, Case No. 33/74 [1974] ECR 1299 (services); *Reyners v. Belgium*, Case No. 2/74 [1974] ECR 631 (establishment); *Criminal proceedings against Sanz de Lera*, Joined Cases C-163, 165 and 250/94 [1995] ECR I-4821 (capital).

to the European Court of Justice (ECJ) via the preliminary rulings procedure, that the most important principles in this area of law have been established.

Since the late 1970s, there have been a number of cases in which individuals have tried to rely on one of the fundamental freedoms, not against the host Member State (e.g., because it had imposed an obstacle to their freedom to move to its territory in the process of performing an economic activity), but also against their own State; and not only when their Member State of origin had imposed an obstacle to their freedom to move to other Member States for an economic purpose (or their freedom to export or import products to and from other Member States), but also, when no other State had been involved on the facts of the case.

One such situation was that in the *Saunders* case,[23] where a British national working in the United Kingdom was relying on Article 39 EC (Article 45 TFEU) before an English court claiming that the United Kingdom had acted contrary to that provision because it had imposed a restriction on her right to move freely *within its territory*. The national court, obviously being of the view that this case was very far removed from the aim of establishing a common market and from the specific aim of Article 39 EC (i.e., to enable Member State nationals to cross inter-state borders in order to be employed in other Member States), referred a question to the ECJ as to whether the situation was caught by the prohibition provided in that provision.

In reply to that question, the Court of Justice held that the situation fell outside the scope of Article 39 EC (Article 45 TFEU) because it was a *wholly internal* one. In its subsequent case-law, the Court made it clear that the purely internal is a cardinal principle to be used in delimiting the scope of *all* the fundamental freedoms provisions.[24]

However, how is it possible to determine whether a situation is a purely internal one? The purely internal rule provides that wholly internal situations fall outside the scope of the fundamental freedoms provisions and thus such situations have to be regulated at Member State level. Any situation which involves products or factors of production that are confined within the territory of their own Member State and which does not involve an impediment to the only aim of those provisions (i.e., the establishment of an internal market by ensuring the inter-state movement of products or factors of production), is considered to be purely internal to that Member State. In cases which are judged to be purely internal to a Member State, the traders and workers involved cannot rely on EC

23. *R v. Saunders*, Case No. 175/78 [1979] ECR 1129.
24. The case-law where this was established and further refined shall be examined in detail in the next chapter of the book. It should be noted that the purely internal rule does not apply only to Treaty Articles but also applies to secondary legislation which complements the fundamental freedoms provisions (unless, of course, it is provided that the legislation also applies to purely internal situations). *See Koua Poirrez v. Caisse d'allocations familiales de la region parisienne, substituée par la Caisse d'allocations familiales de la Seine-Saint-Denis*, Case No. C-206/91 [1992] ECR 6685, para. 11; *Fascicolo and Others v. Regione Puglia and others*, Joined Cases C-10/02 and C-11/02 [2004] ECR I-11107.

law as a source of rights or rules – their position will only be judged by the law of their own Member State.[25]

There are both textual and regulatory reasons behind the development of the purely internal rule.

The first, regulatory, reason has to do with the home State principle and the fact that the purely internal rule is clearly an expression of that principle. According to Bernard, '[t]he Court's vision of the internal market is characterized by regulatory pluralism rather than uniformity'[26] and thus the Community should not provide rules and standards for each and every economic activity that takes place within the common market. Rather, the Community legislature should only intervene by laying down centralized rules in situations where this system of regulatory pluralism fails. In such a system, it is always necessary to provide a principle which will determine the Member State that will be responsible for regulating the economic activities taking place in the internal market, this being necessary for preventing the imposition of a double regulatory burden on persons and products involved in cross-border economic activities.[27] Such a principle is also necessary for ensuring that a regulatory gap is not created in the internal market, since economic activities will always be regulated by one Member State.[28] The free movement case-law of the Court has established, for this purpose, the home State principle, according to which it is the Member State of establishment of persons or the State of production of products that has the competence to lay down the rules for the production of products in its territory and the economic activities of persons that are established within its territory.[29] The purely internal rule is clearly an application of the home State principle. In other words, by providing that the Community cannot interfere in situations that fall outside the scope of EC law as a result of the fact that they do not involve cross-border economic activities, the purely internal rule ensures that the home State is free to regulate in whatever way it considers appropriate the economic activities that take place within its territory.

25. It should be borne in mind that the issue of whether a situation is a purely internal one is mainly a question as to whether a Member State national can rely on EC law against his or her own Member State. For an explanation of this *see* A. Arnull, *The General Principles of EEC Law and the Individual* (London, Leicester, Leicester University Press, 1990), pp. 51 and 57. For an example of a situation in which a national of one Member State may be found to be in a purely internal situation and thus unable to rely on EC law against *another* Member State *see* para. 22 of the Opinion of Advocate General Jacobs in *Bickel and Franz, supra* n. 21. However, it should be kept in mind that the focus of this work will be on instances where a person who is found to be in a purely internal situation, cannot rely on EC law *against his or her Member State of origin because he or she is confined within the territory of that Member State.*
26. N. Bernard, 'Discrimination and Free Movement in EC Law' (1996) *ICLQ* 82, 102-103.
27. This arises when the host State requires migrant workers or the producers of imported products to comply with requirements which are burdensome, *even though they have already complied with (equivalent) requirements imposed by the laws of another Member State.*
28. L. Daniele, 'Non-discriminatory restrictions to the free movement of persons' (1997) 22 *ELRev* 191, 198-199.
29. For an explanation *see* N. Bernard, *supra* n. 26, 106.

The second reason behind the pronouncement of the purely internal rule is a textual one. The need to confine the scope of EC law to cross-border situations seems to have been inspired by the actual wording used in the EC Treaty. More specifically, the wording of (most of) the fundamental freedoms provisions of the EC Treaty[30] coupled with the application of the Court's teleological approach to interpretation, point to the need to ensure that only *cross-border* situations that involve an impediment to the achievement of the main aim of the free movement provisions (i.e., the creation of the internal market) should fall within the scope of those provisions.

In the subsequent part of this section, there will be a presentation of what I call 'the linking factor test' that has (implicitly) been developed by the Court in its case-law through the years, for determining whether a situation is purely internal to a Member State or whether it qualifies for EC protection.

C THE LINKING FACTOR TEST

The first express pronouncement on the issue of purely internal situations was made by the Court of Justice in 1979, in the well-known *Saunders* case.[31] In paragraph 11 of that judgment the Court, somewhat cryptically, stated that

> [T]he provisions of the Treaty on freedom of movement for workers cannot... be applied to situations which are wholly internal to a Member State, in other words, where there is no factor connecting them to any of the situations envisaged by Community law.

As will be seen in the next chapter of the book, despite the lack of clarity embedded in this statement, the Court has repeated it in its case-law in the context of all the fundamental freedoms. And although the Court has never specified exactly when a situation is considered to be 'wholly internal to a Member State', it has, through the years, provided some guidance in relation to the criteria to be used for distinguishing cross-border situations from purely internal ones.

The Court has established that a case presents a link with EC law when it involves the exercise of free movement from one Member State to another[32] which

---

30. *See* the wording of Arts 28 EC (34 TFEU), 29 EC (35 TFEU), 43 EC (49 TFEU), 49 EC (56 TFEU) and Art. 56 EC (63 TFEU). The only free movement provision the wording of which does not make it absolutely clear that only cross-border situations are covered is Art. 39 EC (Art. 45 TFEU).
31. *Supra* n. 23. Note that reference to the notion of 'purely internal' situations was, for the first time, made by the Court one month before the judgment in *Saunders* was delivered in *Knoors v. Secretary of State for Economic Affairs*, Case No. 115/78 [1979] ECR 399, though no further explanation as to the meaning of the phrase was given in that judgment, since the factual background to that case was clearly not purely internal to a Member State.
32. Note that, with the exception of the free movement of capital provisions, movement between a non-member country and a Member State does not suffice for bringing a situation within the scope of the fundamental freedoms provisions. *See Khalil and others v. Bundesanstalt für*

contributes to the construction of the internal market.[33] More specifically, the following three-limb linking factor test can be culled from the Court's jurisprudence on the issue of purely internal situations (though it should be highlighted that the Court has never expressly made reference to a 'test' or specifically to any of the following 'limbs'):

- *First limb*: Is there movement from one Member State to another?
- *Second limb*: Does the movement have an economic aim
- *Third limb*: Would the denial of inclusion within the scope of EC law (and the subsequent denial of EC rights) have a deterrent effect on the exercise of that movement and, thus, a negative impact on the construction of the internal market?

More specifically, the test requires that there is (or will be) inter-state movement for an economic purpose *and* that there is a link between the right claimed under EC law and the exercise of that movement. The latter can be proved by showing that the right claimed is necessary for enabling the economic actor to exercise one of the fundamental freedoms, in other words, that the denial of the grant of this right will deter the exercise of that freedom. If the right claimed is unrelated to the exercise of one of the fundamental freedoms, then the situation cannot (and, rightly, should not) qualify for EC protection.

The reason behind the development of this 'test' has been to provide an easy way for determining whether a situation falls within the scope of EC law or whether it is the national laws of a Member State that must regulate it. The essence of 'the test' comes down to this: since the fundamental freedoms provisions must only apply when there is a negative impact on the achievement of their aim (i.e., the construction of the internal market), any situation which does not involve an impediment to the inter-state movement of products or factors of production must be governed by the law of the Member State where the relevant economic activity takes place.

The most straightforward example of a situation satisfying the linking factor test is that of a person moving from his or her Member State of nationality to another Member State in order to work (as an employed or self-employed person) or provide services *and* the application of the contested national measure (whether of the host State or the home State) impedes that movement (i.e., the movement from the State of origin to the host State). In such a situation, the relevant fundamental freedom requires the national court hearing the case to rule that the contested measure must not be applied to the situation in question, unless this is justified on a non-economic ground acceptable under EC law. Similarly, in the context of EC trade, the linking factor test is satisfied when a situation involves goods or services that have moved from their State of origin to another

Arbeit, Joined Cases C-95/99, C-96/99, C-97/99, C-98/99 and C-180/99 [2001] ECR I-7413, paras 65-72.

33. *See* M. Poiares Maduro, 'The Scope of European Remedies: The Case of Purely Internal Situations and Reverse Discrimination', in *The Future of European Remedies*, C. Kilpatrick, T. Novitz and P. Skidmore (eds) (Oxford, Hart, 2000), pp. 122-123.

Member State, and the application of a State measure results in the imposition of an obstacle to their exportation from their State of origin, or their importation into other Member States.

However, if the application of EC law was confined to the above situations (i.e., where there is merely an exercise of inter-state movement from the State of origin to the host State), a large number of cases would be considered to fall outside the scope of EC law, notwithstanding the fact that the refusal of an EC right in those instances would have a negative impact on the construction of the internal market. Hence, as will be seen more clearly in the next chapter, the Court of Justice has accepted that a link with EC law is also established when a person (or a product), after being involved in an inter-state economic activity, *returns* to his or her Member State of origin and that State treats him or her worse than if he or she had not exercised that cross-border economic activity.[34] The rationale for this is that, had this not been so, Member State nationals might be deterred from exercising one of the fundamental freedoms, as, if their situation was not governed by Community law in their return, they would be disadvantaged *because* of having exercised free movement rights.[35] Thus, in such instances the refusal to extend the protection afforded by EC law would deter the initial exercise of movement from the State of origin to the host State for an economic purpose. In addition, in some other instances, the fundamental freedoms provisions have been held to apply to the situation of re-imported goods or persons returning to their Member State of origin in order to be engaged in an economic activity *there* (i.e., in their State of origin). In these latter instances, it is the movement back to the Member State of origin that is protected, and not the initial exercise of free movement rights.[36]

A significant point which should be kept in mind whilst reading this book is that a Member State national can rely on EC law, either against the host Member State (i.e., the State to which he or she moves in order to exercise an economic activity; or exports his or her products) or, and this is a crucial point, his or her own Member State. In all cases, the important issue is whether a sufficient link with the aims of the fundamental freedoms provisions can be shown. If this is so, then a person can rely on EC law, even against his or her State of nationality.

In its case-law, the Court appears to have been concerned to make sure that the way that has been established for determining whether there is a link with EC law (i.e., in our own words, the 'linking factor test'), is not applied in such a way as to overstretch the scope of application of EC law and take situations within it which are not appropriately included. Therefore, although in the majority of cases the finding of a link with EC law has not proved to be a very complicated exercise, the

---

34. G. Davies, *supra* n. 6, pp. 119-120.
35. *See* para. 45 of the Opinion of Advocate General Kokott in *Mattern and Cikotic v. Ministre du Travail et de l'Emploi*, Case No. C-10/05 [2006] ECR I-3145. For a recent case where the Court employed this line of reasoning *see Criminal proceedings against Van Lent*, Case No. C-232/01 [2003] ECR I-11525.
36. *See*, for example, *De Bobadilla v. Museo Nacional del Prado*, Case No. C-234/97 [1999] ECR I-4773; *Knoors, supra* n. 31.

Court has, nonetheless, provided some qualifications to the more general principles, whenever it had the opportunity to do so.

Firstly, the Court has traditionally highlighted the fact that the movement from one Member State to another must have had some economic aim in order for a link with EC law to be established (this is what I call the 'second limb' of the test)[37] – otherwise, there would be no point in including the situation within the scope of the fundamental freedoms provisions since it would not involve in any way a link with their (economic) aims. Thus, mere residence in another Member State has *traditionally*[38] not been enough for bringing a situation within the scope of the free movement of (economically active) persons provisions, when no economic activity in an inter-state context was involved. Conversely, merely working (without residing) in another Member State from the State of origin has always sufficed for a situation to fall within the scope of EC law.[39]

Secondly, the linking factor test has been held to be satisfied when an inter-state movement involving one of the fundamental freedoms *has been* exercised, or, when such a movement is *definitely* going to be exercised at some point in the near future. The latter can be proved, for example, when a Member State national who is currently in his or her State of origin (and thus has not, already, exercised inter-state movement) has signed a contract for employment in another Member State.[40] The opposite side of the same coin is the fact that a link with EC law cannot be found when the facts of the case before the Court involve a mere hypothetical possibility of movement to another Member State in order to exercise one of the fundamental freedoms.[41]

D REVERSE DISCRIMINATION

Although the application of the purely internal rule has been considered to be a simple solution achieving the right balance between the need to promote the objectives of the Community whilst respecting the sovereignty of the Member States, nevertheless, it has not been an entirely problem-free solution.

---

37. *Gullung v. Conseil de l'Ordre des Avocats*, Case No. 292/86 [1988] ECR 111.
38. *Werner v. Finanzamt Aachen-Innenstadt*, Case No. C-112/91 [1993] ECR I-429. However, as observed by Advocate General Bot in para. 70 of his Opinion in *Commission v. Germany (subsidy for the construction or purchase of a dwelling)*, Case No. C-152/05, judgment of 17 Jan. 2008, not yet reported, the Court abandoned this interpretation in *Ritter-Coulais v. Finanzamt Germersheim*, Case No. C-152/03 [2006] ECR I-1711 and thus it now seems that for the free movement of economically active persons provisions to apply, it suffices that a person resides in a State different from the one where he or she works *even if the State of work and nationality are the same*. *See* Ch. 3 for a criticism of this approach.
39. *Finanzamt Köln-Altstadt v. Schumacker*, Case No. C-279/93 [1995] ECR I-225; *Asscher v. Staatssecretaris van Financiën*, Case No. C-107/94 [1996] ECR I-3089.
40. *See*, for instance, the facts in *Bosman, supra* n. 22, in particular para. 90.
41. *Kremzow v. Republic Österreich*, Case No. C-299/95 [1997] ECR I-2629, para. 16; *Moser v. Land Baden-Württemberg*, Case No. 180/83 [1984] ECR 2539, para. 18; *Höfner and Elser v. Mactroton GmbH*, Case No. C-41/90 [1991] ECR I-1979, para. 39.

The application of the rule when delimiting the scope of the fundamental freedoms provisions may sometimes give rise to a difference in treatment, the so-called 'reverse discrimination'. This is due to the fact that, in order to further the Community's central aim of establishing a common market, EC law often imposes rules on, or grants rights to, persons and traders that fall within its scope by virtue of their contribution to the construction of the internal market, that are more generous or flexible than those that are provided by national laws to persons and traders that are deemed to fall within the scope of application of national law, as a result of the application of the purely internal rule. In other words, persons who remain confined within their Member State of origin have to comply with the (sometimes more restrictive) laws of that State, whereas persons coming from other Member States to the territory of that State, or other nationals of that State that fall within the scope of EC law, may be subject to less restrictive rules as a result of the fact that they fall within the scope of EC law. Accordingly, there may be a difference in treatment between cases which involve very similar factual situations, the only distinguishing factor being that the one situation involves a contribution to the internal market (and thus falls within the scope of the fundamental freedoms), whereas the effects of the other are confined within one and the same Member State.[42]

As already explained, discrimination is characterized as 'reverse', when an unexpected group of persons (or products) is treated less favourably than a group of persons (or products) that is normally treated less beneficially.[43] Hence, the discrimination that is suffered by persons and traders in purely internal situations is defined as 'reverse' since, whilst it is the norm for Member States to be trying to favour their own nationals and products (even if this is not allowed by EC law), in instances of reverse discrimination it is exactly (part of) this group[44] that is treated less favourably.[45]

42. *See* E. Cannizzaro, 'Producing "Reverse Discrimination" through the exercise of EC competences' (1997) 17 *YEL* 29, 32. For further explanation *see* M. Poiares Maduro, *supra* n. 33, pp. 127-128; N. Nic Shuibhne, 'The European Union and Fundamental Rights: Well in Spirit but Considerably Rumpled in Body?', in *Convergence and Divergence in European Public Law*, P. Beaumont, C. Lyons and N. Walker (eds) (Oxford, Hart, 2002), p. 187; H. Staples, *supra* n. 7, p. 15; H.U.J. d'Oliveira, 'Is Reverse discrimination still permissible under the Single European Act?', in *Forty years on: The Evolution of Postwar Private International Law in Europe: symposium in celebration of the 40th anniversary of the Centre of Foreign Law and Private International Law, University of Amsterdam, on 27 October 1998* (The Hague, Kluwer Law International, 1990), pp. 71-72 and 76-81; C. Ritter, 'Purely internal situations, reverse discrimination, Guimont, Dzodzi and Article 234' (2006) 31 *ELRev* 690, 690-692.
43. G. Davies, *supra* n. 6, p. 19.
44. That is, nationals/products of a Member State that have not taken part in the process of the construction of the internal market.
45. Sundberg-Weitman has characterized reverse discrimination as 'the exceptional case that special favours are granted to aliens' – *see* B. Sundberg-Weitman, *Discrimination on Grounds of Nationality – Free Movement of Workers and Freedom of Establishment under the EEC Treaty* (Amsterdam, North-Holland Publishing Company, 1977), p. 113.

In order to make things clearer, it would be appropriate at this point to provide two examples of situations where reverse discrimination emerges as a result of the application of the purely internal rule.

The first instance is where the Court of Justice finds that a national rule which applies equally to wholly internal and cross-border situations violates one of the fundamental freedoms. The Court always confines the effect of its judgment to the persons and products that are *not* in a purely internal situation, and requires that the national legislation becomes inapplicable only to them. As a result of that, the national rules which are considered strict enough to be able to inhibit the exercise of an inter-state economic activity, continue to be applied to the domestic products and persons that do not qualify for EC protection.

In *Commission v. France*,[46] the Court of Justice held that French legislation which restricted the advertising of alcoholic beverages and applied, on its face, to both domestic and imported beverages in the same way, violated Article 28 EC (Article 34 TFEU). In a sequel to this case (*Waterkeyn*[47]) which, also, arose before a French court and involved French alcoholic drinks that were to be marketed on the French market, the main issue was whether the legislation that was found to be contrary to Article 28 EC in *Commission v. France*, should be declared to be inapplicable also in cases involving French beverages that were in a purely internal situation. When the issue was referred to the Court of Justice, the latter made it clear that its previous ruling had declared the French legislation contrary to Article 28 EC *only as long as it affected imported beverages*,[48] since purely internal situations fall outside the scope of Article 28 EC. Accordingly, whereas French producers would continue not being able to advertise their products on the French market, importers of alcoholic beverages from other Member States would, following the Court's judgment, be able to use this method to promote their beverages.[49]

Another instance where the purely internal rule can give rise to reverse discrimination is where EC law, through Treaty provisions or through secondary legislation, bestows supplementary rights upon Member State nationals that fall within the scope of the fundamental freedoms. Persons who fall outside the scope of those provisions because their situation is purely internal to a Member State,

46. *Commission v. France*, Case No. 152/78 [1980] ECR 2299.
47. *Procureur de la République and Comité national de defense contre l'alcoolisme v. Waterkeyn and others*, Joined Cases 314-316/81 and 83/82 [1982] ECR 4337.
48. *Ibid.*, para. 11.
49. For an example of reverse discrimination in the area of persons arising as a result of the fact that the Court's judgments require that national legislation which comes into conflict with EC law is amended/becomes inapplicable only as regards situations that fall within the scope of the fundamental freedoms *see Commission v. Belgium*, Case No. C-278/94 [1996] ECR I-4307. In the subsequent case of *D'Hoop v. Office national de l'emploi*, Case No. C-224/98 [2002] ECR I-6191, the Court remedied (by using the citizenship provisions) the reverse discrimination that was caused as a result of the limited scope of application of *Commission v. Belgium* (*supra* in this footnote).

cannot rely on EC law to claim those rights but can only derive rights (if any are available) from their national laws.

A classic example of such a situation often arises in the context of family reunification cases. EC secondary legislation[50] grants the automatic right to nationals of one Member State who travel to another Member State to work, be established or provide services, to be accompanied by some members of their family. Member State immigration laws, however, have traditionally made it much more difficult for persons who fall within their scope to exercise rights of family reunification, since 'the general practice in most Member States' is to conduct an individual assessment of the situation before family reunification rights are granted, that is, there is no *automatic* right in such situations.[51]

In *Morson and Jhanjan*,[52] two women of Surinamese nationality wished to accompany their adult children, who were Dutch nationals, in the Netherlands (where the children resided and, had always, worked). Following an individual assessment of their situation – as required by Dutch law – their application was rejected, and they subsequently sought to rely on EC secondary legislation to claim that their children had the automatic right to be accompanied by them in the Netherlands. When the issue reached the ECJ, the Court ruled that since the situation of the children was a purely internal one, EC secondary legislation could not be employed for giving them the right to be accompanied in the Netherlands by their mothers: the position of the latter was only to be judged under Dutch immigration legislation (which, in effect, meant that they would not be allowed to stay in the Netherlands). A situation of reverse discrimination, therefore, arose since nationals of other Member States who had gone to work in the Netherlands, or Dutch nationals who could point to a link with Community law, were entitled, as a result of the application of EC law, to be accompanied in the Netherlands by their close family members.

The above two examples have not been selected at random. My aim has been to illustrate the different kinds of problems that arise as a result of the emergence of reverse discrimination.

In the area of trade, the main problem is that reverse discrimination distorts the conditions of competition between traders, as it creates a system whereby the conditions of production and marketing of goods or provision of services differ,

50. 1612/68 (EEC) Regulation on freedom of movement for workers within the Community, OJ L 257/2, 1968; 73/148 (EEC) Directive on the abolition of restrictions on movement and residence within the Community for nationals of Member States with regard to establishment and the provision of services, OJ L 172/14, 1973. Note that the provisions on family reunification of the 1968 Regulation and the 1973 Directive in its entirety, have been repealed by 2004/38 (EC) Directive on the right of citizens of the Union and their family members to move and reside freely within the territory of the Member States, OJ L 158/77, 2004, which, of course, continues to grant family reunification rights to, inter alia, Member State nationals that move to another Member State for an economic purpose.

51. *See* para. 33 of the Opinion of Advocate General Geelhoed in *Jia v. Migrationsverket*, Case No. C-1/05 [2007] ECR I-1.

52. *Morson and Jhanjan v. Netherlands*, Joined Cases 35-36/82 [1982] ECR 3723.

depending on whether inter-state trade is involved. As a result of reverse discrimination, traders competing within one and the same part of the common market (i.e., the State of origin of the products that are in a purely internal situation) compete under different conditions of competition, and traders in purely internal situations may be suffering a competitive disadvantage without this being a result of their own choice (e.g., of choosing to use a cheaper method of promotion of their products). If we take as an example the factual background to *Waterkeyn* and *Commission v. France* above, following the Court's judgments in those cases, importers of alcoholic beverages in France would be entitled to use one of the most effective methods to promote their imports on the French market (advertising), whereas French producers would be deprived of this opportunity.

As regards persons, on the other hand, the main problem is that reverse discrimination often amounts to a difference in treatment with respect to the grant of entitlements or rights in areas that are highly important and sensitive from an emotional point of view. Family reunification cases are the best example to illustrate the bitterness caused by the fact that the protection offered by the fundamental freedoms and secondary legislation supplementing them, is only available to persons contributing to its economic objectives. This bitterness is now increased due to a number of judgments that shall be analyzed in Chapter 3 of the book, in which the scope of the fundamental freedoms provisions was extended to encompass situations that had little or no connection with the aim of creating a common market, making the position of persons falling outside the scope of EC law even more difficult to justify. In addition, like in the context of trade, reverse discrimination against persons (economic actors) that are in a purely internal situation gives rise to competitive distortions – workers who are in a purely internal situation may be less attractive to prospective employers if the latter have to comply with stricter requirements when employing them, than when employing migrant workers.

As was briefly explained in the introduction to this chapter, when the Community requires Member States to treat situations that involve a cross-border economic element more favourably than situations which are confined in all respects within their own territory, its aim is predominantly to achieve substantive equality. As Gareth Davies has noted, '[t]he fact of being a migrant created special disadvantages, which justified migrant-specific treatment aimed at remedying these'.[53]

Therefore, and as will be explained in the last chapter of the book, not all instances of reverse discrimination are problematic from the point of view of Community law. In many cases, the advantages given to migrants in fact redress disadvantages that they would otherwise suffer, and thus in reality merely bring the migrant to the same position as the national of the host State. Hence, in such instances substantive equality is achieved.

53. G. Davies, 'Services, Citizenship and the Country of Origin Principle', *Mitchell Working Paper Series* 2/2007, available at <law.ed.ac.uk/file_download/series/29_servicescitizenshipandthecountryoforiginprinciple.pdf> (accessed on 8 Aug. 2008), at p. 6.

Accordingly, the central issue that always has to be examined is whether, through the exercise of reverse discrimination, substantive equality is achieved. If the more favourable treatment of persons/products that fall within the scope of EC law in reality merely brings them to the same position as persons/products in purely internal situations by compensating them for a disadvantage that they suffer as a result of exercising one of the fundamental freedoms, then this does not amount to discrimination but is, in fact, differential treatment of situations that are not similar. As will be seen in Chapter 6, such instances of reverse discrimination cannot, and should not, be considered as instances of inappropriate discrimination falling within the scope of EC law.

The problem, however, arises in situations where EC law 'clumsily overcompensates for discrimination against foreigners' or where 'substantive free movement law goes "beyond discrimination" to eliminating equally effective obstacles to movement'.[54] As will be seen in Chapter 3 of the book, the effect of the Court's judgments, sometimes, is that of rewarding cross-border movement than solely facilitating or not discouraging it, and, therefore, in such instances, migrants are given 'bonus rights' merely because they have exercised one of the fundamental freedoms, irrespective of whether the situation involves a negative impact on the achievement of the aims of the fundamental freedoms. These are the instances of reverse discrimination that are problematic from the point of view of Community law and, as will be suggested in the final chapter of the book, should be targeted for resolution at EC level.

In the next part of this section, there will be a discussion of the question whether reverse discrimination is, currently, prohibited under EC law.

E Is Reverse Discrimination Prohibited under EC Law?

Under the current state of the law, the answer to the above question is clearly negative. Some scholars[55] have argued that reverse discrimination is a form of discrimination on the grounds of nationality and thus should be considered to be prohibited by Article 12 EC (Article 18 TFEU) and the fundamental freedoms provisions which are, inter alia, a specific application of the principle of non-discrimination on the grounds of nationality. However, the Court of Justice has rejected this argument, being of the view that in order for a difference in treatment to be prohibited by the fundamental freedoms provisions and/or Article 12 EC, it has to have as an effect the imposition of an obstacle to the construction of the

54. G. Davies, *supra* n. 6, p. 131.
55. *See* H.U.J. d'Oliveira, *supra* n. 42; A. Arnull, *supra* n. 25, p. 51; S.D. Kon, 'Aspects of Reverse Discrimination in Community Law' (1981) 6 *ELRev* 75; B. Sundberg-Weitman, *supra* n. 45, Ch. 9; D. Wyatt, 'Social security benefits and discrimination by a Member State against its own nationals' (1978) 3 *ELRev* 488. *See* also Editorial Comment: 'Two-speed European Citizenship? Can the Lisbon Treaty help close the gap?' (2008) 45 *CMLRev* 1, 3.

internal market through inhibiting the exercise of one of the fundamental freedoms. This, obviously, is not the case with reverse discrimination.[56]

However, even if it was accepted that reverse discrimination is a form of discrimination that impedes the free movement of products and factors of production, the argument, again, falters since, as will become more obvious from the case-law analyzed in the next two chapters of the book, reverse discrimination is not discrimination on the grounds of nationality. In cases of reverse discrimination, there is not only a clear-cut difference in treatment between nationals of a Member State and nationals of other Member States, to the detriment of the former. There are, also, many instances where there is a difference in treatment between *some* nationals of a Member State who cannot prove that they fall within the scope of EC law (who are treated less favourably), and other nationals of that same State who can point to a link with EC law (and, thus, can be treated more favourably). Hence, I agree with those scholars who do not accept the argument according to which reverse discrimination is discrimination on the grounds of nationality.[57]

In my view, *reverse discrimination is discrimination based on the ground of 'non-contribution to the internal market'*. This is due to the fact that, in cases of reverse discrimination, the *only* persons/traders that are disadvantaged and discriminated against are those that rely on EC law against their own Member State *and* cannot show the existence of the requisite link with the fundamental freedoms. This is a key point that should be recalled throughout the whole of the book.

That reverse discrimination is not an instance of discrimination on the grounds of nationality, is also obvious from the fact that the Court has ruled that Member States are in violation of the fundamental freedoms provisions when they treat some of their *own* nationals less favourably than they would normally do, *because those persons have exercised one of those freedoms*.[58] In such a situation, a Member State differentiates *between different categories of its own nationals*: someone who has exercised his or her right to free movement is discriminated against because the qualifications he or she has obtained in another Member State,[59] or work he or she has undertaken in another State[60] is not taken into account by his or her State of origin, whereas the qualifications or work of a person from that Member State

56. *See Criminal proceedings against Mathot*, Case No. 98/86 [1987] ECR 809, paras 7-8; *Hurd v. Jones (Her Majesty's Inspector of Taxes)*, Case No. 44/84 [1986] ECR 29, paras 54-56; *Public Prosecutor v. Cognet*, Case No. 355/85 [1986] ECR 3231, paras 10-11.
57. G. Davies, *supra* n. 6, pp. 128-130; A.P. Van der Mei, *Free Movement of Persons Within the European Community: Cross-Border Access to Public Benefits* (Oxford, Hart, 2003), pp. 81-82; N. Nic Shuibhne, 'Free movement of persons and the wholly internal rule: Time to move on?' (2002) 39 *CMLRev* 731, 736-738; C. Hilson, 'Discrimination in Community free movement law' (1999) 24 *ELRev* 445, 460.
58. According to Somek, such a person plays the role of an ' "honorary foreigner" inasmuch as he or she shares with foreigners the essential characteristic of being mobile or having moved'. See A. Somek, 'Solidarity decomposed: being and time in European citizenship' (2007) 32 *ELRev* 787, 793.
59. *Kraus v. Land Baden-Württemberg*, Case No. C-19/92 [1993] ECR I-1663.
60. *Scholz v. Opera Universitaria di Cagliari and Cinzia Porcedda*, Case No. C-419/92 [1994] ECR I-505.

obtained in that same State, are automatically recognized. This kind of discrimination is tantamount to discrimination on the grounds of nationality since a Member State treats some of its own nationals as foreigners *because their situation involves a cross-border element*. In such instances, an obstacle to the inter-state movement of those persons is imposed: due to the fact that those persons know that the reason that they suffer discrimination is caused by the fact that they have exercised one of the fundamental freedoms, this has a deterrent effect on their exercise of that freedom and thus a negative impact on the construction of the internal market. That the EC in such a situation steps-in and requires a Member State to treat some of *its own nationals* in a way that does not conflict with the, until recently, dominant aim of the Treaty (i.e., the construction of the internal market) shows, exactly, that the triggering event for bringing a situation within the scope of EC law is not the fact that a person holds the nationality of another Member State but the exercise of an inter-state economic activity contributing to the establishment of the internal market.

As will be seen more extensively in the subsequent chapter of the book, when the Court was confronted with the question of whether reverse discrimination is a prohibited form of discrimination under EC law, it had no hesitation in ruling that this difference in treatment does not fall within the scope of the fundamental freedoms provisions, since it in no way inhibits the achievement of their main aim, that is, the encouragement of inter-state movement contributing to the internal market;[61] and that it is up to the Member States to provide a solution if they consider it necessary.[62] In addition, it has been implicit in the Court's case-law that instances of reverse discrimination fall outside the general scope of EC law as well. This is, undoubtedly, due to the fact that the Court has, until recently, been of the view that the Community was merely a supranational organization of purely economic aims and, in particular, an organization the main task of which was the establishment of an internal market. Therefore, whenever a difference in treatment has not been detrimental to the aim of building a common market, it has been held to fall outside the general scope of EC law.

It is true that when the EC Treaty was originally drafted, the founding fathers could not have predicted that the system created might give rise to situations of reverse discrimination. Pickup, back in the 1980s, very rightly posed the question: 'what Community pioneer would have expected a Member State to accept a Community-wide standard of protection and then fail to allow

---

61. *See*, for example, *Mathot, supra* n. 56, para. 7; *Hurd v. Jones, supra* n. 56. *See* S. Enchelmaier, 'The Awkward Selling of a Good Idea, or a Traditionalist Interpretation of *Keck*' (2003) 22 *YEL* 249, 272. In a more recent case, the Court of Justice avoided to deal with the issue of whether a specific instance of reverse discrimination was contrary to Arts 12 EC (Art. 18 TFEU), 49 EC (Art. 56 TFEU), 81 EC (Art. 101 TFEU), 82 EC (Art. 102 TFEU) and 87 EC (Art. 107 TFEU) – *see Herrera v. Servicio Cántabro de Salud*, Case No. C-466/04 [2006] ECR I-5341, paras 46-52.
62. *Steen v. Deutsche Bundespost (No. 2)*, Case No. C-132/93 [1994] ECR I-2715; *S. A. Krüger v. Directie van de rechtspersoonlijkheid bezittende Dienst Wegverkeer*, Case No. C-253/01 [2004] ECR I-1191, para.36.

its own nationals the protection it was obliged to afford to nationals of other Member States?'.[63]

Moreover, especially since the emphasis was initially placed on the removal of discriminatory barriers, reverse discrimination was not possible in the first years of the Community's existence.[64] However, when the Court – in the context of the free movement of goods,[65] first, and, subsequently, in the context of the other fundamental freedoms[66] – extended the scope of application of the fundamental freedoms provisions to catch, also, non-discriminatory obstacles to the free movement of products and factors of production, this meant that those provisions would no longer, solely, require Member States to extend national treatment to persons and products coming from other Member States; in certain occasions, they would even define the (more extensive gamut of) rights which Member States must grant to persons that fall within the scope of EC law, this having as a result the emergence of reverse discrimination.

Since, until recently, the sole aim of the EC Treaty was the construction of the internal market, reverse discrimination could not be considered to be an unacceptable difference in treatment that should be prohibited under EC law. However, the EC is a dynamic supranational organization, and certainly some elements which have been considered acceptable in the first decades of its existence, one of them being reverse discrimination, may no longer be so in the context in which it is now working.

III THE MAIN AIM AND QUESTION OF THE BOOK

The main purpose of the book is to examine whether reverse discrimination continues to be a form of differential treatment that escapes the ambit of EC law since it does not impede the aim of establishing an internal market; or whether it should, instead, be considered to be an EC problem which requires an EC solution. More specifically, the main question that this book seeks to answer is whether, viewed against the background of the post-Maastricht developments, reverse discrimination should, now, be considered to be a difference in treatment which falls within the scope of EC law as a result of the fact that it has a negative impact on the achievement of the (now broader) objectives of the Community.

63. D.M.W. Pickup, 'Reverse Discrimination and Freedom of Movement for workers' (1986) 23 *CMLRev* 135, 149.
64. *See* C. Greenwood, 'Nationality and the Limits of the Free movement of Persons in Community Law' (1987) 7 *YEL* 185, 186 and 194; N. Bernard, *supra* n. 26, 86 and 88.
65. *Rewe-Zentrale AG v. Bundesmonopolverwaltung für Branntwein ('Cassis de Dijon')*, Case No. 120/78 [1979] ECR 649.
66. *Bosman, supra* n. 22 (workers); *Säger v. Dennemeyer & Co. Ltd*, Case No. C-76/90 [1991] ECR I-4221 (services); *Gebhard v. Consiglio dell'Ordine degli Avvocato e Procuratori di Milano*, Case No. C-55/94 [1995] ECR I-4165 (establishment).

The catalysts for embarking on research on this topic have been important developments that have taken place in the EC during the 1990s; developments that have to do with the completion of the internal market, but also, and more broadly, with the metamorphosis of the EU into a supranational organization of a wider scope and with wider aims which no longer focuses merely on the construction and maintenance of an internal market. On the one hand, the establishment of the status of Union citizenship by the Treaty of Maastricht in 1993 and the development of that status through the Court's recent jurisprudence, have triggered the question of whether reverse discrimination, as a difference in treatment based on whether a Union citizen has contributed to the economic aims of the Treaty, should now be considered an unjustified difference in treatment between Union citizens and thus a violation of the general principle of equality. On the other hand, the formal completion of the internal market in 1993 as required by the provisions inserted into the EC Treaty by the Single European Act, has brought with it the need to ensure that the (now) completed market is also a properly-functioning market, a market in which important economic (undistorted competition) and non-economic (e.g., environmental protection) values are promoted and respected. In the light of these developments, it becomes questionable whether reverse discrimination (with the resultant competitive distortions) is, still, a side-effect of European economic integration which can be ignored by the Community.

One caveat should precede the main analysis in this book. As seen above, the main question of the book is whether reverse discrimination is still an acceptable difference in treatment in the EC legal system. The further question of what solutions are available for the resolution of this problem once it is decided that reverse discrimination is no longer acceptable in the EC, does not form the subject-matter of this book. Of course, a brief discussion of the available solutions to this problem, and their advantages and disadvantages, is included in the concluding chapter of the book, however this is merely tentative and very little research has been devoted to it.

IV STRUCTURE OF THE BOOK

The book is comprised of this introductory chapter, four main chapters and Chapter 6 which concludes. The four main chapters, in turn, are divided into two parts: Part I under the title 'The Court's traditional and new approaches to purely internal situations' (Chapters 2 and 3); and Part II under the title 'Reverse discrimination as an incongruity in the contemporary EC' (Chapters 4 and 5).

The purpose of the next chapter of the book – Chapter 2 – is to present, through an analysis of the Court's case-law on purely internal situations, the traditional approach followed by the Court when applying the linking factor test and its stance on reverse discrimination. Brief reference is also made to the problems arising from the application of this traditional approach.

The aim of Chapter 3 is to illustrate that in some of its latest case-law in the area of the fundamental freedoms, the Court of Justice has adopted a number of different approaches to be used for delimiting the scope of those provisions, most probably in response to the criticisms voiced against its traditional approach to purely internal situations. It will be seen that one of these new approaches (the one used in the area of the free movement of persons) is greatly problematic and in fact creates more problems than it solves. Conversely, the new approach followed when delimiting the scope of the free movement of goods and services provisions, is a proper response to some of the problems arising as a result of the application of the Court's traditional approach. Yet, the fact remains that even if the way that the Court uses in delimiting the scope of the fundamental freedoms provisions is altered, the scope of those provisions will never be able to be stretched in such a way as to prohibit the emergence of reverse discrimination, since reverse discrimination does not conflict with the sole aim of those provisions that is, the interstate movement of products and factors of production as part of the process of establishing an internal market. Therefore, it will be concluded that some other way should be found for bringing reverse discrimination within the scope of Community law.

Accordingly, the aim of Part II of the book (Chapters 4 and 5) is to examine whether there is any other way in which instances of reverse discrimination can be brought within the scope of Community law. For this purpose, two developments that have taken place in the EC during the 1990s are analyzed. In Chapter 4, there will be an explanation of how the institution of the status of citizenship of the Union by the Treaty of Maastricht and the interpretation afforded to that status by the Court of Justice in its latest case-law has, now, broadened the scope of Community law to include within its ambit Member State nationals that in no way contribute to its economic aims. This will form the basis for my argument that unjustified instances of reverse discrimination[67] should, now, fall within the scope of EC law and, in particular, be held to amount to a violation of the principle of equality between Union citizens. In Chapter 5 it will be explained that, although the fundamental freedoms provisions are merely concerned with ensuring that products and factors of production can move uninhibited from one Member State to another, nonetheless, the (more general) internal market provisions have a broader focus: the proper-functioning of the internal market. In fact, following the formal completion of the internal market, the focus seems to have been placed on ensuring that the internal market is a properly-functioning market. Since a market that functions properly is a market where a system of undistorted competition is maintained, unjustified instances of reverse discrimination[68] appear, now, to fall within the scope of the internal market provisions as those provisions prohibit any

67. In Ch. 6, it will be explained that the doctrine of mandatory requirements should be made available to Member States for justifying any instances of reverse discrimination that fall within the scope of EC law. Thus, if such instances of reverse discrimination can be justified on a (valid) ground other than the desire to grant EC rights only to persons/traders that have contributed to the economic aims of the Treaty, then the Member State which resorts to such differential treatment can continue doing so.

68. *Ibid.*

difference in treatment which distorts competition in the internal market and which has come about as a side-effect of the process of European integration.

In the final chapter, there is a summary of the findings of this study and an explanation of how the analysis provided in this work has answered the main question of the book. Reference is also made to the various solutions that are available for the resolution of the reverse discrimination conundrum and a brief assessment of the advantages and disadvantages of each of those solutions is provided.

V METHODOLOGY

Traditional legal method has been used in conducting the research necessary for this study. The main tools that have been employed are the case-law of the Court of Justice (both, the judgments of the Court and the Opinions of its Advocates General); selected case-law of the Court of First Instance; the EC Treaty; Community secondary legislation; books and scholarly articles; and selected jurisprudence of national courts. In addition, use has been made of non-binding measures of the Community institutions such as Commission notices, communications and reports.

The above tools have been used in three ways. Firstly, they have been employed for illustrating the Court's traditional approach to purely internal situations and for presenting the Court's formal stance on the issue of reverse discrimination. Secondly, they have been utilized for exploring the real impact that the post-Maastricht developments have had in the development of the contemporary EC as a supranational organization of broader scope and aims which is not merely concerned with the construction of an internal market. And thirdly, and more importantly, they have been used for showing how the developments that have taken place in the EC during the 1990s have already (implicitly) affected the Court's position towards purely internal situations and reverse discrimination; and for illustrating how these developments can now be used in support of the argument that reverse discrimination is an incongruity in the contemporary EC.

It should be noted that the study examines the issue of reverse discrimination from the perspective of the EC – the question is whether reverse discrimination is contrary to *EC law*. The opposite side of the same coin, that is, the question of whether reverse discrimination is incompatible with national law, does not fall within the scope of this study and is only very sparingly touched, where this contributes to the clarity of the analysis.

Obviously, like with every other study, some outer boundaries need to be placed on the scope of this work. The study's central theme is reverse discrimination in purely internal situations. As already explained, this is discrimination which arises in situations that do not involve the exercise of one of the fundamental freedoms *and* where an individual seeks to rely on one of the fundamental freedoms provisions *against his or her own Member State*. Therefore, the case-law that will be analyzed in this book will mainly involve such a factual background.

Hence, although there has been an immense amount of case-law in the area of the fundamental freedoms, which involved all sorts of imaginative arguments for bringing a situation within the scope of the fundamental freedoms provisions even though the facts were unrelated to the exercise of one of those freedoms, it is only such case-law which, also, involved an individual relying on EC law against his or her own Member State that is analyzed here.

As will be seen, in its main part the book adopts a blend of expository and evaluative approaches. For example, Chapter 2 includes a purely expository analysis of the law on purely internal situations and reverse discrimination, as has traditionally been laid down by the Court of Justice. In Chapter 3, on the other hand, there is an interplay between expository and evaluative approaches. Thus, there is an explanation of the law on purely internal situations, as has been developed by the Court (expository); whilst at the same time this description of the development of the law is used to show how the Court has departed from its traditional approach in finding a link with EC law; and what are the advantages and disadvantages of these new approaches now followed by the Court (evaluative). A similar pattern is followed in Chapters 4 and 5 which start by providing an expository analysis of current jurisprudence of the Court, which is subsequently used to support the argument that the Court should depart from its traditional stance on reverse discrimination and rule that this difference in treatment is, now, contrary to EC law.

A final point – regarding presentation – has to be made. At the time of writing the EU is awaiting ratification of the new Lisbon Treaty[69] by all Member States. Once the Lisbon Treaty comes into force, it will amend the current Treaty on European Union (TEU) and replace the current EC Treaty with the Treaty on the Functioning of the European Union (TFEU). In this work, the current numbering is used, however, next to each Treaty Article the equivalent Treaty provision that will replace the current numbering following the entry into force of the Lisbon Treaty is provided in brackets. Quotations do not include the Lisbon renumbering. They include the current numbering unless the old numbering is included in the original, in which case the current numbering is included in square brackets.

69. *Supra* n. 8.

Part I

The Court's Traditional and New Approaches to Purely Internal Situations

Chapter 2

The Traditional Approach of the Court

I INTRODUCTION

The second chapter of the book has as its purpose to present the traditional approach followed by the Court in determining whether a situation is purely internal to a Member State. In particular, the traditional approach followed when applying the linking factor test seen in the previous chapter of the book will be analyzed, using the Court's case-law as a point of reference. Specific emphasis will be placed on explaining how reverse discrimination emerges as a result of the application of the purely internal rule and what has been the Court's approach to this form of differential treatment. The chapter will conclude with a brief explanation of the reasons behind the Court's insistence on applying its traditional approach to purely internal situations and reverse discrimination; and of the objections that may be raised to the application of this approach.

As will be noticed, the chapter is mainly a descriptive one and, therefore, the author should be forgiven for the lack of a sufficiently intellectually stimulating analysis and the heavy reliance on the Court's case-law.

II PURELY INTERNAL RULE, REVERSE DISCRIMINATION AND THE FUNDAMENTAL FREEDOMS: THE COURT'S TRADITIONAL APPROACH

The Court's traditional approach to purely internal situations is a unitary one, as the Court applies exactly the same principles when delimiting the scope of all the fundamental freedoms provisions. In its traditional case-law, the Court of Justice follows a consistent and, to a certain extent, simplistic approach in finding a link with EC law, always requiring *all three limbs* of the linking factor test to be satisfied *on the specific facts from which a case arose*. The Court appears to begin its enquiry by examining whether the first limb of the test (i.e., inter-state movement) – which is the most straightforward of the three to apply – is satisfied on the facts of the case and, if not, this signals the end of the matter; if the first limb of the test is satisfied on the facts of the case, then the Court moves on to examine whether the second and third limbs are also satisfied.

According to this approach, once the three limbs of the test are satisfied on the specific facts of the case, the Court is content that the contested measure is capable of inhibiting the free movement of products or factors of production and thus further examination of the question as to whether that measure actually amounts to a breach of the relevant EC Treaty provision has to take place.[1] Conversely, failure of one of the limbs of the test to be satisfied *on the specific facts of the case* signifies the end of the enquiry as to a possible violation of one of the fundamental freedoms provisions, since the issue is deemed to be wholly internal to the relevant Member State. Further, deeper, examination of the actual impact that the contested measure may have on inter-state movement for an economic purpose is altogether ruled out by the Court.

Obviously, under this approach the Court draws particular attention to the specific facts from which a case arose and only accepts that a situation falls within the scope of EC law if a *specific* person or product can be identified, the movement of which is hampered as a result of the application of the measure that is contested before it.[2] Therefore it would appear that under the Court's traditional approach, even if it can be proved with sufficient certainty that the measure the compatibility of which with EC law is questioned actually has an effect on the inter-state movement of products or factors of production, this does not suffice for satisfying the linking factor test, if the inter-state movement of the specific products or persons that are involved on the facts before the Court is not impeded.

As regards the question of the permissibility of reverse discrimination, it will be seen below that the Court has expressly ruled in its case-law that any instances of reverse discrimination arising as a result of the application of the purely internal rule escape the ambit of EC law and, in particular, the remit of the fundamental

---

1. It should be noted that in the Court's case-law there is, usually, no real clear-cut division between those two stages (i.e., firstly deciding whether the situation is a purely internal one, and then determining whether there is a violation of EC law). In other words, the questions of whether the situation is purely internal to a Member State and whether there is a violation of one of the fundamental freedoms are usually answered together and the second stage of the enquiry – if it is found that there is a prima facie violation – consists in determining whether there is a justification for the contested measure. This latter stage in the Court's judgments will not be discussed when cases are analyzed since it is not relevant to this study.
2. This becomes obvious from the Court's traditional case-law in all the fundamental freedoms, but it has also been expressly suggested by Advocate General Cosmas in para. 14 of his Opinion in *Belgapom v. ITM and Vocarex*, Case No. C-36/94 [1995] ECR I-2647: 'the connecting factor bringing a given situation within the ambit of Article 30 [now Article 28] of the Treaty should be sought in the provenance of the *goods allegedly affected in the specific case*, by a given national measure' (emphasis added).

freedoms provisions. This is due to the fact that this form of differential treatment does not inhibit the achievement of the aim of those provisions and, more broadly, the (until recently) dominant aim of the Community, that is, the establishment of an internal market through the removal of obstacles to the free movement of goods, persons, services and capital.[3]

The doctrine of purely internal situations has also had important implications for the delimitation of the scope of the Court's jurisdiction in Article 234 EC (Article 267 TFEU) cases (i.e., preliminary ruling proceedings). Under the Court's traditional approach, whenever the facts of a case are found to be purely internal to a Member State, the Court lacks jurisdiction to provide a reply to any questions that have arisen from those facts and which have been referred to it by a national court via the preliminary rulings mechanism. The answer to the question(s) has to wait until another case arises before a national court which involves a situation that falls within the scope of EC law.

Finally, it should be noted that the Court's traditional approach used in finding a link with EC law is still the 'default' approach, and this is not surprising as the main issue that the Court always needs to examine first is whether the linking factor test is satisfied on the specific facts of the case. If this is so, no further enquiry needs to be undertaken: the situation is not a purely internal one and thus falls within the scope of EC law. If, however, the linking factor test is not satisfied on the specific facts of the case, this is the end of the matter under the traditional approach.

In the rest of this section, I shall provide examples from the case-law of the Court in the context of all the fundamental freedoms, where the Court has applied its traditional approach in finding a link with EC law and in dealing with instances of reverse discrimination. I consider that in those cases the Court has followed its traditional approach because it found that the situation was not a purely internal one since the linking factor test was satisfied *on the specific facts of the case*; or that the situation fell outside the scope of EC law as a result of the fact that the linking factor test was *not satisfied on the facts before the Court*. In that case-law, the impact that the contested measure might have on the inter-state movement of products or persons not involved on the specific facts of the case was not examined at all (and, after all, this would be an unnecessary exercise where the linking factor test was satisfied on the specific facts of the case, and thus the situation was deemed to fall within the scope of EC law).

A FREE MOVEMENT OF GOODS

The traditional approach towards the application of the purely internal rule in the context of the free movement of goods,[4] has contributed to the development of

3. *See* S. Enchelmaier, 'The Awkward Selling of a Good Idea, or a Traditionalist Interpretation of *Keck*' (2003) 22 *YEL* 249, 272.
4. For an explanation of the purely internal rule and reverse discrimination in relation to the free movement of goods *see* J. Steiner, L. Woods and C. Twigg-Flesner, *Textbook on EC Law* (8th

case-law which is 'clear and consistent, and faithfully [reflects] the language of the Treaty'.[5] Whenever a product is imported into Member State A from Member State B, there is clearly a cross-border element, the situation is not a wholly internal one, and any rules imposed by Member State A on that product must not violate Article 28 EC (Article 34 TFEU). Similarly, if a product is manufactured in Member State B and is to be exported to another Member State, any rules imposed by Member State B on that product have to comply with Article 29 EC (Article 35 TFEU). In contrast, according to the Court's traditional approach, whenever a case concerns the application of the rules of a Member State to goods that have not moved between Member States, it clearly involves a purely internal situation and Articles 28 and 29 EC are not applicable. In such instances, the State of production of the goods is free to impose its own rules on producers/traders.[6] This may give rise to reverse discrimination as EC law may impose through secondary legislation a more flexible standard on goods that fall within the scope of EC law, or, it may simply require that goods that comply with less burdensome requirements in their home State are accepted in the host State, prohibiting the latter from applying its stricter rules to them. In certain other instances, goods moving between regions of *one and the same Member State* and which are thus in a purely internal situation may be (reversely) discriminated against when compared with goods that move between Member States and enjoy the protection offered by EC law.

Below, I shall analyze the jurisprudence of the Court of Justice where the traditional approach to the application of the linking factor test has been followed in delimiting the scope of Articles 28 and Article 29 EC (Articles 34 and 35 TFEU respectively), as well as of secondary Community legislation. The emphasis will be placed on instances where the application of the test has given rise to reverse discrimination since, in this context, the issue of whether the linking factor test is satisfied on the facts of the case does not usually need to be extensively examined: it is often quite clear whether the specific facts of a case involve goods that have moved between Member States and whether the contested measure has raised an obstacle to the free movement of *those* goods.

Towards the end of this subsection, there will be a brief analysis of the application of the Court's traditional approach when delimiting the scope of the customs duties provisions of the Treaty (Articles 23-25 EC),[7] despite the fact that these provisions do not, formally, fall within the 'group' of the fundamental freedoms provisions. Since the customs duties provisions are considered equally important, with Articles 28 and 29 EC (Articles 34 and 35 TFEU), in protecting the free movement of goods within the EC, and since the recent case-law of the Court

---

edn, Oxford, OUP, 2003), pp. 222-223; P. Oliver, 'Some further reflections on the scope of Articles 28-30' (1999) 36 *CMLRev* 783, 783-785; T. Van Rijn, 'A review of the case-law of the Court of Justice on Articles 30 to 36 EEC in 1986 and 1987' (1988) 25 *CMLRev* 593, 611-612.

5. P. Oliver, *Free movement of goods in the European Community* (4th edn, London, Sweet and Maxwell, 2003), p. 149.
6. *Oosthoek's Uitgeversmaatschappij BV*, Case No. 286/81 [1982] ECR 4575, para. 9.
7. Articles 28-30 TFEU.

on the scope of those provisions has played an important role in questioning the appropriateness of applying the Court's traditional approach when establishing a link with EC law, the analysis in this chapter would be deficient if no reference was made to the results of the application of the Court's traditional approach when delimiting the scope of those provisions.

1 Reverse Discrimination Exercised by a Member State against its Own Goods

Early on in its case-law, the Court made it clear that reverse discrimination exercised by a Member State against its own goods is not a form of a difference in treatment that is prohibited by Article 28 EC (Article 34 TFEU), since it does not inhibit the inter-state movement of goods and thus does not obstruct the achievement of the aim of that provision.[8]

In *Mathot*[9] at issue was the compatibility with Article 28 EC (Article 34 TFEU) of Belgian legislation which required Belgian producers of butter to indicate on the package of their goods their name and address, whilst (obviously in order to comply with EC law) it did not impose such a requirement on butter produced in other Member States and imported into Belgium. As a result of that requirement, Belgian producers that destined their butter for the Belgian market were disadvantaged, since Belgian supermarkets preferred to market butter which did not include the name and address of its producer on its packaging.[10]

When the ECJ was asked whether this difference in treatment between Belgian butter and imported butter was contrary to Article 28 EC (Article 34 TFEU), it replied, without hesitation, that

> A difference of treatment as between goods which is not capable of restricting imports or of prejudicing the marketing of imported goods does not fall within the prohibition contained in that Article.[11]

Since the contested legislation put Belgian butter, as opposed to imported butter, at a disadvantage, it did not give rise to an obstacle to the importation into Belgium of butter from other Member States and thus was not contrary to Article 28 EC (Article 34 TFEU).

---

8. This view seems to have also been taken by the Community legislature since it is obvious from the provisions of Directive 70/50 that it is only discrimination against imported goods that amounts to an MEQR. *See* 70/50 (EEC) Directive on the abolition of measures which have an effect equivalent to quantitative restrictions on imports and are not covered by other provisions adopted in pursuance of the EEC Treaty OJ L 13/29, 1970 (only formally applicable during the Community's transitional period).
9. *Criminal proceedings against Mathot*, Case No. 98/86 [1987] ECR 809. For a more recent case confirming this *see Commission v. Italy (Chocolate)*, Case No. C-14/00 [2003] ECR I-513, paras 71-73.
10. *Mathot, supra* n. 9, para. 3.
11. *Ibid.*, para. 7.

2 Reverse Discrimination Arising as a Result of the ECJ Confining the Application of its Judgments to Imported Goods

In many instances, reverse discrimination arises as a result of a judgment delivered by the Court of Justice. As seen in Chapter 1, when the Court rules that a national measure is contrary to one of the fundamental freedoms, it requires that the measure becomes inapplicable only in situations that fall within the scope of EC law; purely internal situations can continue to be regulated by the (restrictive) national measure in question. And, like reverse discrimination which is exercised by a Member State against its own goods simply because this is the policy of the State (see, for instance, *Mathot* above), these instances of reverse discrimination are, also, permissible under Article 28 EC (Article 34 TFEU) since they do not contravene its aim.

In the *3 Glocken* case,[12] a German manufacturer of pasta brought an action in an Italian court claiming that Italian legislation which prohibited the marketing of pasta in Italy unless it was solely made from durum wheat, was contrary to Article 28 EC (Article 34 TFEU). The ECJ found that such legislation was contrary to Article 28 EC because it was an obstacle to the importation of pasta produced lawfully in other Member States using common wheat or a mixture of common and durum wheat, however, it further pointed out that

> [I]t is the extension of the law on pasta products to imported products which is at issue, and . . . Community law does not require the legislature to repeal the law as far as pasta producers established on Italian territory are concerned.[13]

Accordingly, following the approach adopted in *Waterkeyn*[14] (seen in Chapter 1), the Court itself created a situation of reverse discrimination by confining the effect of its judgment to products which were not in a purely internal situation – Italian producers of pasta would still have to comply with the more burdensome Italian rules in order to be able to market their pasta on the Italian market; they would still have to use (the more expensive) durum wheat whilst competing on the Italian market with producers who could produce their products using cheaper raw materials.[15] And, applying the Court's reasoning in *Mathot*, it would seem

12. *Drei Glocken GmbH and Gertraud Kritzinger v. USL Centro-Sud and Provincia autonoma di Bolzano*, Case No. 407/85 [1988] ECR 4233.
13. *Ibid.*, para. 25.
14. *Procureur de la République and Comité national de defense contre l'alcoolisme v. Waterkeyn and others*, Joined Cases 314-316/81 and 83/82 [1982] ECR 4337.
15. It should be noted, however, that as opposed to giving rise to a competitive disadvantage, the use of better quality, and thus more expensive, raw materials in cases such as this may, in reality, provide a competitive advantage for national products. This argument is particularly pertinent in the case of Italian pasta, since Italians know that their domestic pasta tastes good because it is made from durum wheat and, thus, the lower price of (lower quality) imported pasta does not seem to be capable of switching demand towards the latter. This is, also, evident from the Court's judgment in *Drei Glocken*: 'trends in the export markets demonstrate that competition

that the resultant difference in treatment would not be found to be contrary to EC law since it did not impede the inter-state movement of goods.[16]

3 Reverse Discrimination Arising as a Result of the Implementation of EC Minimum Harmonization Legislation

Minimum harmonization occurs when Community legislation sets minimum requirements which must always be respected by Member States, whilst allowing Member States to impose stricter requirements from those provided by the legislation, as long as the latter do not conflict with EC law. Some minimum harmonization measures include a 'market access' clause. This means that the Member State which imposes stricter requirements than those laid down by the Community legislation, must provide access to its market to goods that comply with the minimum requirements of the Community legislation *and* are lawfully produced *in another Member State*, notwithstanding the fact that they do not comply with the stricter requirements imposed by it.

In cases where a piece of minimum harmonization legislation contains a 'market access' clause, reverse discrimination may emerge since Member States can only impose stricter requirements than the minimum provided in that piece of legislation, in situations involving domestic products which are in a purely internal situation.[17] In contrast, when the Community legislation does not contain a 'market

---

based on quality operates in favour of durum wheat. The statistics supplied to the Court show a steady increase in the market share held by pasta products made exclusively from durum wheat in other Member States in which they already face competition from pasta made from common wheat or from a mixture of common wheat and durum wheat' (para. 27 of the judgment in *Drei Glocken, supra* n. 12). For an argument that a requirement for the use of better quality raw materials for national products may not give rise to a competitive disadvantage but may actually improve the competitive position of domestic products and, thus, even create an obstacle to the importation of goods from other Member States *see* G. Davies, *Nationality Discrimination in the European Internal Market* (The Hague, Kluwer Law International, 2003), p. 133; S. Weatherill, *Cases and Materials on EU Law* (8th edn, Oxford, OUP, 2007), pp. 385-386; H.C. Von Heydebrand u.d. Lasa, 'Free movement of foodstuffs, consumer protection and food standards in the European Community: has the Court of Justice got it wrong?' (1991) 16 *ELRev* 391, 404. In my view, the question of whether a competitive advantage is enjoyed by imported products as a result of reverse discrimination requires an examination of (a) the exact requirements imposed by the legislation (i.e., whether the legislation requires national producers to use raw materials which are of better quality and thus more expensive, or whether the legislation requires the use of, simply, more burdensome production procedures) and (b) the basis of competition on the relevant market (i.e., whether competition is based on price or quality).

16. *See* to the same effect *SARPP v. Chambre syndicale des raffineurs et conditionneurs de sucre de France and others*, Case No. C-241/89 [1990] ECR I-4695, para. 33; *Commission v. Greece (Greek Beer)*, Case No. 176/84 [1987] ECR 1193, para. 21; *Commission v. Germany (German Beer)*, Case No. 178/84 [1987] ECR 1227; *Nederlandse Bakkerij Stichting and Others v. Edah BV*, Joined Cases 80 and 159/85 [1986] ECR 3359, para. 18.
17. For an explanation of the relationship between minimum harmonization Directives and reverse discrimination *see* J. Steiner, L. Woods and C. Twigg-Flesner *supra* n. 4, pp. 266-267; M. Poiares Maduro, *We the Court: The European Court of Justice and the European Economic*

access' clause, national legislation can impose stricter requirements on *both* domestic and imported goods which fall within its jurisdiction, provided that those requirements comply with EC law.[18]

Gallaher[19] is an example of a case in which reverse discrimination emerged as a result of the implementation of minimum harmonization legislation with a 'market access' clause. That case involved EC legislation laying down minimum requirements for the packaging of tobacco products. The Directive (which included a 'market access' clause) required that the health warnings that cigarette packets must carry shall cover 'at least' 4% of the surface of the packet. The United Kingdom regulations implementing the Directive required that cigarettes *which were not imported* should be sold in packets on which the health warnings referred to in the said Directive would cover not less than 6% of the surface of the packet. A number of companies which produced cigarettes in the United Kingdom, brought an action before an English court in order to have the United Kingdom legislation declared void for violating the Directive by not permitting cigarettes produced in the United Kingdom to be marketed there when complying with the (less strict)

Constitution (Oxford, Hart, 1998), pp. 134-135; S. de Vries, *Tensions within the Internal Market: The Functioning of the Internal Market and the Development of Horizontal and Flanking Policies* (Groningen, Europa Law Publishing, 2006), pp. 254-255; C. Barnard, *The Substantive Law of the EU: The Four Freedoms* (2nd edn, Oxford, OUP, 2007), pp. 601-604. It is important to remember that when the EC legislature harmonizes by means of exhaustive (total) harmonization, Member State action is preempted in all situations (including situations which do not include goods crossing inter-state frontiers – *see* J. Currall, 'Some Aspects of the Relation between Articles 30-36 and Article 100 of the EEC Treaty, with a Closer Look at Optional Harmonisation' (1984) 4 *YEL* 169, 178), and thus there are no instances of reverse discrimination. For an explanation of exhaustive (total) harmonization *see* C. Barnard, (*supra* in this footnote), pp. 591-599. For a very well-known example of exhaustive harmonization and its effects *see Commission v. UK (Dim-Dip Headlights)*, Case No. 60/86 [1988] ECR 3921. Note that in the early years of the Community, total harmonization was the mostly used method of harmonization – *see* A. Young and H. Wallace, 'The Single Market: A New Approach to Policy', in *Policy-Making in the European Union*, H. Wallace and W. Wallace (eds) (5th edn, Oxford, OUP, 2000), p. 88; W. Sauter and E. Vos, 'Harmonisation under Community Law: The comitology issue', in *Lawmaking in the European Union*, P. Craig and C. Harlow (eds) (The Hague, Kluwer Law International, 1998), p. 171. This method of harmonization, in combination with the discrimination-based approach to the delimitation of the scope of the fundamental freedoms, meant that reverse discrimination would not – or, only very seldom – arise.

18. Weatherill has pointed out that the *Tobacco Advertising I* case (*Germany v. Parliament and Council*, Case No. C-376/98 [2000] ECR I-8419) appears to insist that a harmonization measure must include a market access clause – S. Weatherill, 'Supply of and demand for internal market regulation: strategies, preferences and interpretation', in *Regulating the Internal Market*, N. Nic Shuibhne (ed.) (Cheltenham, Northampton, Edward Elgar, 2006), p. 46. This would give rise to an increase in the instances of reverse discrimination.

19. *The Queen v. Secretary of State for Health, ex parte Gallaher Ltd, Imperial Tobacco Ltd and Rothmans International Tobacco (UK) Ltd*, Case No. C-11/92 [1993] ECR 3545. *See* S. Weatherill, 'Regulating the Internal Market: Result orientation in the Court of Justice' (1994) 19 *ELRev* 55. For a similar approach but in the context of export restrictions *see R v. Minister of Agriculture, Fisheries and Food ex parte Compassion in World Farming*, Case No. C-1/96 [1998] ECR I-1251.

requirements of it. The ECJ held that the Directive allowed Member States to impose stricter requirements than those provided in the Community legislation, but only on domestic goods. It was only imported goods which complied with the minimum standards imposed by the secondary legislation that could enjoy free access to the United Kingdom market.[20] Accordingly, Member States are free to exercise reverse discrimination against their own goods, when implementing Community minimum harmonization legislation.[21]

4 Reverse Discrimination as a Difference in Treatment between Domestic Goods in a Purely Internal Situation and Re-imported Domestic Goods

Domestic goods which are exported and then re-imported into the Member State in which they were manufactured are considered to fall within the scope of the Treaty, and the Court extends the protection afforded to foreign (imported) goods to such products.[22] When national legislation imposes stricter requirements on domestic goods which have not crossed any borders, these goods are treated differently both in relation to (foreign) imported goods and in relation to (domestic) re-imported goods. However, according to the Court, this instance of differential treatment does not violate Article 28 EC (Article 34 TFEU) since it does not impede the importation of goods from other Member States.[23]

An example should be used to view this in practice. In *Cognet*[24] French legislation required that books made in France and put directly on the market in that country should comply with a system of fixed prices, whereas the price of books made in France which were exported to another Member State and then re-imported into France and put on the market in the latter Member State (France), was freely determinable. Mr Cognet, a French national, was charged with having

20. *See* also *Smit Transport BV v. Commissie Grensoverschrijdend Beroepsgoederenvervoer*, Case No. 126/82 [1983] ECR 73.
21. For further discussion of this *see* M. Dougan, 'Minimum harmonization and the internal market' (2000) 37 *CMLRev* 853, 867-868; B. Kurcz, 'Harmonisation by means of Directives – never-ending story?' (2001) *EBLRev* 287, 298-299; P. Slot, 'Harmonisation' (1996) 21 *ELRev* 378, 384-386. It should be noted that the maintenance of different conditions of competition in the internal market has been considered a natural and acceptable consequence of the degree of harmonization sought by minimum harmonization legislation. *See Gallaher, supra* n. 19, para. 22; *Hönig v. Stadt Stockach*, Case No. C-128/94 [1995] ECR I-3389, para. 17; para. 84 of the Opinion of Advocate General Jacobs in *ARD v. PRO Sieben Media*, Case No. C-6/98 [1999] ECR I-7599. However, in practical terms, it seems unlikely that Member States would want to engage in reverse discrimination by insisting that their own traders should comply with stricter rules, this leading to the danger of a regulatory race to the bottom – *see* S. Weatherill, *supra* n. 18, pp. 46-47.
22. *Association des Centres disributeurs Édouard Leclerc and others v. SARL 'Au blé vert' and others*, Case No. 229/83 [1985] ECR 1, para. 26.
23. *See Ministère Public v. Verbrugge*, Case No. 160/86 [1987] ECR 1783; *Procureur Général v. Rousseau*, Case No. 168/86 [1987] ECR 995.
24. *Public Prosecutor v. Cognet*, Case No. 355/85 [1986] ECR 3231.

sold books in France (which had never crossed any borders), without complying with the system of fixed prices. In the criminal proceedings brought against him, Mr Cognet argued that the difference in treatment caused by the existence of two systems in the determination of prices for books violated, inter alia, Article 28 EC (Article 34 TFEU). When the issue was referred to the Court of Justice, it was held that the French legislation did not breach Article 28 EC as a difference in treatment between goods which is not capable of restricting imports or of prejudicing the marketing of imported or re-imported goods falls outside the scope of the prohibition in Article 28 EC.[25]

5 Article 29 EC and the Application of the Linking Factor Test: The Traditional Approach

Although in the context of Article 29 EC (Article 35 TFEU) the Court has never had the chance to deliver a judgment expressly ruling that the purely internal rule applies in delimiting the scope of that provision, nevertheless, it appears to be implicit in the Court's case-law that Article 29 EC governs only the situation of goods exported from one Member State to another, that is, there is a requirement of *inter-state* movement before a situation can be accepted within the scope of Article 29 EC. However, the non-applicability of Article 29 EC in situations which involve the imposition by a Member State of its rules on its own goods that are in a purely internal situation, cannot give rise to reverse discrimination since Article 29 EC merely prohibits the exercise of discrimination against goods that are exported to other Member States and, thus, non-discriminatory obstacles to exports of goods to other Member States do not fall within the scope of Article 29 EC.[26] Therefore, since Article 29 EC merely requires Member States to extend the treatment that they apply to their own goods that are marketed within their territory to goods that are exported to other Member State, reverse discrimination cannot arise.

Nonetheless, a more complicated situation arises when a piece of national legislation imposes restrictive rules only on goods that are despatched from a region of a Member State *both* to other regions of that State and to other States.[27] In such a situation, Article 29 EC (Article 35 TFEU) has been held to prohibit merely the application of the legislation to goods exported to other Member States.[28] Under the Court's traditional approach, a case which involves goods which move solely between regions of a single Member State fails to satisfy the first limb (i.e., inter-state movement) of the linking factor test and thus falls outside the scope of Article 29 EC. The application of the traditional approach in this

25. *Ibid.*, para. 10. Note that the Court made clear in *Leclerc, supra* n. 22 (para. 26), that the reason for extending EC protection to re-imported goods is in order to protect their movement *back to the Member State of origin* that is, their (re)-importation into their Member State of origin.
26. *P. B. Groenveld BV v. Produktschap voor Vee en Vlees*, Case No. 15/79 [1979] ECR 3409.
27. That is, goods that remain confined within that region are not subject to the restrictive regime.
28. *Établissements Delhaize Freres et Compagnie Le Lion SA v. Promalvin and AGE Bodegas Unidas*, Case No. C-47/90 [1992] ECR I-3669, para. 13; *Belgium v. Spain*, Case No. C-388/95 [2000] ECR I-3121.

context gives rise to a difference in treatment between, on the one hand, goods moving from one region of a Member State to another region of that same State (that continue being subject to the restrictive legal regime applicable to exports from the area in question) and, on the other, goods exported to other Member States that, by virtue of EC law, are no longer subject to the contested legal regime[29] – a form of reverse discrimination.[30] However, the traditional rulings of the Court in the context of Article 28 EC (Article 34 TFEU) point out that, if the Court was confronted with the question of whether this instance of reverse discrimination is contrary to Article 29, it would simply rule that this difference in treatment should be considered to fall outside the scope of EC law since it in no way inhibits the exportation of goods to other Member States.

6 Articles 23-25 and the Application of the Linking Factor Test: The Traditional Approach

Article 25 EC (Article 30 TFEU) prohibits the imposition of customs duties on imports and exports and charges having equivalent effect (CEEs). In accordance with the traditional application of the purely internal rule in the context of the fundamental freedoms, it has been generally considered that Article 25 EC governs only the situation of goods moving between two or more Member States. Any other movement of goods (e.g., between two parts of one and the same Member State) would seem not to satisfy the first limb of the linking factor test and thus such a situation would fall outside the scope of Article 25 EC. The Court has not expressly ruled on the application of the purely internal rule to the customs duties provisions to date, though it appears that the linking factor test – as applied traditionally – has been applicable in this area as well,[31] at least until the mid-1990s.[32]

---

29. Note that a difference in treatment also arises between goods despatched to other regions of the same Member State and goods confined within their region of production to which the restrictive rules are not applied (the region which applies the restrictive regime). This, however, is not a form of reverse discrimination since the difference in treatment is between two groups of products that fall within the scope of national law and are thus (both) regulated by national legislation.
30. It should be noted that this form of reverse discrimination can, also, arise in the context of Art. 28 EC (Art. 34 TFEU), when a region of a Member State imposes stricter rules on goods that have been imported into that region, both from other Member States and from other regions of that State. Under the Court's traditional approach, the Member State would be required not to apply this stricter regime to goods being imported into that region *from other Member States*, whereas goods imported into that region from other regions of the same State would be the only group of products remaining within the scope of application of the stricter legal regime, in other words, the only group of products suffering reverse discrimination. However, in no case to date has the Court been confronted with such a situation in the context of Art. 28 EC.
31. For a judgment where this was implied *see Società Italiana per l'Oleodotto Transalpino (SIOT) v. Ministero delle finanze, Ministero della marina mercantile, Circoscrizione doganale di Trieste and Ente autonomo del porto di Trieste*, Case No. 266/81 [1983] ECR 731.
32. In the next chapter, it will be seen that in a series of judgments starting in the mid-1990s, the Court has expressly departed from its traditional approach used in finding a link with EC law in this area.

The application of the purely internal rule in delimiting the scope of the customs duties provisions may in some instances lead to the emergence of reverse discrimination. Under the traditional approach to purely internal situations, Article 25 EC (Article 30 TFEU) merely requires Member States not to impose customs duties on goods coming from other Member States or goods exported to other Member States. However, the limited scope of application of Article 25 EC means that such dues may continue being imposed on goods moving between regions of one and the same State. Accordingly, a difference in treatment may arise between, on the one hand, goods moving between Member States (that will not be subject to the imposition of customs duties) and, on the other, goods moving between regions of one and the same State but which do not cross an inter-state frontier (that will be subject to the imposition of customs duties). This will give rise to reverse discrimination and, consequently, to different conditions of competition within the domestic market since goods confined within their domestic market (that have moved between regions of a single Member State) will incur further costs that will have to be reflected in the final price of the product, whereas goods that have crossed inter-state frontiers will escape the imposition of such customs duties.[33] However, under the traditional approach of the Court, again, this difference in treatment escapes the ambit of EC law, and in particular the scope of application of the customs duties provisions, since it does not seem capable of affecting the inter-state movement of goods.[34]

B Free Movement of Workers

A national of a Member State cannot rely on Article 39 EC (Article 45 TFEU) when his or her situation is considered purely internal. Nor can he or she rely on secondary legislation bestowing supplementary rights upon persons falling within the personal scope of that provision. Hence, persons working in their own Member

33. Note that like in the context of Art. 29 EC (Art. 35 TFEU), in this context as well, a difference in treatment may arise between goods *moving* within the territory of one Member State and goods confined within their region of production (the region which imposed the restrictive regime). However, again, this difference in treatment cannot be considered a form of reverse discrimination since it merely exists as a result of the application of national law to situations that fall within the scope of national law.
34. Note that the purely internal rule has been applied, also, in delimiting the scope of Art. 90 EC (Art. 110 TFEU) which prohibits Member States from imposing on imported goods internal taxation in excess of that imposed on domestic products. The ECJ has made it clear that Art. 90 EC does not prohibit the reverse situation that is, the imposition of internal taxation on domestic goods in excess of that imposed on imported products and thus the latter may suffer reverse discrimination as a result of the limited scope of application of Art. 90 EC. *See SA des grandes distilleries Peureux v. Directeur des Services fiscaux de la Haute-Saône et du territoire de Belfort*, Case No. 86/78 [1979] ECR 897, paras 32-33; *Eismann Alto Adige Srl v. Ufficio IVA di Bolzano*, Case No. C-217/94 [1996] ECR I-5287. For an explanation *see* S. Weatherill and P. Beaumont, *EU Law* (3rd edn, London, Penguin, 1999), pp. 470-471; A. Evans, *A Textbook on EU Law* (Oxford, Hart, 1998), pp. 457-458.

State who are unable to demonstrate a link with EC law can be the victims of reverse discrimination, as a result of the fact that the national legal regime governing their situation may be less generous than the rules (if any) applicable in situations governed by EC law.[35]

As already explained, a situation can escape the characterization of 'purely internal' if the three-limb test set out in Chapter 1 can be satisfied on the specific facts of the case. In other words, a Member State national can rely on Article 39 EC (Article 45 TFEU) against his or her own Member State if he or she has moved to another Member State in order to work. In such a situation, if national legislation is found to be interfering with that person's freedom to move as a worker, either by being discriminatory on the ground of 'migration' or by simply imposing an obstacle to that person's inter-state movement, it violates Article 39 EC and becomes inapplicable. Further, when someone moves to another Member State to work or obtain a qualification and then *returns to his or her own State in order to work*, his or her situation is no longer a purely internal one[36] – the situation is regarded as equivalent to that of any other person relying, as against the host State, on the rights and liberties guaranteed by the Treaty and therefore that person must be treated in the same way as his or her State of nationality is obliged to treat, by virtue of EC law, workers having the nationality of another Member State.[37]

Member State nationals who move to other Member States in order to work there can, naturally, also rely on Article 39 EC (Article 45 TFEU) against the host Member State whenever a measure of the latter imposes an obstacle to that movement.

As will be seen, the application of the purely internal rule in the context of Article 39 EC (Article 45 TFEU) can lead to the emergence of reverse discrimination. However, the Court in its case-law has ruled out the possibility of outlawing this form of differential treatment through the use of the fundamental freedoms.

Below, there will be an exposition of the Court's traditional case-law in the context of the free movement of workers, where the purely internal rule was

---

35. For an explanation of the purely internal rule and reverse discrimination in the context of the free movement of workers *see* P. Craig and G. de Búrca, *EU Law: Text, Cases and Materials* (4th edn, Oxford, OUP, 2008), pp. 762-763; A. Arnull (ed.), *Wyatt and Dashwood's European Union Law* (4th edn, London, Sweet & Maxwell, 2000), pp. 383-384; A. Arnull, *The European Union and its Court of Justice* (Oxford, OUP, 1999), pp. 321-324; D. Martin and E. Guild, *Free Movement of Persons in the European Union* (London, Edinburgh, Butterworths, 1996), pp. 25-26; R.C.A. White, *Workers, Establishment and Services in the European Union* (Oxford, OUP, 2004), pp. 42-46; E. Johnson and D. O'Keeffe, 'From discrimination to obstacles to free movement: recent developments concerning the free movement of workers 1989-1994' (1994) 31 *CMLRev* 1313, 1334-1340; C. Greenwood, 'Nationality and the Limits of the Free movement of Persons in Community Law' (1987) 7 *YEL* 185, 199-203.
36. *See* A. Arnull, *The General Principles of EEC Law and the Individual* (London, Leicester, Leicester University Press, 1990), pp. 60-61; P. Oliver, 'Non-Community nationals and the Treaty of Rome' (1985) *YEL* 57, 64.
37. Gareth Davies has drawn a parallelism between this 'assimilation to a foreigner' reasoning of the Court in the free movement of persons case-law and the Court's rulings on re-imported goods. *See* G. Davies, *supra* n. 15, p. 123.

applied; where the issue of reverse discrimination was discussed by the Court; and where, despite the fact that a person was relying on Article 39 EC against his or her Member State of nationality, a link with EC law was established. A similar structure will be followed in the following two subsections dealing with the free movement of persons in the context of the freedom of establishment and the freedom to provide services, respectively.

1 Article 39 EC and Purely Internal Situations

An example of a situation which was confined within the territory of a Member State and, clearly, did not involve any hindrance to the free movement of a worker is the case of *Iorio*.[38] Mr Iorio was an Italian lawyer who was residing and working in Italy. Italian regulations allowed access to certain trains that operated within Italian territory (in particular, express trains), only to persons who held first class tickets. In a case brought against him as a result of not complying with those regulations, Mr Iorio argued that the regulations were contrary to Article 39(3)(b) EC (Article 45(3)(b) TFEU) according to which workers have the right to move freely within the territory of Member States. When the issue reached the Court of Justice in the form of a preliminary ruling question, the Court merely pointed out that the situation of Mr Iorio contained no factor connecting it to the provisions of Community law concerning the freedom of movement for workers and thus Article 39 EC (Article 45 TFEU) was not applicable.[39] The fact that an Italian national who was a worker in Italy might find it difficult, due to the contested Italian rules, to move *within* Italy, could not, in any way, affect his right to move to other Member States in order to work, and thus the impugned rules could not amount to a violation of Article 39 EC.[40]

2 Article 39 EC and Reverse Discrimination

Some of the judgments of the Court where it was ruled that the factual background to a case was purely internal to a Member State and thus fell outside the scope of EC law, have led to the emergence of reverse discrimination.[41] We saw in Chapter 1 of the book the infamous *Morson and Jhanjan* case,[42] where the

38. *Iorio v. Azienda autonoma delle ferrovie dello Stato*, Case No. 298/84 [1986] ECR 247.
39. *Ibid.*, para. 15.
40. *See* also *Criminal proceedings against Morais*, Case No. C-60/91 [1992] ECR I-2085; *R v. Saunders*, Case No. 175/78 [1979] ECR 1129.
41. *Criminal proceedings against Peralta*, Case No. C-379/92 [1994] ECR I-3453, paras 27-28; *Steen v. Deutsche Bundespost*, Case No. C-332/90 [1992] ECR I-341.
42. *Morson and Jhanjan v. Netherlands*, Joined Cases 35 and 36/82 [1982] ECR 3723. For other cases involving reverse discrimination as regards the availability of rights derived from EC law to the family members of Member State nationals who were in a purely internal situation, *see Land Nordrhein-Westfalen v. Uecker and Jacquet*, Case No. C-64/96 [1997] ECR I-3171; *Zaoui v. Cramif*, Case No. 147/87 [1987] ECR 5511; *Petit v. Office National des Pensions*, Case No. C-153/91 [1992] ECR I-4973; *Koua Poirrez v. Caisse d'allocations familiales de la region*

third-country national parents of Dutch nationals who were in a purely internal situation, could not rely on EC secondary legislation in order to be allowed to accompany their children there. This gave rise to reverse discrimination, as other Dutch nationals who could show a link with EC law or nationals of other Member States who went to work in the Netherlands could, under Community law, be accompanied by their family members in that State.

Like in the context of the free movement of goods, the Court of Justice has ruled that reverse discrimination exercised by a Member State against its own nationals who fall outside the scope of Article 39 EC (Article 45 TFEU), is not a form of differential treatment that violates EC law. In *Hurd v. Jones*[43] it was held that the United Kingdom was not in violation of Article 12 EC (Article 18 TFEU) read in conjunction with Article 39 EC when it subjected to income tax both the basic salary paid by the United Kingdom to British teachers in the European School in Britain and the 'European supplement' paid to them by the European School, whilst it did not require other Member State nationals who worked in the same school to pay to the British Government tax on the 'European supplement'. Since, according to the Court, the situation of the former was a purely internal one, this difference in treatment fell outside the scope of EC law. It seems that the rationale behind the Court's judgment in this case is the same as that in the case of *Mathot* in the context of the free movement of goods (though the Court, in this case, has not stated this expressly): since the difference in treatment which formed the subject-matter of the case was not prejudicial to the achievement of the aim of establishing an internal market in labour, it fell outside the scope of EC law.

Again, like in the area of the free movement of goods, in this area as well reverse discrimination may emerge when a regional law applies a more favourable legal regime only to persons who both reside and work in the territory of that region and the ECJ requires the extension of this favourable regime to persons who work in that region (even though they do not reside there) *and* whose situation falls within the scope of EC law. Because of the doctrine of purely internal situations, EC law does not require the region to extend this (more favourable) regime to persons who work in that region but reside in a different region in the same Member State *and* whose situation is a wholly internal one. Such an instance of reverse discrimination has emerged following the Court's ruling in *Government of the French Community and Walloon Government v. Flemish Government.*[44] In that case, at issue was the compatibility with, inter alia, Article 39 EC (Article 45

---

perisienne, substituée par la Caisse d'allocations familiales de la Seine-Saint-Denis, Case No. C-206/91 [1992] ECR 6685, paras 10-14. For cases where national courts reached the same conclusion without making a reference for a preliminary ruling to the ECJ *see The Queen v. Secretary of State for the Home Department ex parte Muhammad Ayub*, [1983] 3 CMLR 140 (English High Court); *Re Residence Permit for an Egyptian National*, [1975] 2 CMLR 402 (German Oberverwaltungsgericht Rheinland-Pfalz).

43. *Hurd v. Jones (Her Majesty's Inspector of Taxes)*, Case No. 44/84 [1986] ECR 29.
44. *Government of the French Community and Walloon Government v. Flemish Government*, Case No. C-212/06, judgment of 1 Apr. 2008, not yet reported. It should be noted that such instances of reverse discrimination can arise in the context of all the free movement of persons provisions.

TFEU) of certain features of the Flemish care insurance scheme.[45] The impugned (Flemish) regional laws provided that affiliation to the care insurance scheme was only open to persons residing in the Dutch-speaking (Flemish) region of Belgium.[46] The Court found that the free movement of workers provisions[47] require the extension of the availability of the care insurance scheme to nationals of other Member States who work in that region whilst residing outside that region; and to Belgian nationals who work in that region whilst residing outside that region *provided that they can demonstrate that their situation falls within the scope of EC law as a result of having made use of their right to freedom of (inter-State) movement.* In contrast, the Court held that Belgian nationals who work in the Flemish region whilst residing outside that region *and* cannot point to a link with EC law, can continue being excluded from the Flemish care insurance scheme. Hence, following the Court's judgment in this case, reverse discrimination emerged.[48] And, following its classic approach to the permissibility of reverse discrimination, the Court, in a recent case in the context of Article 43 EC (Article 49 TFEU), seems to have hinted that this form of reverse discrimination is also not contrary to the free movement of persons provisions.[49]

3 Establishing a Link with EC Law: Export Restrictions

Under the Court's traditional approach, a Member State national can rely on Article 39 EC (Article 45 TFEU) against his or her own Member State, provided that a link with EC law can be proved on the facts of the case. Such a link can be established when the Member State of origin imposes an 'export restriction'; in other words, when a person wishes to move to another Member State to work and the application of a specific piece of national legislation will have the effect of impeding that movement.

To avoid repetition, this point should be kept in mind when reading the subsequent parts of the chapter.

45. The questions referred also asked whether the Flemish care insurance scheme was contrary to Art. 43 EC (Art. 49 TFEU) and Art. 18 EC (Art. 21 TFEU).
46. In fact, it also provided that the scheme was open to persons residing in the bilingual region of Brussels-Capital. It should be noted that, in order to comply with the requirements of EC law, in 2004 a Decree of the Flemish Parliament extended the availability of the care insurance scheme to persons working in the territory of the Flemish region and residing in a Member State other than Belgium.
47. This referring to Art. 39 EC (Art. 45 TFEU) and Art. 43 EC (Art. 49 TFEU).
48. For an explanation *see* para. 151 of the Opinion of Advocate General Sharpston in this case.
49. *See Commission v. Germany (psychotherapists)*, Case No. C-456/05, judgment of 6 Dec. 2007, not yet reported, paras 44 and 74-75. Also, again as in the context of goods, a further instance of differential treatment arises between, on the one hand, nationals of that Member State who work in that region *but* reside outside it *and* do not fall within the scope of EC law (and thus are not entitled to the benefit), and, on the other, nationals of that Member State who reside within the said region and do not fall within the scope of EC law (who are the persons who were in the first instance entitled to the benefit).

In the landmark case of *Bosman*,[50] the Court of Justice held that Article 39 EC (Article 45 TFEU) prohibited the application of rules of, inter alia, the *Belgian* football association which required the payment of 'transfer fees' by the destination team to the originating team, before a transfer of a *Belgian* professional footballer *from a Belgian team to a French team* could take effect. The reason for this was that the application of the contested legislation to the specific situation in question was, in effect, an 'export restriction'.[51] Since Member State nationals have the right to leave their country in order to move to another Member State to pursue an economic activity in its territory,[52] national laws which preclude or deter a national of a Member State from leaving his or her country of origin in order to exercise his or her right to freedom of movement constitute an obstacle to that freedom and are therefore contrary to Article 39 EC.[53] Accordingly, Mr Bosman could rely on Article 39 EC *against his State of origin* since all three limbs of the linking factor test were satisfied on the facts before the Court: he was definitely going to move from Belgium to France (he had already signed a contract to this effect); this movement was for an economic purpose (to work); the refusal to apply Article 39 EC in the case and, thus, the application of the contested transfer rules, would have deterred Mr Bosman from exercising that movement.[54]

4 Establishing a Link with EC law: Obstacles to the Free Movement of a Person Back to his or her Member State of Origin in Order to Work

As in the context of the free movement of goods and, in particular, the case-law on re-imported goods seen above, in the area of the free movement of workers the Court has accepted that the *return* of a Member State national to his or her State of nationality in order to work there, brings that person's situation within the scope of Article 39 EC (Article 45 TFEU).

---

50. *Union Royal Belge des Société de Football Association ASBL & others v. Bosman*, Case No. C-415/93 [1995] ECR I-4921.
51. *Ibid.*, para. 100.
52. *Roux v. Belgium*, Case No. C-363/89 [1991] ECR I-273, para. 9.
53. *Masgio v. Bundesknappschaft*, Case No. C-10/90 [1991] ECR I-1119, paras 18-19.
54. *See* also *Criminal proceedings against Ledoux*, Case No. 127/86 [1988] ECR 3741. For subsequent case-law where this reasoning was affirmed *see Criminal proceedings against Van Lent*, Case No. C-232/01 [2003] ECR I-11525; *Commission v. Denmark (motor vehicles)*, Case No. C-464/02 [2005] ECR I-7929; *F.W.L. de Groot v. Staatssecretaris van Financiën*, Case No. C-385/00 [2002] ECR I-11819; *Terhoeve v. Inspecteur van de Belastingdiens Particulieren/Ondernemingen Buitenland*, Case No. C-18/95 [1999] ECR I-345; *Sehrer v. Bundesknappschaft*, Case No. C-302/98 [2000] ECR I-4585; *Kranemann v. Land Nordrhein-Westfalen*, Case No. C-109/04 [2005] ECR I-2421; *Gilly v. Directeur des Services Fiscaux du Bas-Rhin*, Case No. C-336/96 [1998] ECR I-2793; *Schilling v. Finanzamt Nürnberg-Süd*, Case No. C-209/01 [2003] ECR I-13389, paras 23-25; *Rijksdienst voor Pensioenen v. Robert Engelbrecht*, Case No. C-262/97 [2000] ECR I-7321; *Commission v. Germany (subsidy for the construction or purchase of a dwelling)*, Case No. C-152/05, judgment of 17 Jan. 2008, para. 22.

In *De Bobadilla*,[55] Ms Fernandez de Bobadilla was a Spanish national who, after obtaining a postgraduate qualification in fine arts restoration in the United Kingdom, returned to Spain and applied to take part in a competition for the post of restorer in the museum of Prado. In order to allow her to participate in the competition, the Spanish authorities required her to sit a number of examinations to prove that the knowledge she acquired in the United Kingdom was equivalent to that acquired by possession of Spanish qualifications. Ms De Bobadilla refused to sit the examinations because, in her view, the action of the Spanish authorities was contrary to EC law.

When the issue was referred to the ECJ, it was held that a Member State national who had left her State of origin in order to obtain a qualification in another Member State and later returned to the former to work, was in the same position as migrant workers and thus could rely on Article 39 EC (Article 45 TFEU).[56] In particular, Article 39 EC required the authorities of her Member State of origin to compare the knowledge and qualifications certified by her diploma with the knowledge and abilities required by the national rules. It was only if the former were found not to correspond to the latter that the home State authorities would be able to require her to sit the examination. If recognition of the qualification was automatically ruled out (and thus EC rights were not extended to require Spain to conduct an assessment to establish equivalence), this would deter Ms De Bobadilla from moving back to Spain in order to work there and thus would deprive her of the right to exercise free movement *back to her Member State of origin* to work.[57] Therefore, although Ms De Bobadilla was relying on EC law against her Member State of nationality, the situation was not a purely internal one, as a sufficient link with one of the fundamental freedoms was established on the facts before the Court. Ms De Bobadilla had exercised movement from one Member State (the United Kingdom) to another (Spain – her State of nationality); in order to work; and the refusal to apply Article 39 EC would have deterred that movement.

C FREEDOM OF ESTABLISHMENT

The purely internal rule is one of the limits placed on the scope of application of Article 43 EC (Article 49 TFEU). Indeed, it would be peculiar if the purely internal

55. *De Bobadilla v. Museo Nacional del Prado*, Case No. C-234/97 [1999] ECR I-4773.
56. *Ibid.*, para. 30.
57. For very recent cases which involved similar situations as *De Bobadilla*, but where the issue of a purely internal situation was not discussed *see Aslanidou v. Ypourgos Ygeias & Pronoias*, Case No. C-142/04 [2005] ECR I-7181; *Peros v. Technico Epimelitirio Ellados*, Case No. C-141/04 [2005] ECR I-7163. For another case where the same approach was implicit, though the Court had based its judgment on a finding of indirect discrimination on the grounds of nationality *see Scholz v. Opera Universitaria di Cagliari and Cinzia Porcedda*, Case No. C-419/92 [1994] ECR I-505.

rule was found not to be applicable to Article 43 EC, as the wording of the provision itself points to the need for an inter-state element.[58]

A person who cannot show that he or she has moved to another Member State and that his or her movement has contributed to the realization of the internal market, cannot rely on Article 43 EC (Article 49 TFEU) against any Member State, including his or her own. However, like in the area of the free movement of workers, a link with EC law can be found in two instances: firstly, where a national of Member State A moves to Member State B in order to establish a business and work there in a self-employed capacity; secondly, where a national of Member State A moves to Member State B, for example in order to work or obtain a qualification, and then returns to Member State A to become established. In all instances, of course, the third limb of the test (i.e., the need to prove that there is a link between the right claimed and the exercise of inter-state movement for an economic purpose) must also be satisfied.

Like in the context of the other fundamental freedoms, the application of the purely internal rule when delimiting the scope of application of Article 43 EC (Article 49 TFEU) can give rise to reverse discrimination. This can, of course, occur both when delimiting the scope of Article 43 EC as such and when delimiting the scope of secondary legislation applying to persons who have made use of the freedom of establishment. As will be seen below, like in the context of the other fundamental freedoms, reverse discrimination has been held by the Court to fall outside the scope of Article 43 EC.[59]

1 Article 43 EC and Purely Internal Situations

Niño[60] is the classic example of the application of the purely internal rule in the context of the freedom of establishment. The case concerned four Italian nationals who, without authorization to practise as medical doctors as was required by Italian law, had provided biotherapy and pranotherapy treatment in Italy. Criminal proceedings were brought against them and they relied on Article 43 EC (Article 49 TFEU) to claim that the Italian legislation in question violated Community law. The Court of Justice found that since, on the facts, all the accused were Italian nationals who qualified as biotherapists and pranotherapists in Italy and who had been charged under Italian legislation as a result of treatment administered solely

58. '[R]estrictions on the freedom of establishment of nationals of a Member State in the territory of another Member State shall be prohibited'. *See*, however, the approach of Advocate General Mayras in *Thieffry v. Conseil de l'Ordre des Avocats à la Cour de Paris*, Case No. 71/76 [1977] ECR 1199, p. 792.
59. For an explanation of the purely internal rule and reverse discrimination in the context of the freedom of establishment, *see* P. Craig and G. de Búrca, *supra* n. 35, pp. 803-805; F. Weiss and F. Wooldridge, *Free Movement of Persons Within the European Community* (The Hague, Kluwer Law International, 2002), pp. 104-105; R.C.A. White, *supra* n. 35, pp. 42-46. *See* also the comments of Stanley in his annotation of *Asscher* in (1997) 34 *CMLRev* 713, 717-723.
60. *Criminal proceedings against Niño and others*, Joined Cases 54 and 91/88 and 14/89 [1990] ECR 3537.

within Italy, they were in a purely internal situation and thus Article 43 EC was not applicable to their case.[61] Accordingly, the ECJ did not have to answer the specific question referred to it by the national court.

2 Article 43 EC and Reverse Discrimination

In the context of Article 43 EC (Article 49 TFEU), reverse discrimination usually arises when a national who has obtained his or her qualifications or has worked in his or her own Member State and seeks to derive a right from EC law, cannot rely on Article 43 EC because the situation is found to be purely internal to that Member State. That person may be in a situation less favourable than the situation of a person who comes to that Member State from another Member State in order to establish business there, since the latter can rely on the provisions of EC law governing the freedom of establishment which may require the grant of more extensive rights or the imposition of less burdensome requirements, than those that are laid down by national laws.

In this context as well, the Court has held that reverse discrimination is not contrary to EC law. This can be seen in the case of *Aubertin*.[62] In that case at issue was French legislation which required French hairdressers to have a hairdressing diploma or master's diploma to be able to practise in France, whereas, in order to comply with the requirements of EC law, no such requirement had been imposed on Member State nationals (including French nationals) who had worked for a number of years as hairdressers in other Member States. A group of French hairdressers who operated a hairdressing salon in France without being in possession of the required diplomas and without having worked in other Member States were prosecuted under that French legislation. The accused claimed that the legislation in question was contrary to Article 43 EC (Article 49 TFEU) because it discriminated against French nationals in a purely internal situation. The Court found that Article 43 EC did not preclude France from imposing stricter requirements on

61. *Ibid.*, paras 10-11. *See* also, *Kapasakalis, Skiathitis and Kougiagkas v. Greek State*, Joined Cases C-225/95, 226/95 and 227/95 [1998] ECR I-4239 where it was held that 89/48 (EEC) Directive on a general system for the recognition of higher education diplomas awarded on completion of professional education and training of at least three years' duration, OJ L 19/16, 1989, could not be relied on by Greek nationals who had obtained their higher education in Greece and worked in Greece. The purely internal situations doctrine has also been applied in delimiting the scope of the successor to Directive 89/48: Art. 2(1) of 2005/36 (EC) Directive on the recognition of professional qualifications, OJ L 255/22, 2005, provides that Directive 2005/36 applies only to applicants who seek to practise in a State other than the State in which their qualifications were obtained. *See* also, in a broader context, *Criminal proceedings against Van Buynder*, Case No. C-152/94 [1995] ECR I-3981; *Criminal proceedings against Lopez Brea*, Joined Cases C-330/90 and C-331/90 [1992] ECR I-323; *Morais supra* n. 40; *Ministère Public v. Gauchard*, Case No. 20/87 [1987] ECR 4879; *Criminal proceedings against Bekaert*, Case No. 204/87 [1988] ECR 209; *Criminal proceedings against Gervais et al.*, Case No. C-17/94 [1995] ECR I-4353.
62. *Criminal proceedings against Aubertin and others*, Joined Cases C-29/94, C-30/94, C-31/94, C-32/94, C-33/94, C-34/94 and C-35/94 [1995] ECR I-301.

hairdressers who were in a wholly domestic situation. According to the Court, this form of difference in treatment fell outside the scope of Article 43 EC since it did not impede the exercise of the freedom of establishment of Member State nationals to other Member States.[63]

3 Establishing a Link with EC Law: Export Restrictions

Like in the very similar context of the free movement of workers, the Court of Justice has made it clear in its case-law that the provisions of the Treaty on the freedom of establishment include within their scope 'export restrictions'. Accordingly, situations that involve a restriction imposed by their Member State of origin on persons (whether natural or legal) interested in exercising their freedom of establishment, fall within the scope of those provisions and thus, in such cases, those persons can rely on EC law against their own Member State.[64]

4 Establishing a Link with EC Law: Obstacles to the Free Movement of a Person Back to his or her Member State of Origin in Order to Work in a Self-employed Capacity

In the same way as traders can rely on Article 28 EC (Article 34 TFEU) against their own Member State when a case involves goods re-imported to their State of production; and like in the context of the free movement of workers, where Article 39 EC applies (Article 45 TFEU) to ensure that a national of a Member State is not deterred by rules of that State from returning there to work; the Court has accepted that the *return* of a Member State national to his or her State of nationality in order to work in a self-employed capacity brings the situation within the scope of Article 43 EC.

The landmark case on this issue is *Knoors*.[65] In that case, a Dutch national who had worked for a number of years in Belgium as a plumber, returned to the Netherlands and applied for an authorization to carry on the same trade there in a self-employed capacity. His application was refused because he did not possess the qualifications required for that trade by Dutch legislation. Furthermore, the Dutch authorities were of the view that Knoors (as a Dutch national) could not, on the

---

63. *Ibid.*, para. 13.
64. *See The Queen v. H.M. Treasury and Commissioners of Inland Revenue ex parte Daily Mail and General Trust plc*, Case No. 81/87 [1988] ECR 5483, para. 16. This was subsequently confirmed in *Marks & Spencer plc v. David Halsey (HM Inspector of Taxes)*, Case No. C-446/03 [2005] ECR I-10837, para. 31; *Criminal proceedings against Nadin, Nadin-Lux SA and Durré*, Joined Cases C-151/04 and C-152/04 [2005] ECR I-11203; *C. Baars v. Inspecteur der Belastingdienst Particulieren/Ondernemingen Gorinchem*, Case No. C-251/98 [2000] ECR I-2787, paras 28-30; *Finanzamt Offenbach am Main-Land v. Keller Holding GmbH*, Case No. C-471/04 [2006] ECR I-2107, para. 30; *The International Transport Workers' Federation and The Finnish Seamen's Union v. Viking Line ABP and OÜ Viking Line Eesti*, Case No. C-438/05, judgment of 11 Dec. 2007, not yet reported, paras 68-69; *Commission v. Germany (subsidy for the construction or purchase of a dwelling), supra* n. 54, para. 22.
65. *Knoors v. Secretary of State for Economic Affairs*, Case No. 115/78 [1979] ECR 399.

alternative, rely on Community secondary legislation under which Member States had to recognize as a sufficient proof of trade qualifications, the actual practice in another Member State of the activity in question. When the issue was referred to the ECJ, the Court found that a person in the position of Knoors could rely on the relevant Community legislation and be allowed to exercise his trade *in his Member State of origin* by having his experience acquired in another Member State taken into account – in other words, he was entitled to be treated like any other Member State national wishing to be established in the Netherlands and work as a plumber.[66]

In this case, the finding of a link with EC law was based on the existence of movement from a Member State where a person was working (Belgium) to another Member State in order to establish a business (the Netherlands). The fact that the State of destination was, also, the State of which Mr Knoors was a national, seems to have played no part in determining whether the situation fell within the scope of EC law. Since the refusal to accept the qualification of Mr Knoors, would impose an obstacle to the movement of Mr Knoors from Belgium back to the Netherlands for an economic purpose (i.e., to work as a self-employed person), there was a, prima facie, violation of Article 43 EC (Article 49 TFEU).

D Free Movement of Services

Throughout the years, it has been made clear that the purely internal rule is also applicable in the context of the free movement of services. Thus, in the case of *Debauve* the ECJ pointed out that

> [T]he provisions of the Treaty on freedom to provide services cannot apply to activities whose relevant elements are confined within a single Member State.[67]

---

66. *Ibid.*, para. 24. *See* also *C. C. van de Bijl v. Staatssecretaris van Economische Zaken*, Case No. 130/88 [1989] ECR 3039; and more recently, *Conseil National de l'Ordre des Architects v. Dreessen*, Case No. C-31/00 [2002] ECR I-663 (very similar to the case of *De Bobadilla*). Note that the Court in its initial case-law after *Knoors*, interpreted that case restrictively, to the effect that Knoors was only entitled to use his qualifications obtained in another Member State against his Member State of origin because there was secondary legislation which established equivalence and thus he had acquired rights in the host State which were recognized by the provisions of Community law: *Ministère Public v. Auer*, Case No. 136/78 [1979] ECR 437; *Auer v. Ministère Public (No. 2)*, Case No. 271/82 [1983] ECR 2727; *Criminal proceedings against Bouchoucha*, Case No. C-61/89 [1990] ECR I-3551; *Broekmeulen v. Huisarts Registratie Commissie*, Case No. 246/80 [1981] ECR 2311; *Middleburgh v. Chief Adjudication Officer*, Case No. C-15/90 [1991] ECR I-4655. *See* A. Arnull *supra* n. 36, pp. 52-57; C. Greenwood *supra* n. 35, 195-197 and 203; S.D. Kon, 'Aspects of Reverse Discrimination in Community Law' (1981) 6 *ELRev* 75. The Court has, however, made it clear in subsequent case-law (*Kraus v. Land Baden-Württemberg*, Case No. C-19/92 [1993] ECR I-1663) that this is no longer the case.
67. *Procureur du Roi v. Debauve and others*, Case No. 52/79 [1980] ECR 833, para. 9. This was subsequently affirmed in *Commission v. France (tourist guides)*, Case No. C-154/89 [1991] ECR I-659, para. 9.

Hence, when a case involves the provision of services within one and the same Member State, Article 49 EC (Article 56 TFEU) cannot be of any assistance to the parties. Any claims they have can only be based on national law. In this context, a link with EC law is found as soon as the facts of a case involve some kind of movement, from or towards a Member State, whether this is a movement of persons (to receive[68] or provide[69] services)[70] or of services themselves.[71] Lorna Woods has explained that '[t]he internal situation can be seen as describing the position when none of the service provider, the service recipient or the service itself cross a border'.[72] Accordingly, the freedom to provide services may be relied on by a provider of services against the Member State in which he or she is established, where the services are provided for recipients established in another Member State or, more generally, where he or she offers services in a Member State other than the one in which he or she is established.[73] In addition, a link with EC law is established when a person moves from his or her Member State of origin to another Member State to receive services; or, even if a recipient does not move to another Member State, a link may nonetheless be established if he or she receives services provided by a person established in another Member State (and, even if the latter does not move to the former's State).

The requirement of inter-state movement is particularly important in the area of services, and this is evident from the fact that such a movement must be continuously taking place in order for a situation to fall within the scope of these

---

68. *Luisi and Carbone v. Ministero del Tesoro*, Joined Cases 286/82 and 26/83 [1984] ECR 377; *Cowan v. Le Trésor Public*, Case No. 186/87 [1989] ECR 195.
69. *Corsica Ferries Italia Srl v. Corpo dei Piloti del Porto di Genova*, Case No. C-18/93 [1994] ECR I-1783, para. 30; *Peralta supra* n. 41, paras 40-42; *Deliège v. Ligue Francophone de Judi et Disciplines Associées ASBL*, Joined Cases C-51/96 and C-191/97 [2000] ECR I-2549, para. 58; *Alpine Investments BV v. Minister van Financiën*, Case No. C-384/93 [1995] ECR I-1141, para. 30.
70. Note that a situation also falls within the scope of EC law when both the provider of the service and the beneficiary go to a Member State that is not their own. *See* First biennial report on the application of the principle of mutual recognition in product and services markets, SEC (1999) 1106, not published in the Official Journal.
71. *Alpine Investments, supra* n. 69; *Scorpio Konzertproduktionen GmbH*, Case No. C-290/04 [2006] ECR I-9461, paras 63-65. Advocate General Mancini in *Bond van Adverteerders v. Netherlands*, Case No. 352/85 [1988] ECR 2085 had even suggested that in respect of certain services which are 'without frontiers' such as broadcasting services, the situation should never be qualified as a purely internal one. Note, however, that the Court in that case avoided to deal with that issue, since it found that on the facts the provider and the recipient of the services in question were established in two different Member States and thus the situation fell within the scope of EC law as a result of that factor.
72. L. Woods, *Free Movement of Goods and Services within the European Community*, (Aldershot, Ashgate, 2004), p. 204. It should be noted that the link with EC law does not have to be present from the beginning of the relationship between a provider and a recipient; it is sufficient if the activities meet the inter-state movement criterion at some (subsequent) stage: *Société Générale Alsacienne de Banque SA v. Koestler*, Case No. 15/78 [1978] ECR 1971.
73. *United Pan-Europe Communications Belgium SA and others v. État belge*, Case No. C-250/06, judgment of 13 Dec. 2007, not yet reported, para. 31.

provisions.[74] To that effect, the Court in the *Sodemare* case[75] held that when a company establishes itself in a Member State for providing services on a long-term basis to persons residing permanently there, rights under Article 49 EC (Article 56 TFEU) are exhausted and the matter falls to be treated as purely internal to the Member State in question.[76]

In this context as well, the application of the purely internal rule can give rise to reverse discrimination – the provision of services in a purely national context may be subject to a more restrictive trading regime than the one applicable to cross-border services that fall within the scope of EC law.[77]

1 Article 49 EC and Purely Internal Situations

Although it seems that it is not overly problematic to establish a link with EC law in the area of the free movement of services, nevertheless, there have been a number of cases where the ECJ found that the facts were purely internal to a Member State and thus outside the scope of application of EC law.[78] For example, in *Jägerskiöld* it was held that Article 49 EC (Article 56 TFEU) was not applicable as the facts of the case involved a purely internal situation – they involved:

> [L]egal proceedings . . . between two Finnish nationals, both established in Finland, concerning the right of one of them to fish in waters belonging to the other situated in Finland.[79]

2 Article 49 EC and Reverse Discrimination

The application of the purely internal rule when delimiting the scope of Article 49 EC (Article 56 TFEU) has, sometimes, given rise to reverse discrimination. In *Höfner and Elser*,[80] at issue was German legislation which prohibited anybody,

---

74. Contrast this with the position in the area of the free movement of workers and the freedom of establishment, where, for a situation to fall within the scope of EC law, it is sufficient if the exercise of inter-state movement has taken place once.
75. *Sodemare SA, Anni Azzuri Holdings SpA & Anni Azzuri Rezzato Srl v. Regione Lombardia*, Case No. C-70/95 [1997] ECR I-3395, paras 36-40.
76. *See* also *Zhu and Chen v. Secretary of State for the Home Department*, Case No. C-200/02 [2004] ECR I-9925, para. 22 for the position of a recipient of services who moves permanently to another Member State in order to receive services from a provider established in that Member State.
77. For an explanation of the purely internal rule and reverse discrimination in the area of the free movement of services *see*: P. Craig and G. de Búrca, *supra* n. 35, pp. 817-818; D. Martin and E. Guild *supra* n. 35, pp. 71-72; R.C.A. White, *supra* n. 35, pp. 42-46; D.M.W. Pickup, 'Reverse Discrimination and Freedom of Movement for workers' (1986) 23 *CMLRev* 135, 149-151.
78. *Gervais supra* n. 61; *RI.SAN. Srl v. Comune di Ischia*, Case No. C-108/98 [1999] ECR I-5219, paras 21-23; *USSL No. 47 di Biella*, Case No. C-134/95 [1997] ECR I-195.
79. *Jägerskiöld v. Gustafsson*, Case No. C-97/98 [1999] ECR I-7319, para. 43.
80. *Höfner and Elser v. Mactroton GmbH*, Case No. C-41/90 [1991] ECR I-1979.

apart from authorized bodies, to carry out employment procurement activities. Messrs Höfner and Elser, German nationals established in Germany, had a contract with Macrotron GmbH (a German company) under which they would assist the latter in the recruitment of a sales director. Höfner and Elser presented to Macrotron a German candidate for the post and subsequently claimed their fees. Macrotron refused to pay the fees, claiming that the contract was void under the German civil code because it violated the legislation on employment procurement. When the case was brought before a German court, the question arose as to whether the German legislation on employment procurement was in violation of Article 49 EC.

The ECJ found that since Höfner and Elser were German recruitment consultants, Macrotron was a German company and the candidate proposed by the former was a German national, this was a purely internal situation and thus Article 49 EC (Article 56 TFEU) was not applicable. The Court went on to say that

> [T]hat finding cannot be invalidated by the fact that a contract concluded between the recruitment consultants and the undertakings concerned includes the theoretical possibility of seeking German candidates resident in other Member States or nationals of other Member States.[81]

This latter comment of the Court implies that if the recruitment consultants had presented to Macrotron a national of another Member State or a German national who would be able to show that his situation entailed a cross-border element, things would be different, and the German legislation would be assessed under Article 49 EC (Article 56 TFEU), and most probably, would be found to be in violation of that provision.[82] Accordingly, the application of the purely internal rule in this instance might lead to the emergence of discrimination against German nationals who might be suitable candidates but who would be unable to show a link with EC law. German candidates in purely internal situations might be disadvantaged when competing with candidates falling within the scope of EC law since procurement consultants might, after the ECJ's judgment in this case, prefer to present a candidate who would be able to demonstrate a link with EC law. Only in the latter case would the application of Article 49 EC (Article 56 TFEU) (be likely to) require the non-application of the contested German legislation and any contracts made between the public procurement company and the company/person employing their services, would be valid.

---

81. *Ibid.*, para. 39.
82. For a very recent case the facts of which involved a German recruitment agency relying on, inter alia, Art. 49 EC (Art. 56 TFEU) against Germany but where, nevertheless, the situation was not found to be a purely internal one since the recruitment agency had found employment for a German national in another Member State (the Netherlands) *see ITC Innovative Technology Center GmbH v. Bundesagentur für Arbeit*, Case No. C-208/05 [2007] ECR I-181, in particular paras 58 and 59.

3 Establishing a Link with EC Law: Export Restrictions

Like in the context of the other fundamental freedoms, measures amounting to 'export restrictions' have been considered to be contrary to Article 49 EC (Article 56 TFEU). Thus, the Court has held that a person can rely on Article 49 EC against his or her Member State when that State imposes a restriction on that person's movement to another Member State for the purpose of providing or receiving services.

In *Corsica Ferries*[83] the Court found that the situation was not purely internal to a Member State, even though the facts involved an Italian company relying on Article 49 EC (Article 56 TFEU) against Italy, since the contested measure would prevent that company from exporting its services to other Member States. Corsica Ferries was a company established under Italian law which provided liner services between Italian ports and ports in other Member States. The Corporation of Pilots of the Port of Genoa charged it tariffs for piloting services it received in the port of Genoa, which were higher than the tariffs imposed on companies which provided liner services exclusively between Italian ports. The Court of Justice stated in paragraph 30 of its judgment that

> [T]he freedom to provide maritime transport services between Member States, and in particular the prohibition of discrimination on grounds of nationality, may be relied on by an undertaking as against the State in which it is established if the services are provided for persons established in another Member State.

Therefore, the situation fell within the scope of Article 49 EC (Article 56 TFEU), since the specific facts of the case involved an impediment to the provision of services from a company established in one Member State to persons established in other Member States.

4 Establishing a Link with EC Law: Obstacles to the Freedom of a Person to Provide Services to Persons Established in his or her Member State of Origin

In *Van Binsbergen*,[84] at issue was Dutch legislation which provided that only persons established in the Netherlands could act as legal representatives before Dutch courts. Relying on the above legislation, the Dutch authorities questioned the capacity of a Dutch national *established in Belgium* (Mr Kortmann) to represent another Dutch national (Mr Van Binsbergen) before a Dutch court.

---

83. *Supra* n. 69.
84. *Van Binsbergen v. Bestuur van de Bedrijfsvereniging voor de Metaalnijverheid*, Case No. 33/74 [1974] ECR 1299.

When the issue reached the Court of Justice, it was ruled that national legislation such as that at issue was capable of infringing Article 49 EC (Article 56 TFEU), since it inhibited the inter-state provision of services:

> [A] requirement that the person providing the service must be habitually resident within the territory of the State where the service is to be provided may, according to the circumstances, have the result of depriving Article 59 [now 49 EC] of all useful effect.[85]

The issue of whether the situation was a purely internal one since a Dutch national was relying on Article 49 EC (Article 56 TFEU) against the Netherlands (his own Member State), was not expressly discussed by the Court, however, it appears that a link with EC law was established by virtue of the fact that the recipient of the services in question would receive services from a person established in another Member State (Belgium). The fact that the provider of services held the same nationality as that of the recipient (i.e., the nationality of the Member State the legislation of which was contested), did not qualify the situation as a purely internal one, since an extraneous element (establishment in another Member State) was present.[86]

It seems that in this case the Court followed an approach similar to that followed in the context of the free movement of workers (*De Bobadilla*) and establishment (*Knoors*), where EC law was found to be applicable in order to protect the movement of a person back to his or her Member State to work or become established. In *Van Binsbergen* the aim of the Court was to protect the freedom of persons to provide services from other Member States to persons residing in their Member State of origin.

E FREE MOVEMENT OF CAPITAL

In the context of Article 56 EC (Article 63 TFEU) no case, to date, has been found to be purely internal to a Member State. Nonetheless, it is clear that the purely internal rule applies in this area as well.[87] Therefore, in order for a measure to fall within the scope of Article 56 EC, it must amount to a restriction on the movement of capital *between Member States*. It should be noted, however, that, unlike in the context of the other fundamental freedoms, even movement of capital between a Member State and a third country (i.e., where no second Member State is involved)

85. *Ibid.*, para. 11.
86. *See* also *Gullung v. Conseil de l'Ordre des Avocats*, Case No. 292/86 [1988] ECR 111, especially paras 12-13; *Coenen v. Sociaal-Economische Raad*, Case No. 39/75 [1975] ECR 1547.
87. For cases where this was made clear *see Heirs of M.E.A. van Hilten-van der Heijden v. Inspecteur van de Belastingdienst/Particulieren/Ondernemingen buitenland te Heerlen*, Case No. C-513/03 [2006] ECR I-1957, para. 42; *Jäger v. Finanzamt Kusel-Landstuhl*, Case No. C-256/06, judgment of 17 Jan. 2008, not yet reported, para. 25.

falls within the scope of Article 56 EC.[88] In this area as well, a person can rely on Article 56 EC against his or her own Member State, provided that a link with EC law can be established.[89]

Obviously, the application of the purely internal rule may, also in this area, give rise to reverse discrimination. If a particular piece of Member State legislation is found to restrict the inter-state movement of capital and is thus held inapplicable to inter-state transactions by virtue of Article 56 EC (Article 63 TFEU), similar transactions confined within the territory of a single Member State will continue to be subject to that restrictive legal regime, and thus persons (physical or legal) involved in such transactions will be the victims of reverse discrimination. And, like in the context of the other free movement provisions, reverse discrimination arising as a result of the limited scope of application of Article 56 EC will escape the ambit of that provision, since it is unlikely that it will give rise to an impediment to the free movement of capital.

III THE PROBLEMS WITH THE TRADITIONAL APPROACH OF THE COURT

The main advantage of the Court's traditional approach used in finding a link with EC law has been its simplicity, and probably this has been the reason that the Court has stuck to it for such a long time and still continues to apply it as the 'default' approach in determining whether a situation falls within the scope of the free movement provisions.

Whether the three limbs of the linking factor test are satisfied *on the specific facts of a case* is a question that can be answered easily and effectively, without the need to have recourse to hypothetical issues and detailed assessments. The question of whether the first limb of the test (inter-state movement) is satisfied in the context of a specific case is an overly easy, and thus not time-consuming, exercise for the Court (or the national courts). As regards the second and third limbs of the test

88. *See van Hilten, supra* n. 87, para. 37; *Fidium Finanz AG v. Bundesanstalt für Finanzdienstleistungsaufsicht*, Case No. C-452/04 [2006] ECR I-9521, para. 25. This is, also, obvious from the text of Art. 56 EC: 'all restrictions in the movement of capital between Member States and between Member States and third countries shall be prohibited . . . all restrictions on payments between Member States and between Member States and third countries shall be prohibited'. The same wording will be maintained in Art. 63 TFEU, following the entry into force of the Treaty of Lisbon (Treaty of Lisbon amending the Treaty on European Union and the Treaty establishing the European Community, OJ C 306/1, 2007). For an explanation of the application of the purely internal rule in the area of the free movement of capital *see* L. Flynn, 'Coming of Age: The free movement of capital case-law 1993-2002' (2002) 39 *CMLRev* 773, 784.

89. For an early example of a case where Member State nationals could rely on the free movement of capital provisions of the Treaty against their own Member State since a cross-border element was existent *see Svensson and Gustavsson v. Ministre du Logement et de l'Urbanisme*, Case No. C-484/93 [1995] ECR I-3955. For a more recent case where the ECJ examined whether the facts involved a purely internal situation but found that they did not *see X and Y v. Riksskatteverket*, Case No. C-436/00 [2002] ECR I-10829.

which may require a closer look at the specific facts of the case, the Court has, again, managed to simplify things by establishing, through its case-law, a number of general principles that can easily be applied in the context of specific situations, thus allowing national courts to decide cases consistently and without continuously having recourse to the preliminary rulings procedure.

The simplicity of the traditional approach derives, also, from the fact that under this approach, further, deeper, inquiry into the real impact a measure may have on other areas of human life in general, or on the smooth functioning of the internal market in particular, does not take place. In particular, under this approach, the Court does not have to be engaged in an examination of the implications of its judgments, this being justified, until recently, by the principle that the scope of EC law only extends to situations in which the Community has competence to act (the principle of attributed competence – Article 5(1) EC[90]) or situations which involve an impediment to the achievement of its objectives. Since the dominant aim of the Community has, until recently, been the construction of the internal market, the general scope of EC law (i.e., not only the scope of the free movement provisions) was rightly considered to include only situations that involved an impediment to that aim. Accordingly, the Court's 'myopic' traditional approach which ignored the spillover effects that the application of the purely internal rule can have in areas and issues not strictly related to the process of building an internal market, could be justified by the fact that the Community lacked competence in areas and situations that did not involve an impediment to the Community's objectives.

Yet, the traditional approach of the Court to purely internal situations and reverse discrimination has not always been an unmitigated success. Through the continuous application of this approach over the years, some of its weaknesses have come to the fore.

First of all, the insistence of the traditional approach on the existence of inter-state movement (first limb) *on the specific facts of the case* before the Court, may lead to decisions that are very far removed from the economic realities of a case. O'Keeffe and Bavasso have cautioned against a merely superficial application of the linking factor test: 'The existence of a cross-border element is still a useful tool to determine if Community rules should come into play . . . However, one should not overstate the benefits of this approach. One could easily imagine a transnational case with little impact on the common market and [an] internal matter with a major effect on the common market'.[91]

Accordingly, although the application of the linking factor test (and, in particular, the first limb) is useful in straightforward factual situations where it is clear that there is no effect whatsoever on the construction of the internal market,

90. Following the Treaty of Lisbon (*supra* n. 88) coming into force, Art. 5(1) EC will be replaced, in substance, by the new Art. 5(2) TEU (as amended by the Treaty of Lisbon).
91. D. O'Keeffe and A. Bavasso, 'Four freedoms, one market and national competence: in search of a dividing line', in *Liber Amicorum in Honour of Lord Slynn of Hadley: Judicial Review in European Union Law*, D. O'Keeffe and A. Bavasso (eds) (The Hague, Kluwer Law International, 2000), pp. 554-555.

nevertheless, in certain more complicated cases, whether the test is satisfied or not on the specific facts of a case cannot be conclusive as to whether the situation before the Court actually involves an impediment to the free movement of products and factors of production. An example of this is situations which involve the application of rules which require public authorities or bodies to reserve a proportion of a public supply contract to producers located within a particular region of national territory. If such a rule is challenged by a producer of goods who is established in another region of the same State, the facts of the case do not involve inter-state movement and thus, under the traditional approach, the case falls outside the scope of EC law. Yet, it cannot be excluded that the authorities and public bodies which have to comply with the challenged rules may have been interested in being supplied, not only with goods from other regions of the State but, also, with goods from other Member States. Therefore, in such a situation, just because the case happens to be brought before a court by a national producer of goods and thus there is no inter-state movement on the facts before the Court, this does not mean that the application of the measure to the relevant public bodies does not have, also, an effect on inter-state trade.

Closely connected to the above argument is the fact that, following the (formal) completion of the internal market which, according to Article 14(2) EC (Article 26(2) TFEU), is an area 'without internal frontiers', it seems increasingly out of place to attach so much importance to the crossing of internal (inter-state) frontiers, for a situation to fall within the scope of EC law. In the words of d'Oliveira, '[a]iming at an internal market, or completing it, while at the same time continuing to attach importance to the crossing of national frontiers is self-contradictory'.[92]

Another problem with the Court's traditional approach is that it reflects a view according to which different areas of law can be divided into watertight compartments. This is clearly an erroneous approach, since the operation of the law in one area often has spillover effects into other areas. More specifically, we saw in Chapter 1 that the application of the purely internal rule in the area of the fundamental freedoms has negative effects both in that area of law (i.e., the internal market) – in the form of reverse discrimination resulting in a distortion of the conditions of competition – and, also, in other areas far removed from inter-state trade, such as that of family reunification rights. If we take as an example the latter area, the fact that the free movement of persons provisions grant the *automatic* right to be accompanied by their family members only to Member State nationals that have exercised their freedom to move for an economic purpose, has led to the emergence of reverse discrimination against persons who cannot point to a link with EC law. Member State nationals that fall outside the scope of EC law do

92. H.U.J. D'Oliveira, 'Is Reverse discrimination still permissible under the Single European Act?', in *Forty years on: The Evolution of Postwar Private International Law in Europe: symposium in celebration of the 40th anniversary of the Centre of Foreign Law and Private International Law, University of Amsterdam, on 27 October 1998* (The Hague, Kluwer Law International, 1990), p. 84.

not derive from EC law an *automatic* right to be accompanied by their family members in their State of origin and since national laws on the matter are usually more difficult to satisfy,[93] we are often left with two 'groups' of persons: the 'favoured ones' who fall within the scope of EC law and thus can easily move with their family members; and the 'reversely discriminated ones' who, by virtue of the fact that they remain confined within the boundaries of their Member State of nationality, can only enjoy the company of their loved ones if and when they satisfy the more burdensome requirements that may be imposed by the immigration legislation of their Member State.

It is true that nobody really 'aims' at creating this difference in treatment[94] – reverse discrimination is merely 'a consequence of the existence of overlapping spheres of competence in the same matter'.[95] Yet, the fact remains that a difference in treatment based on the contribution of a person to the economic aims of the Treaty persists, in an area which is so much removed from inter-state trade and where the raw logic of the need to delimitate the different spheres of competence of the EC and its Member States, seems to be entirely out of place. In areas such as that of family reunification '[w]hat remains is the material difference in treatment',[96] the reverse discrimination, that 'is likely to arouse considerable irritation among'[97] a State's citizens.

Of course, it cannot be disputed that since reverse discrimination does not inhibit the exercise of the fundamental freedoms, it has rightly been considered to fall outside the scope of the free movement provisions. However, the main aim of the book is to prove that, although reverse discrimination caused as a result of the limited application of EC law, indeed, rightly falls outside the scope of the free movement provisions, nevertheless it should now be considered to fall within the

93. *See* paras 26 and 33 of the Opinion of Advocate General Geelhoed in *Jia v. Migrationsverket*, Case No. C-1/05 [2007] ECR I-1.
94. *See* M. Poiares Maduro, 'The Scope of European Remedies: The Case of Purely Internal Situations and Reverse Discrimination', in *The Future of European Remedies*, C. Kilpatrick, T. Novitz and P. Skidmore (eds) (Oxford, Hart, 2000), pp. 127-128.
95. E. Cannizzaro, 'Producing "Reverse Discrimination" through the exercise of EC competences' (1997) 17 *YEL* 29.
96. N. Nic Shuibhne, 'Free movement of persons and the wholly internal rule: Time to move on?' (2002) 39 *CMLRev* 731, 738 (comment made in a broader context, that is, not only for family reunification cases).
97. B. Sundberg-Weitman, *Discrimination on Grounds of Nationality – Free Movement of Workers and Freedom of Establishment under the EEC Treaty* (Amsterdam, North-Holland Publishing Company, 1977), p. 116 (comment made in a broader context, that is, not only for family reunification cases). Back in 1982, Advocate General Slynn considered the emergence of reverse discrimination in the area of family reunification rights as a necessary evil of the system: 'This it is said causes incongruous results if a non-national can come in with his family, or if, as the Commission contend, a national can come back with his family, but a national cannot bring in his family to join him in the place where he has always been. Since the rights conferred derive from the principle of a freedom of movement for workers, and not from a right of residence, throughout the Community, gaps in the right of a family to live with an individual are at the least possible and perhaps inevitable' – *see* the Opinion of Advocate General Slynn in *Morson and Jhanjan, supra* n. 42, p. 3742.

(broader) scope of EC law. The Court can no longer simply ignore the potentially negative effects the process of economic integration may have on the achievement of a number of Community aims that have recently been added either through Treaty revision, or through its own case-law, and the importance of which has been highlighted in its own rulings.

Before concluding this chapter, it would be wise to add a few comments in order to enable the reader to view the Court's traditional approach to the issue of purely internal situations and reverse discrimination, through a lens that places this approach in context, taking into account the different priorities of the Community in the various phases of its development.

First of all, it is worth recalling that the traditional approach of the Court was developed at a time when the first building blocks were placed on the common market construct. As a result of that, and since the Court of Justice would have to allocate its limited resources in a balanced way so as to be able to give the necessary guidance in as many areas of EC law as possible, a filtering mechanism for determining which situations fall within the scope of EC law which was more straightforward and quicker to apply was more appropriate. The Court, quite rightly, seemed to be unwilling to delve into a complex inquiry as to the real (potential) impact a national measure might have on the establishment of the internal market, at a time when basic principles still had to be laid down and interpretations of Community legislation provided.

Moreover, since the dominant aim of the Community until the early 1990s was the construction of a common market through the removal of obstacles to the inter-state movement of products and persons, any side-effects that arose as a result of the construction of that market which did not come into conflict with that goal in any way, were rightly considered to fall outside the scope of EC law. Consequently, as already explained, reverse discrimination was considered to be a difference in treatment that fell outside the scope of EC law as it did not inhibit the achievement of the Community's dominant aim at the time. What is more, reverse discrimination could actually be effectively utilized as an instrument through which to facilitate the achievement of the Community's main aim as, by ensuring that certain rights would not be denied to migrant workers or persons engaged in inter-state trade, the exercise of an economic activity in an inter-state context would, in fact, be encouraged. The fact that this form of 'positive action' in favour of persons and traders that contributed to the main aim of the Community also gave rise to a difference in treatment to the detriment of persons or traders that in no way promoted the (purely economic) aims of the Treaty, could not be considered to lead to a violation of EC law since, even when it overcompensated 'free-movers' and thus amounted, in effect, to discrimination, it did not conflict with the (limited) economic aims of the Community.

Hence, it would be grossly superficial to hastily castigate the Court for the somewhat simplistic and narrow approach it has followed with regard to the issues of reverse discrimination and purely internal situations, without taking into account the context within which it had been working and the priorities that the Community had set for itself at the time of the development of the purely internal rule (i.e., the late 1970s). Yet, without speculating too much, the fact remains that the traditional approach of the Court to purely internal situations and reverse discrimination has proved too simplistic and inadequate in certain instances. On the one hand, it sometimes fails to reflect economic reality by excluding from the scope of the fundamental freedoms provisions, situations which involve a substantial impediment to the free movement of products. On the other hand, the fact that the application of the purely internal rule may have as a direct result the emergence of reverse discrimination, can no longer be ignored by the ECJ and this has become all the more so since the early 1990s, as a result of two important developments that have taken place in the EC: the development of a meaningful notion of citizenship of the Union; and the completion of the internal market.

It will be seen in the next chapter that the Court's approach to reverse discrimination and its approach followed when finding a link with EC law has, at least to a certain extent, altered over time in tune with judicial moods in Luxembourg and with the overall reassessment of the Community's priorities.

Chapter 3

The Court's New Approaches to a Link with EC Law: Responding to the Problems of the Traditional Approach

I INTRODUCTION

In Chapter 2 of the book, the Court's traditional approach to purely internal situations and the context in which this approach was developed were presented. It was argued that, through the continuous application of this approach over the years, some of its weaknesses have come to the fore, and this has increasingly been so during the 1990s as a result of important developments that have taken place in the EC, such as the introduction of the status of citizenship of the Union and the completion of the internal market.

The main aim of this chapter will be to present the reaction of the Court of Justice to the problems emerging from the application of its traditional approach to purely internal situations. More specifically, there will be a presentation of the new approaches that have been followed in (some) of the recent judgments of the Court for determining whether a situation is purely internal to a Member State. It will be noticed that, at first glance, the Court in its case-law appears to have merely changed its approach towards the application of the linking factor test – not its approach towards the question of whether reverse discrimination is a difference in treatment that is prohibited under EC law. However, it will be argued that, although the Court has not explicitly modified its traditional stance on the permissibility of reverse discrimination, nonetheless, (some) of its new approaches to the issue of finding a link with EC law may, in reality, have been fuelled by an (implicit) recognition of the fact that reverse discrimination is no longer an acceptable difference in treatment in the EC of today. An assessment of the potential success or failure of the Court's new approaches towards finding a link with EC law will also be provided.

II SOME GENERAL COMMENTS ON THE COURT'S CASE-LAW WHERE THE TRADITIONAL APPROACH TOWARDS FINDING A LINK WITH EC LAW WAS NOT FOLLOWED

In this chapter it will be seen that, as a result of the problems caused by the application of its traditional approach when finding a link with EC law, the Court has departed, in some of its case-law, from that approach. It will be explained that, although the basic elements of the linking factor test are still maintained (i.e., the need to prove that the application of the contested national measure impedes the free movement of products or factors of production), the exact method of application of that test has been differentiated. The relevant case-law can be divided into two groups.

The first group (section III of the chapter) is comprised of case-law in the area of EC trade (the free movement of goods and services) the facts of which involved the application of a national measure to products confined within the territory of a single Member State; or the challenging of acts of a Member State by service-providers whose situation did not involve an inter-state element. In this case-law, it seems that the Court accepted that a situation falls within the scope of EC law, when it involves the application of a measure that is capable of having a sufficiently negative impact on the free movement of goods and services, irrespective of whether such an effect can be proved on the specific facts from which the case arose. Under this approach, even though the factual background to the case before the Court involves goods and services confined within the territory of a single Member State, this does not result in the *automatic* exclusion of the situation from the scope of EC law. The Court accepts that the contested Member State action or the application of the impugned measure to goods or services that are in a purely internal situation may, *at the same time*, have an effect on the inter-state movement of goods and services that are not involved on the facts of the case (i.e., of goods/services that cannot be specifically identified at the time of the judgment). Therefore, in these cases, all three limbs of the linking factor test are satisfied, but only when the test is applied to (potential) situations involving traders that are not parties to the case from which the question referred to the ECJ arose. In this group of cases, the aim of the Court seems to have been to include within the scope of the free movement of goods and services provisions all national measures the application of which involves a sufficiently negative impact on inter-state trade, thus responding to the concern that the Court's traditional approach sometimes fails to reflect economic reality.

The second group (section IV of the chapter) includes case-law in the area of the free movement of persons where the Court, without admitting it, extended the scope of EC law to cover purely internal situations. Here, the Court in its judgments uses wording which suggests that it sticks to its traditional approach towards the application of the linking factor test, since it finds that an impediment to the inter-state movement of the persons involved on the facts of the case arises as a result of the application of the contested national measure. Yet, as will be seen, in this group of cases the test is, in reality, far from satisfied on the facts of the case. In this group of case-law, the Court accepts that there is a link with EC law even if the third limb, or even in some cases both the second and third limbs, of the linking factor test are not satisfied. The main characteristic of this case-law is that the existence of inter-state movement (i.e., first limb of the test) on the facts of the case suffices for bringing the situation within the scope of EC law. This flies in the face of the Court's traditional approach according to which *all three limbs* of the linking factor test must be satisfied *on the specific facts of a case*. In this group of cases, the aim of the Court seems to have been to include within the scope of the free movement of persons provisions as many situations as possible, thereby reducing the number of instances of reverse discrimination.

In order to be able to have a better understanding of the approaches followed by the Court in the two groups of cases presented in sections III and IV of this chapter, the analysis offered by d'Oliveira in an important article on reverse discrimination should be recalled. D'Oliveira[1] has pointed out that in private international law, two approaches are followed when distinguishing between internal and international cases: the 'geographical' and the 'juridical' approaches. Under the geographical approach, emphasis is placed on the factual aspect of the legal relationship – the main question is whether the facts involve elements which turn a case into an international one. Conversely, under the juridical approach, the main question is whether more than one legal system is connected with the case – if the answer is yes, the case is an international one, irrespective of the actual factual background to the case.

D'Oliveira notes that when deciding in the context of EC law whether a situation is purely internal to a Member State, the Court 'overwhelmingly favours the geographical approach'[2] – the Court attaches great importance to the question of whether *the facts of the case* involve products or persons that have moved (or are going to move) between Member States. However, he is of the view that in Community law it would be more appropriate to follow the juridical approach and instead of seeking for facts which involve inter-state movement, the Court should examine whether the national legislation or measure in question has a detrimental impact on the aims of the Treaty.

As was seen in the previous chapter of the book, the Court's traditional approach used in finding a link with EC law corresponds, largely, to d'Oliveira's

1. *See* H.U.J. d'Oliveira, 'Is Reverse discrimination still permissible under the Single European Act?', in *Forty years on: The Evolution of Postwar Private International Law in Europe: symposium in celebration of the 40th anniversary of the Centre of Foreign Law and Private International Law, University of Amsterdam, on 27 October 1998* (The Hague, Kluwer Law International, 1990), pp. 73-74.
2. *Ibid.*, p. 74.

'geographical approach'. As explained, under the Court's traditional approach all three limbs of the linking factor test must be satisfied *on the specific facts of the case* in order for a situation to be considered as falling within the scope of EC law and the contested measure to be examined for its compatibility with one of the fundamental freedoms provisions. Any other consideration, such as the detrimental effect a measure may have on the achievement of the aim of the fundamental freedoms provisions potentially and in an abstract context (i.e., not on the specific facts of the case), is excluded from the Court's analysis.

In its more recent case-law, however, the Court is using both of the above approaches. On the one hand, in the context of the free movement of goods and services the Court is perhaps trying to use an approach closer to the juridical one, that is, it (rightly) does not attach great importance to the issue of whether the specific facts of the case involve goods or services the movement of which is impeded, but is satisfied that the situation falls within the scope of EC law if it is certain that the inter-state movement of *some* (unidentified, though identifiable) products is negatively affected as a result of the contested Member State action. On the other hand, in cases in the field of the free movement of persons, the Court is still following an approach closer to the geographical, described above: it still examines closely the specific facts of the case and finds that there is a link with EC law if (in its view) the linking factor test is satisfied on those specific facts.

The final group of cases that will be (briefly) analyzed in section V of this chapter, has nothing to do with the question of which is the exact approach that the Court uses in determining whether a situation is a purely internal one. Rather, the issue is one having to do with the Court's jurisdiction in preliminary ruling proceedings. In this group of cases, the Court accepted jurisdiction to rule on such proceedings even in cases the facts of which were purely internal to a Member State, confining, however, the effects of its judgment to future situations which would involve a link with EC law. Although in this group the Court does not appear to be differentiating the traditional approach to the application of the linking factor test in any way – it still applies all three limbs of that test when determining whether a situation is purely internal to a Member State – nonetheless, the Court's approach to the limits of its jurisdiction in preliminary rulings cases was differentiated in order to facilitate national courts to remedy instances of reverse discrimination, when this is required by their national law. Accordingly, it is necessary to include this group of cases within this chapter so as to provide a complete picture of the Court's recent attempts to contribute to the resolution of the reverse discrimination conundrum.

It should be borne in mind that the different approaches followed when determining whether a case involves a link with EC law – the traditional and each of the new approaches – do not fall into neatly packaged periods of time, and in fact, the traditional approach is still extensively followed. Therefore, it should by no means be taken that Chapter 2 of the book presents an 'old and forgotten' approach to the application of the linking factor test; or that Chapter 3 presents the approaches that are now overwhelmingly used by the Court for establishing whether a case falls within the scope of EC law.

III THE COURT'S NEW APPROACH TOWARDS FINDING A LINK WITH EC LAW IN SOME OF ITS CASE-LAW IN THE AREA OF THE FREE MOVEMENT OF GOODS AND SERVICES

The Court's traditional approach to the application of the linking factor test in the context of the free movement provisions, rules out the possibility that a situation which involves products that remain confined within the territory of a single Member State can be found to fall within the scope of Articles 28 EC (Article 34 TFEU) or 49 EC (Article 56 TFEU). This comes into stark contrast with the approach followed in EC competition law when determining whether a situation falls within the scope of the competition law provisions.

In this part of the chapter, it will be seen that the new approach that has been used in some of the Court's case-law in the context of the free movement of services and goods is, now, coming much closer to the approach followed in the area of EC competition law. This is because, under this case-law, provided that an effect on the inter-state movement of products is proved, a national measure can be found to be in violation of the free movement provisions even when it is applied to products confined within the territory of a single Member State.

A The Approach Followed by the Court in Finding a Link with EC Law in Competition Law Cases

The Community's competition policy has two – equally important – objectives: first, the maintenance of competitive markets; and, second, the single market objective which entails the aim of preventing anti-competitive practices from undermining the single market's achievements and, in particular, the opening-up of national markets.[3] Accordingly, 'in addition to the general goals pursued by any competition system, EC competition law fulfils the function of contributing to the achievement of the single market'.[4]

As a result of that, for the EC competition law provisions to become applicable, a situation must involve an effect on inter-state trade; otherwise, the situation does not fall within the scope of those provisions. This requirement of an effect on inter-state trade before a situation can fall within the scope of EC competition law, serves the same purpose as the purely internal rule does in the context

3. *See* paras 2 and 3 of the Commission's XXIXth Report on Competition Policy 1999, SEC (2000) 720 Final, not published in the Official Journal.
4. A. Albors-Llorens, *EC Competition Law and Policy* (Cullompton, Willan Publishing, 2002), p. 6. For an excellent explanation of the interrelationship between competition law and free movement law in the process of attaining the single market objective *see* G. Davies, *EU Internal Market Law* (2nd edn, London, Cavendish, 2003), pp. 136-137.

of the fundamental freedoms, that is, it defines the boundary between the areas respectively covered by Community law and the law of the Member States.[5]

The requirement that a situation must involve an effect on inter-state trade is reflected in both Articles 81 and 82 EC (Articles 101 and 102 TFEU), the Treaty provisions that have constituted the cornerstone of the Community's competition policy. Accordingly, those provisions have been applied by the Community in order to prohibit, inter alia, anti-competitive agreements by undertakings which divide the markets of the Member States along national lines (and, thus, inhibit the free movement of goods and services); and situations where the abuse of a dominant position – a position of economic strength in the relevant market – can restrict the access of products to the market of a Member State and thus, similarly, inhibit inter-state trade.

However, what is the actual approach followed by the Court in delimiting the scope of the EC competition law provisions? According to Goyder, '[i]nitially it was believed that agreements and practices that had effect merely within a single Member State and upon undertakings whose business was operating only there, could always claim to be outside the scope of the Article'.[6] This, obviously, is very similar to the traditional approach followed by the Court when delimiting the scope of the free movement provisions of the Treaty.

Nevertheless, the above belief soon proved to be too simplistic in the area of competition law, and the Court laid down in *STM v. Maschinenbau* a (very broadly worded) test for deciding whether an agreement, decision or concerted practice within the meaning of Article 81 EC (Article 101 TFEU) has an effect on inter-state trade. According to the 'STM test', for an effect on inter-state trade to be proved

> [I]t must be possible to foresee with a sufficient degree of probability on the basis of a set of objective factors of law or of fact that the agreement in question may have an influence, direct or indirect, actual or potential, on the pattern of trade between the Member States.[7]

---

5. For an explanation *see Hugin Kassaregister AB and Hugin Cash Registers Ltd v. Commission*, Case No. 22/78 [1979] ECR 1869, para. 17; *see* also (for Art. 81 EC [Art. 101 TFEU] only) *Etablissements Consten SA and Grundig-Verkaufs-GmbH v. Commission*, Joined Cases 56 and 58/64 [1966] ECR 229, p. 341; *Istituto Chemioterapico Italiano S.p.A. and Commercial Solvents Corporation v. Commission*, Joined Cases 6 and 7/73 [1974] ECR 223, para. 31. For further explanation *see* R. Lane, *EC Competition Law* (Harlow, Longman: Pearson Education, 2000), p. 68. *See* also paras 12, 13 and 35 of the Commission's Notice on the effect on trade concept contained in Arts 81 and 82 of the Treaty, OJ C 101/81, 2004.
6. D. Goyder, *EC Competition Law* (4th edn, Oxford, OUP, 2003), at p. 83.
7. *Société Technique Minière v. Maschinenbau Ulm*, Case No. 56/65 [1966] ECR 235, p. 249. The test has been endorsed and applied by the Court of Justice and the Court of First Instance in their subsequent case-law. *See*, for example *Tréfilunion SA v. Commission*, Case No. T-148/89 [1995] ECR II-1063, para. 102; *Musique Diffusion Française and others v. Commission*, Joined Cases 100-103/80 [1983] ECR 1825, para. 84.

Moreover, the Court has always included a *de minimis* test in its analysis applied for finding whether an agreement has an effect on intra-Community trade, requiring that the effect on inter-state trade must not be insignificant.[8]

More importantly for our purposes, the Court has held that even if the parties to an agreement operate in the same Member State and the agreement takes place wholly within that Member State, the agreement may nonetheless fall within the scope of EC competition law and, in particular, Article 81 EC (Article 101 TFEU), provided that an effect on inter-state trade can be proved.[9]

Similar principles have been applied when drawing the boundary between the scope of application of Article 82 EC (Article 102 TFEU), on the one hand, and national competition law, on the other. The 'STM test' has been applied also in determining whether a situation falls within the scope of Article 82 EC.[10] In this context as well, the Court has held that there is no need for the involvement of two or more Member States, for a situation to fall within the scope of Article 82 EC. In particular, in *Michelin* the Court said that:

> [W]hen the holder of a dominant position obstructs access to the market by competitors, it makes no difference whether such conduct is confined to a

---

8. *Völk v. Vervaecke*, Case No. 5/69 [1969] ECR 295, paras 5-7; *Béguelin Import v. SAGL Import-Export and Others*, Case No. 22/71 [1971] ECR 949, para. 16; *Miller International Schallplatten GmbH v. Commission*, Case No. 19/77 [1978] ECR 131; *Bagnasco and Others v. Banca Popolare di Novara soc. Coop. arl. (BNP) and Cassa di Risparmio di Genova e Imperia SpA (Carige)*, Joined Cases C-215/96 and C-216/96 [1999] ECR I-135, para. 34; *Dutch Banks*, Commission Decision 1999/87/EC [2000] 4 CMLR 137.
9. *SC Belasco and others v. Commission*, Case No. 246/86 [1989] ECR 2117, para. 33; *Salonia v. Poidomani and Baglieri, née Giglio*, Case No. 126/80 [1981] ECR 1563 paras 11-16; *Vereeniging van Cementhandelaren v. Commission*, Case No. 8/72 [1972] ECR 977, paras 26-32; *Re Vacuum Interrupters Ltd*, Commission Decision 77/160/EEC [1977] 1 CMLR D67; *Remia BV v. Commission*, Case No. 42/84 [1985] ECR 2545, paras 22-24; *Commission v. Italy*, Case No. C-35/96 [1998] ECR I-3851; *SA Brasserie de Haecht v. Consorts Wilkin-Janssen*, Case No. 23/67 [1967] ECR 407; *BNIC v. Clair*, Case No. 123/83 [1985] ECR 391; *Italian Flat Glass*, Commission Decision 81/881/EEC [1982] 3 CMLR 366; *Italian Cast Glass*, Commission Decision 80/1334/EEC [1982] 2 CMLR 61; *Eirpage*, Commission Decision 91/562/EEC [1993] 4 CMLR 64; *Tate & Lyle plc and others v. Commission*, Joined Cases T-202, 204 & 207/98 [2001] ECR II-2035, para. 79; *Publishers Association v. Commission*, Case No. T-66/89 [1992] ECR II-1995, para. 57. This is also reflected, and further explained, in paras 77-92 of the Commission's Notice on the effect on trade concept contained in Arts 81 and 82 of the Treaty, *supra* n. 5. For further explanation of the application of the requirement of an effect on inter-state trade in Art. 81 (Art. 101 TFEU) cases *see* R. Whish, *Competition Law* (5th edn, London, Butterworths, 2003), pp. 137-146; A. Jones and B. Sufrin, *EC Competition Law: Texts, Cases and Materials* (2nd edn, Oxford, OUP, 2004), pp. 168-176; A. Albors-Llorens, *supra* n. 4, pp. 28-34; R. Lane, *supra* n. 5, pp. 68-77; J. Steiner, L. Woods and C. Twigg-Flesner, *EU Law* (9th edn, Oxford, OUP, 2006), pp. 585-586; D. Goyder, *supra* n. 6, pp. 83-90; V. Korah, *An Introductory Guide to EC Competition Law and Practice* (8th edn, Oxford, Hart, 2004), pp. 59-65; P. Craig and G. de Búrca, *EU Law: Text, Cases and Materials* (4th edn, Oxford, OUP, 2008), at p. 975.
10. *See*, for example, *Gøttrup-Klim e.a. Grovvareforeninger v. Dansk Landbrugs Grovvareselskab AmbA*, Case No. C-250/92 [1994] ECR I-5641, para. 54; *Compagnie maritime belge transports SA and Compagnie maritime belge SA, Dafra-Lines A/S, Deutsche Afrika-Linien GmbH & Co. and Nedlloyd Lijnen BV v. Commission*, Joined Cases T-24/93, T-25/93, T-26/93 and T-28/93 [1996] ECR II-1201, para. 201.

single Member State as long as it is capable of affecting patterns of trade and competition in the common market.[11]

The definition of 'measure(s) having equivalent effect to quantitative restrictions' (MEQRs) in the context of Article 28 EC (Article 34 TFEU) that was laid down in the case of *Dassonville*[12] is very similar to the definition of the term 'agreements which may affect trade between the Member States' in the context of Article 81 EC (Article 101 TFEU) as established in the *Consten and Grundig* case.[13] According to one commentator, the rationale behind the concurrence between the jurisprudence on the free movement provisions on the one hand, and the competition law provisions on the other, is the principle of 'unity of the (common) market', according to which, 'there has to be an uninhibited flow of goods between Member States, just as there is free movement of goods within the internal market of a single Member State'.[14] Therefore, one might have expected that a very similar approach would be used in delimiting the scope of, respectively, the internal market provisions and the competition law provisions. In fact, Advocate General Poiares Maduro – in an article written before his appointment as an Advocate General – argued that there seems to be no point in adopting a different approach in the two areas.[15]

However, the Court seems to have had a different view.[16] The approach followed in competition law contrasts with that followed, traditionally, in internal

---

11. *Michelin v. Commission*, Case No. 322/81 [1983] ECR 3461, para. 103. *See* also *BPB Industries Plc and British Gypsum Ltd v. Commission*, Case No. T-65/89 [1993] ECR II-389; *Cipolla v. Portolese* and *Macrino and Capodarte v. Meloni*, Joined Cases C-94/04 and C-202/04 [2006] ECR I-11421, para. 45. For further explanation of this *see* paras 93-99 of the Commission's Notice on the effect on trade concept, *supra* n. 5. For an explanation of the requirement of an effect on inter-state trade in the context of Art. 82 EC (Art. 102 TFEU) *see* V. Korah, *supra* n. 9, pp. 65-66; R. Whish, *supra* n. 9, p. 178; A. Jones and B. Sufrin, *supra* n. 9, pp. 287-289; A. Albors-Llorens, *supra* n. 4, at pp. 105-107.
12. According to the *Dassonville* formula, 'all trading rules enacted by Member States which are capable of hindering, directly or indirectly, actually or potentially, intra-Community trade are to be considered as measures having an effect equivalent to quantitative restrictions' – *Procureur du Roi v. Dassonville*, Case No. 8/74 [1974] ECR 837, para. 5.
13. *Consten and Grundig, supra* n. 5, at p. 341: the agreement must be 'capable of constituting a threat, either direct or indirect, actual or potential, to freedom of trade between Member States in a manner which might harm the attainment of the objectives of a single market between States'. For a commentator who shares this view *see* K. Mortelmans, 'Towards convergence in the application of the rules on free movement and on competition?' (2001) 38 *CMLRev* 613, 623. *See* also paras 21-22 of the Opinion of Advocate General Van Gerven in *Torfaen BV v. B & Q plc*, Case No. 145/88 [1989] ECR 765.
14. R. Barents, 'New Developments in measures having equivalent effect' (1981) 18 *CMLRev* 271, 274.
15. M. Poiares Maduro, 'The Scope of European Remedies: The Case of Purely Internal Situations and Reverse Discrimination', in *The Future of European Remedies*, C. Kilpatrick, T. Novitz and P. Skidmore (eds) (Oxford, Hart, 2000), p. 122 (n. 28).
16. *See Höfner and Elser v. Macrotron GmbH*, Case No. C-41/90 [1991] ECR I-4695, para. 16. For an explanation *see* K. Mortelmans, *supra* n. 13, 631-632; S. de Vries, *Tensions within the Internal Market: The Functioning of the Internal Market and the Development of Horizontal and Flanking Policies* (Groningen, Europa Law Publishing, 2006), p. 113.

market law since in the context of the latter, it has been well-established that an effect on inter-state trade can only be proved if the specific situation under scrutiny involves products that have moved (or are going to move) between Member States. In other words, the traditional approach requires the *existence and impediment* of inter-state movement *on the specific facts of a case*, before the free movement provisions can be ruled to be applicable.

Nonetheless, it is possible to discern a differentiated ('new') approach that is followed when delimiting the scope of the free movement provisions, in some of the Court's latest case-law in the area of the free movement of goods and services. Under this approach, the focus is placed on the effect that a specific measure can have on the inter-state movement of goods and services in general; not, only, the specific goods and services that are involved on the facts of a case. Under this new approach, the important and only question is whether a national action or measure has an appreciable effect on inter-state trade, that is, whether it raises a substantial obstacle to the (inter-state) movement of goods or services, even when this comes as a result of its application to products confined within the territory of a single Member State. Hence, it appears that the approach followed by the Court in delimiting the scope of the fundamental freedoms and, in particular, the free movement of goods and services provisions, becomes very similar to that followed in the area of EC competition law.[17]

B THE NEW APPROACH FOLLOWED BY THE COURT WHEN DELIMITING THE SCOPE OF THE CUSTOMS DUTIES AND FREE MOVEMENT OF GOODS PROVISIONS

In this part of the section, there will be an analysis of the case-law in which the Court followed its new approach to the application of the linking factor test when delimiting the scope of Articles 23-25, 28 and 29 EC (respectively, Articles 28-30, 34 and 35 TFEU).[18]

17. For a commentary on possible convergence between the fundamental freedoms and competition law in relation to internal situations/requirement of an effect on inter-state trade *see* K. Mortelmans, *supra* n. 13, 630-632.
18. For literature where most of this case-law is discussed *see*: P. Oliver and W.H. Roth, 'The internal market and the four freedoms' (2004) 41 *CMLRev* 407, 430-431; P. Oliver, *Free Movement of Goods in the European Community* (4th edn, London, Sweet & Maxwell, 2003), pp. 149-152 (paras 6.103-6.105); P. Oliver, 'Some further reflections on the scope of Articles 28-30 EC' (1999) 36 *CMLRev* 783, 785-788; K. Mortelmans, 'The Common Market, the Internal Market and the Single Market, What's in a Market?' (1998) 35 *CMLRev* 101, 133-134; P. Oliver and S. Enchelmaier, 'Free movement of goods: Recent developments in the case law' (2007) 44 *CMLRev* 649, 651-656.

1 The Application of the New Approach of the Court when Delimiting the Scope of the Customs Duties Provisions

The wording of the customs duties provisions of the Treaty suggests that Community law prohibits the imposition of customs duties and charges having equivalent effect on goods that have moved from one Member State to another.[19] The rationale behind this prohibition is to ensure that the inter-state movement of goods is not inhibited as a result of the imposition of additional costs on goods by reason of the fact that they cross a frontier.

It has widely been considered – though in no case, to date, has the Court ruled on this expressly – that the linking factor test (as applied traditionally) should be used, also, when delimiting the scope of the customs duties provisions.[20] Therefore, the imposition of customs duties has traditionally been considered to amount to a violation of those provisions, *only* if those duties had been imposed on goods that had moved from one Member State to another.

Nevertheless, the Court departed from that position in 1994, in the landmark case of *Lancry*[21] where it held that when customs duties are imposed on *all* goods entering a specific region of a Member State, those duties are contrary to Article 25 EC (Article 30 TFEU) *even when they are imposed on goods crossing merely the internal frontiers of a Member State* (i.e., goods that merely move between regions of the same Member State).

In *Lancry*, at issue was the compatibility with the EC Treaty provisions on customs duties of dock dues levied in the French overseas departments on *all* goods (even goods from metropolitan France) entering the overseas department concerned. The main question was whether such dues constituted charges having equivalent effect to customs duties *in so far as they were imposed on goods coming from metropolitan France* (i.e., goods moving within one and the same Member State). In a previous case, *Legros*,[22] the Court had held that when the same dues were imposed on *imported* goods (i.e., goods coming from other Member States) entering that *region*, they were charges having equivalent effect

19. Article 23(1) EC: 'The Community shall be based upon a customs union which shall cover all trade in goods and which shall involve the prohibition *between Member States* of customs duties on *imports* and *exports* and of all charges having equivalent effect' (emphasis added). Once the Treaty of Lisbon (Treaty of Lisbon amending the Treaty on European Union and the Treaty establishing the European Community, OJ C 306/1, 2007) will come into force this will be provided in Article 28 TFEU, though it should be noted that there will be a slight (though insignificant) change in the wording. Article 25 EC (Article 30 TFEU): 'Customs duties on *imports* and *exports* and charges having equivalent effect shall be prohibited *between Member States*.' (emphasis added).
20. G. Tesauro, 'The Community's internal market in the light of the recent case-law of the Court of Justice' (1995) *YEL* 1, 11.
21. *Lancry SA v. Direction Générale des Douanes*, Joined Cases C-363/93, C-407/93, C-409/93 and C-411/93 [1994] ECR I-3957.
22. *Administration des Douanes et Droits Indirects v. Legros and Others*, Case No. C-163/90 [1992] ECR I-4625.

to a customs duty within the meaning of Article 25 EC (Article 30 TFEU) and thus prohibited.[23]

The Court did not accept the arguments put forward by the Council and the Spanish government, to the effect that the customs duties provisions were not applicable to dock dues imposed on goods moving between regions of the same Member State.[24] The Court pointed out that:

> [T]he levying of charges exhibiting the features of dock dues could be classified as a purely internal situation only if the dues were levied *exclusively* on products from the same Member State.[25]

It was concluded that the situation in question was not purely internal to a Member State. The main reason put forward was that, since the contested legislation applied equally to *all* products entering the overseas department concerned (i.e., goods coming from other Member States and goods coming from other regions of France), it would be inconsistent to hold, on the one hand, that dock dues constitute charges having equivalent effect in so far as they are levied on goods from other Member States and to concede, on the other, that those dues do not constitute charges having equivalent effect when they are levied on goods from metropolitan France.[26]

Moreover, the Court in its judgment stressed that legislation which applies equally to goods moving between Member States and goods staying confined within the territory of a single Member State should be held inapplicable in its entirety since now it is

23. The Court in *Legros* made it clear that regional frontiers are to be treated in the same way as State frontiers. When customs duties are imposed by regional authorities on goods *imported from one Member State into a region of another*, those customs duties are equally prohibited by the Treaty Articles on customs duties, as are customs duties imposed on goods by reason of the fact that they cross a State frontier (*see* para. 16 of the judgment in *Legros, ibid.*).
24. Note also that the Court did not follow the Opinion of Advocate General Tesauro who was of the view that, following the well-established case-law on purely internal situations, when dues are imposed on domestic goods moving to another region of the Member State, this is a purely internal situation and thus the dues are not prohibited by Art. 25 EC (Art. 30 TFEU). In para. 28 of his Opinion, however, the Advocate General admitted that 'the solution of the problem as dictated by the interpretation of the Treaty and the case-law of the Court may seem somewhat paradoxical. An experienced lawyer will also notice the paradox of a single market in which barriers to trade between Portugal and Denmark are prohibited, whilst barriers to trade between Naples and Capri are immaterial. Neither the Treaty nor the Court in its decisions can, or could, find a way out of such paradox'. For a similar view *see* para. 116 of the Opinion of Advocate General Sharpston in the free movement of persons case *Government of the French Community and Walloon Government v. Flemish Government*, Case No. C-212/06, judgment of 1 Apr. 2008, not yet reported.
25. *Lancry, supra* n. 21, para. 30 (emphasis added).
26. *Ibid.*, para. 30. This statement seems, also, to be concealing a concern on the part of the Court for the emergence of reverse discrimination as a result of it delivering a judgment which only partly rules a piece of national legislation inapplicable. For an extensive discussion of this *see* Ch. 5.

> [V]ery difficult, if not impossible, in practical terms, to distinguish between products of domestic origin and products originating in other Member States.[27]

This is due to the fact that, following the formal completion of the internal market as required by the '1992 project', all frontier controls on goods moving within the internal market have been abolished and, therefore, it is now very difficult to distinguish between goods that have crossed inter-state frontiers and goods that have remained confined within the territory of a single Member State. Thus, according to Oliver and Roth, the Court by making this observation 'clearly has a point'[28] and it has been suggested that this was one of the main concerns behind the Court's 'revolutionary' approach in *Lancry*.[29]

Accordingly, it appears that the Court has not abolished the purely internal rule in the area of customs duties. The Court is still requiring an effect on the inter-state movement of goods, before a situation can be considered to fall within the customs duties provisions. Since it is now impossible to specify exactly when (i.e., when applied to which specific products) legislation which imposes customs duties on *all* goods crossing a regional frontier will, indeed, have an effect on inter-state trade, the Court has chosen to prohibit such legislation in its entirety, even if this means that certain situations that are purely internal to a Member State are included within the scope of the prohibition.

Advocate General Tesauro writing extra-judicially shortly after *Lancry* was decided, wondered whether the case was an accident or the beginning of another revolution.[30] That *Lancry* was not merely an accident but the first in a new line of cases, was affirmed by the subsequent cases *Simitzi v. Kos*[31] and *Carbonati Apuani*,[32] where the Court repeated that whenever national legislation imposes customs duties on *all* goods (i.e., imported and domestic) crossing the frontiers of a region of a Member State, it must be struck down *in its entirety* for being in violation of Articles 23-25 EC (Articles 28-30 TFEU).

In a more recent case, *Jersey Potatoes*,[33] the issue was whether the legislation of the Island of Jersey[34] under which charges having equivalent effect to customs duties would be levied on potatoes despatched from Jersey to other parts of the

---

27. *Lancry, supra* n. 21, para. 31.
28. P. Oliver and W.H. Roth, *supra* n. 18, 431.
29. *See* C. Ritter, 'Purely Internal situations, reverse discrimination, Guimont, Dzodzi and Article 234' (2006) 31(5) *ELRev* 690, 705.
30. *Supra* n. 20, p. 10.
31. *Simitzi v. Dimos Kos*, Joined Cases C-485/93 and C-486/93 [1995] ECR I-2655.
32. *Carbonati Apuani Srl v. Comune di Carrara*, Case No. C-72/03 [2004] ECR I-8027 – annotated by A. Tryfonidou, '*Carbonati Apuani Srl v Comune di Carrara*: Should we reverse "reverse discrimination"?' (2005) 16 *KCLJ* 373.
33. *Jersey Produce Marketing Organisation Ltd v. States of Jersey and Jersey Potato Export Marketing Board,* Case No. C-293/02 [2005] ECR I-9543 – annotated by A. Tryfonidou, (2006) 43 *CMLRev* 1727.
34. The Island of Jersey is considered to be part of the United Kingdom for the purposes of the free movement of goods provisions. Therefore, goods moving from Jersey to other parts of the United Kingdom and *vice-versa* are considered to move between two parts of the same Member State.

United Kingdom, was contrary to Articles 23-25 EC (Articles 28-30 TFEU). One of the significant points of this case was that the contested legislation regulated only the imposition of customs duties on goods despatched from a region of a Member State (Jersey) to another region of the same State (the mainland United Kingdom). It did not apply to regulate the export of potatoes from Jersey to other Member States. Thus, on its face, it was unlike the measures that were contested in *Lancry, Simitzi* and *Carbonati Apuani* which imposed customs duties on *all* goods entering or leaving a region of a Member State.

In its ruling, the Court pointed out that, *due to the specific characteristics of the situation in question* (i.e., that almost all Jersey potatoes are despatched to the United Kingdom), it was almost certain that the imposition of customs duties by Jersey on goods despatched to the mainland United Kingdom would *also* have a potential effect on the further movement of (some of) those goods from the United Kingdom to other Member States. Therefore, the impugned legislation amounted to a violation of Articles 23-25 EC (Articles 28-30 TFEU) since, given the specific situation of the Jersey market in potatoes, it was virtually certain that a portion of the potatoes sent to the United Kingdom would be further exported to other Member States, and thus any restrictive impact the contested legislation might have on the movement of potatoes within the United Kingdom, would also be felt by *those* Jersey potatoes that would be re-exported to other Member States through the United Kingdom.[35] And since it would be impossible to identify at the time of application of the contested rules, *exactly which potatoes* sent from Jersey to the United Kingdom would be further exported to other Member States (and, thus, fall within the scope of EC law), the Court preferred to rule that the legislation fell within the scope of EC law in its entirety, and thus in practical terms be held inapplicable to *all* potatoes despatched from Jersey, even if this meant that some potatoes that would never be re-exported to other Member States (and were thus in a purely internal situation) were included within the scope of EC law.

This comes down to the same principle that was followed in the *Lancry-Simitzi-Carbonati Apuani* trilogy: when it is impossible to identify the specific goods the inter-state movement of which will be negatively affected as a result of the imposition of the contested dues, the Court rules that the imposition of customs duties on all goods is contrary to EC law, even if this will mean that some goods that will not be involved on inter-state trade will also benefit from the application of EC law.

Accordingly, as a general rule, it can be concluded that in the area of customs duties (like in the context of the free movement of goods and services to be analyzed below), in order for a situation to fall within the scope of Articles 23-25 EC (Articles 28-30 TFEU), it is no longer necessary that it involves the imposition of customs duties on goods that move between Member States *and* that the imposition of those dues impedes the inter-state movement of *those* (or, in this context, *all* those) goods. As long as it is virtually certain that the imposition of specific dues will raise an obstacle to the free movement of some goods, this

35. *See Jersey Potatoes, supra* n. 33, paras 65-66.

suffices for bringing the situation within the scope of EC law and declare the national measure inapplicable.

2 The Application of the New Approach of the Court when Delimiting the Scope of Article 28 EC

The 1980s was the decade in which the real difficulties caused by the development of the law on the free movement of goods (Article 28 EC [Article 34 TFEU]) came to the fore. After the initial enthusiasm with *Dassonville* and *Cassis de Dijon*[36] which were considered a panacea for the difficulties caused by the eurosclerosis of the 1970s, the first clouds on this otherwise fairly clear horizon started to appear.[37] In particular, there was a general feeling that in some instances[38] the Court had gone too far in the opposite direction and was now becoming too interventionist, by including within the scope of Article 28 EC national measures that seemed to have no impact on the free movement of goods, over and above that which is inherent in every market regulation regime.

As a response to the above criticisms, the Court in 1993 in the famous *Keck* case,[39] limited the scope of Article 28 EC (Article 34 TFEU) by excluding from it national measures regulating selling arrangements, which apply to all traders within the national territory and which affect in the same manner, in law and in fact, the marketing of domestic and imported products. According to the Court, the application by a Member State of rules regulating selling arrangements on goods coming from other Member States is not such as to prevent their access to the market of that State or to impede their access to that market more than it does for domestic goods, and therefore such rules should escape the ambit of Article 28 EC.[40]

---

36. *Dassonville, supra* n. 12; *Rewe-Zentrale AG v. Bundesmonopolverwaltung für Branntwein*, Case No. 120/78 [1979] ECR 649.
37. For literature criticizing the case-law of the Court in the area of the free movement of goods before *Keck see* D. Chalmers, 'Free Movement of goods within the European Community: An unhealthy addiction to Scotch Whisky?' (1993) 42 *ICLQ* 269; J. Steiner, 'Drawing the line: Uses and abuses of Article 30 EEC' (1992) 29 *CMLRev* 749; K. Mortelmans, 'Article 30 of the EEC Treaty and legislation relating to market circumstances: Time to consider a new definition?' (1991) 28 *CMLRev* 115; E. White, 'In search of the limits to Article 30 of the EEC Treaty' (1989) 26 *CMLRev* 235.
38. *See*, among others, *Torfaen supra* n. 13; *Stoke-on-Trend and Norwich City Councils v. B & Q plc*, Case No. C-169/91 [1992] ECR I-6635; *Cinéthèque SA and others v. Fédération nationale des cinemas français*, Joined Cases 60 and 61/84 [1985] ECR 2605.
39. *Criminal proceedings against Keck and Mithouard*, Joined Cases C-267/91 and C-268/91 [1993] ECR I-6097. There is an immense amount of literature on *Keck* and its ramifications. *See*, among others: J. Snell, *Goods and Services in EC Law: A Study of the Relationship Between the Freedoms* (Oxford, OUP, 2002), pp. 70-127; M. Poiares Maduro, '*Keck*: The end? The beginning of the end? Or just the end of the beginning?' (1994) 1 *IJEL* 30; S. Weatherill, 'After *Keck*: Some Thoughts on How to Clarify the Clarification?' (1996) 33 *CMLRev* 885; P. Koutrakos, 'On groceries, alcohol and olive oil: More on free movement of goods after *Keck*' (2001) 26 *ELRev* 391; N. Reich, 'The November Revolution of the European Court of Justice: Keck, Meng and Audi revisited' (1994) 31 *CMLRev* 459; L. Gormley, 'Two years after *Keck*' (1996) 19 *Fordham Int'l LJ* 866; N. Reich, 'Europe's Economic Constitution, or: A New Look at Keck' (1999) 19 *OJLS* 337; S. Moore, 'Re-visiting the limits of Article 30 EEC' (1994) 19 *ELRev* 195.
40. *Keck, supra* n. 39, para. 17.

The *Keck* solution, itself, has not been without its problems, however. Many commentators have criticized it for being too formalistic.[41] Moreover, not only was the definition of the term 'selling arrangements' not clarified in the case itself (or, as a matter of fact, in any of the Court's subsequent rulings) but also, the *Keck* formula has been claimed, by some, to be a return to the more restrictive nationality discrimination approach.[42] In addition, various commentators have been particularly opposed to the distinction drawn between product requirements and selling arrangements, and the application of different tests to each category of rules.[43] Some members of the Court,[44] the first of them being Advocate General Jacobs,[45] suggested that the question whether a measure falls within the scope of Article 28 EC (Article 34 TFEU) should not depend on whether a measure belongs to a specific category of rules, but rather, on its impact on the access of goods to the market of a Member State[46] – an approach which is much more sensitive to economic reality.[47]

---

41. C. Barnard, 'Fitting the remaining pieces into the goods and persons jigsaw' (2001) 26 *ELRev* 35, 42; D. O'Keeffe and A. Bavasso, 'Four freedoms, one market and national competence: In search of a dividing line', in *Liber Amicorum in Honour of Lord Slynn of Hadley: Judicial Review in European Union Law*, D. O'Keeffe and A. Bavasso (eds) (The Hague, Kluwer Law International, 2000).
42. *See* J. Snell and M. Andenas, 'Exploring the Outer Limits: Restrictions on the Free Movement of Goods and Services', in *Services and Free Movement in EU Law*, M. Andenas and W.H. Roth (eds) (Oxford, OUP, 2003), p. 105; M. Poiares Maduro, 'The Saga of Article 30 EC Treaty: To Be Continued' (1998) 5 *MJ* 298; N. Bernard, 'Discrimination and Free Movement in EC Law' (1996) 45 *ICLQ* 82; D. Wilsher, 'Does Keck discrimination make any sense? An assessment of the non-discrimination principle within the European Single Market' (2008) 33 *ELRev* 3.
43. *See*, for example, M. Poiares Maduro, *supra* n. 39; J.H.H. Weiler, 'The Constitution of the Common Market Place: Text and Context in the Evolution of the Free Movement of Goods', in *The Evolution of EU Law*, P. Craig and G. de Búrca (eds) (Oxford, OUP, 1999).
44. *See*, for example, paras 51-65 of the Opinion of Advocate General Elmer in *Criminal proceedings against Franzén*, Case No. C-189/95 [1997] ECR I -5909; para. 8 of the Opinion of Advocate General Gulmann in *Lucien Ortscheit GmbH v. Eurim-Pharm Arzneimittel GmbH*, Case No. C-320/93 [1994] ECR I-5243; paras 62-64 of the Opinion of Advocate General Geelhoed in *Douwe Egberts NV v. Westrom Pharma NV and Christophe Souranis, carrying on business under the commercial name of 'Etablissements FICS' and Douwe Egberts NV v. FICS-World BVBA*, Case No. C-239/02 [2004] ECR I-7007; Opinion of Advocate General Lenz in *Commission v. Greece (Baby milk)*, Case No. C-391/92 [1995] ECR I-1621; Opinion of Advocate General Poiares Maduro in *Alfa Vita Vassilopoulos AE v. Elliniko Dimosio and Nomarkhiaki Aftodiikisi Ioanninon*, Joined Cases C-158/04 and C-159/04 [2006] ECR I-8135.
45. *See* paras 38-49 of the Opinion of Advocate General Jacobs in *Leclerc-Siplec v. TF1 Publicité*, Case No. C-412/93 [1995] ECR I-179.
46. A strong advocate of this view is Weatherill (S. Weatherill, *supra* n. 39). *See* also L. Woods, *Free Movement of Goods and Services within the European Community* (Aldershot, Ashgate, 2004), pp. 64-67; L. Prete, 'Of Motorcycle Trailers and Personal Watercrafts: the Battle over *Keck*' (2008) 35 *LIEI* 133. For a commentator who strongly opposes the introduction of a market to access approach *see* G. Davies, *Nationality Discrimination in the European Internal Market* (The Hague, Kluwer Law International, 2003), Ch. 6.
47. Even before the Court's judgment in *Keck*, a similar view was expressed by Advocate General Van Gerven in *Torfaen, supra* n. 13. The Advocate General pointed out that Art. 28 EC (Art. 34 TFEU) should apply 'where rules, either on their own or as part of an entire legal and economic context, can lead to a national market being screened off, or access to that market being made

Although the Court of Justice seemed, at first, to be ignoring these continuous calls for a refinement of its approach in *Keck*, nonetheless, it appears that in its more recent case-law,[48] it diffidently adopts an approach much closer to economic reality. What is important, now, in deciding whether a measure falls within the scope of Article 28 EC (Article 34 TFEU), is not whether it is a measure regulating selling arrangements or a measure specifying the characteristics of a product. Furthermore, it is not important whether the measure is discriminatory (whether directly or indirectly), or not. Instead, what is important in deciding whether a situation falls within the scope of EC law is whether there is a substantial restriction on the access to the market of a Member State of goods from other Member States,[49] that is, a substantial negative impact on the free movement of goods.[50] In some of its recent case-law the Court even appears to base its reasoning heavily on the notion of market access, without making use of the distinction between selling arrangements and product requirements established in *Keck*.[51]

Seen in this light, *Keck* can now be considered as a turning point, as the case which changed the way that the scope of Article 28 EC (Article 34 TFEU) is delimited. *Keck* illustrates the Court's concern to ensure that Article 28 EC catches only those rules that have a real and substantial negative impact on inter-state trade: national measures that raise a real obstacle to the free movement of goods. And perhaps the fact that *Keck* was decided less than a month after the Treaty of Maastricht came into force, the Treaty that for the first time inserted into the

---

unacceptably difficult, less profitable or less attractive for economic operators from other Member States' (para. 17 of the Opinion).

48. *Konsumentombudsmannen (KO) v. De Agostini (Svenska) Förlag AB and TV-Shop I Sverige AB*, Joined Cases C-34/95, C-35/95 and C-36/95 [1997] ECR I-3843; *Deutscher Apothekerverband eV v. 0800 DocMorris NV and Jacques Waterval*, Case No. C-322/01 [2003] ECR I-14887, paras 73-75; *Konsumentombudsmannen v. Gourmet International Products AB (GIP)*, Case No. C-405/98 [2001] ECR I-1795.

49. *See* para. 78 of the Opinion of Advocate General Stix-Hackl in *DocMorris, supra* n. 48. This view has been advocated by various commentators, *see*, for example, S. Enchelmaier, 'The Awkward Selling of a Good Idea, or a Traditionalist Interpretation of *Keck*' (2003) 22 *YEL* 249; P. Oliver and W.H. Roth, *supra* n. 18, 413-414; N. Nic Shuibhne, 'The Free Movement of Goods and Article 28 EC: An evolving Framework' (2002) 27 *ELRev* 408; A. Dashwood, 'Non-Discriminatory trade restrictions after *Keck*' (2002) *CLJ* 35; D. O'Keeffe and A. Bavasso, *supra* n. 41; S. Weatherill, 'Current Developments, European law, Free movement of goods' (2006) 55 *ICLQ* 457, 457-459; A. Kaczorowska, 'Gourmet can have his *Keck* and eat it!' (2004) 10 *ELJ* 479; P. Koutrakos, *supra* n. 39, 394-395 and 397-398.

50. For an explanation of the application of the *Keck* principle in the Court's recent case-law *see* A. Tryfonidou, 'Was *Keck* a half-baked solution after all?' (2007) 34 *LIEI* 167. One commentator has rightly noted that '[t]hough the basic application of the selling arrangement has become clear, there is an inherent ability to manipulate it to changing circumstances' – *see* T. Connor, 'Accentuating the positive: the "selling arrangement", the first decade and beyond' (2005) 54 *ICLQ* 127, 160.

51. *Franzén, supra* n. 44; *Parfums Christian Dior SA and Parfums Christian Dior BV v. Evora BV*, Case No. C-337/95 [1997] ECR I-6013, paras 49-54; *Monsees v. Unabhängiger Verwaltungssenat für Kärnten*, Case No. C-350/97 [1999] ECR I-2921; *Société Civile Agricole du Centre d'insémination de la Crespelle v. Coopérative D'Elevage et d'Insémination Artificielle du Département de la Mayenne*, Case No. C-323/93 [1994] ECR I-5077, para. 29.

EC Treaty a general provision requiring respect of the principle of subsidiarity, is not entirely coincidental: *Keck* gives back to the Member States the freedom to regulate the marketing of goods in their territory, as long as this does not impede the inter-state movement of goods.[52] Therefore *Keck*, despite appearances to the contrary, seems to have introduced a more pragmatic approach, an approach which, although based on presumptions, nevertheless, where necessary, allows those presumptions to be rebutted in order to reflect economic reality. *Keck* was thus the Court's reaction to the failure of its early case-law to reflect, in some instances, the economic realities of a case by *including* within the scope of Article 28 EC situations that were not sufficiently connected to the aim of that provision.

As seen in Chapter 2, one of the major disadvantages of the Court's traditional approach to purely internal situations has been its failure to reflect the economic realities of a case. In the context of purely internal situations, however, this failure is due to the fact that the Court's traditional approach automatically *excludes* from the scope of Article 28 EC (Article 34 TFEU) situations that may, on further examination, prove to be sufficiently harmful to the attainment of the aim of that provision.

Accordingly, once the dust from the *Keck* ruling settled, the Court turned its attention towards the difficulties caused by the application of its traditional approach to purely internal situations. As will be explained below, the Court, in some of its Article 28 EC (Article 34 TFEU) case-law in the late 1990s and onwards, decided to follow the tide and refine its traditional approach in such a way as to be able to reflect the economic realities of a case. More specifically, in its (relatively) recent jurisprudence, the Court has expressly recognized that it is wrong *automatically* to exclude a situation from the scope of Article 28 EC merely because it involves the application of a measure to goods that are in a purely internal situation. The application of a measure to such goods can, at the same time, have a sufficiently negative impact on the inter-state movement of *other* goods and thus, in certain instances, Article 28 EC requires a national measure not to be applied even to goods that are in a purely internal situation.

Consequently, *Keck* and the Court's recent jurisprudence on purely internal situations share the underlying connecting theme of the need to delimit the scope of Article 28 EC (Article 34 TFEU) in such as way as to *include* within it all rules that are capable of sufficiently impeding the inter-state movement of goods whilst *excluding* from the scope of that provision any rules that are incapable of having such an effect.[53]

---

52. For a similar view *see* J.H.H. Weiler, *supra* n. 43, pp. 371-372; C. Barnard, *The Substantive Law of the EU: The Four Freedoms* (2nd, edn, Oxford, OUP, 2007), p. 165.
53. *See* A. Tryfonidou, *supra* n. 50. It should be noted that the factual background in *Keck* involved, in reality, a purely internal situation: it involved the application of French rules regulating the *marketing* of (allegedly French) goods in France by French supermarkets. Such rules are, by nature, incapable of impeding the inter-state movement of goods as they (usually) impose an equal burden on imported and domestic goods; moreover, whereas it is for the home State to regulate the production of goods, the regulation of the marketing of goods (i.e., a subsequent stage in the trading process) should be left to the host State (i.e., the State in which the goods are

Let us now turn to the analysis of the case-law where the Court developed its new approach towards finding a link with EC law in the context of Article 28 EC (Article 34 TFEU). The most prominent example is the case of *Pistre*.[54] In that case, the question was whether Article 28 EC precluded French legislation which allowed the description 'mountain' to be used *only* in relation to products prepared on national territory from domestic raw materials, after the producer had obtained an authorization from the French authorities. The contested legislation was, therefore, in effect, discriminatory against goods imported from other Member States, since it reserved use of the description 'mountain' for national products.[55]

The question referred to the Court arose from criminal proceedings brought against Pistre and others (who were *French* nationals) for selling in *France* (*French*) cooked meat products under a label on which appeared the description 'mountain', despite the fact that they had not obtained the authorization required by the contested legislation. The Court accepted that the facts from which the question arose did not involve goods that had moved between Member States, however, in its view this could not be conclusive as to whether the situation was purely internal to France:

> [W]hilst the application of a national measure having no actual link to the importation of goods does not fall within the ambit of Article 30 [now 28] of the Treaty, Article 30 [now 28] cannot be considered inapplicable simply because all the facts of the specific case before the national court are confined to a single Member State. In such a situation, the application of the national measure may also have effects on the free movement of goods between Member States, in particular when the measure in question facilitates the marketing of goods of domestic origin to the detriment of imported goods. In such circumstances, the application of the measure, even if restricted to domestic producers, in itself creates and maintains a difference of treatment between those two categories of goods, hindering, at least potentially, intra-Community trade.[56]

The legislation in *Pistre* was held to be in violation of Article 28 EC (Article 34 TFEU) because, even when it was solely applied to domestic goods, it had the effect of (potentially) inhibiting the importation of 'mountain' goods from other Member States. Since the impugned legislation did not allow, under any circumstances, the use of the designation 'mountain' on products imported from other Member States (i.e., in effect, it was directly discriminatory against imports), this

---

marketed) which can apply its rules to all goods marketed within its territory, whether they are also produced there or not. Therefore, some commentators have been of the view that the *Keck* ruling reinforces the purely internal rule – *see* C. Barnard, *supra* n. 41, n. 57; G. Davies, *supra* n. 4, p. 172; L. Gormley, *supra* n. 39, 867. Moreover, in his Opinion in the *Keck* case Advocate General Van Gerven was, also, of the view that the situation was in reality an 'internal' one.

54. *Criminal proceedings against Pistre*, Joined Cases C-321/94, C-322/94, C-323/94 and C-324/94 [1997] ECR I-2343.
55. *Ibid.*, para. 49.
56. *Ibid.*, para. 45.

meant that imported products that could demonstrate the qualities associated by the consumer with products coming from mountain areas would not be able to bear that label of quality, and would thus be sold as normal products. By allowing the use of a label of quality ('mountain products') only on the packaging of meat products that were manufactured within French territory, the contested legislation improved the position of domestic mountain products in the eyes of the French consumer, thereby raising an invisible obstacle to the importation of such products from other Member States.[57]

It appears, therefore, that the Court in *Pistre* made its first tentative steps in the area of Article 28 EC (Article 34 TFEU), towards the reform of the approach applied in determining whether a situation is purely internal to a Member State. The Court seems to have accepted that, in order to decide whether a situation is not purely internal to Article 28 EC, the question to be asked should be whether there is an (actual or potential) effect on intra-Community trade; something which can be proved to exist even when national legislation has been applied in a situation involving goods that have been confined within the territory of a single Member State.[58]

The innovation in *Pistre* lies in the fact that, although the specific goods to which the contested legislation was applied were not imported products and thus the application of the contested legislation did not impede the inter-state movement *of those specific goods*, nonetheless, the Court did not consider this factor to be sufficient in itself for qualifying the situation as purely internal. The Court, contrary to its traditional approach, did not interrupt its inquiry as soon as it found that the specific facts of the case did not involve an impediment to the free movement of the goods involved. Rather, in order to reflect economic reality, the Court moved on with its assessment and, after finding that it was obvious that the contested legislation, even when applied to domestic goods, was such as to impede the importation of goods from other Member States (though, it was not possible to specify exactly which 'mountain' products from other Member States would be affected), held that the situation was not a purely internal one.

---

57. For an excellent explanation *see* G. Davies, *supra* n. 4, pp. 169-172; G. Davies, *supra* n. 46, pp. 134-135. *See* also *Commission v. France (foie gras)*, Case No. C-184/96 [1998] ECR I-6197, para. 17. The same reasoning can be used generally in order to challenge any national legislation which allows the use of a quality label *only* on the packaging of domestic products. *See Commission v. Germany (Label of origin and quality)*, Case No. C-325/00 [2002] ECR I-9977, para. 23; *Eggers v. Freie Hansestadt Bremen*, Case No. 13/78 [1978] ECR 1935, paras 23-25. Note, however, that this should not be taken to mean that Member States can never take measures in order to ensure that their goods are of high quality. Such measures can be taken since they comply 'with the requirement of sound and fair competition', provided they do not discriminate against imports – *see Jongeneel Kaas BV and others v. The Netherlands and Stichting Centraal Orgaan Zuivelcontrole*, Case No. 237/82 [1984] ECR 483, para. 20.
58. Another commentator advocating this view is Woods who, very rightly, explains that the Court 'has divided trading rules into two categories: those that have an impact on trade; and those which do not and which therefore constitute an internal situation'. *See* L. Woods, *supra* n. 46, p. 56.

Woods has very rightly pointed out that, in the light of the Court's recent case-law such as *Pistre*, it can safely be concluded that the Court no longer attaches great importance to the facts before the referring court, in order to decide whether a situation is a purely internal one: 'The ECJ has thus turned the question of the internal situation into an abstract, objective test rather than a test that relates to the facts in the case'.[59]

The Court's approach in *Pistre* has been criticized by commentators who support a more straightforward and simple approach conducive to legal certainty, such as the traditional approach to purely internal situations.[60] On the other hand, it has been pointed out that the fact that in *Pistre* the ECJ accepted, for the first time, that Article 28 EC (Article 34 TFEU) could be invoked in a case involving facts which were confined to a single Member State, 'is to be welcomed as a positive step towards achieving a genuine internal market'.[61]

The ECJ's reasoning in *Pistre* was confirmed, subsequently, in the case of *PreussenElektra*.[62] In that case, at issue was the compatibility with Article 28 EC (Article 34 TFEU) of German legislation which required electricity supply undertakings to purchase the electricity produced from renewable energy sources in their area of supply, in order to satisfy their needs in such electricity. The interveners in the main proceedings and the German Government had argued before the Court that the issue was a purely internal one since the dispute in the main proceedings did not entail any cross-border elements, pointing out that the plaintiff and the defendant were both German undertakings and no other kind of cross-border element was present. The Court, however, in response to that argument noted that

> [A]n obligation placed on traders in a Member State to obtain a certain percentage of their supplies of a given product from a national supplier limits to that extent the possibility of importing the same product by preventing those traders from obtaining supplies in respect of part of their needs from traders situated in other Member States.[63]

Therefore, the application of the contested legislation to national suppliers of electricity had, at the same time, an effect on the free movement of goods (electricity produced from renewable energy sources) from other Member States.

As with *Pistre*, the Court therefore accepted that there can be an effect on inter-state trade, and thus a violation of Article 28 EC (Article 34 TFEU), even if a piece of national legislation is applied to undertakings that are established in that Member State and the specific facts from which a question arises do not involve inter-state movement. On the facts of the case, it was not possible to show that a

---

59. L. Woods, *supra* n. 46, p. 79.
60. *See*, for example, P. Oliver, *Free Movement of Goods in the European Community, supra* n. 18, pp. 146-154; P. Oliver and S. Enchelmaier, *supra* n. 18, 657-658.
61. M.A. Jarvis, *The application of EC Law by National Courts: The Free Movement of Goods* (Oxford, Clarendon Press, 1998), p. 156.
62. *PreussenElektra AG v. Schleswag AG*, Case No. C-379/98 [2001] ECR I-2099.
63. *Ibid.*, para. 70. *See* also *Du Pont de Nemours Italiana SpA v. Unità sanitaria locale No 2 di Carrara*, Case No. 21/88 [1990] ECR I-889, para. 11.

specific trader from another Member State had been harmed. And yet, the effect on inter-state trade was so direct and immediate that Article 28 EC should apply. Notwithstanding the fact that it only applied to national traders, the German legislation had the effect of discriminating against electricity produced in other Member States and thus was per se capable of hindering the free movement of goods. It was as if the contested legislation directly prohibited the importation of 'green' electricity from other Member States.

In *Pistre* and *PreussenElektra* the Court was correct in finding that an effect on inter-state trade was felt, even when the contested legislation was applied to domestic goods. In those cases the legislation was, by nature, only applicable to domestic goods so one, at first sight, could have concluded that it would be impossible for such legislation to have a negative impact on inter-state trade. And yet, this may have been the aim of the astute drafters of those pieces of legislation. The legislation may have been drafted in such a way as, on its face, to apply only to goods confined within the territory of a single Member State, so that, under the traditional approach used in finding a link with EC law, it would in all circumstances fall outside the scope of EC law. However, the laws contested in *Pistre* and *PreussenElektra* were, in fact, discriminatory against goods coming from other Member States. Their application, solely, to goods confined within the territory of a single Member State was such as to directly affect the position of imported goods.[64]

64. More recently, another judgment of the Court appears to have the potential of extending the scope of application of Art. 28 EC (Art. 34 TFEU) even further. In the *A-Punkt* case (*A-Punkt Schmuckhandel v. Schmidt*, Case No. C-441/04 [2006] ECR I-2093, para. 9), the Court accepted that as long as the trader involved on the facts of the case can point to a cross-border element (e.g., he or she is established in a Member State other than that where the goods are marketed), this suffices for bringing the situation within the scope of Art. 28 EC, notwithstanding the fact that the goods involved have not crossed State borders. In this case the Court seems to have followed an approach similar to that applied in the area of the free movement of services where, apart from the situation where the service itself moves, an inter-state element is also deemed to exist if the provider of the service is established in a State different from the one where the recipient resides, even if the actual provision of the service takes place within one and the same Member State (e.g., if the provider has travelled to the Member State of the recipient to provide a service, or *vice-versa*). This approach appears to be totally justified in the context of the free movement of services since a large number of services (e.g., services which require a specific skill to be possessed by the provider) require the provider to *physically* move in order to provide them and Art. 49 EC (Art. 56 TFEU) aims, inter alia, at enabling such movement to take place. Conversely, with goods, the situation is different since the sole aim of Art. 28 EC is to enable goods that have been manufactured in one Member State to move to the territory of another. The movement of a trader is not something that falls within the scope of Art. 28 EC – and, after all, this is obvious from the fact that for Art. 28 EC to apply, the producer of goods or the trader involved on the facts of the case, does not need to hold the nationality of a Member State, whereas it is only nationals of Member States that can enjoy the rights provided by Arts 39, 43, 49 and 18 EC (respectively, Arts 45, 49, 56 and 21 TFEU). If the Court wishes to protect the freedom of traders to move between Member States, then Arts 43 EC or 49 EC can be applied. Of course, the fact that the judgment in *A-Punkt* was delivered by a three-judge Chamber and that its value as a precedent still has to be confirmed (since there has been no other case, to date, where the Court affirmed this principle) means that we are unable at

3 The Application of the New Approach of the Court when Delimiting the Scope of Article 29 EC

In the *Jersey Potatoes* case,[65] at issue was not only the compatibility of a national measure with Articles 23-25 EC (Articles 28-30 TFEU). Another issue was whether the same piece of legislation, which required potatoes grown in the territory of a region of a Member State (Jersey) to satisfy a number of requirements before they could be despatched to other regions of the same State (the mainland United Kingdom), was contrary to Article 29 EC (Article 35 TFEU). When the questions reached the Court of Justice, Jersey, whilst not denying the fact that its legislation might be an obstacle to exports to the United Kingdom (i.e., an obstacle to the movement of goods between two regions of the same Member State), argued that there was no violation of Article 29 EC as there was no negative impact on the *inter-state movement* of goods.

The Court, however, found that although the impugned legislation was applicable only to goods (potatoes) exported from Jersey to other parts of the United Kingdom and its immediately apparent effect was to establish a difference in treatment between Jersey's domestic trade and its export trade to the United Kingdom in such a way as to provide a particular advantage for the island's production or its domestic market,[66] nevertheless,

> [T]here is nothing to rule out the possibility that such potatoes, once within the United Kingdom, might then be re-exported to other Member States.[67]

The Court, having in mind the particular situation of the market in question (i.e., that almost all Jersey potatoes are exported to the United Kingdom),[68] noted that such a pattern of re-exports was 'certainly conceivable'. As a result of that, the impugned legislation was

> [A]lso likely to be an obstacle to the export of those goods to other Member States and to have, with regard to the latters' markets, the same negative effect as that observed in respect of the United Kingdom market.[69]

Accordingly, the contested legislation violated Article 29 EC (Article 35 TFEU) since, even when merely applied to domestic goods, it was almost certain that, at least in respect of a portion of those goods, it would have an effect on inter-state

---

this stage to conclude with certainty whether the Court has extended the scope of application of Art. 28 EC in this inordinate way. For a criticism of the Court's approach in this case *see* P. Oliver and S. Enchelmaier, *supra* n. 18, 658.

65. *Supra* n. 33.
66. *Ibid.*, para. 76.
67. *Ibid.*, para. 79. *See* also para. 80 of the judgment.
68. *Ibid.*, para. 81.
69. *Ibid.*, para. 80. For a strong criticism of the application of the Court's new approach in the context of Art. 29 EC (Art. 35 TFEU) *see* A. Dawes, 'Importing and exporting poor reasoning: worrying trends in relation to the case law on the free movement of goods' (2007) 8 *GLJ* 761, 770-772.

trade by inhibiting the further exportation of those goods to other Member States. Hence, the new approach followed by the Court when finding a link with EC law seems to have been applied in this area as well, and the finding of a (potential) discriminatory treatment against goods exported to other Member States was held to be sufficient to bring the situation within the scope of EC law, even though the specific goods the movement of which would be hampered could not be identified.

C THE NEW APPROACH FOLLOWED BY THE COURT WHEN DELIMITING THE SCOPE OF THE FREE MOVEMENT OF SERVICES PROVISIONS

As was seen in detail in Chapter 2, the Court has established through its case-law that for a situation to fall within the scope of Article 49 EC (Article 56 TFEU) it must involve the exercise of inter-state movement. In particular, under the Court's traditional approach, a situation is held to fall within the scope of Article 49 EC if the specific facts of the case before the Court involve services (or service-providers) that have moved (or are definitely going to move) between Member States, and the application of the contested measure to those services/service-providers is such as to inhibit that specific movement.

Nonetheless, the Court's judgment in *Alpine Investments* illustrates that the Court no longer insists on the existence of a *specific* exercise of inter-state movement on the facts before the referring court, for a situation to fall within the scope of the free movement of services provisions.[70] As long as a substantially negative impact on the access of services to the market of Member States other than their State of origin can be proved, there is no need to show that a *specific* movement of services has been realized or is going to be realized *with particular recipients*.[71]

Hence, *Alpine Investments* opened the way for the application of the Court's new approach to purely internal situations, also in the area of the free movement of services. In particular, the Court has accepted in its very recent case-law in the area of public procurement, that an effect on the inter-state provision of services can be found to exist, even if the dispute from which a question for a preliminary ruling

---

70. *Alpine Investments BV v. Minister van Financiën*, Case No. C-384/93 [1995] ECR I-1141, para. 19. For other cases where the Court did not insist on the need to specifically identify the one party to the transaction *see Syndesmos ton en Elladi Touristikon kai Taxidiotikon Grafeion v. Ypourgos Ergasias (SETTG)*, Case No. C-398/95 [1997] ECR I-3091 (there, the [identified] recipients of services brought an action against their Member State of establishment, claiming that a national measure prevented [unidentified] providers of services from other Member States to provide services to them); *Freskot AE v. Elliniko Dimosio*, Case No. C-355/00 [2003] ECR I-5263, paras 61-63; *Deliège v. Ligue Francophone de Judi et Disciplines Associées ASBL*, Joined Cases C-51/96 and C-191/97 [2000] ECR I-2549, para. 58. *See*, also, para. 68 of the Opinion of Advocate General Jacobs in *Gourmet, supra* n. 48.
71. For an explanation *see* V. Hatzopoulos, 'Recent Developments of the Case law of the ECJ in the field of services' (2000) 37 *CMLRev* 43, 58. *See* also V. Hatzopoulos and T.U. Do, 'The case law of the ECJ concerning the free provision of services: 2000-2005' (2006) 43 *CMLRev* 923, 925.

arose does not involve an identifiable service provider established in another Member State and the parties to the dispute are both situated in the same State.

Before going further with an analysis of the Court's new approach to the application of the linking factor test in public procurement cases, it may be useful to reflect, for a moment, on a case in this area where the Court applied its traditional approach. In *RI.SAN*,[72] the Municipality of Ischia in Italy entrusted, by decision, to an Italian company the solid urban waste collection service. By two actions, RI.SAN (another Italian company) challenged the municipal council decision claiming, in particular, that the choice of private partner should have been made through public tender procedure and that the waste collection service should also have been awarded under such a procedure. RI.SAN was relying on, inter alia, the free movement of services provisions of the Treaty. When the issue reached the Court of Justice, the Court held that the situation did not fall within the scope of the free movement of services provisions:

> RI.SAN . . . has its seat in Italy and does not operate on the Italian market in reliance on freedom of establishment or freedom to provide services. Such a situation does not therefore have any connecting link with one of the situations envisaged by Community law in the area of the free movement of persons and services.[73]

Accordingly, it seems that since, on the specific facts of the case, the opportunity of a specific company established in the territory of another Member State to provide the said services was not proved to have been affected as a result of the failure of the municipality to resort to the use of the public tender procedure, the situation qualified as a purely internal one.

Yet, in a number of recent cases, the Court appears to have differentiated its approach, accepting as a sufficient connection with EC law the fact that the failure to advertise competitions for the provision of public services, directly impedes the provision of such services by companies established in other Member States. In this context, like in the context of Article 28 EC (Article 34 TFEU), the fact that a specific company established in another State did not bring the action against the relevant municipality, and thus a company from another Member State that was negatively affected by the contested action could not be specifically identified on the facts before the Court, did not take the situation outside the scope of EC law.

In *Parking Brixen*[74] the main issue was whether the municipality of Brixen in Italy could award, without putting it to tender, the management of car-parks within that municipality (a public service concession) to Stadtwerke Brixen, a company which resulted from the conversion of a special undertaking of that public authority established in that municipality. In particular, it was claimed that the failure to put to tender the above economic activity was a violation of Articles 43 and 49 EC

72. *RI.SAN. Srl v. Comune di Ischia and others,* Case No. C-108/98 [1999] ECR I-5219.
73. *Ibid.*, paras 21-22.
74. *Parking Brixen GmbH v. Gemeinde Brixen and Stadtwerke Brixen AG*, Case No. C-458/03 [2005] ECR I-8612.

(respectively, Articles 49 and 56 TFEU). Although the facts from which the question arose did not involve inter-state movement since all of the interested parties were established within Italy, nevertheless, the Court held that this was not a purely internal situation since

> It is possible that, in the main proceedings, undertakings established in Member States other than the Italian Republic might have been interested in providing the services concerned... In the absence of advertising and the opening to competition of the award of a public service concession such as that at issue in the main proceedings, there is discrimination, at least potentially, against undertakings of the other Member States which are prevented from making use of the freedom to provide services and of the freedom of establishment provided for by the Treaty.[75]

Admittedly, in such cases the effect on inter-state trade is not purely hypothetical – the mere act of awarding a concession to a local company without holding an invitation to tender is itself an obstacle to the freedom of establishment and services, since service-providers established in other Member States are, by virtue of this action, entirely foreclosed from the market. The requirement of the traditional approach, that a specific person or company in a cross-border situation should be identified before a situation could escape the characterization of 'purely internal', seems to be entirely inappropriate in the context of public procurement.[76] However, taking into account the specific nature of public procurement and the importance of transparency for this process to work, it is not entirely clear whether the Court intended this 'new' approach to purely internal situations to be applied generally in all free movement of services cases, or whether the Court merely refined its approach to a link with EC law in order to reflect the special nature of public procurement cases. Hence, only time will tell whether the Court is eager to apply its revised approach in all cases in the context of the free movement of services and, thus, how far the Court will follow further down this road in the future.[77]

---

75. *Ibid.*, para. 55. For similar rulings (though not as explicit as this one) *see Coname v. Comune di Cingia de' Botti*, Case No. C-231/03 [2005] ECR I-7287, paras 17-19; *ANAV v. Comune di Bari and AMTAB Servizio Spa*, Case No. C-410/04 [2006] ECR I-3303; ASM *Brescia SpA v. Comune di Rodengo Saiano*, Case No. C-347/06, judgment of 17 Jul. 2008, not yet reported, paras 59-63. Note that this approach is also implicit in a rather older case, *ARGE Gewässerschutz v. Bundesministerium für Land- und Forstwirtschaft*, Case No. C-94/99 [2000] ECR I-11037, paras 33-38.
76. *See* para. 27 of the Opinion of Advocate General Stix-Hackl in *Coname, supra* n. 75.
77. It should be noted that in a 2008 judgment, the Court seems to have extended this approach to a services case which did not involve public procurement as such – *see Centro Europa 7 Srl v. Ministero delle Comunicazioni e Autorità per le garanzie nelle comunicazioni and Direzione generale per le concessioni e le autorizzazioni del Ministero delle Comunicazioni*, Case No. C-380/05, judgment of 31 Jan. 2008, not yet reported, para. 66. However, this does not seem to be sufficient for establishing that the Court has decided to extend its 'new' approach to 'general' free movement of services cases since, as explained by Advocate General Poiares Maduro in his Opinion in this case (*see* paras 34-36), situations involving facts such as those in the main

The fact that there can be an effect on inter-state trade even where a specific case before a national court involves only national traders or companies (and no specific company or person from another Member State that is affected can be identified), is also implicit in the Opinion of Advocate General Poiares Maduro in the *Alfa Vita Vassilopoulos* case (a case in the area of the free movement of goods). In his Opinion in that case, the Advocate General explained that some measures which restrict the freedom to trade within the market of the Member State of the trader by allowing only specific traders to be involved in a specific area of the economy (i.e., a situation similar to that arising in public procurement cases), may also be considered as restricting the access of traders from other Member States to that market since such measures may maintain the 'status quo' in the local market and thus make the access of new traders (including traders from other Member States) to that market more difficult.[78]

D Some General Comments on the Court's New Approach to the Application of the Linking Factor Test

In the preceding parts of this section, an analysis of the Court's case-law in the context of the free movement of goods and services was provided, where the new approach used in finding a link with EC law was applied. In particular, it was explained that in those cases, the Court did not follow its traditional approach since it did not require the linking factor test to be satisfied *on the facts of the case*. Under the Court's new approach, a national measure falls within the scope of EC law as long as its application may potentially have an effect on the inter-state movement of products. That the movement of the specific products that are involved on the facts of the case is not affected (or the movement of *all* those products is not affected), is no longer of any importance in determining whether the situation is a purely internal one.

This new approach of the Court is by no means a revolutionary one. This is for two reasons. Firstly, when applied in the context of Article 28 EC (Article 34 TFEU), the Court's new approach is a pure reflection of *Dassonville*,[79] according to which a measure is an MEQR and, thus, contrary to Article 28 EC if it is, inter alia, capable of hindering *potentially* intra-Community trade. And, despite the fact that there is not an equally explicit judicial pronouncement to support this argument as regards the other provisions to which this new approach has been applied by the Court (i.e., Articles 25 EC, 29 EC and 49 EC [respectively 30, 35 and 56

---

proceedings in the case (i.e., where the Member State awards the right to provide certain services to a limited number of economic operators) are very similar to public procurement cases.

78. Para. 38 of the Opinion of Advocate General Poiares Maduro in *Alfa Vita Vassilopoulos, supra* n. 44. The negative impact that the maintenance of the 'status quo' in the local market can have on inter-state trade seems to have been acknowledged by the Court in the free movement of goods cases of *Gourmet* (*supra* n. 48) and, more subtly, *De Agostini* (*supra* n. 48).
79. *Supra* n. 12, para. 5.

TFEU]), it would appear somewhat anomalous if those other provisions which share the same objective as Article 28 EC (i.e., the establishment of the single market) were not interpreted in a similar way. Secondly, the Court in some of its pronouncements on purely internal situations has pointed out that a situation is purely internal if it has no factor linking it with any of the situations governed by Community law *and* is wholly internal to a Member State (this meaning that it does not involve inter-state movement).[80] The use of the word 'and' points to the fact that the above two conditions (i.e., (a) no linking factor and (b) no inter-state movement) are cumulative and thus must both be satisfied for a situation to qualify as purely internal to a Member State. In other words, the Court (even) in its (early) case-law has hinted that it is possible to have a situation that is confined in all relevant respects within a single Member State, *and yet* have a link with EC law because it involves an effect on the achievement of the aim of the free movement provisions.

The Court's new approach could be considered as giving birth to a simplified linking factor test, though one which, in effect, poses the same question as the classic linking factor test, that is, whether a measure impedes the free movement of goods and services. This revised linking factor test could be reduced to only one limb and should be as follows: Does the application of the contested measure have a substantial effect on inter-state trade and, in particular, on the free movement of goods or services between Member States?

A substantial effect on the free movement of products can be proved in two ways: either where the application of the contested measure results in discrimination against goods and services involved in inter-state trade; or where, in the absence of discrimination, a substantial impact on the inter-state movement of goods and services can be proved, following an examination of the virtually certain (though potential) impact the contested measure can have on the inter-state movement of (identifiable though not identified) goods or services.[81]

Whether a situation involves discrimination against goods or services that have moved or are going to move between Member States, is readily apparent and no deeper inquiry into the specific characteristics of the relevant market and the potential effect of the legislation on the free movement of products needs to be undertaken.

The most difficult part of this revised test seems to be its application to situations which do not involve discrimination based on the origin of goods or services. In such situations, in order for the test to be satisfied, a deeper analysis of the specific effects of the measure under scrutiny has to be conducted, in order to determine whether the situation involves a substantial effect on inter-state trade. In particular, it will have to be proved that on the specific situation in question, and

80. *See*, for example, para. 55 of *Hurd v. Jones (Her Majesty's Inspector of Taxes)*, Case No. 44/84 [1986] ECR 29; *Metock and Others v. Minister for Justice, Equality and Law Reform*, Case No. C-127/08, judgment of 25 Jul. 2008, not yet reported, para.77.

81. For another commentator advocating the adoption of such a test *see* N. Nic Shuibhne, *supra* n. 49.

viewed in the light of the circumstances under which the relevant market in question operates, the application of the contested measure either to products confined within the territory of a single Member State or to products involved in inter-state trade, indeed, has a substantial (actual or potential) effect on the inter-state movement of products.[82]

A test aiming at reflecting the economic realities of a case (such as the revised linking factor test) would necessarily involve the application of two principles: remoteness and the *de minimis* rule.

In a great number of cases since the early years of its existence, the Court has accepted that the notion of remoteness applies in determining whether a situation falls within the scope of the fundamental freedoms provisions of the Treaty.[83] This rule – which is also applicable in the area of competition law[84] – has attained increasing importance through the years and will continue to be highly significant in the process of applying the revised linking factor test. Nonetheless, despite the importance attached to it, the Court has never provided a clear explanation of the meaning of remoteness.[85] The only indication offered by the Court is that a situation is too remote from inter-state trade, if the restrictive effects it has on the free movement of products and factors of production are too uncertain and indirect. A more specific explanation of the principle of remoteness has been provided by Advocate General La Pergola in his Opinion in the *BASF* case, where he pointed out that the object of this principle is to verify whether a causal link exists between the national measure concerned and the pattern of imports.[86]

The second important rule that has to be applied as part of the revised test is the *de minimis* rule. According to this rule, a situation escapes the ambit of a specific provision if it only has a small and insignificant negative effect on the aims of that provision. Although in EC competition law, a *de minimis* approach applies,[87] this has traditionally been rejected by the Court in the context of the free movement provisions.[88] Nonetheless, some of the Court's latest case-law may be suggesting

82. For a similar view *see* L. Prete, *supra* n. 46, 149.
83. *See*, among others, *Centro Servizi Spediporto Srl v. Spedizioni Marittima del Golfo Srl*, Case No. C-96/94 [1995] ECR I-2883, para. 41; *DIP SpA et al. v. Comune di Bassano del Grappa et al*, Joined Cases C-140/94, C-141/94 and C-142/94 [1995] ECR I-3527, para. 29; *Esso Española v. Comunidad Autónoma de Canarias*, Case No. C-134/94 [1995] ECR I-4223, para. 24; *ED Srl v. Italo Fenocchio*, Case No. C-412/97 [1999] ECR I-3845, paras 4 and 10; *Krantz GmbH & Co. v. Ontvanger der Directe Belastingen and Netherlands*, Case No. 69/88 [1990] ECR I-583; *BASF AG v. Prasident des Deutschen Patentamts*, Case No. C-44/98 [1999] ECR I-6269, para. 16; *Graf v. Filzmoser Maschinenbau GmbH*, Case No. C-190/98 [2000] ECR I-493, para. 25.
84. K. Mortelmans, *supra* n. 13, 634.
85. *See* A. Biondi, 'In and Out of the Internal Market', (1999/2000) *YEL* 469, 485-488. For literature on the notion of remoteness *see* S. Enchelmaier, *supra* n. 49, 290-291; P. Oliver, 'Some further reflections on the scope of Articles 28-30 EC', *supra* n. 18, 788-789.
86. *See* para. 18 of the Advocate General's Opinion in *BASF, supra* n. 83.
87. *See* the cases in n. 8.
88. L. Woods, *supra* n. 46, pp. 33, 55 and 212 (both in the area of goods and services); K. Mortelmans, *supra* n. 13, 633; P. Oliver, 'Some further reflections on the scope of Articles 28-30 EC', *supra* n. 18, 789-793. *See Criminal proceedings against Van de Haar*, Joined Cases 177 and 178/82

that the Court is tentatively moving towards the adoption of such a test in delimiting the scope of Articles 28 and 49 EC (Articles 34 and 35 TFEU, respectively). In *Burmanjer*, for example, when examining whether a piece of national legislation violated Article 28 EC, the Court noted that such was not the case since even if there might be some kind of effect on the inter-state movement of goods, nevertheless

> [I]t would be too *insignificant* and uncertain to be regarded as being such as to hinder or otherwise interfere with trade between Member States.[89]

The application of the rule of remoteness and of a *de minimis* test are necessary steps that have to be followed if the Court's new approach to a link with EC law is to be successful. Since this approach can include within the scope of EC law more situations than before (since the limiting requirement of the *existence* of inter-state movement on the specific facts of the case has lost its significance), another limiting principle should be applied. This new 'filter' is the need for a situation to involve a *substantial* effect on the inter-state movement of goods and services, which, in its turn, involves the need to exclude from the scope of EC law situations where there is only limited (if at all) negative impact on the inter-state movement of goods and services; and situations which do not involve a causal link between the application of the contested national measure *and* a negative impact on the inter-state movement of products (i.e., are too remote).

Finally, the importance attached, in the Court's new approach, to reflecting the economic realities of a case means that the specific economic context from which the situation on the facts arises must now be taken into account by the Court when making its assessment as to whether the situation presents a sufficient link with EC law. The difficulties that this entails become obvious from a judgment of the Court delivered in the period between *Pistre* and *PreussenElektra* (*TK-Heimdienst*) which illustrates that this requirement of a more 'mature' analysis of the economic context of a case may prove to be the Achilles' heel of the Court's new approach.

In *TK-Heimdienst*[90] at issue was Austrian legislation that provided that bakers, butchers and grocers were permitted to offer for sale goods on rounds, only if they also carried on their trade from a permanent establishment in the Austrian

---

[1984] ECR 1797, para. 13; *Commission v. France*, Case No. 269/83 [1985] ECR 837, para. 10; *Commission v. Italy*, Case No. 103/84 [1986] ECR 1759, para. 18; *Criminal proceedings against Prantl*, Case No. 16/83 [1984] ECR 1299, para. 20; *Leclerc-Siplec supra* n. 45; *Criminal Proceedings against Bluhme*, Case No. C-67/97 [1998] ECR I-8033.

89. *Criminal proceedings against Burmanjer, Van Der Linden and De Jong*, Case No. C-20/03 [2005] ECR I-4133, para. 31 (emphasis added). For an Art. 49 EC (Art. 56 TFEU) case where the Court seems to have applied the *de minimis* rule *see Viacom Outdoor Srl v. Giotto Immobilier SARL*, Case No. C-134/03 [2005] ECR I-1167, para. 38. However, in a recent Grand Chamber judgment, the Court seems to have affirmed its traditional position according to which the *de minimis* rule does not apply when determining whether a measure falls within the scope of the free movement provisions – *see Government of the French Community and Walloon Government v. Flemish Government, supra* n. 24, para. 52.

90. *Schutzverband gegen unlauteren Wettbewerb v. TK-Heimdienst Sass GmbH*, Case No. C-254/98 [2000] ECR I-151 – annotated by E. Spaventa, (2000) 37 *CMLRev* 1265.

administrative district in which the rounds would take place or in a municipality adjacent thereto. The facts from which the question arose involved an Austrian retail trader (TK-Heimdienst) who violated the above legislation by offering for sale goods on rounds in a municipality which was not the same or adjacent to the municipality from which it was established. Before the national court, the question arose whether the national legislation was in violation of Article 28 EC (Article 34 TFEU).

When the issue was referred to the ECJ, the main question was whether legislation such as that at issue had effects confined within one Member State, or whether it was capable of constituting a potential impediment to intra-Community trade. The Court, applying *Keck*, found that although such legislation related to the selling arrangements for certain goods, nevertheless, it did constitute a violation of Article 28 EC (Article 34 TFEU) as it did not affect in the same manner the marketing of domestic products and that of products from other Member States.[91] It imposed an obligation on bakers, butchers and grocers who wanted to sell goods in an Austrian municipality but who already had a permanent establishment in another Member State, to set up another permanent establishment in that administrative district (thus incurring additional costs), whilst local economic operators already met the requirement as to a permanent establishment.

In my view, the application of the contested legislation to goods confined within the territory of Austria (or, as a matter of fact, to any goods) would not seem to be such as to affect, to a substantial degree, the inter-state movement of goods.

Firstly, the legislation in question was not directly discriminatory against goods coming from other Member States: it applied, equally, to Austrian traders and traders coming from other Member States. Moreover, unlike the contested pieces of legislation in *Pistre* and *PreussenElektra*, the legislation in *TK-Heimdienst* did not have as an effect the total foreclosure of the Austrian market to goods coming from other Member States. As the Court concluded, the legislation in question would merely create an *impediment* (as opposed to a total ban) to the access of imported goods in the Austrian market. The retailers of both domestic and imported goods would merely have to find alternative methods for marketing their goods.

Finally, and most fundamentally, the specific goods that are sold on rounds (bread, groceries and meat) – highly perishable goods – are not, by nature, commodities that are marketable in an inter-state context,[92] and even if in theory the contested legislation might have an effect on the inter-state movement of goods, the practical realities of the relevant market were such that no substantial effect on

91. *TK-Heimdienst, supra* n. 90, paras 24-25.
92. Note that there is no inter-state trade in goods that are highly perishable – *Morellato v. Comune di Padova*, Case No. C-416/00 [2003] ECR I-9343, para. 23. *See* G. Wagner, 'The Economics of Harmonization: the case of Contract law' (2002) 39 *CMLRev* 995, 1016.

inter-state trade could be proved. To this effect, Advocate General La Pergola stressed, in paragraph 12 of his Opinion in the case,[93] that

> [I]t is not realistic to argue that imports have fallen because a baker, butcher or any other retailer of food products established, for example, in Brussels, Paris or Berlin, cannot sell products not ordered in advance from his van in Austria, for the simple reason that in commercial practice, there are natural limits, so to speak, on the area covered by this form of distribution.

Accordingly, the Court in *TK-Heimdienst* seems to have followed a purely legalistic, as opposed to a pragmatic, approach and, without taking into account the nature of the market involved and the prospect of foreign retailers being interested in accessing that market, it found that the legislation imposed an impediment to the access of traders from other Member States to the Austrian market and thus was contrary to Article 28 EC (Article 34 TFEU).

Hence, the real challenge now facing the Court seems to be to ensure that economic reality is actually taken into account, when making an assessment as to whether a situation falls within the scope of EC law. Useful lessons can be learned from the Court's competition law jurisprudence. In particular, account should be taken of the 'economic and legal conditions'[94] of the relevant (product and geographic) market to determine whether the application of the measure can, indeed, have an effect on the free movement of goods.[95] Only in this way will the Court's new approach reflect the view that the internal market is a mature market, the rules of which apply only to situations that involve a real impediment to the achievement of one of its aims. A failure by the Court to take into account the economic and legal context in which a challenged measure is applied, questions the rationale, and puts into danger the effectiveness, of the new approach.

Consequently, although the new approach followed by the Court in finding a link with EC law, should be applauded, the Court should take care not to take a mechanical, *ex ante* approach in a context in which it is wholly inappropriate. In order for the new approach to be successful, a more detailed examination of the practical realities of the relevant market is now called for, and the Court should not conduct a purely superficial examination of whether the specific kind of goods

93. For another case where the Court replied to a question whether a piece of national legislation which was applied to national products was capable of being contrary to Art. 28 EC (Art. 34 TFEU), without confining the effect of its judgment to potential situations where the legislation would be applied to imported goods *see Sapod Audic v. Eco-Emballages SA*, Case No. C-159/00 [2002] ECR I-5031, paras 64-75.
94. This phrase can be found in a number of competition law cases. *See*, for example, para. 13 of *Béguelin, supra* n. 8.
95. Note that Biondi (*supra* n. 85, at p. 485) has called for the exercise of some caution when deciding that even a case involving facts purely internal to a Member State, may have an effect on intra-Community trade. He has argued that, 'in the absence of objective "tangible" factors which could affect intra-Community trade, Community law should not be invoked. This, after all, is the approach taken in the field of competition law when examining whether there is an effect on intra-Community trade'.

involved on the facts of a case may form the subject-matter of inter-state trade. If the Court does not feel ready to follow this more 'mature' approach when deciding whether a situation falls within the scope of EC law, then it would be more appropriate to retreat to its traditional approach and only accept that a case falls within the scope of EC law, if its specific facts satisfy the linking factor test. If the new approach of the Court is applied wrongly, it will have the negative consequence of overstretching the scope of EC law in a pre-*Keck*-like manner by catching any national measure regulating trade, irrespective of its actual effect on the inter-state movement of goods.[96]

E Conclusion

In this part of the chapter I have analyzed the new approach that has been followed in some of the Court's recent judgments, in determining whether a situation presents a link with EC law in the area of the free movement of goods and services. The Court has rightly responded to the criticisms voiced towards its traditional approach to the application of the linking factor test and its insistence on the test being satisfied on the specific facts of the case, by accepting that a situation can have an effect on inter-state trade even if a national measure is applied to goods and services that are confined within the territory of a single Member State.

The question that remains to be asked is whether this new approach used in delimiting the scope of Articles 25, 28, 29 and 49 EC (Articles 30, 34, 35 and 56 TFEU) is now capable of including within the scope of those provisions, instances of reverse discrimination. I would like to suggest that the answer is clearly a 'no', since reverse discrimination does not normally create an obstacle to the inter-state movement of goods and services. Accordingly, since the linking factor test (whether as applied traditionally, or under the Court's new approach) still (and very rightly) requires the creation of an impediment to the inter-state *movement* of goods and services for a situation to fall within the scope of the relevant provisions, it cannot be satisfied when a situation involves reverse discrimination. Hence, although the new approach of the Court to the application of the linking factor test seems to be capable of solving some of the deficiencies of the traditional approach (i.e., the failure to reflect the economic realities of a case), the Court, through this new approach, has not managed to address its other, equally important, concern: to find a solution for the reverse discrimination conundrum.

96. Note that some scholars are of the view that in order to avoid such difficulties, Art. 28 EC (Art. 34 TFEU) should only catch discriminatory measures (including double-burden rules) *and* measures *preventing* (as opposed to merely impeding) market access. In that way, only non-discriminatory measures which totally prevent access to market would be caught be Art. 28 EC. *See* M. Poiares Maduro, 'Harmony and Dissonance in Free Movement' (2001) 4 *CYELS* 315; J.H.H. Weiler, *supra* n. 43, 372.

IV FREE MOVEMENT OF (ECONOMICALLY ACTIVE) PERSONS: THE COURT TWEAKS ITS TRADITIONAL APPROACH TO PREVENT THE EMERGENCE OF REVERSE DISCRIMINATION

In Chapter 2 of the book, it was explained that one of the main disadvantages of the Court's traditional approach to purely internal situations is that it induces us to adopt a view according to which different areas of law can be divided into watertight compartments – an approach that is somewhat unrealistic, in view of the fact that the operation of the law in one area often has spillover effects into other areas. More specifically, reverse discrimination suffered by persons who cannot point to a contribution, on their part, to the construction of the internal market may often have as a side-effect the non-extension to those persons of a number of rights that are related to areas of human life that are far-removed from inter-state trade and which are highly significant from an emotional point of view – the most prominent example being family reunification rights.

Although it is true that the Court has been correct in delimiting the scope of the fundamental freedoms provisions in such a way as to include within it only situations that involve a sufficient link with the aims of those provisions, it is difficult to perceive that a person would be comforted by being told that the emerging difference in treatment (i.e., reverse discrimination) is, actually, a justified difference in treatment which escapes the ambit of EC law and, for this reason, is not prohibited by Community law. And, as will be seen in the next part of the book, reverse discrimination is now a difference in treatment that, not only causes inconvenience and irritation among Union citizens, but also a difference in treatment that comes on a collision course with the Community's (new) aims.

The main argument of this part of the chapter is that the Court, in some of its recent case-law in the context of the free movement of persons, has tried to avoid the emergence of reverse discrimination, by making it overly easy for a link with EC law to be established. As will be seen, this 'artificial' approach to a link with EC law has been applied in case-law in the area of family reunification rights; a case in the area of educational qualifications; and, in a cluster of cases in the context of Articles 39 and 43 EC (respectively, Articles 45 and 49 TFEU). It is my contention that, most probably, the roots of this case-law can be traced to a realization, on the part of the Court, that reverse discrimination is no longer an acceptable difference in treatment in the Community.[97]

In this section of the chapter, there will be a presentation of these three groups of cases, where the Court's lax approach to a link with EC law has been followed. Their main characteristic is that the search for an equitable solution in the individual case is of higher importance for the Court, than preserving a coherent

97. White, back in 1993, noted that the Court in order to avoid the emergence of reverse discrimination, is making it increasingly easy for a link to be established in cases involving family reunification rights. *See* R. C. A. White, 'A fresh look at reverse discrimination?' (1993) 18 *ELRev* 527.

approach respecting cardinal principles of Community law such as the purely internal rule. It will be explained that the traditional approach to the application of the linking factor test was not followed in those judgments, since the Court had accepted that each of the situations fell within the scope of EC law, even though the third limb of the linking factor test was not satisfied (cases to be analyzed in subsections A and B), or even though the second (and, consequently, also the third) limb of the test was not satisfied (cases to be analyzed in subsection C). In other words, in all groups of cases to be analyzed in this section, once the first limb of the linking factor test (i.e., inter-state movement) was found by the Court to be satisfied, the Court did not further engage in a real enquiry as to whether the other limbs of the test were also satisfied. As Poiares Maduro has, very rightly, noted, 'the confusion between the aim of protecting free movement and the exercise of free movement as the element ascertaining a connection with EC law may lead the Court to apply EC rules even when that goal is not at stake. In other words, once a cross-border element exists, EC law will apply even if there is no impact on free movement'.[98]

This body of case-law appears to be the most controversial of the three categories discussed in this chapter and, as will be seen, has attracted increasing scholarly attention. If the Court follows this approach in the future, it is highly likely that it will be accused of an unwarranted intrusion into the internal affairs of the Member States. Accordingly, after presenting the Court's case-law where this new approach to a link with EC law has been applied, the problems emerging from this approach will be analyzed, and it will be concluded that its application is entirely inappropriate as a remedy to the problem of reverse discrimination.

A CASE-LAW IN THE AREA OF FAMILY REUNIFICATION RIGHTS

The Community legislature had early on spotted the close interrelationship between inter-state movement for the purpose of exercising an economic activity and the need to grant family reunification rights. If migrants were denied by the immigration authorities of the host State the right to be accompanied in its territory by their family members, this would form a serious deterrent to mobility. This is because family – in whatever way this term is defined – always plays a hugely important part in a person's life, and family-related reasons often tilt the balance in favour of, or against, a decision to migrate.

As a result of that, and as seen in Chapter 1, the Community legislature in the 1960s and early 1970s made provision for the grant of family reunification rights to migrant economic actors. However, back then, the Community was simply a European *Economic* Community and, thus, the Community legislature was acting

98. *Supra* n. 15, p. 124. For a similar criticism *see* N. Nic Shuibhne, 'The European Union and Fundamental Rights: Well in Spirit but Considerably Rumpled in Body?', in *Convergence and Divergence in European Public Law*, P. Beaumont, C. Lyons and N. Walker (eds) (Oxford, Hart, 2002), p. 194.

as an institution of an economic organization that viewed Member State nationals merely as instruments to be used in promoting its economic objectives. Accordingly, Community legislation bestowed family reunification rights solely in order to encourage Member State nationals to move between Member States and exercise one of the fundamental freedoms, furthering in that way the Community's principal aim of creating a common market.[99]

In a similar vein the Court of Justice, until quite recently, interpreted the provisions of the Community's secondary legislation as bestowing family reunification rights upon migrant economic actors only when this was *necessary* for encouraging or, more accurately, not deterring a Member State national from exercising one of the fundamental freedoms. Hence, the mere fact that a person satisfied the necessary familial link with a migrant economic actor was not, until recently, a sufficient reason by itself for that person to derive an automatic right from EC law to join the migrant economic actor in another Member State. There was a further requirement that the denial of family reunification rights would have a negative impact on the related economic actor's decision as to whether or not to move between Member States for an economic purpose. This, in effect, was satisfied when the exercise of the relevant movement would result in the loss of the right to live with close family members which was enjoyed in the Member State from which the migrant moved. Obviously, this reflects the requirements of the linking factor test: it is only where there has been (or will be) an exercise of inter-state movement (first limb) for an economic purpose (second limb) *and* the denial of family reunification rights will impede that movement (third limb), that EC law should apply to require the bestowal of such rights in a specific situation.

Nonetheless, the Court of Justice in a number of cases since the 1990s seems to have accepted that family reunification rights can be granted in situations where there is no real link with the exercise of a fundamental freedom; or, in other words, in situations where the denial of the automatic bestowal by EC law of family reunification rights on Member State nationals, will not, in reality, affect their decision as to the exercise of one of the fundamental freedoms. As will be seen, the mere fact that someone satisfies the required familial link with a migrant economic actor in combination with the fact that there has been some kind of inter-state movement seems, now, to suffice for a situation to be brought within the scope of EC law. As argued elsewhere,[100] it is therefore safe to say that the jurisprudence of the Court of Justice overwhelmingly exhibits a tendency of following a liberal approach as regards the bestowal of family reunification rights on migrant Member State nationals; and, more broadly, that this may be an implicit

99. *See* para. 69 of Advocate General Geelhoed's Opinion in *Jia v. Migrationsverket*, Case No. C-1/05 [2007] ECR I-1; G. Barrett, 'Family matters: European Community law and third-country family members' (2003) 40 *CMLRev* 369, 375-376. For an excellent explanation of what have traditionally been the implications of this *see* T.K. Hervey, 'Migrant workers and their families in the European Union: the pervasive market ideology of Community law', in *New Legal Dynamics of European Union*, J. Shaw and G. More (eds) (Oxford, Clarendon Press, 1995).

100. A. Tryfonidou, 'Family reunification rights of (migrant) Union citizens: Towards a liberal approach' (2009) 15 *ELJ* (forthcoming).

acceptance of the principle suggested by Advocate General Jacobs in the *Konstantinidis* case[101] that the fundamental (human) rights of all *moving* Union citizens must be protected, *as a matter of EC law*, irrespective of whether there is a link between the need to protect the specific right in question *and* the exercise of interstate movement by the person concerned.[102]

Below, there will be an analysis of the Court's case-law where this more liberal approach towards the bestowal of family reunification rights was followed. It will be seen that the recent cases of *Carpenter, Jia* and *Eind* fall squarely within this 'group', as well as the 1992 *Singh* case, of which the initial (and much-criticized) interpretation (what I call 'Interpretation I' of *Singh*) was affirmed, in 2007, by the Court's judgment in *Eind.*

Taking a chronological order, the first case to be analyzed is *Singh.*[103] Mr Singh, an Indian national, entered the United Kingdom and married a British national in 1982. The subsequent year the couple moved to Germany where they were employed for two years. At the end of 1985, they returned to the United Kingdom to open a business there where Mrs Singh would work as a self-employed person. The British authorities refused to grant Mr Singh a permanent right of residence in the United Kingdom as a husband of a British national and subsequently a deportation order was made against him. Mr Singh lodged an appeal against the order. In the judicial proceedings which arose from those facts, the High Court of Justice made a reference for a preliminary ruling to the ECJ, asking the latter whether a Member State could refuse to grant a permanent residence right to the third-country national spouse of a Community national in Mrs Singh's position.

The Court of Justice replied that the free movement provisions require a Member State to grant the right to enter and reside in its territory to the third-country national spouse of one of its nationals, when the latter (accompanied by his or her third-country national spouse) has moved to another Member State and worked there for a number of years, and subsequently returned to his or her Member State of origin in order to work as a self-employed person. The Court, in reaching this conclusion, made use of the 'deterrence' principle:

> A national of a Member State might be deterred from leaving his country of origin in order to pursue an activity as an employed or self-employed person as envisaged by the Treaty in the territory of another Member State if, on returning to the Member State of which he is a national in order to pursue an activity there as an employed or self-employed person, the conditions of his entry and

101. *Konstantinidis v. Stadt Altensteig-Standesamt*, Case No. C-168/91 [1993] ECR I-1191.
102. For a similar view *see* C. Schiltz, '*Akrich*: A Clear delimitation without limits' (2005) 12 *MJ* 241, 251-252.
103. *The Queen v. Immigration Appeal Tribunal and Singh, ex parte Secretary of State for the Home Department*, Case No. C-370/90 [1992] ECR I-4265. *See* R.C.A. White, *supra* n. 97; P. Watson, 'Free Movement of Workers: a one way ticket?' (1993) 22(1) *ILJ* 68. *See* also the comments of N. Nic Shuibhne, 'Free movement of persons and the wholly internal rule: Time to move on?' (2002) 39 *CMLRev* 731, 744-748; M. Poiares Maduro, *supra* n. 15, pp. 124-125; P. Craig and G. de Búrca, *supra* n. 9, pp. 782-783.

> residence were not at least equivalent to those which he would enjoy under the Treaty or secondary law in the territory of another Member State.
>
> He would in particular be deterred from so doing if his spouse and children were not also permitted to enter and reside in the territory of his Member State of origin under conditions at least equivalent to those granted them by Community law in the territory of another Member State.[104]

This case has attracted an immense amount of criticism. True, it was not the first time that the Court of Justice had accepted that in certain cases a person could rely on rights derived from EC law against his or her Member State of origin. In the previous chapter a well-settled line of case-law starting with *Knoors*[105] was mentioned, where the Court accepted that a national of a Member State could rely on EC provisions against his own Member State, after returning from another Member State where he moved in order to obtain a qualification or exercise one of the fundamental freedoms. However, some of those cases can fit to the explanation given by the Court in *Singh*, according to which, had the Member State national who had exercised his or her free movement rights not been granted EC protection, he or she would be deterred from moving to another Member State in order to work in the first place.[106]

Nonetheless, it is questionable whether a sufficient element of deterrence to move to a Member State other than that of her nationality, could be proved in the case of Mrs Singh. The right of residence of the spouse of a British national who had never exercised his or her freedom of movement to work in another Member State was governed by United Kingdom law. When the Singhs returned to England the British authorities, applying United Kingdom legislation, refused to grant Mr Singh an indefinite leave to remain. Thus, Mr Singh's situation was governed by United Kingdom law, as would have been, had his wife not exercised her freedom of movement to work in Germany. Hence, he was not granted fewer rights than he would be granted had his wife not exercised her right to free movement to another Member State; in other words, Mrs Singh's movement did not result in the loss of rights in the United Kingdom that would otherwise be enjoyed.

The application of the deterrence principle on the facts of the case illustrates that the third limb of the linking factor test fails to be satisfied. Although there had been movement from one Member State to another that had an economic aim (Mrs Singh moved to Germany and was employed there for two years), nevertheless, if the Community right to be accompanied by her husband in the United Kingdom was not afforded to Mrs Singh, this would not have affected her decision to move to Germany in the first place.[107] Advocate General Poiares Maduro

104. *Singh, supra* n. 103, paras 19-20.
105. *Knoors v. Secretary of State for Economic Affairs*, Case No. 115/78 [1979] ECR 399.
106. *See*, for example, *Criminal proceedings against Van Lent*, Case No. C-232/01 [2003] ECR I-11525.
107. For a case which arose shortly before *Singh* and where the Advocate General adopted a more cautious approach *see Middleburgh v. Chief Adjudication Officer*, Case No. C-15/90 [1991] ECR I-4655. In his Opinion in that case, Advocate General Mischo wondered: 'might a British

(writing extra-judicially) has observed that 'the cross-border element in *Singh* led the Court to give some nationals *vis-à-vis* their home State a "bonus" right that is in no way linked with the protection of their freedom of movement to another Member State'.[108]

However, I would like to suggest that the Court in its judgment in *Singh* had arrived at the right conclusion: that the refusal to Mr Singh of a right of residence in the United Kingdom would, indeed, have a negative impact on the exercise by Mrs Singh of inter-state movement for an economic purpose. The relevant movement, nonetheless, is not the one that was suggested by most critics[109] of the judgment, that is, the movement of Mrs Singh from England to Germany in order to work in the latter State. Rather, the relevant movement which could appropriately bring the situation within the scope of EC law was the movement of Mrs Singh from Germany *back to the United Kingdom,* in order to pursue an activity as a self-employed person in the latter State (i.e., this reasoning is similar to that followed in *Knoors* analyzed in Chapter 2). Since Mrs Singh had the right to live in Germany with her husband by virtue of EC law if, when moving to the United Kingdom, she lost that right then, most probably, she would not have exercised her freedom to move back to the United Kingdom to work as a self-employed person (this is what I call 'Interpretation II' of *Singh*).[110]

However, as will be explained subsequently, in the recent *Eind*[111] case the Court seems to have read *Singh* in the way interpreted by most commentators, that is, that the movement that would be deterred as a result of the refusal to extend

national forgo his right to pursue an occupational activity in another Member State by reason of the fact that when he returns to his country he will not be entitled to British child benefit if the child born during his period of residence abroad does not return with him?' (para. 52 of the Opinion). The Advocate General explained that 'the resultant impediment to the pursuit of occupational activities outside the United Kingdom would be so indirect and hypothetical that it could only with great difficulty amount to a restriction on the freedom of movement prohibited under Community law. It would depend on the occurrence of events following the exercise of the right of freedom of movement, namely the birth of a child and the return of the person concerned to his State of origin: his return, moreover, without the child born in the intervening period' (para. 53). The Court avoided dealing with this issue in its judgment in that case.

108. *Supra* n. 15, p. 125. *See* also E. Johnson and D. O'Keeffe, 'From Discrimination to Obstacles to Free Movement: Recent developments concerning the Free Movement of Workers 1989-1994' (1994) 31 *CMLRev* 1313, 1338.

109. *See* M. Poiares Maduro, *supra* n. 15, pp. 124-125; N. Nic Shuibhne, *supra* n. 103, 744-748; L. Woods, *supra* n. 46, p. 225. This appears also to be the view of Advocate General Stix-Hackl in her Opinion in *Carpenter, infra* n. 113, para. 66.

110. Advocate General Tesauro followed this line of reasoning in his Opinion in *Singh*. This view is also reflected in the work of another scholar: *see* G. Barrett, *supra* n. 99, 379. For a more far-reaching attempt to reconcile the *Singh* case with the 'deterrence' argument *see* G. Davies, *supra* n. 46, p. 122. This reasoning is also evident in the more recent case *Secretary of State for the Home Department v. Akrich*, Case No. C-109/01 [2003] ECR 9607 where the Court (perhaps in reply to the criticisms of its reasoning in *Singh)* was concerned with avoiding a situation whereby a person would be deterred from exercising her freedom to move back to her Member State of origin (*see* para. 54 of the judgment).

111. *Infra* n. 121.

family reunification rights to Mrs Singh would be her *initial* movement from the United Kingdom to Germany (i.e., the Court adopted 'Interpretation I' of *Singh*). In this way, *Singh* can be included in the 'liberal approach' group of family reunification cases, even though, on the specific facts of that case, there was, indeed, an impediment to inter-state movement for an economic purpose (though, not the one suggested by the Court).[112]

Although one might have expected that, in the light of the attack that it had received as a result of its judgment in *Singh*, the Court would subsequently be more cautious in accepting that a situation presents a link with EC law, things were taken one step further in *Carpenter*,[113] where the Court 'went so far as to accept on the most tenuous of bases, that the requisite inter-state element was present'.[114]

Mr Carpenter was a British national who was providing services to persons established in other Member States, whilst retaining his permanent residence and business in the United Kingdom. The problems for Mr Carpenter began when his Philippines national wife applied for a permanent residence permit in the United Kingdom. The British authorities refused to grant Mrs Carpenter a residence permit on the ground that she did not satisfy the requirements of the United Kingdom legislation on the issue; and they issued a deportation order against her. Although most of the parties who submitted observations to the Court considered the facts of the case to be purely internal to the United Kingdom, both the Advocate General[115] and the Court[116] found that the case was not a purely internal one as Mr Carpenter provided services to persons established in other Member States, and often travelled to other Member States for that purpose.

The Court noted:

> [T]he separation of Mr and Mrs Carpenter would be detrimental to their family life and, therefore, to the conditions under which Mr Carpenter exercises a fundamental freedom. That freedom could not be fully effective if Mr Carpenter were to be deterred from exercising it by obstacles raised in his country of origin to the entry and residence of his spouse.[117]

In this case, the element that served as the link with EC law is even more artificial than the one that was found by the Court in *Singh*. Would Mr Carpenter be deterred

112. For more on this *see* A. Tryfonidou, *supra* n. 100.
113. *Carpenter v. Secretary of State for the Home Department*, Case No. C-60/00 [2002] ECR 6279 – annotated by H. Toner (2003) 5 *EJML* 163. *See* also A. Tryfonidou, '*Mary Carpenter v. Secretary of State for the Home Department*: The beginning of a new era in the European Union?' (2003) 14 *KCLJ* 81; S. Acierno, 'The Carpenter Judgment: Fundamental Rights and the Limits of the Community Legal Order' (2003) 28 *ELRev* 398; Editorial comment: 'Freedoms unlimited? Reflections on Mary Carpenter v. Secretary of State' (2003) 40 *CMLRev* 537. For an excellent analysis *see* L. Woods, *supra* n. 46, pp. 222-226.
114. P. Oliver and W.H. Roth *supra* n. 18, 432. For a similar view *see* V. Hatzopoulos and T.U. Do, *supra* n. 71, 943-944.
115. *See* paras 60-73 of the Opinion.
116. Paras 29, 30 and 37 of the judgment in *Carpenter, supra* n. 113.
117. *Carpenter, supra* n. 113, para. 39.

from providing services to persons established in other Member States, if his wife was not granted the rights granted by EC law in family reunification cases? This is improbable. How can it be said that Mr Carpenter would cease travelling to other Member States in order to provide services (or, even more extraordinarily, stop providing services from the United Kingdom to persons established in other Member States), just because his wife was not given a right to reside *in the United Kingdom*? Mr Carpenter was not confronted with the dilemma of either not exercising his freedom to provide services and maintaining the right to reside with his wife, or exercising that freedom and, as a result of that, losing that right.[118] Therefore, although the first limb of the linking factor test was satisfied on the facts of the case (there clearly was inter-state movement); and the second limb was also satisfied since the movement was for an economic purpose (the provision of services); the third limb of the test fails to be satisfied since it seems unlikely that a person would stop providing services from his Member State of origin to other Member States (or stop travelling temporarily to other Member States in order to provide services), just because EC law does not grant him the right to be accompanied by his spouse *in his State of origin*. Finally, the reasoning in *Carpenter* cannot even be re-read, as can be done with *Singh*, in order to find another kind of link with EC law: no inter-state movement back to the Member State of origin which would result in the loss of the right to be accompanied by family members can be shown.[119]

---

118. For a similar explanation *see* L. Woods, *supra* n. 46, p. 224.

119. It could be argued that *Akrich* (*supra* n. 110) confined *Carpenter* to its own facts in two important ways: Firstly, in *Akrich* it was held that, in order for a third-country national spouse to be able to derive a right of residence in the Member State of origin of his/her (EC national) spouse from EC provisions, he/she must have been lawfully resident in his/her spouse's Member State of origin. The reason behind this condition of prior lawful residence within the territory of the EU is obvious: if the aim of the grant of family reunification rights is, *purely*, to enable Member State nationals to move freely between Member States, the refusal of such rights can be considered as impeding that movement only if a Member State national who was, previously, residing lawfully with his family members in the territory of one Member State will, *as a result of his movement to another Member State*, lose the right to live together with his close family members. Conversely, if no such right was enjoyed in the territory of the State from which the migrant moved, then it seems that the refusal of a right of residence for family members in the receiving State would not have any impact on the exercise of the freedom to move. In *Carpenter* there had been a deportation order against Mrs Carpenter because she overstayed her leave in the United Kingdom and thus she was not lawfully resident in the United Kingdom – nonetheless, the fact that Mrs *Carpenter* (unlike Mr Akrich) did not have any serious problems with the authorities and did not present a danger to public security, must have weighed in the Court's reasoning in allowing her to rely on EC law in order to gain entry to the EC without her situation ever being assessed under national immigration law. It should be noted, however, that in the subsequent cases of *Jia, Eind* and *Metock* the Court confined the application of the *Akrich* condition to the specific facts of the *Akrich* case – *Jia, supra* n. 99, paras 31-33; *Eind, infra* n. 121, paras 41-44; *Metock, supra* n. 80, paras 48-80. Secondly, the Court in *Akrich* translated the *Singh* judgment to the effect that the obstacle caused by the denial of a right of residence to the third-country national spouse, is an obstacle to the freedom to move *back to the Member State of origin* and not, as was initially suggested and followed in subsequent case-law (including *Carpenter* and *Eind*) to the freedom to move to

A very similar approach was followed by the Court, subsequently, in the *Jia* case.[120] There, the failure of the host Member State (Sweden) to grant family reunification rights to the Chinese mother-in-law of a German national who had moved from Germany to its territory in order to exercise her freedom of establishment eight years before, did not seem capable of interfering with the exercise of the latter's freedom to move. Yet, the Court held that Ms Jia (the Chinese mother-in-law) was entitled, under EC law, to be granted the right to accompany her daughter-in-law in Sweden. The main difference from *Carpenter* is that the State where the right of residence was claimed by the third-country national, was not the State of nationality of the migrant worker, and, therefore, this is not a case where if the situation was found to fall outside the scope of EC law, *reverse* discrimination would emerge (i.e., discrimination by a Member State against *its own nationals*). However, like in *Carpenter*, in *Jia* there was not a link between the failure to grant family reunification rights and a deterrent effect on the exercise of inter-state movement in furtherance of the Community's (economic) aims. How can it be said that a person who has exercised her freedom to move and establish business in the territory of another Member State, would be deterred if her mother-in-law from a non-EU country was not allowed to come directly to join her in the host Member State eight years after that initial movement?

More recently, in the *Eind* case,[121] the Court seems to have employed, once more, its liberal approach in a case in which, like *Carpenter*, reverse discrimination would emerge if the situation was excluded from the scope of application of EC law. In 2000 Mr Runaldo Eind, a Dutch national, left the Netherlands and went to the United Kingdom in order to work. He was subsequently joined by his daughter Rachel, a national of Surinam, who joined him directly from her country of nationality. The United Kingdom authorities informed Mr Eind that he (as a migrant worker) and his daughter (as a family member) had a right to reside in the United Kingdom by virtue of EC law. In 2001, Mr Eind and Rachel entered the

---

another Member State – that is, the Court in *Akrich* applied 'Interpretation II' of *Singh*. This reasoning justified the Court's judgment in *Singh* but highlighted that *Carpenter* had been wrongly decided as in the latter case there was no issue at all of a return to the Member State of origin: Mr and Mrs Carpenter had always been (and intended to be always) established in the United Kingdom and thus the *Akrich* reasoning (and 'Interpretation II' of *Singh*) could not be applied in that case. However, as will subsequently be explained in the main text, in the *Eind* case the Court seems to have embraced the initial (much-criticized) 'Interpretation I' of *Singh*, according to which the movement that was going to be deterred as a result of the refusal of family reunification rights was the *initial movement* from the United Kingdom to Germany for the purpose of working as an employed person in the latter (for an explanation of this *see* A. Tryfonidou, *supra* n. 100). For further discussion of the relationship between *Carpenter* and *Akrich see* C. Schiltz, *supra* n. 102, 247-249.

120. *Supra* n. 99. The fact that there was no link with EC law and, in particular, the exercise of the right to freedom of establishment, is advocated by Advocate General Geelhoed in his Opinion in this case (*see* paras 69-71 of the Opinion); and A. Tryfonidou, '*Jia* or "*Carpenter* II": The edge of reason' (2007) 32 *ELRev* 908.

121. *Minister voor Vreemdelingenzaken en Integratie v. R. N. G. Eind*, Case No. C-291/05, judgment of 11 Dec. 2007, not yet reported.

Netherlands. Because of poor health, Mr Eind had not been employed, nor had he actively sought employment. Once in the Netherlands, Rachel applied for a residence permit so that she could stay with her father. The Dutch authorities rejected her application on the basis that Mr Eind was neither a migrant worker within the meaning of EC law, nor was he an (economically inactive) Union citizen whose situation fell within the scope of EC law. When Rachel appealed this decision, the matter was referred to the ECJ. The gist of the Court's reply was that Rachel derived from EC law the right to accompany her father in his State of nationality since, otherwise, Mr Eind's right to exercise his freedom of movement as a worker from the Netherlands to the United Kingdom would be impeded.

The Court arrived at that conclusion by making use of the 'deterrence principle' which, as previously explained, was firstly applied in the *Singh* case. The Court began its analysis by explaining that

> [T]he right of the migrant worker to return and reside in the Member State of which he is a national, after being gainfully employed in another Member State, is conferred by Community law, to the extent necessary to ensure the useful effect of the right to free movement for workers under Article 39 EC and the provisions adopted to give effect to that right, such as those laid down in Regulation 1612/68.[122]

The Court then moved on to explain this in more detail and pointed out in paragraphs 35 and 36 of its judgment that:

> A national of a Member State could be deterred from leaving that Member State if he does not have the certainty of being able to return to his Member State of origin, irrespective of whether he is going to engage in economic activity in the latter State.
>
> That deterrent effect would also derive simply from the prospect, for that same national, of not being able, on returning to his Member State of origin, to continue living together with close relatives, a way of life which may have come into being in the host Member State as a result of marriage or family reunification.

In *Eind* the Court appears to have been determined to clarify a number of outstanding issues, the most important ones being whether the *Akrich* condition according to which a third-country national must be lawfully resident in one Member State before he or she can accompany a Member State national to another Member State,[123] should be applied as a general condition in family reunification cases; and, more implicitly, which interpretation of *Singh* should prevail. Clearly, the clarification provided by the Court in *Eind* as regards these issues illustrates that the Court's reasoning exhibits a tendency of increasingly moving towards the 'liberal approach' side.

In its written observations in *Eind*, the Netherlands government emphasized that Mr Eind could not have been deterred from exercising his freedom *to move to*

---

122. *Ibid.*, para. 32.
123. *See supra* n. 119.

the United Kingdom in order to take up gainful employment, by the fact that it would be impossible for his daughter to reside with him once he returned to his Member State of origin, having in mind that at the time of the initial move Miss Eind did not have a right to reside in the Netherlands.[124] In reply to that point, the Court noted that that approach cannot be accepted and, as already seen, making use of the 'deterrence principle' and applying reasoning akin to the much-criticized 'Interpretation I' of *Singh*,[125] it pointed out that Mr Eind's right to exercise his *initial movement from the Netherlands to the United Kingdom* as a worker, would have been deterred as a result of the refusal of the Netherlands to grant a right of residence to Rachel. As regards, in particular, the '*Akrich* condition', the Court observed, somewhat ambiguously, that the fact that Rachel was not lawfully resident in the territory of the Netherlands prior to moving to the United Kingdom, does not affect the finding that Mr Eind would be deterred from moving from the Netherlands to the United Kingdom in case the former State refused to grant Rachel a right of residence on his return.[126] This appears to have been a subtle affirmation of the principle established in *Jia*, that the application of the '*Akrich* condition' should be confined to cases involving facts similar to *Akrich*.[127]

Moreover, in practical terms, the facts in *Eind* did not appear to involve a sufficient link with EC law. More specifically, there does not seem to be any link between the exercise by Mr Eind of his right under Article 39 EC (Article 45 TFEU) to move from his home State to the United Kingdom to work, and the refusal of the Netherlands to grant his daughter a right to reside in its territory on his return from the United Kingdom. In other words, the refusal of the Dutch authorities to grant Rachel a residence permit did not come as a result of Mr Eind's movement to the United Kingdom. Rachel did not enjoy a right of residence in the Netherlands before Mr Eind exercised his freedom of movement to the United Kingdom and, similarly, on Mr Eind's return to the Netherlands the Dutch

---

124. *Eind supra* n. 121, para. 33.
125. In his Opinion in the *Eind* case, Advocate General Mengozzi also adopted 'Interpretation I' of *Singh* – *see*, in particular, para. 97 of the Opinion. It should be noted that although the Advocate General applied the 'deterrence principle' in the same way as the Court (*see* paras 101-103 of the Opinion), nonetheless he complemented his reasoning by looking at alternative ways for bringing the situation within the scope of EC law: (a) he examined whether Rachel could derive from EC law a right of residence in the Netherlands as a family member of a job-seeker; and (b) he enquired whether Rachel could, in the alternative, derive a right of residence in the Netherlands as a family member of a migrant Union citizen falling within the scope of Art. 18 EC (Art. 21 TFEU) read in conjunction with 90/364 (EEC) Directive on the right of residence, OJ L 180/26, 1990. Perhaps the Advocate General was suspecting that the Court might prefer to apply its original approach to the grant of family reunification rights and require a *real link* between the refusal of the grant of family reunification rights and the exercise of an inter-state economic activity and, therefore, in such an instance, the free movement of workers provisions and the 'deterrence principle' would be of no use to the Einds.
126. *Eind, supra* n. 121, paras 41-44.
127. This is more directly expressed in the Opinion of Advocate General Mengozzi in *Eind*, paras 42-46; and by the Court itself in *Metock, supra* n. 80, paras 48-80.

authorities, applying Dutch law, did not grant her a right of residence. Hence, the exercise by Mr Eind of his right to move to another Member State to work could not have been deterred as a result of the Dutch authorities' refusal to grant his daughter a residence permit in the Netherlands. Accordingly, like *Carpenter, Jia* and *Singh* (where 'Interpretation I' was adopted), *Eind* is another example of a case where the Court accepted that there was a link with EC law, even though the third limb of the linking factor test was not satisfied on the facts of the case.

B Case-Law in the Area of Educational Qualifications

Another case which has attracted a large amount of attention by commentators is *Angonese*,[128] the result of which has been characterized as 'uncomfortably vague and incomplete'.[129]

Mr Angonese, an Italian national, applied to take part in a competition for a post with a bank in Bolzano (an Italian town in the region of Alto Adige). The bank imposed as a condition for entry to the competition the possession of the 'Patentino', a certificate of bilingualism in Italian and German. The 'Patentino' was issued by the public authorities of the province of Bolzano after the candidates sat an examination which took place only in that province. The problem for Mr Angonese was that he did not possess a 'Patentino', though it was established that he was perfectly bilingual in German and Italian. In order to be allowed to take part in the competition for the post, Mr Angonese submitted certificates attesting to his studies (which were not yet completed) of languages (other than German and Italian) at the University of Vienna. The bank refused him admission to the competition because he did not possess a 'Patentino'; any other evidence of his knowledge of German and Italian was inadmissible.

Mr Angonese complained that by requiring the possession of a 'Patentino' in order to allow someone to take part in the competition for the post, the bank had acted contrary to Article 39 EC (Article 45 TFEU). The national court, taking the view that the requirement could have been prejudicial to Mr Angonese who had made use of the opportunities offered by Community law and resided in another Member State for the purpose of studying there, stayed the proceedings and made a reference for a preliminary ruling to the Court of Justice.

In their submissions to the ECJ, the Italian Government and the bank contended that the situation had no connection with EC law since Mr Angonese was an Italian national who was relying on Article 39 EC (Article 45 TFEU) against Italy. In reply to those submissions, the Court stressed that it is for the national courts to determine the need for a preliminary ruling and the relevance of the questions which they refer to the Court.[130] It then went on to make the obscure observation that

128. *Angonese v. Cassa di Risparmio di Bolzano Spa*, Case No. C-281/98 [2000] ECR I-4139 – annotated by R. Lane and N. Nic Shuibhne, (2000) 37 *CMLRev* 1237.
129. R. Lane and N. Nic Shuibhne, *supra* n. 128, 1243.
130. *Angonese, supra* n. 128, para. 18.

> [I]t is far from clear that the interpretation of Community law it seeks has no relation to the actual facts of the case or the subject-matter of the main action and concluded that the question submitted should be answered.[131]

The Court found that the requirement imposed by the bank was (indirectly) discriminatory on the grounds of nationality, and thus was contrary to Article 39 EC (Article 45 TFEU). This was a correct conclusion to reach, albeit a conclusion which could only be applied to facts involving a person possessing the nationality of a Member State other than Italy. The facts before the Court, however, involved an Italian national. If we leave aside, for a moment, the Court's finding of indirect discrimination on the grounds of nationality, the question is whether the facts in *Angonese* involved an impediment to inter-state movement for an economic purpose and, thus, could in this way, be brought within the scope of Article 39 EC.

The only movement that would be capable of bringing the situation within the scope of Article 39 EC (Article 45 TFEU) was the movement of Angonese from Austria back to Italy in order to work. This is the same approach that was followed by the Court in *De Bobadilla*,[132] seen in Chapter 2. In that case it was held that the fact that a Member State refuses to examine the equivalence of an educational qualification obtained in another Member State with the qualifications offered in its territory, may have a negative impact on the movement of its nationals back to its territory in order to work. In *De Bobadilla* the said qualification was a postgraduate qualification in fine arts restoration obtained in the United Kingdom; a qualification that was directly relevant to the post the claimant was applying for (a post in the museum of Prado) and thus was necessary in order to enable her to gain access to that profession.

The question, now, is whether the *De Bobadilla* reasoning can appropriately be applied in the case of *Angonese*. In *Angonese*, the Court seems to have taken as a sufficient connection with EC law the fact that Mr Angonese wished to return to his Member State of nationality to work, using a qualification he had (not yet) obtained in another Member State (Austria). If the qualification was a qualification that certified his bilingualism in Italian and German, the situation would be the same as that in *De Bobadilla*, and thus the same result could have rightly been reached, that is, the bank would be required by Article 39 EC (Article 45 TFEU) to examine the equivalence of any qualifications which satisfy the same aim as the 'Patentino' (i.e., they attest to the bilingualism in German and Italian of the person possessing them).

However, in *Angonese*, the Court seems to have accepted as a sufficient connection with EC law the studies which Mr Angonese followed at the University of Vienna; studies that were neither equivalent to the 'Patentino' (they did not establish the bilingualism of Mr Angonese), nor were they (even more remotely) relevant to the post for which he was applying. If the three-limb test mentioned in

131. *Ibid.*, para. 19.
132. *De Bobadilla v. Museo Nacional del Prado*, Case No. C-234/97 [1999] ECR I-4773.

Chapter 2 is applied, it is obvious that the connection found by the Court with EC law is very artificial. The first limb of the test is satisfied: there would have been movement from one Member State (Austria) to another Member State (Italy, Angonese's Member State of origin) once the job was offered to Angonese. The second limb is also satisfied as Mr Angonese's movement back to Italy would be for the purpose of being employed by the Italian bank. Nonetheless, the third limb of the test is not satisfied. If Mr Angonese knew that his qualification (which, in fact, was not yet obtained) that was totally unrelated to the subject-matter of the post applied for or to the requirement required for access to the competition, would not be accepted as equivalent to a national qualification, that would not, really, deter his movement to Italy from Austria. This is because a person cannot expect the authorities of a Member State (or a private body as the one involved on the facts before the national court) to accept a foreign qualification which in no way proves possession of the knowledge which is required for the post.[133] Had Mr Angonese obtained from the University of Vienna a degree which certified his bilingualism in Italian and German, then the situation might rightly be considered to fall within the scope of EC law.

C Case-Law in the Area of Freedom of Establishment and the Free Movement of Workers

In a cluster of recent cases in the area of the free movement of (economically active) persons, the Court seems to have, once more, side-stepped the linking factor test. In this group, however, the Court has gone further than in the two groups of cases seen above, by accepting within the scope of Articles 39 EC (Article 45 TFEU) and 43 EC (Article 49 TFEU) situations which only satisfied the first limb of the linking factor test. In other words, the mere exercise of movement from one Member State to another, sufficed for bringing a situation within the scope of the free movement of economically active persons provisions. In this case-law, the Court dispenses with the need that the inter-state movement is exercised for an economic purpose, that is, that the claimant moves *in order to work (as an employed or self-employed person) in the host State*.

Starting with the freedom of establishment, in the case of *N*[134] the question was whether the situation of a Dutch national who was the sole shareholder of three limited liability Dutch companies and who, at some point in time, decided to move from the Netherlands to the United Kingdom 'where he did not pursue an economic activity for a number of years',[135] fell within the scope of Article 43 EC (Article 49 TFEU).

133. For a very good explanation of this *see* para. 28 of the Opinion of Advocate General Fennelly in *Angonese, supra* n. 128.
134. *N v. Inspecteur van de Belastingdienst Oost/kantoor Almelo*, Case No. C-470/04 [2006] ECR I-7409.
135. *See* para. 3 of the Opinion of Advocate General Kokott in *N, ibid.*

In its judgment, the Court firstly pointed out that

> [W]here a Community national lives in one Member State and has a shareholding in the capital of a company established in another Member State which gives him substantial influence over the company's decisions and allows him to determine its activities ... may ... fall within the freedom of establishment.[136]

Applying this principle to the specific facts of the case, the Court found that the situation fell within the scope of EC law – and in particular Article 43 EC (Article 49 TFEU) – since the claimant was a 'Community national who, since the transfer of his residence, has been living in one Member State and holding all the shares of companies established in another'.[137]

It is true that the situation of N involved inter-state (physical) movement: Mr N moved from the Netherlands to reside permanently in the United Kingdom. However, that specific inter-state movement (from the Netherlands to the United Kingdom) was not for an economic purpose: N did not move to the United Kingdom in order to exercise his freedom of establishment. The traditional case-law of the Court on the establishment of companies would require a person *to establish and manage a company* (or a subsidiary) in *another* Member State, in order for a situation to fall within the scope of Articles 43 and 48 EC (Articles 49 and 54 TFEU, respectively). Under that case-law, it does not suffice for a link with EC law to be established, that a person who establishes and manages a company in a Member State, subsequently moves to another Member State for reasons entirely unrelated to that economic activity. On the facts in *N*, the relevant shares were already owned by N at the time that he exercised his freedom to move and reside in another Member State, that is, Mr N was resident in the Netherlands (i.e., the country where the relevant companies were established) and so the inter-state movement that was exercised was not, in any way, connected with the exercise of his right to establish and manage an undertaking in the territory of another Member State. Therefore, the second limb of the linking factor test was not satisfied on the facts of the case.

The lack of a sufficient link with EC law in this case was extensively discussed by Advocate General Kokott in her Opinion, where she advocated the view that, on the one hand, the situation of Mr N would fall within the scope of Article 43 EC (Article 49 TFEU) only once economic activity was taken up in the United Kingdom (since merely owning shares in a company in another Member State is not an economic activity within the meaning of Community law[138]) and, on the other, that Article 18 EC (Article 21 TFEU) could be relied on by Mr N against the

136. *N, supra* n. 134, para. 27.
137. *Ibid.*, para. 28. This reasoning has been recently affirmed in *Geurts and Vogten v. Administratie van de BTW, registratie en domeinen, Belgische Staat*, Case No. C-464/05, judgment of 25 Oct. 2007, not yet reported, para. 14, where the claimants, however, were relying on Art. 43 EC (Art. 49 TFEU) *against the host Member State.*
138. *See* paras 34-35 of the Opinion of Advocate General Kokott in *N, supra* n. 134.

Netherlands in order to question the compatibility of the contested Dutch tax legislation with Community law. The reason behind the Court's approach in this case (preferring to find an (artificial) link with Article 43 EC rather than, as rightly suggested by the Advocate General, bringing the case within the scope of Article 18 EC) remains a mystery since the contested legislation would probably be found to be in violation of EC law even if the case was decided under Article 18 EC.

The approach followed by the Court in the above case had also been applied, earlier the same year (i.e., 2006), in the 'sister area' of the free movement of workers, in the case of *Ritter-Coulais.*

In *Ritter-Coulais*[139] Mr and Mrs Ritter-Coulais were German nationals.[140] Both worked as teachers in Germany and received all their income in that country whilst they resided in a house owned by them in France. The problems for them began when the German authorities taxed the couple without taking into account rental income losses relating to their own use of a private dwelling, because the dwelling was not situated in Germany. In the judgment, the Court accepted that the situation of the couple fell within the scope of the free movement of workers provisions since they worked in a Member State other than that of their actual place of residence.[141]

In this case, like in the case of *N*, the Court seems to be considering that the mere fact that someone works in a State different from the one where he or she resides, suffices for bringing the situation within the scope of the free movement of (economically active) persons provisions.[142] The Ritter-Coulais had always worked in Germany – they never moved from Germany to another Member State in order to engage in an economic activity. Yet, the Court found that their situation fell within the scope of EC law since they resided in a Member State different from the State in which they worked.

In reaching this conclusion, the Court employed the following principle:

> [A]ny Community national who, irrespective of his place of residence and his nationality, has exercised the right to freedom of movement for workers and who has been employed in a Member State other than that of residence falls within the scope of the free movement of (economically active) persons provisions.[143]

---

139. *Ritter-Coulais v. Finanzamt Germersheim*, Case No. C-152/03 [2006] ECR I-1711

140. In fact, Mrs Ritter-Coulais had dual German and French nationality, however, for the purposes of the Court's reasoning this did not make a difference since the Court in its judgment applied exactly the same principles to the situation of Mr Ritter-Coulais (who only possessed German nationality) and the situation of Mrs Ritter-Coulais.

141. *Supra* n. 139, para. 32.

142. For a strong view that the facts of the case did not fall within the scope of the free movement of (economically active) persons provisions since there was no movement *for an economic purpose see* the Opinion of Advocate General Léger in *Ritter-Coulais, ibid.*, paras 33-77.

143. *Ritter-Coulais, supra* n. 139, para. 31. This principle was subsequently repeated in, among others, *Hartmann v. Freistaat Bayern*, Case No. C-212/05 [2007] ECR I-6303, para. 17; *Government of the French Community and Walloon Government v. Flemish Government,*

A proper reading of this statement, taking into account the aim of the free movement of economically active persons provisions, is that any Community national who has exercised the right to freedom of movement for workers *and* has been employed in a Member State other than that of residence falls within the scope of those provisions.[144] In other words, the first part of the proposition is a necessary condition for making the second part sufficient to satisfy the linking factor test. Thus, if someone resides in a Member State different from that of his or her State of employment, the situation falls within the scope of EC law *if this situation has emerged as a result of the prior exercise by that person of his or her freedom to move between Member States for an economic purpose*. This is satisfied, for example, when a Member State national has moved from his or her State of nationality to work in the territory of another Member State and, yet, retains his place of residence in the former State. Therefore, the orthodox reading of the principle quoted above is that, merely residing in a State different from that of the State of employment does not suffice for bringing a situation within the scope of the free movement of (economically active) persons provisions, in the absence of prior exercise of movement *for the purpose of employment or self-employment in the territory of another Member State*.

Nonetheless, the interpretation afforded to the quoted principle by the Court of Justice in its latest case-law, departs from the suggestion put forward in the previous paragraph. This was clearly seen in *Ritter-Coulais*; a similar approach was followed in the establishment case of *N*, seen above (though the principle was not quoted as such); and, below, one more case in the area of the free movement of

---

supra n. 24, para. 34; *Commission v. Germany (subsidy for the construction or purchase of a dwelling)*, Case No. C-152/05, judgment of 17 Jan. 2008, not yet reported, para. 20.

144. In fact, in the first cases in which the Court employed this principle, this was the interpretation afforded to it. Thus, for example, in *Terhoeve v. Inspecteur van de Belastingdiens Particulieren/Ondernemingen Buitenland*, Case No. C-18/95 [1999] ECR I-345, the facts involved a Dutch national who was relying on the free movement of workers provisions against the Netherlands and his situation was found to fall within the scope of Art. 39 EC (Art. 45 TFEU) since he had moved from the Netherlands *to work in the United Kingdom* (therefore, there was exercise of the freedom of movement of workers) and it was *because of this movement* that he was placed at a disadvantage as regards the payment of social security contributions (*see* paras 27-28). Similarly, in an older case (*Scholz v. Opera Universitaria di Cagliari and Cinzia Porcedda*, Case No. C-419/92 [1994] ECR I-505), the Court made the quoted statement (*see* para. 9 of the judgment) and found that there was a link with EC law on the facts because the claimant was an Italian national *who had exercised her freedom to move as a worker*, by having been employed in Germany. This reinforces the argument that the Court has *only recently* altered its approach regarding the linking factor test, and this may have been a corollary of the development of the status of Union citizenship through its latest case-law in that area. For more recent cases where this principle has been repeated and a link with EC law was found as a result of the exercise of inter-state movement *for an economic purpose* (i.e., all limbs of the linking factor test were satisfied on the facts) *see Schilling v. Finanzamt Nürnberg-Süd*, Case No. C-209/01 [2003] ECR I-13389, paras 23 and 27; *F.W.L. de Groot v. Staatssecretaris van Financiën*, Case No. C-385/00 [2002] ECR I-11819, paras 76 and 80.

workers will be analyzed, where the Court seems to have affirmed that this unorthodox interpretation of the principle is here to stay.

In the case of *Hartmann*[145] Ms Hartmann, an Austrian national residing in Austria, sought to obtain a German child-raising allowance for her three children. The children were the product of the marriage of Ms Hartmann with Mr Hartmann, a German national who was residing in Austria since their marriage in 1990 but who was working in Germany as a civil servant before (since 1986) and during their marriage. The German authorities refused to grant Ms Hartmann the child-raising allowance on the ground that she was neither resident in Germany nor did she work in that country. The main question was whether Mr Hartmann fell within the scope of the free movement of workers provisions and the accompanying secondary legislation; and if yes, whether the refusal of the grant of the said allowance to his wife amounted to a violation of EC law.

The ECJ found that, firstly, Mr Hartmann's situation fell within the scope of the free movement of workers provisions and the relevant secondary legislation; and, secondly, Article 7(2) of Regulation 1612/68[146] precluded Germany from refusing the grant of the child-raising allowance to Ms Hartmann on the ground that she was not permanently resident within its territory. The child-raising allowance, even when granted to the wife of a worker (and not directly to the worker himself), was a 'social advantage' within the meaning of Article 7(2) of the Regulation and, therefore, should be enjoyed by migrant workers on the same basis as is enjoyed by a national worker.[147]

The issue of whether the refusal of the child-raising allowance could have any negative impact on the exercise of the freedom to move as a worker (i.e., the third limb of the test) does not need to be discussed here. This is because, as will be seen, not even the second limb of the linking factor test is satisfied on the facts of the case.

The German, Dutch and United Kingdom Governments, as well as the Commission, submitted that 'a person such as Mr Hartmann, who never left his employment in the Member State of which he is a national and merely transferred his residence to the Member State of his spouse, could not therefore benefit from the Community provisions on freedom of movement for workers'.[148] In response to that, the Court noted that that argument should be considered in the light of the judgment in *Ritter-Coulais*[149] and went on to note:

> The situation which gave rise to the main proceedings is that of a person who, since the transfer of his residence, resides in one Member State and works in another Member State. That Mr Hartmann settled in Austria for reasons not connected with his employment does not justify refusing him the status of

145. *Supra* n. 143.
146. 1612/68 (EEC) Regulation on freedom of movement for workers within the Community, OJ L 257/2, 1968.
147. *Hartmann, supra* n. 143, paras 26-27.
148. *Ibid.*, para. 16.
149. *Ibid.*, para. 17.

> migrant worker which he acquired as from the time when, following the transfer of his residence to Austria, he made full use of his right to freedom of movement for workers by going to Germany to carry on an occupation there.[150]

It is true that the mere fact that someone moves to another Member State in order to reside there, should not lead to the denial of the status of migrant worker, provided that there has been an exercise of the right to freedom of movement for workers. However, the question is, was there such an exercise in the case of Mr Hartmann?

In the *Hartmann* case, like in *N* and *Ritter-Coulais*, there had been inter-state movement. Firstly, Mr Hartmann moved from Germany to Austria to reside permanently in the latter; and, secondly, since his movement to Austria, Mr Hartmann travels daily from Austria to Germany where he works. However, Mr Hartmann worked in Germany before moving to Austria, and continued working there since his relocation to Austria. Therefore, it cannot be said that any one of the inter-state movements that he exercised (i.e., the permanent movement from Germany to Austria in order to reside in the latter or, later, the short-term daily movements from Austria to Germany) had the purpose of enabling him to *start* employment in the receiving State and, thus, further the aim of Article 39 EC (Article 45 TFEU). Mr Hartmann had his post and he would keep it, even if he never moved from Germany to Austria or *vice-versa*. Hence, it cannot be accepted that in this case there was an exercise of the freedom to move *in order to be engaged in employment* in another Member State.[151]

The number of cases in which this 'new' approach in the context of Article 39 EC (Article 45 TFEU) and Article 43 EC (Article 49 TFEU) has been followed suggests that the approach may be here to stay. This will mean that the Court will no longer engage in an exhaustive scrutiny of whether the facts of a case involve the exercise of inter-state movement *for an economic purpose*, but will accept within the scope of the above provisions any situations involving some kind of a cross-border element, even if it is totally unrelated to the economic aims of those provisions. This 'new' approach followed by the Court, however, makes it necessary for the Court to ask itself what is the actual aim of Articles 39 EC (Article 45 TFEU)[152] and 43 EC (Article 49 TFEU). Is the aim of these provisions, now, something more than the mere opening-up of national frontiers in order to enable factors of production and self-employed persons to move *in order to work*

---

150. *Ibid.*, para. 18.
151. For other cases where the same approach was followed *see Hendrix v. Raad van Bestuur van het Uitvoeringsinstituut Werknemersverzekeringen*, Case No. C-287/05 [2007] ECR I-6909, para. 46; *A.J. van Pommeren-Bourgondiën v. Raad van Bestuur van de Sociale verzekeringsbank*, Case No. C-227/03 [2005] ECR I-6101. For a view that the Court's approach in these cases has been correct *see* paras 29-49 of the Opinion of Advocate General Kokott in *Hendrix*.
152. For an excellent analysis of the issue of the appropriate scope of Art. 39 EC (Art. 45 TFEU) (i.e., what must be the aim of the exercise of inter-state movement by a Member State national, for a situation to fall within the scope of the free movement of workers provisions) *see* paras 28-43 of the Opinion of Advocate General Geelhoed in *Hartmann, supra* n. 143.

permanently in the Member State of their choice? In other words, do these provisions, now, have not only a market-building aim, but also, the aim to ensure that once a cross-border element is present (even if this is totally unrelated to the economic aims of the Treaty), Member State nationals must enjoy a number of rights as a matter of EC law?

The case-law analyzed in this subsection of the chapter would seem to answer these questions in the affirmative. However, I am in total disagreement with this approach. Situations which do not present a link with the economic aims of the Treaty can, following the introduction of the status of Citizenship of the Union, be included within the scope of the citizenship provisions and, thus, it is not necessary to inordinately extend the scope of the free movement of economically active persons provisions to cover such situations. In any event, it would seem that if the Court continues to apply this lenient approach in establishing a link with EC law in Article 39 and 43 EC cases, then it appears questionable whether there is any point in maintaining different categories of provisions governing the situation of economically active and economically inactive Union citizens. This would point towards the abolition of the different categories of claimant under EC law and the need to subsume all rights into Article 18 EC (Article 21 TFEU). Something which, as will be argued briefly in the next chapter is, also, the necessary corollary of the convergence achieved in the position of economically active and economically inactive Union citizens through the Court's latest case-law on citizenship.

D PROBLEMS CAUSED BY THE APPROACH FOLLOWED BY THE COURT IN THE ABOVE CASE-LAW

1 Inordinate Extension of the Scope of EC Law

In *Singh*, Advocate General Tesauro stressed that

> [T]he simple exercise of the right of free movement within the Community is not in itself sufficient to bring a particular set of circumstances within the scope of Community law; there must be some connecting factor between the exercise of the right of free movement and the right relied on by the individual.[153]

The cases analyzed in this section of the chapter illustrate that the Court is more and more straying from the path suggested by the Advocate General. Although this has as a result the granting of more extensive rights to individuals in a greater number of cases and thus can be considered desirable if looked at solely from a humanitarian point of view, nevertheless, it has the important disadvantage of creating an enormous cloud of uncertainty in the demarcation of the boundaries

153. Para. 5 of the Opinion in *Singh, supra* n. 103.

between the scope of EC law and that of national law.[154] This can be tremendously disadvantageous to the proper working of the internal market and might even lead to a questioning of the legality of action on the part of the EC, since it can give rise to an *unjustified* interference by the Community in areas which are considered to fall within the traditional realm of Member States' sovereignty – issues of competence and subsidiarity will arise, which are two of the most important cornerstones of the Community edifice.

Of the cases mentioned above, *Carpenter* provides the most dramatic illustration of the dire consequences of the Court's approach. The main problem that arises as a result of *Carpenter* has to do with the specific freedom that was applicable in that case – the free movement of services. Although a great number of persons *provide* services in cross-border situations (in fact, a much greater number than persons moving permanently to another Member State in order to work), an even greater number of persons (in fact almost anyone) *receive* cross-border services.[155] Accordingly, by extending the scope of EC law to cover providers of services in situations which do not, in reality, present a link with EC law, and *by leaving it open that even recipients of services* could be covered by EC law in analogous situations, the Court has potentially included within the scope of EC law almost anyone who is a Member State national.

Consequently, the extension of the scope of Article 49 EC (Article 56 TFEU) to cover the situation of persons who exercise the right to provide services, without a requirement that there must be a sufficient link between the exercise of that freedom and the right relied on, makes us wonder whether any situation can now fall outside the scope of EC law. This seems to present problems, both, from the point of view of the Community, as a supranational organization of *limited scope* which covers only situations that promote or interfere with its aims and, on the other hand, from the point of view of Member States that have always been guarding against an unjustified intrusion

154. N. Nic Shuibhne, *supra* n. 103, 744; G. Barrett, *supra* n. 99, 380. R. Lane and N. Nic Shuibhne, *supra* n. 128, 1245.

155. N. Nic Shuibhne, *supra* n. 103, 758; S. Acierno *supra* n. 113, 403-404. R. Lane and N. Nic Shuibhne (*supra* n. 128, p. 1242) writing after *Singh* but before *Carpenter*, characterized *Singh* 'as a particularly vermicular can of worms' wondering how far the Court could go in finding a link with EC law: 'Has a Belgian who went on holiday to Crete 15 years ago, or from time to time watches TF1 on cable television – both involving the exercise of a Community right – earned the right to invoke Articles 39 or 43 and their attendant legislation in Belgium?'. *Carpenter* seems to have the potential effect of replying the above questions in the affirmative. Gavin Barrett (*supra* n. 99, 407) poses the question whether, as a consequence of *Carpenter*, 'third-country family members of providers of goods will now be held to have the same entitlements as third-country family members of providers of services'. *See* also N. Foster, 'Family and welfare rights in Europe: the impact of recent European Court of Justice decisions in the area of the free movement of persons' (2003) 25(3) *JSWFL* 291, 297; V. Hatzopoulos, 'A (more) social Europe: a political crossroad or a legal one-way? Dialogues between Luxembourg and Lisbon' (2006) 42 *CMLRev* 1599, 1607; S. Weatherill, *Cases and Materials on EU Law* (8th edn, Oxford, OUP, 2007), p. 478.

by the EC into sensitive areas of their sovereignty, such as that of immigration control.[156]

If such an approach is followed in the future, then this will lead to a situation where only very few (if any) situations will escape the ambit of EC law. According to Oliver and Roth, 'the decisive issue raised by the judgment in *Mary Carpenter* is . . . whether *all* measures of the State of origin that are even-handedly applied to the provider of the service and that may impose an incidental burden on the inter-state provision of services will in the future by scrutinized as well'.[157]

The above concerns can, and should, be allayed by the Court of Justice itself. Hence, the Court should begin considering the possibility of delivering a judgment, in the context of the free movement of persons, which will have the same effect as *Keck* has had on the principles applicable to the free movement of goods; that is, of setting the proper boundaries between cases which are within the scope of EC law and those which escape its ambit because they are very far-removed from inter-state trade.[158]

2 Instead of Removing the Harsh Consequences of the Strict Application of the Purely Internal Rule, the Injustice of the Situation is Enhanced

The Court seems to have been aware of the adverse consequences that the purely internal rule has had, especially in the context of family reunification cases,[159] and

156. For an excellent, detailed, explanation of the need to maintain the proper boundaries between the EC competence to regulate the free movement of persons in furtherance of the Community's aims, on the one hand and, national competences in the field of immigration policy, on the other, *see* the Opinion of Advocate General Geelhoed in *Jia, supra* n. 99.
157. P. Oliver and W.H. Roth *supra* n. 18, 418-419.
158. *See* the suggestion of Advocate General Tizzano in paras 29-76 of his Opinion in *CaixaBank France v. Ministere de l'Economie, des Finances et de l'Industrie*, Case No. C-442/02 [2004] ECR I-8961. Of course, to a certain extent, some limits have been put to the extension of the scope of EC law by *Akrich* (*see* the comments *supra* n. 119 – though note that recent case-law seems to have confined the principles established in *Akrich* to its specific facts) and *Graf supra* n. 83.
159. A Directive on family reunification (2003/86 (EC) Directive on the right to family reunification, OJ L 251/12, 2003) has been adopted which grants to refugees and third-country nationals lawfully resident in (the participating) Member States, the right to be accompanied by their spouse and minor children in the Member State in which they reside (without, of course, the need for the prior exercise of free movement within the EU). Note, however, that this Directive does not apply to citizens of the EU who want to be accompanied by their family members in their Member State of origin – thus, they still must point to a link with EC law in order to derive any family reunification rights by virtue of EC law in their State of origin. According to White, 'the restriction of the beneficiaries of the rules in the Directive to third-country nationals and refugees, and the exclusion of family members of citizens of the Union could result in some anomalies. If the immigration rules of the Member State are restrictive, then it could result in third-country nationals being treated more favourably than nationals . . . This could perpetuate – even extend – reverse discrimination' – *see* R.C.A. White, 'Conflicting competences: free movement rules and immigration laws' (2004) 29 *ELRev* 385, 395. It should be noted that in the *Metock* case in 2008, the Court seems to have been aware of a possible injustice arising as a

perhaps this has been one of the reasons that have led it to adopt a much more liberal approach in finding a link with EC law in some of its most recent cases.

Nonetheless, despite the fact that bringing more situations within the scope of EC law means the granting of more beneficial rights to more individuals, at the same time it should not be forgotten that there will always be a (perhaps small) number of persons who will not be able to establish a link with EC law and thus will suffer reverse discrimination. Hence, instead of remedying the adverse consequences of the emergence of reverse discrimination, the current approach of the Court may in reality enhance them as now the difference in treatment that emerges as a result of the limited scope of EC law will not even have the justification of being due to the actual contribution the inter-state movement exercised by the claimant makes to the completion of the internal market.[160] Nic Shuibhne has very rightly noted that 'it is precisely the . . . ease with which Community law *can* be triggered which sours the logic of leaving the rest aside'.[161]

3 Abuse of EC Law

The Court has always been alert to the danger that, since a link with the common market is the ticket to the application of much more beneficial regulations, people would be eager to establish such a link, artificially, in order to bring their situation within the scope of EC law and take advantage of the (more extensive) rights granted by it.[162] The Court expressed its concern for this possibility in its case-law in all the fundamental freedoms[163] and, in particular, it pointed out in paragraph 24 of its judgment in *Singh* that

> [A]s regards the risk of fraud . . . it is sufficient to note that . . . the facilities created by the Treaty cannot have the effect of allowing persons who benefit

result of a restrictive approach towards the grand of family reunification rights to *migrant* Union citizens: another form of reverse discrimination but this time exercised by the Community itself against its own citizens, when their situation is compared with third-country nationals who wish to be accompanied in a Member State by their family members. The Court acknowledged that the requirement of a prior lawful residence in the territory of another Member State, before family members of a Union citizen could accompany the latter in the host Member State by virtue of EC law (i.e., the *Akrich* condition), 'would lead to the paradoxical outcome that a Member State' would be obliged under Directive 2003/86 to authorize 'the entry and residence of the spouse of a national of a non-member country lawfully resident in its territory where the spouse is not already lawfully resident in another Member State, but would be free to refuse the entry and residence of the spouse of a Union citizen in the same circumstances' – *see Metock, supra* n. 80, para. 69.

160. A. Tryfonidou *supra* n. 113, 86. This was also pointed out, more recently, by Advocate General Geelhoed in his Opinion in *Jia, supra* n. 99, paras 74-75 of the Opinion.

161. N. Nic Shuibhne, *supra* n. 103, 738 (*see* also p. 758). *See* also N. Nic Shuibhne, *supra* n. 98, p. 192. For another scholar supporting this argument *see* B. Hofstotter, 'A cascade of rights, or who shall care for little Catherine? Some reflections on the Chen case' (2005) 30 *ELRev* 548, 552-553.

162. *See* S. Weatherill and P. Beaumont, *EU Law* (3rd edn, London, Penguin, 1999), p. 714.

163. *See*, among others, *Cadbury Schweppes plc & Cadbury Schweppes Overseas Ltd v. Commisioners of Inland Revenue*, Case No. C-196/04 [2006] ECR I-7995, paras 34-38; *Kamer van*

from them to evade the application of national legislation and of prohibiting Member States from taking measures necessary to prevent such abuse.

Nonetheless, because of the difficulties of proof involved, the Court's approach can be characterized as anything but strict in cases of this kind.[164] The problem of abuse appears to have been aggravated as the ease with which nowadays the Court accepts the establishment of a link with EC law may encourage and, in fact, facilitate people to abuse the opportunities offered by Community law. Gavin Barrett has observed that following the *Singh* judgment, the obvious 'solution in order to attract the optimum level of protection . . . is for the Community national in the family to exercise free movement rights as a worker or self-employed person in another Member State of the EU'.[165]

Indeed, it is well-known that it is a usual phenomenon for British nationals married to third-country nationals to travel to Ireland with their spouse and work for a limited period of time there, so that the (third-country national) spouse will be awarded a right of residence, automatically, under EC law in their return to the United Kingdom.[166]

E CONCLUSION

The analysis in this section of the chapter illustrates that the Court now, most probably in response to the criticisms levelled towards its stance on the problem of reverse discrimination, has accepted in some of its case-law that a link with EC

Koophandel en Fabrieken voor Amsterdam v. Inspire Art, Case No. C-167/01 [2001] ECR I-10155, paras 95-97; *Centros Ltd v. Erhvervs- og Selskabsstyrelsen*, Case No. C-212/97 [1999] ECR I-1459; *Veronica Omroep Organisatie*, Case No. C-148/91 [1993] ECR I-487; *TV10*, Case No. C-23/93 [1994] ECR I-4795; *Coenen and others v. the Sociaal-Economische Raad*, Case No. 39/75 [1975] ECR 1547, para. 9.

164. In *Emsland-Stärke GmbH v. Hauptzollamt Hamurg-Jonas*, Case No. C-110/99 [2000] ECR I-11569, paras 52 and 53, the Court laid down two cumulative conditions which have to be satisfied before abuse of EC law can be established: (a) a combination of objective circumstances in which, despite formal observance of the conditions laid down by the Community rules, the purpose of those rules has not been achieved, (b) a subjective element consisting in the intention to obtain an advantage from the Community rules by creating artificially the conditions laid down for obtaining it.

165. *Supra* n. 99, p. 379. *See* also D. O'Keeffe and P. Osborne, 'The European Court Scores a Goal' (1996) *IJCLLIR* 111, 124; A. Arnull, *The European Union and its Court of Justice* (Oxford, OUP, 1999), p. 324; S. Weatherill (annotation of *Bosman*), (1996) 33 *CMLRev* 991, 1020; L. Woods, *supra* n. 46, pp. 225-226.

166. *See* B. Ingoldsy, 'Free movement – A Department of Justice perspective', in *The Free Movement of Workers Within the European Union*, N. Hyland (ed.) (ICEL, 1999), p. 26. For an example of this *see* the factual background to the *Akrich* case, *supra* n. 110. For a similar case decided in a national court *see Wael Kweder v. Minister for Justice*, [1996] IR 381. Such an issue has, more recently, also arisen in Denmark: *see* 'Denmark, immigration and the EU: Hoist by its own policy', published in *The Economist*, 14 Aug. 2008, available at <www.economist.com/world/europe/displaystory.cfm?story_id=11921278&fsrc=RSS> (accessed on 1 Sep. 2008).

law was established, even if a situation merely involved the exercise of inter-state movement. That the exercise of such a movement did not, in fact, have any connection with the EC right that a person sought to rely on by trying to bring his or her case within the scope of EC law, seems to have been ignored by the Court in its attempt to avoid the emergence of reverse discrimination.

It is true that reverse discrimination arising as a result of the application of the purely internal rule, is a difference in treatment which, although it does not interfere with the exercise of the free movement of persons to work or provide services in different Member States, nonetheless, is increasingly seen as inappropriate, especially when viewed in the light of recent developments in the EC and, in particular, the creation of the status of citizenship of the Union. However, the method used by the Court for solving this problem in some of its recent case-law is not an appropriate one. By refusing to deal with the problem head-on and by trying to solve it in indirect ways by accepting within the scope of EC law as many situations as possible, the Court has only scratched the surface of the problem. In fact, it has been illustrated above how this new approach raises more problems than it solves.

Remedying (or preventing the emergence of) instances of reverse discrimination in the area of persons is, indeed, a noble aim however this should not be done by inappropriately extending the scope of the fundamental freedoms provisions. Those provisions should only include within their ambit situations that have a sufficient link with their sole aim, that is, the free movement of persons for an economic aim. Accordingly, since the Community appears to be concerned about the emergence of instances of reverse discrimination in the area of the free movement of persons, some other way for the resolution of this conundrum should be found.

V THE NEW APPROACH FOLLOWED BY THE COURT WHEN DELIMITING THE SCOPE OF ITS JURISDICTION IN PRELIMINARY RULINGS PROCEEDINGS

In Chapter 2, it was explained that, traditionally, when a question was referred to the ECJ from a national court dealing with a case the facts of which were purely internal to a Member State, the Court declined jurisdiction and refused to reply to the question referred. The Court was of the view that, a reply to the question of whether the contested measure is such as to violate one of the fundamental freedoms provisions would have to be postponed until a case involving facts that were not purely internal to a Member State would arise before a national court.

However, the Court seems to have changed its approach in its (mostly) recent case-law: because it wishes to give the national court a useful reply as to the interpretation of EC law in instances where national law has extended the application of EC law to purely internal situations, and thus assist the national court in preventing the emergence of reverse discrimination, the Court rules that it is bound to give a reply to the question referred.[167] It should be noted, nonetheless, that the fact that the Court gives a reply to the questions referred in such cases (even though it recognizes that the facts before it involve a purely internal situation), does not in any way extend the boundaries of the scope of application of EC law – it is purely a matter concerning the Court's jurisdiction under the Article 234 EC (Article 267 TFEU) procedure[168] since, after all, the Court makes it clear that the effect of its judgment is confined to potential situations that will involve facts that are not purely internal to a Member State.

Advocate General Geelhoed in *Reisch*,[169] commenting on the Court's approach in delimiting its jurisdiction in preliminary rulings cases, stressed that the main question is this:

> [I]s it the facts in the main proceedings that determine whether the Court must answer the questions referred to it for a preliminary ruling, or is it the nature and substance of the national measure?'.[170]

He went on to explain the results that follow from the application of each of these approaches:

> If it is the facts in the main proceedings that are decisive, the Court clearly will not answer the question where the main proceedings have no cross-border elements.[171]
>
> If it is the substance of the national measure that is decisive, the Court should consider how far the national legislation may have an external effect. Only if there is no – potential – external effect should the Court refrain from answering the question referred to it.[172]

This distinction drawn by the Advocate General seems to be reflecting the differentiation made by d'Oliveira (seen in section 2 of this chapter) between the two approaches that are followed for distinguishing between internal and international cases in private international law: the 'geographical' and the 'juridical' approaches. And, in this context as well, the Court, in some of its case-law seems to have moved away from a 'geographical' approach towards a 'juridical' approach. In other words, in a substantial number of cases in – almost – all the fundamental freedoms, the Court has accepted jurisdiction to give a reply to a question as to the interpretation of EC law, even though the facts in the main

167. *See* n. 39 of the Opinion of Advocate General Poiares Maduro in *Carbonati Apuani, supra* n. 32. *See* also paras 69-75 of the Opinion of Advocate General Léger in *Ritter-Coulais, supra* n. 139. For literature dealing with this case-law *see*: C. Ritter, *supra* n. 29; P. Oliver and W-H. Roth *supra* n. 18, 431-432; P. Oliver, *Free Movement of Goods in the European Community, supra* n. 18, pp. 152-153 (para. 6.105).
168. P. Oliver and W.H. Roth, *supra* n. 18, 431; P. Oliver, *supra* n. 18, p. 149 (para. 6.101).
169. *Reisch and Others*, Joined Cases C-515/99, C-519/99 to C-524/99 and C-526/99 to C-540/99 [2002] ECR I-2157.
170. *Ibid.*, para. 80 of the Opinion.
171. *Ibid.*, para. 81 of the Opinion.
172. *Ibid.*, para. 82 of the Opinion.

proceedings presented no cross-border element. This, of course, is subject to the qualification that the contested measure must be such that its application will have an effect on the exercise of one of the fundamental freedoms, in case it is applied to situations involving a cross-border element.

Accordingly, if it is obvious that a Member State measure, when applied to products or factors of production involved in an inter-state economic activity will be contrary to one of the fundamental freedoms, this is sufficient for urging the Court to give a reply to the question referred as to the compatibility of that measure with one of the fundamental freedoms provisions. As will be seen, however, the Court in its judgments makes it clear that EC law only requires the contested measure to become inapplicable in situations that are not purely internal to a Member State. It is up to the national courts to determine whether a measure that is found contrary to EC law and thus inapplicable in situations that are not purely internal to a Member State, should also be held inapplicable in purely internal situations. And, as will be seen, this is usually required by Member State laws or the Constitutions of Member States in order to prevent the emergence of reverse discrimination.

A THE NEW APPROACH FOLLOWED BY THE COURT WHEN DELIMITING THE SCOPE OF ITS JURISDICTION IN INSTANCES WHERE NATIONAL LAW PROHIBITS THE EMERGENCE OF REVERSE DISCRIMINATION

The new approach followed by the Court when determining whether it has jurisdiction to provide a reply to a question referred for a preliminary ruling, has been applied in case-law in the fields of the free movement of goods, capital,[173] services[174] and establishment.[175] It should be borne in mind that in this case-law, the Court specifically mentions the fact that its reply might be useful if national law requires that purely internal situations should be treated in the same way as situations falling within the scope of EC law, that is, if national law prohibits the emergence of reverse discrimination. The root of this case-law seems to be the fact that in some Member States – such as France, Italy and Austria – the national courts have held that reverse discrimination is prohibited by the principle of equality protected by their Constitution and thus there has been an extension of the rules

173. *Reische, supra* n. 169; *Salzmann*, Case No. C-300/01, [2003] ECR I-4899. *See* L. Flynn, 'Coming of age: The free movement of capital case law 1993-2002' (2002) 39 *CMLRev* 773, 784-785.

174. *Anomar v. Estado português*, Case No. C-6/01 [2003] ECR I-8621 (annotated by G. Straetmans (2004) 41 *CMLRev* 1409); *Cipolla supra* note 11; *Servizi Ausiliari Dottori Commercialisti Srl v. Giuseppe Calafiori*, Case No. C-451/03 [2006] ECR I-2941; *Europa 7, supra* n. 77, paras 64-70.

175. *Mauri v. Ministero della Giustizia, Commissione per gli esami di avvocato presso la Corte d'appello di Milano*, Case No. C-250/03 [2005] ECR I-1267; *Calafiori, supra* n. 174.

imposed by Community law, to purely internal situations, this being required by the Member States' own Constitution.[176]

Exigencies of space mean that it is only possible to analyze one case belonging to this group. Accordingly, I have chosen the most well-known: the *Guimont* case.[177] In that case, at issue was French legislation which, in effect, prohibited the manufacture and marketing in France of a cheese without rind under the designation *Emmenthal*. The issue arose when criminal proceedings were brought against Mr Guimont (a French national) for manufacturing and marketing cheese in France, in contravention of the above legislation. Mr Guimont claimed that the French legislation was contrary to Article 28 EC (Article 34 TFEU). When the issue reached the Court of Justice, the Court noted that as the legislation in question could have a potential effect on inter-state trade, it fell within Article 28 EC, but only in so far as it applied to situations that were linked to the importation of goods.[178]

When dealing with the issue of its jurisdiction, the Court merely pointed out that

> [I]t is for the national courts alone to determine, having regard to the particular features of each case, both the need for a preliminary ruling in order to enable them to give their judgment and the relevance of the questions which they refer to the Court.[179]

It then continued to rule that in the case under discussion,

> [I]t is not obvious that the interpretation of Community law requested is not necessary for the national court. Such a reply might be useful to it if its national law were to require, in proceedings such as those in this case, that a national producer must be allowed to enjoy the same rights as those which a producer of another Member State would derive from Community law in the same situation.[180]

---

176. *See* E. Spaventa, annotation of *TK-Heimdienst, supra* n. 90, 1267. For an explanation of how the Italian Constitutional Court has quite recently ruled in Decision 30 Dec. 1997, No 443, Riv dir Internaz (1998) that reverse discrimination is prohibited by the Italian Constitution (and, in particular, the principle of equality enshrined in it) *see* A. Adinolfi, 'The Judicial application of Community law in Italy (1981-1997)' (1998) 35 *CMLRev* 1313, 1326-1327. *See* also n. 11 of the Opinion of Advocate General Poiares Maduro in *Cipolla, supra* n. 11; para. 36 of the Opinion of Advocate General Ruiz-Jarabo Colomer in *Calafiori, supra* n. 174. This was also mentioned by the Commission in its 'Sixteenth Annual Report on Monitoring the Application of Community Law' COM (99) 301 final, OJ C 354/1, 1999, at p. 190.
177. *Criminal proceedings against Guimont*, Case No. C-448/98 [2000] ECR I-10663. For similar cases *see Proceedings for a compulsory reconstruction against Smanor SA*, Case No. 298/87 [1988] ECR 4489; *Tridon v. Fédération départementale des cahsseurs de l'Isère*, Case No. C-510/99 [2001] ECR I-7777, paras 46-48; *Douwe Egberts, supra* n. 44, paras 57-58; *Karner Industrie-Auktionen GmbH v. Troostwijk GmbH*, Case No. C-71/02 [2004] ECR I-3025; *Bluhme, supra* n. 88.
178. *Guimont, supra* n. 177, para. 21.
179. *Ibid.*, para. 22.
180. *Ibid.*, para. 23 (emphasis added). Note the difference of this case-law with the case-law analysed in section III of this chapter, where the legislation even when applied to domestic

B THE NEW APPROACH FOLLOWED BY THE COURT WHEN DELIMITING THE SCOPE OF ITS JURISDICTION IN INSTANCES INVOLVING '*RENVOI*'

In the previous chapters of the book, it was explained that EC law does not prohibit reverse discrimination as it considers it a problem outside its scope which, if at all, should be addressed by the Member States.[181] As a result of that, some Member States have responded to the problem of reverse discrimination by transposing Community law into purely internal situations through national legislation (this is called 'voluntary adoption', 'spontaneous harmonization' or '*renvoi*').

It should be noted that this does not extend the scope of EC law to purely internal situations: purely internal situations continue to be considered as such, however, national legislation refers to a Community provision in order to ensure that reverse discrimination is eliminated by extending to persons in purely internal situations, the rights granted by EC law to persons falling within its scope. The issue that arises in such situations is whether national courts, faced with a question in relation to their national legislation (which reproduces EC law), should be able to request the ECJ to provide them with a ruling as to the meaning of the relevant EC provision, which they would then be able to use in deciding the issue which arose on the purely national setting in question.

Albeit the fact that someone might expect that the Court would decline jurisdiction in situations of this kind, as clearly the facts in issue are purely internal to a Member State, nevertheless, the Court (disregarding the Opinions of most of its Advocates General to the contrary)[182] has developed a consistent line of case-law (the so-called '*Dzodzi* jurisprudence'),[183] according to which the

---

goods had an effect on inter-state trade. G. Davies, *supra* n. 46, pp. 135-136, explains that *Guimont* is different from *Pistre* in that the application of stricter requirements only to domestic goods (since, in practice, the legislation was not applied to imported goods) did not give a competitive advantage to them in comparison with imported ones – no one would consider French Emmenthal better than imported Emmenthal because it had a rind.

181. *Steen v. Deutsche Bundespost (No. 2)*, Case No. C-132/93 [1994] ECR I-2715.

182. Note, however, that Advocate General Geelhoed in his Opinion in *Poseidon Chartering BV v. Marianne Zeeschip VOF and others*, Case No. C-3/04 [2006] ECR I-2505, seems to be of the view that the Court of Justice does not lack jurisdiction in such cases (*see* paras 11-18 of the Opinion).

183. *Dzodzi v. Belgian State*, Joined Cases 297/88 and 197/89 [1990] ECR I-3763, paras 31-43; *Thomasdunger GmbH v. Oberfinanzdirektion Frankfurt am Main*, Case No. 166/84 [1985] ECR 3001; *Gmurzynska-Bsher*, Case No. C-231/89 [1990] ECR I-4003, paras 15-26; *Criminal proceedings against Tomatis and Fulchiron*, Case No. C-384/89 [1991] ECR I-127; *Fournier v. Van Werven*, Case No. C-73/89 [1992] ECR I-5621 (EC law transposed into national context by private law agreements); *Federconsorzi v. Azienda di Stato per gli Interventi nel Mercato Agricolo*, Case No. C-88/91 [1992] ECR I-4035, paras 6-10 (EC law transposed into national context by a contractual provision); *Giloy v. Hauptzollamt Frankfurt am Main-Ost*, Case No. C-130/95 [1997] ECR I-4291; *Leur-Bloem v. Inspecteur der Belastingdienst/Ondernemingen Amsterdam 2*, Case No. C-28/95 [1997] ECR I-4161, paras 24-34 (annotated by G. Betlem (1999) 36 *CMLRev* 1656); *Schoonbroodt*, Case No. C-247/97 [1998] ECR I-8095, paras 13-16; *Kofisa Italia Srl v. Ministero delle Finanze*, Case No. C-1/99 [2001] ECR I-207, paras 20-33;

Court has jurisdiction to reply to such a question when referred to it by a national court.[184]

In *Dzodzi*,[185] Mrs Massam Dzodzi, a Togolese national married to a Belgian national who had never exercised one of the fundamental freedoms, claimed the right to stay in Belgium as the spouse of a Belgian worker. It was clear that she could not derive a right from EC law to stay in Belgium as a family member of a Community worker.[186] However, an interpretation of EC law on family reunification rights was sought by the national court since, in order to avoid the emergence of reverse discrimination, Belgian legislation extended to aliens married to Belgian nationals who were in a purely internal situation, the same family reunification rights that were available, by virtue of EC law, to the spouses of nationals of other Member States residing in Belgium.

When the question was referred to the ECJ, the Belgian Government and the Commission pointed out that the Court did not have jurisdiction to reply to this question as in issue was the interpretation of a provision of national law. The Court,

---

Andersen og Jensen ApS v. Skatteministeriet, Case No. C-43/00 [2002] ECR I-379, paras 14-19; *Urbing-Adam v. Administration de l'enregistrement et des domains*, Case No. C-267/99 [2001] ECR I-7467; *BIAO v. Finanzamt für Groβunternehmen in Hamburg*, Case No. C-306/99 [2003] ECR I-1, paras 88-94; *Poseidon Chartering, supra* n. 182, paras 15-18; *Confederación Española de Empresarios de Estaciones de Servicio v. Compañía Española de Petróleos SA*, Case No. C-217/05 [2006] ECR I-11987, paras 19-22; *Staatssecretaris van Financiën v. Feron*, Case No. C-170/03 [2005] ECR I-2299, para. 11; *Government of the French Community and Walloon Government v. Flemish Government, supra* n. 24, para. 40. *See*, however, *Kleinwort Benson Ltd v. City of Glasgow*, Case No. C-346/92 [1995] ECR I-615, paras 14-25, where the Court declined jurisdiction because the national legislation took the Community provisions only as a model and made express provision for modifications, and the national legislation did not require national courts to apply absolutely and unconditionally the interpretation given by the Court of Justice. Note, also, that in *Berliner Kindl Brauerei AG v. Andreas Siepert*, Case No. C-208/98 [2000] ECR I-1741, Advocate General Léger drew a distinction between cases of the *Dzodzi*-type (the facts of which fall outside the scope of EC law), and cases where a Member State extends the application of a minimum harmonization Directive to situations not expressly covered by it, 'in pursuance of the Directive itself and in a manner entirely consistent with the intentions of the Community legislature'. In the latter cases, since the minimum harmonization Directive explicitly authorizes Member States to retain or adopt more stringent provisions in furtherance of its aims, the extension of the scope of such a Directive by virtue of national law has a basis in Community law and thus falls within the scope of EC law (*see* paras 22-28 of the Opinion).

184. For an explanation *see* S.L. Kaleda, 'Extension of the preliminary rulings procedure outside the scope of Community law: "The Dzodzi line of cases"', European Integration online Papers (EIoP), Vol. 4, No. 11, 19 Oct. 2000 available at <eiop.or.at/eiop/texte/2000-011a.htm> (accessed on 10 Sep. 2008); S. Douglas-Scott, *Constitutional law of the European Union* (London, Longman, 2002), pp. 240-241; K. Mortelmans *supra* n. 18, at p. 134; C. Barnard and E. Sharpston, 'The changing face of article 177 references' (1997) 34 *CMLRev* 1113, 1128-1133; G. Davies, *supra* n. 46, pp. 137-141; D. Anderson, 'The admissibility of Preliminary References' (1994) 14 *YEL* 179, 184-185; D. O'Keeffe, 'Is the spirit of Article 177 under attack? Preliminary references and admissibility' (1998) 23 *ELRev* 509, 518-519.

185. *Supra* n. 183, annotated by M. Bravo-Ferrer Delgado and N. La Casta Muñoa, (1992) 29 *CMLRev* 152.

186. *Supra* n. 183, paras 20-28.

however, refused to lend credence to those arguments as it was of the view that the questions submitted by the national court in fact concerned the interpretation of a provision of Community law. Accordingly, under Article 234 EC (Article 267 TFEU), it was obliged to give a ruling in order to achieve uniformity of interpretation of EC law, which is the main aim of that provision.[187] The backbone of the Court's reasoning can be found in paragraphs 36 and 37 of the judgment:

> It does not appear either from the wording of Article 177 [now 234] or from the aim of the procedure introduced by that article that the authors of the Treaty intended to exclude from the jurisdiction of the Court requests for a preliminary ruling on a Community provision in the specific case where the national law of a Member State refers to the content of that provision in order to determine rules applicable to a situation which is purely internal to that State.
>
> On the contrary, it is manifestly in the interest of the Community legal order that, in order to forestall future differences of interpretation, every Community provision should be given a uniform interpretation irrespective of the circumstances in which it is to be applied.

Therefore, in its judgments in the Dzodzi-line of cases the Court appears to be willing to deliver a judgment in order to clarify the meaning of a specific provision of EC law, if this will facilitate national courts to remedy instances of reverse discrimination by extending, by operation of national law, to purely internal situations the protection afforded to situations falling within the scope of EC law.

Although there has been an animated discussion between commentators and members of the Court of Justice for[188] and against[189] the Court's new approach used in the two groups of cases above (i.e., *Guimont*-type cases and *Dzodzi*-type cases), the fact remains that reverse discrimination is increasingly considered to be an *EC* problem.[190] Since two of the ways in which reverse discrimination can be remedied are 'spontaneous harmonization' or 'renvoi' as well as the use of the Member States' Constitutional Articles on equality, it seems worthwhile for the Court of Justice to use its resources in order to facilitate national courts to apply those solutions to the reverse discrimination conundrum in the most effective way.

Consequently, when a national court is requesting an interpretation of a provision of Community law in order to remedy instances of reverse discrimination, this should be considered sufficient for enabling (and perhaps requiring) the Court of Justice to exercise its jurisdiction.

---

187. *See* S. Douglas-Scott, *supra* n. 184, p. 241; S.L. Kaleda, *supra* n. 184, pp. 29-30.
188. *See*, for example, G. Davies, *supra* n. 46, pp. 138-139.
189. *See* the Joined Opinion of Advocate General Jacobs in *Leur-Bloem* and *Giloy, supra* n. 183; C. Ritter, *supra* n. 29, 699-700; paras 17-53 of the Opinion of Advocate General Ruiz-Jarabo Colomer in *Kofisa Italia, supra* n. 183.
190. *See* M. Poiares Maduro, *supra* n. 15, p. 132.

VI CONCLUSION

The Court of Justice is not an isolated body which delivers judgments without having any contact with the outside world. The members of the Court of Justice deliver informed rulings which often take into account the criticisms voiced towards particular areas of law as well as calls for changes to well-established principles which need to be reformed in such a way as to conform to the developments in the broader European context.

In Chapter 1 of the book, I highlighted the problems caused by the emergence of reverse discrimination as a result of the application of the purely internal rule. In the final sections of Chapter 2, I also explained briefly the main problems with the Court's traditional approach to the issue of finding a link with EC law. The Court of Justice has, of course, been aware of those problems. And although the Court, at first, found it easy and appropriate to adopt a 'Pilate solution' to some of those problems by pointing out that reverse discrimination falls outside the scope of EC law since it does not inhibit its main aim (i.e., the construction of the internal market), nonetheless, this solution has become increasingly inappropriate due to a number of recent developments in the EC context.

There is a general feeling in academic circles as well as among certain members of the Court of Justice, that reverse discrimination can no longer be ignored by the EC. Apparently, it is time for a solution to be found to this problem. The Court, itself, has tried to provide a solution by applying a different approach towards the root of the problem, that is, the purely internal rule. However, both in the area of EC trade and in the area of persons, it seems that whatever way is used for delimiting the scope of the free movement provisions, reverse discrimination will not, appropriately, be remedied since those provisions prohibit only the emergence of situations that inhibit their main aim: the construction of the internal market. Since reverse discrimination does not affect that aim, it cannot, under any circumstances, be considered to fall within the scope of those provisions.

Hence, how can one solve, if at all, the reverse discrimination conundrum? Or better, how can instances of reverse discrimination be brought within the scope of EC law and thus, where appropriate, enable the Community to provide a solution? In order to answer this question, EC law will have to be analyzed in a broader context. Reverse discrimination seems to be no longer sustainable in the light of two important developments in the EC: a) the establishment of EU citizenship in 1993 and the growing importance it has attained; and b) the goal of the establishment and maintenance of an internal market 'without internal frontiers' which functions smoothly. Each of these developments, and the contribution it has made to the debate concerning reverse discrimination, will be discussed, respectively, in the two following chapters of the book.

Part II

Reverse Discrimination as an Incongruity in the Contemporary EC

Chapter 4

Reverse Discrimination and the Free Movement of Persons: An Incongruity in a Citizens' Europe

I INTRODUCTION

Is reverse discrimination, as a difference in treatment based on whether a Member State national has contributed to the economic aims of the Treaty, still acceptable in a Citizens' Europe? If not, how can instances of reverse discrimination be brought within the scope of EC law, since it was made clear in the previous part of the book that reverse discrimination can never fall within the scope of the fundamental freedoms provisions? These are the questions that I aim to answer in this chapter.[1]

I will begin my analysis with a brief presentation of pre-1993 case-law of the Court of Justice and secondary legislation, which have been seen by many as creating 'an incipient form of citizenship'. It will be explained that although through that case-law and pieces of legislation, rights were granted to Member State nationals where this was not necessary for enabling them to exercise a cross-border economic activity, some kind of (indirect) contribution to the economic aims of the Treaty was still required before a person could enjoy the protection of EC law. Therefore, until very recently, the EC was still mainly – if not solely – an *economic* organization of limited scope and aims and thus a difference in treatment based on a person's contribution to the internal market was justified by the need to confine the Community's scope to situations where the application of EC law was necessary for the attainment of the Community's economic aims.

---

1. Chapter 4 and parts of Chapter 3 of the book have formed the basis for an article published in LIEI: A. Tryfonidou, 'Reverse discrimination in purely internal situations: an incongruity in a Citizens' Europe' (2008) 35 *LIEI* 43.

This will be followed by a section that will present the Court's early reaction to the formal introduction of the status of Union citizenship and to the question of whether this new status requires a change in its stance on reverse discrimination. It will be seen that the ECJ has – until quite recently – taken a rather conservative approach towards this new status and held in its case-law that citizenship of the Union has in no way affected the well-established principle that reverse discrimination is not prohibited by EC law.

The subsequent section of the chapter will examine the question of whether the citizenship provisions are, in fact, merely of a symbolic nature and thus, in reality, Community law still includes within its scope only persons that have contributed, in one way or another, to its economic aims. It will be argued that since, through the Court's latest case-law, Community rights have been granted to economically inactive Union citizens who could not point in any way to a link with the economic aims of the Treaty, the status of Union citizenship is no longer merely symbolic but a status through which Member State nationals have attained importance in the Community legal system not only as factors of production but also as citizens.

The final section will deal with the main question of the chapter, that is, whether reverse discrimination is now a form of discrimination that falls within the scope of EC law. It will be explained that, due to the fact that the Court in its recent case-law has brought economically active and economically inactive persons to the same position as regards the bestowal of some of the rights that are available under EC law and, thus, a person's contribution to the completion of the internal market seems to bear little importance in determining whether he or she should enjoy rights deriving from EC law, reverse discrimination is no longer a difference in treatment justified by the need to confine the scope of application of EC law to situations involving a contribution to the economic aims of the Community. And since reverse discrimination is a difference in treatment that emerges as a result of the limited scope of application of EC law (i.e., is a 'residual' situation from the point of view of Community law), it falls within its scope and thus may amount to a violation of the Community principle of equality, unless justified.[2]

As explained in Chapter 1 – and as will be seen in more detail in Chapter 6 – not all instances of reverse discrimination are problematic. Some of them do not even amount to discrimination, as the situations (internal and cross-border) that are treated differently are, in fact, not similar. Therefore, it should be kept in mind that the analysis provided in this chapter is only relevant to instances of reverse discrimination that actually amount to a form of differential treatment of similar situations and are thus problematic from the point of view of Community law.

---

2. In Ch. 6, it will be explained that the doctrine of mandatory requirements should be made available to Member States for justifying any instances of reverse discrimination that fall within the scope of EC law. Thus, if such instances of reverse discrimination can be justified on a (valid) ground other than the desire to grant EC rights only to persons that have contributed to the economic aims of the Treaty, then the Member State which resorts to such differential treatment can continue doing so.

II DEFINITION OF THE TERMS TO BE USED THROUGHOUT THE CHAPTER

As is obvious from the whole of the study, the term 'fundamental freedom(s)' collectively covers the cross-border *economic* freedoms granted to persons by the Treaty, that is, the free movement of workers, the freedom to provide services and the freedom of establishment. Similarly, the term 'migrant economic actor' refers to a person who is a worker in another Member State, a provider of cross-border services, or a person who has established business in a Member State other than that of his or her nationality. In contrast, when use of the phrases 'citizenship provisions' or 'citizenship rights' is made, it means the provisions enshrined in Part Two of the EC Treaty. Finally, the term 'fundamental rights' refers to the human rights that have been held to form part of the general principles that must be respected in the Community legal system.

It will be observed that the terms 'direct' and 'indirect' contribution to the construction of the internal market will be widely used to show how the scope of application of EC law has evolved. In this chapter, when reference is made to a direct contribution to the establishment of the internal market, it means that the scope of EC law has been held to cover a situation where a person bears the status of a traditional economic actor (i.e., a migrant worker, a *provider* of services or a person who establishes business in the territory of another Member State) *and* the right granted by virtue of application of EC law is *necessary* in order to enable that person to exercise *that* cross-border economic activity. Conversely, *indirect* contribution to the internal market may occur in one of two ways: firstly, when an EC right is granted to a person who is not a traditional economic actor in order to enable that person to exercise his or her right to move to another Member State to receive services, purchase goods or receive vocational training; secondly, when an EC right is granted to a person (e.g., a worker) when this is *not necessary* for enabling him or her to exercise one of the fundamental freedoms.

III MARKET CITIZENSHIP AND REVERSE DISCRIMINATION

As explained in Chapter 1 of the book, the EEC Treaty, signed in 1957, had a limited, yet ambitious, aim: to construct a common market. All the provisions of the Treaty (and secondary legislation) were interpreted by the Court of Justice, at least in the first years of the Community's existence, with merely that objective in mind. Any situation not furthering in any sense the above aim would, accordingly, not be governed by those provisions, but, on the contrary, would be a matter for other legal systems, and more specifically, the legal systems of the Member States.

The Treaty provisions on the free movement of persons[3] could not form an exception. In the early years of the Community's existence, Member State

3. Until 1993, the Treaty provisions on the free movement of persons were Art. 39 EC (workers), Art. 43 EC (self-employed) and Art. 49 EC (providers and recipients of services). Following the coming into force of the Lisbon Treaty (Treaty of Lisbon amending the Treaty on European

nationals were merely seen as factors of production, as instruments to be used in the process of establishing a common market and thus EC rights were granted to them only where this was *necessary* in order to enable them to exercise one of the fundamental freedoms;[4] or, using terminology of this chapter, where there was a *direct* contribution to the internal market.

Nonetheless, it will be seen in this section that, in its case-law from the 1970s onwards, the Court did not stick to this narrow approach, but extended the bestowal of rights on Member State nationals in situations where this would make no direct contribution to the internal market. This occurred in two ways. Firstly, rights were granted to workers in situations where the denial of those rights would not have a real negative impact on the exercise of a fundamental freedom – they were granted in situations involving matters that were 'peripheral and essentially non-economic in nature'.[5] Secondly, rights were granted to persons who did not belong to the traditional groups of economically active persons but who, nevertheless, contributed indirectly to the completion of the internal market by moving to another Member State as university students, consumers or recipients of services.[6]

As a result of this, a 'citizenship rhetoric' had started developing:[7] Member State nationals were granted EC rights where this did not make a *direct* contribution to the completion of the internal market. Nonetheless, as will be explained below, economic activity of some kind remained a prerequisite for the enjoyment of rights granted by EC law. Therefore, the only notion of citizenship which could be said to have existed at the time (and until very recently) was that of 'market citizenship': the Community considered as its 'citizens' only those persons who contributed to its economic objectives by participating in the construction of the common market.

A THE MARKET CITIZENSHIP CASE-LAW

1 Rights under Article 7(2) of Regulation 1612/68

Regulation 1612/68[8] enumerates a number of rights that workers should be entitled to in the Member State of their employment, in order to ensure that the primary

---

Union and the Treaty establishing the European Community, OJ C 306/1, 2007), these articles will be respectively renumbered as follows: Art. 45 TFEU; Art. 49 TFEU; Art. 56 TFEU.

4. S. O'Leary, *The Evolving Concept of Community Citizenship: From the Free Movement of Persons to Union Citizenship* (The Hague, Kluwer Law International, 1996), p. 69.
5. Para. 18 of the Opinion of Advocate General Jacobs in *Phil Collins v. Imtrat Handelsgesellschaft mbH*, Joined Cases C-92/92 and C-326/92 [1993] ECR I-5145.
6. *See Blaizot v. University of Liège and Others*, Case No. 24/86 [1988] ECR 379; para. 33 of the Opinion of Advocate General Tizzano in *Lidl Belgium GmbH & Co. KG v. Etablissementen Franz Colruyt NV*, Case No. C-356/04 [2006] ECR I-08501; *Cowan v. Le Trésor Public*, Case No. 186/87 [1989] ECR 195; and the case-law mentioned *infra* in n. 16-19.
7. F. Mancini, 'The making of a Constitution for Europe' (1989) 26 *CMLRev* 595, 606-608.
8. 1612/68 (EEC) Regulation on freedom of movement for workers within the Community, OJ L 257/2, 1968.

right granted by the Treaty through Article 39 EC (Article 45 TFEU) is protected and its exercise facilitated. To that effect, Article 7(2) of this Regulation provides that Member State nationals who work and reside in a Member State other than their State of nationality are entitled to the same tax and social advantages as the nationals of that State.

The Court of Justice has, as usual, been entrusted with the task of interpreting the above provision. And although the Court has always insisted that a person would first have to prove that he or she is a 'worker'[9] before being able to take advantage of the rights granted by this Article, it has nonetheless stretched the interpretation of that provision to such an extent that rights have been granted in situations which would have been difficult to envisage at the early stages of the Community's existence. In particular, the Court has interpreted the term 'social advantages' very broadly[10] and rights have been granted to workers and their family members[11] in situations which had little to do with the worker's contribution towards the establishment of the internal market.[12]

The first case in which the Court applied this broad approach was *Cristini*.[13] In that case, the Court held that the widow of an Italian worker in France was entitled, by virtue of Article 7(2) of the 1968 Regulation, to a reduction card for rail fares for large families since such a reduction was granted to large French families. The Court stressed that

> [I]n view of the equality of treatment which the provision seeks to achieve, the substantive area of application must be delineated so as to include all social and tax advantages, *whether or not attached to the contract of employment*, such as reductions in fares for large families.[14]

---

9. Note, however, that the Court has interpreted the term 'worker' very widely. *See Levin v. Staatssecretaris van Justitie*, Case No. 53/81 [1982] ECR 1035; *Kempf v. Staatsecretaris van Justitie*, Case No. 139/85 [1986] ECR 1741; *Steymann v. Staatsecretaris van Justitie*, Case No. 196/87 [1988] ECR 6159; *Lawrie-Blum v. Land Baden-Württemberg*, Case No. 66/85 [1986] ECR 2121.
10. *See Fiorini (neé Cristini) v. Société Nationale des Chemins de Fer Français*, Case No. 32/75 [1975] ECR 1085; *Reina v. Landeskreditbank Baden-Werttemberg*, Case No. 65/81 [1982] ECR 33; *State of Netherlands v. Reed*, Case No. 59/85 [1986] ECR 1283; *Mutsch v. Ministère public*, Case No. 137/84 [1985] ECR 2681; *Frascogna v. Caisse des Dépôts et consignations*, Case No. 157/84 [1985] ECR 1739; *O'Flynn v. Adjudication Officer*, Case No. C-237/94 [1996] ECR I-2617.
11. *Office national de l'emploi v. Deak*, Case No. 94/84 [1985] ECR 1873; *Inzirillo v. Caisse d'allocations familiales de l'Arrondissement de Lyon*, Case No. 63/76 [1976] ECR 2057; *Castelli v. ONPTS*, Case No. 261/83 [1984] ECR 3199; *Schmid v. Belgian State*, Case No. C-310/91 [1993] ECR I-3011; *Mr and Mrs F. v. Belgian State*, Case No. 7/75 [1975] ECR 679.
12. For an authoritative analysis of the Court's jurisprudence concerning Art. 7(2) of Regulation 1612/68 *see* D. O'Keeffe, 'Equal Rights for Migrants: the Concept of Social Advantages in Article 7(2), Regulation 1612/68' (1985) 5 *YEL* 93. *See* also J. Steiner, 'The Right to Welfare: Equality and Equity under Community Law' (1985) 10 *ELRev* 21, 35-39.
13. *Supra* n. 10.
14. *Ibid.*, para. 13 (emphasis added).

Obviously, the Court in this case extended the non-discrimination principle to cover a situation where this was not necessary in order to enable a person to exercise inter-state movement contributing to the internal market. It seems difficult to perceive in practical terms that an Italian worker would be deterred from exercising his freedom to move if he knew before deciding to move to France to work that he (and his family) would not be entitled to such a reduced rail fare; or, if we take the argument from the opposite side, that a worker who was aware of the availability of such an advantage, would decide to move to France in order to take advantage of it. Moreover, if Mr Cristini was still alive, it equally seems somewhat untenable to argue that the failure to grant him the social advantage at issue would induce him to take his family and leave France.

Commenting on cases such as the one that was described in the immediately preceding paragraph, O'Keeffe has correctly observed that 'the causal link between extending a particular benefit to migrants and the consequences for mobility do not seem ever to have been subjected to exhaustive scrutiny'.[15] In such cases, the extension of the grant of social advantages to migrant workers made only an *indirect* contribution to the internal market – the worker would not really be deterred from exercising his or her initial movement if he or she knew that the specific right in question would be refused in the host Member State. In view of the fact that workers are, also, human beings and not merely factors of production, it seems that the Court's underlying objective in such cases has been to achieve a certain degree of equality of treatment between migrant workers and the nationals of the host State.

2 Students

In the 1980s in the landmark case of *Gravier*,[16] the Court ruled that Member State nationals who move to another Member State with the sole aim of following a vocational training course, fall within the scope of EC law and are entitled to claim the right not to be discriminated against on grounds of nationality with regard to access to such education. This was an important step to be made by the Court since, for the first time, persons who were not involved in an economic activity of some kind were granted rights by virtue of EC law.

Nonetheless, the Court in its judgment acknowledged the fact that students who follow a course of higher education are potential contributors to the internal market since their aim is to prepare themselves for work in the future. By being granted rights under EC law which facilitate the commencement of a course of study in another Member State, their ability to work, subsequently, in Member States other than their own is enhanced.[17] Therefore, although in *Gravier* EC rights were extended to persons not contributing to the establishment of the internal

15. D. O'Keeffe, *supra* n. 12, 106.
16. *Gravier v. City of Liège*, Case No. 293/83 [1985] ECR 593. *See* also *Raulin v. Minister van Onderwijs en Wetenschappen*, Case No. C-357/89 [1992] ECR I-1027.
17. *See* para. 24 of *Gravier, supra* n. 16.

market in the traditional sense, nonetheless, after further reflection, it can be concluded that the Court was, once again, granting EC rights to Member State nationals in order to *indirectly* promote the economic aims of the Treaty.

3 Service Recipients and Consumers

In the early years of the Community's existence, it was widely considered that only *direct* contributors to the completion of the internal market were entitled to EC rights. Consequently, it was only workers, producers/traders of goods that were involved in inter-state trade, providers of services, and self-employed persons who had exercised their right to establish in another Member State that were considered to be the beneficiaries of EC rights. Nonetheless, in the early 1980s, the Court extended the scope of application of the EC Treaty to include other – *indirect* – contributors to the internal market. These were Member State nationals who moved to the territory of another Member State in order to receive a service[18] or make purchases of goods.[19]

B A General Right of Residence for Economically Inactive (but Economically Self-sufficient) Persons

Judicial developments are usually followed by legislative drafting, either consolidating those developments or, even, expanding them. As explained in the immediately foregoing part of this section, through its wide interpretation of Treaty provisions and secondary legislation, the Court had, in effect, created a form of citizenship during the 1970s and 1980s.

Nonetheless, these developments had not, until quite recently, been mirrored at legislative level. This, however, was not due to a lack of interest in cementing a notion of European citizenship through legislative means. Far from it. In fact, in 1979 the Commission drafted a proposal for a Directive on the free movement of economically inactive persons which would allow persons to move across borders and reside in the Member State of their choice, without having to be workers or self-employed persons. Nevertheless, the Commission's proposal had gone through a tortuous path and, in the end, quite disappointingly, after ten years was abandoned. However, from the ashes of that proposal immediately grew a new proposal for three Directives which became law in the early 1990s. These were

18. *Luisi and Carbone v. Ministero del Tesoro*, Joined Cases 286/82 and 26/83 [1984] ECR 377, para. 16. It should be noted, however, that this right had already been conferred on Member State nationals by Community legislation and in *Luisi and Carbone* the Court seems to have merely endorsed that legislative right. *See*, for example, Art. 1(1)(b) of 73/148 (EEC) Directive on the abolition of restrictions on movement and residence within the Community for nationals of Member States with regard to establishment and the provision of services, OJ L 172/14, 1973 (now repealed).
19. *GB-INNO-BM v. Confédération du commerce luxembourgeois*, Case No. 362/88 [1990] ECR I-667.

Directives 90/365,[20] 93/96[21] and 90/364[22] which granted a right of free movement and residence to, respectively, employed and self-employed persons who had ceased to work, students exercising the right to receive vocational training, and to all Member State nationals who did not enjoy a right of residence under any other provision of Community law.[23]

It has been submitted that the reason behind this quick and relatively unproblematic legislative development was the fact that the Directives put to rest the fears of the Member States that an unrestricted right to free movement and residence in any Member State of the Union by all Member State nationals would have, as an effect, that persons with insufficient means would move to the Member States with the most attractive benefit schemes (the so-called problem of 'benefit tourism').[24] This was achieved by the requirement, in all three Directives, that Member State nationals moving to reside in Member States other than that of their nationality, were entitled to do so as long as they did not pose an 'unreasonable burden' on the social assistance schemes of those Member States. The Directives provided to that effect that the right to reside in the territory of another Member State would be granted and protected by EC law, as long as the migrant could prove that he or she had adequate resources not to become a burden on the social assistance scheme of the host Member State and that he or she was covered by sickness insurance in respect of all risks.[25]

Having in mind the above two prerequisites that had to be satisfied under those Directives, it is immediately apparent that, once again, a meaningful status of European citizenship had failed to be established. True, the three Directives did not require a *direct* contribution to the completion of the internal market, as had

20. 90/365 (EEC) Directive on the right of residence for employees and self-employed persons who have ceased their occupational activity, OJ L 180/28, 1990.
21. 93/96 (EC) Directive on the right of residence for students, OJ L 317/59, 1993.
22. 90/364 (EEC) Directive on the right of residence, OJ L 180/26, 1990.
23. For an account of the history of the Directives (including the older 1979 proposal) *see* A.P. Van der Mei, *Free Movement of Persons Within the European Community: Cross-Border Access to Public Benefits* (Oxford, Hart, 2003), pp. 43-46. Note that these Directives are no longer in force since they have been repealed by 2004/38 (EC) Directive on the right of citizens of the Union and their family members to move and reside freely within the territory of the Member States, OJ L 158/77, 2004.
24. For an explanation of the problem of 'benefit tourism' *see* M. Dougan, 'Free Movement: The Workseeker as Citizen' (2001) *CYELS* 93, 106-110.
25. Note that the new Directive (Directive 2004/38, *supra* n. 23) consolidates, to a great extent, the previous legislative provisions (including the three 1990 Directives) as well as the case-law on the free movement of persons. It should be noted that this Directive still includes self-sufficiency requirements for economically inactive persons who reside in the territory of the host Member State for more than three months (*see* Arts 7(1)(b) and 7(1)(c) of the Directive); and any Union citizen who moves from his or her Member State of nationality to another Member State (even for a limited period of time – that is, for even less than three months) must not become an unreasonable burden on the social assistance system of the host Member State (*see* Art. 14 of the 2004 Directive).

been the case (at least initially) with the Treaty provisions on the fundamental freedoms. However, they did not, either, do away, entirely, with the requirement of an economic element.[26] The Directives provided that Member State nationals could rely on them in order to derive a right of residence from EC law only if they were economically self-sufficient. This, without a doubt, preserved a requirement of contribution, albeit indirect, to the completion of the internal market. This is because self-sufficient persons are able to purchase goods or services in the host Member State. Therefore, by giving them the right to move and reside in another Member State, EC law also encourages them to purchase goods and receive services in the host State and, thus, contribute *indirectly* to the completion of the internal market.[27] Accordingly, these Directives did not go much further than establishing, or actually consolidating, the status of market citizen.

C MARKET CITIZENSHIP AND REVERSE DISCRIMINATION

The steps that were taken by the Community institutions (both the judiciary and the legislature) in the 1980s and 1990s may, indeed, be seen as the main pillars of a rudimentary form of European citizenship.[28] And, having in mind that the EC was still, at the time, seen as a Community of primarily economic aims, these steps could, indeed, be considered as contributing to the emergence of a Europe with a more 'human face'. Nonetheless, this should not conceal the fact that this form of citizenship was a pale shadow of a meaningful notion of citizenship. At best, this form of citizenship could be characterized as 'market citizenship'[29] – rights were granted to persons in situations where there was an *indirect* contribution to the completion of the internal market.[30]

Under this form of citizenship, all that seems to be required is that Member State nationals who move to another Member State to work, become established or provide services or even to receive services or purchase goods, should be granted

26. A. Castro Oliveira, 'Workers and other persons: step-by-step from movement to citizenship – Case-law 1995-2001' (2002) 39 *CMLRev* 77, 78.
27. *See* n. 73 of the Opinion of Advocate General Cosmas in *Criminal proceedings against Wijsenbeek*, Case No. C-378/97 [1999] ECR I-6207.
28. For an excellent explanation of Community legislation and the Court's case-law creating an 'incipient form of Union citizenship' *see* D. O'Keeffe, 'Trends in the Free Movement of persons within the European Communities', in *Human Rights and Constitutional Law: Essays in honour of Brian Walsh*, J. O'Reilly (ed.) (Dublin, The Round Hall Press, 1992), pp. 267-276.
29. For an authoritative article on market citizenship *see* M. Everson, 'The Legacy of the Market Citizen', in *New Legal Dynamics of European Integration*, J. Shaw and G. More (eds) (Oxford, Clarendon Press, 1995). *See* also S. Douglas-Scott, *Constitutional Law of the European Union* (London, Longman, 2002), pp. 486-493; G. Peebles, ' "A very Eden of the Innate Rights of Man"? A Marxist Look at the European Union Treaties and Case Law' (1997) 22 *Law and Social Inquiry* 581.
30. For an author sharing this view *see* S. O'Leary, *supra* n. 4, p. 70.

exactly the same rights (at least in most fields) with that State's nationals.[31] This is because, to use the words of Advocate General Jacobs in *Konstantinidis*,

> Community law does not regard the migrant worker (or the self-employed migrant) purely as an economic agent and a factor of production entitled to the same salary and working conditions as nationals of the host State; it regards him as a human being who is entitled to live in that State 'in freedom and dignity' . . . and to be spared any difference in treatment that would render his life less comfortable, physically or psychologically, than the lives of the native population.[32]

However, in order to be a member of the 'EC club' and claim a right to equality in other Member States, a person, until very recently, still had to further the Community's economic aims. He or she still had to be a migrant worker, a self-employed person or an indirect contributor to the internal market, in order to be entitled to live in the host State 'in freedom and dignity'.[33] Hence, at that stage in the development of Community law, the Court still attached great importance to the performance of an economic activity, before a Member State national would be able to enjoy a right granted by EC law: [34] '[t]he instrumental nature of market citizenship rights has undermined the ability of the EU to create a culture in which rights are meaningful to all'.[35]

Therefore, at that stage in the development of Community law, reverse discrimination could still be considered a difference in treatment not prohibited by EC law. Instances of reverse discrimination were rightly considered to fall outside the scope of EC law because this form of discrimination does not come into conflict with the economic aims of the Community. As already explained, the fundamental freedoms provisions do not prohibit reverse discrimination as this form of discrimination does not impede the exercise by persons of inter-state movement for an economic purpose. Similarly since, until quite recently, the Community viewed Member State nationals merely as factors of production to be used as instruments in the process of constructing the common market, reverse discrimination against persons who did not contribute in any way to the internal market was not a difference in treatment that fell within the (*broader* scope) of EC law. The EC was, until very recently, an organization which was primarily concerned with the construction of a common market and thus it was not illogical to grant rights only to persons who furthered its economic aspirations.[36]

---

31. For an explanation of this *see* paras 10 and 11 of the Opinion of Advocate General Jacobs in *Phil Collins, supra* n. 5.
32. *Konstantinidis v. Stadt Altensteig-Standesamt*, Case No. C-168/91 [1993] ECR I-1191, para. 24.
33. A.G. Toth, 'The European Union and Human Rights: The way forward' (1997) 34 *CMLRev* 491, 498.
34. N. Reich, 'A European Constitution for Citizens: Reflections on the Rethinking of Union and Community Law' (1997) 3 *ELJ* 131, 131-133.
35. S. Douglas-Scott, *supra* n. 29, p. 492.
36. M. Dougan, *supra* n. 24, 102.

IV REVERSE DISCRIMINATION AND THE NEW STATUS OF UNION CITIZENSHIP: THE FIRST REACTIONS

Following the Paris summit in 1974, a 'citizenship rhetoric' had been in circulation in Europe as the next logical step in a successful economic union.[37] Nonetheless, as seen in the previous section, notwithstanding the fact that there had been attempts, since the late 1970s, to take the first steps towards the establishment of a citizenship status, the obdurate reluctance of the Member States, eager to protect their sovereignty and their public funds, allowed the development of a merely rudimentary form of citizenship. It was only at Maastricht that the Member States' governments agreed on the insertion of a new Part Two in the EC Treaty, which constitutionalized the status of Union citizenship for the first time.[38]

Part Two of the EC Treaty is comprised of six Articles. Article 17(1) EC (Article 20(1) TFEU) limits the availability of citizenship of the Union to Member State nationals[39] and makes it clear that Union citizenship is complementary to

---

37. E. Marias, 'From Market Citizen to Union Citizen', in *European Citizenship*, E. Marias (ed.) (Maastricht, EIPA, 1994), p. 1. For some early views on European citizenship *see* A. Evans, 'European Citizenship: A Novel Concept in EEC Law' (1984) 32 *AJCL* 679; A. Evans, 'European Citizenship' (1982) 45 *MLR* 497; A. Durand, 'European Citizenship' (1979) 4 *ELRev* 3; R. Plender, 'An incipient form of European Citizenship', in *European Law and the Individual*, F.G. Jacobs (ed.) (Amsterdam, North-Holland Publishing Company, 1976).
38. The introduction of the status of Union citizenship in the EC Treaty has sparked virulent debate among academic commentators. *See*, among others, D. Kostakopoulou, 'Ideas, Norms and European Citizenship: Explaining Institutional Change' (2005) 68 *MLR* 233; C. Barnard, *The Substantive Law of the EU: The Four Freedoms* (Oxford, OUP, 2004), Chapter 15; N. Reich, 'Union Citizenship – Metaphor or Source of Rights?' (2001) 7 *ELJ* 4; C. Lyons, 'The Limits of European Union Citizenship', in *The European Union and its Order: The Legal Theory of European Integration*, Z. Bańkowski and A. Scott (eds) (Oxford, Blackwell, 2000); C. Lyons, 'Citizenship in the Constitution of the European Union: rhetoric or reality?', in *Constitutionalism, Democracy and Sovereignty: American and European Perspectives*, R. Bellamy (ed.) (Aldershot, Avebury, 1996); D. O'Keeffe and M. Horspool, 'European Citizenship and the Free Movement of Persons' (1996) 31 *The Irish Jurist* 145; D. O'Keeffe, 'Reflections on European Union Citizenship' (1996) 49 *CLP* 347; H.U.J. d'Oliveira, 'European Citizenship: Its Meaning, Its Potential', in *Europe after Maastricht: An ever closer Union*, R. Dehousse (ed.) (Munich, Beck, 1994); D. O'Keeffe, 'Union Citizenship', in *Legal Issues of the Maastricht Treaty*, D. O'Keeffe and P. Twomey (eds) (London, Chancery/Wiley, 1994); C. Closa, 'The Concept of Citizenship in the Treaty on European Union' (1992) 29 *CMLRev* 1137. For some more theoretical discussions on Union citizenship *see* J. Shaw, 'The Interpretation of European Union Citizenship' (1998) 61 *MLR* 293; J.H.H. Weiler, 'To be a European Citizen: Eros and Civilization', in *The Constitutions of Europe*, J.H.H. Weiler (ed.) (Cambridge, Cambridge University Press, 1999).
39. It is well-established that the question of who is a Member State national remains for each Member State to decide. The Union, as such, has no competence whatsoever to grant its citizenship to any person. *See* to this effect the Declaration on Nationality of a Member State appended to the TEU. This is affirmed by Directive 2004/38/EC (*supra* n. 23), Art. 2(1). For case-law on the issue *see Micheletti v. Delegación del Gobierno en Cantabria*, Case No. C-369/90 [1992] ECR I-4239; *R v. Secretary of State for the Home Department, ex p. Kaur*, Case No. C-192/99 [2001] ECR I-1237. For an explanation of this *see* S. O'Leary, 'Nationality Law and Community Citizenship: A Tale of Two Uneasy Bedfellows' (1992) 12 *YEL* 353; C. Closa,

Member State citizenship. The second paragraph of that Article provides that citizens of the Union shall enjoy the rights conferred by the Treaty and shall be subject to the duties imposed thereby. Article 18 EC (Article 21 TFEU), which is the provision of this Part that has been most widely examined by the Court, provides in its first paragraph: 'Every citizen of the Union shall have the right to move and reside freely within the territory of the Member States, subject to the limitations and conditions laid down in this Treaty and by the measures adopted to give it effect'.

The subsequent provisions of Part Two (Articles 19-21 EC [Articles 22-24 TFEU]) provide for passive and active rights in local and European Parliament elections in the Member State of residence; a right to diplomatic protection in third countries where the Member State of nationality fails to do so; as well as rights to petition the European Parliament and apply to the Ombudsman. The Treaty of Amsterdam has also added the right to write to any of the listed Community institutions or bodies in one of the official Community languages and to receive a reply in that language.

It was not long after the introduction of this new status that a strong wave of criticism was levelled against it. For many, citizenship, as established in the EC Treaty, was nothing more than a consolidation of the existing *acquis*.[40] The rights of economically active Union citizens would continue to be protected under the fundamental freedoms provisions of the Treaty; and economically inactive (but self-sufficient) persons had already been covered by the three 1990 Residency Directives which included the limitations to which the Article 18 EC (Article 21 TFEU) right was – also – subject. Accordingly, there was a feeling that the new status of citizenship was nothing more than a glittering notion that was introduced to overshadow the much dreaded issue of democratic deficit in the EU.[41]

The Court, on its part, during the early years of existence of this new status had done little to disavow those initial criticisms, and its approach increasingly fuelled the negative discussions around the ability of the status of citizenship to solve the problem of lack of support of the EU by its citizens. In particular, until quite recently, it was well-established that the self-sufficiency requirements were still the conditions that had to be satisfied *before* a right to reside in the territory of another Member State could be derived from Article 18 EC (Article 21 TFEU), that is, it seemed that it was only economically active persons and economically inactive self-sufficient persons (i.e., direct and indirect contributors to the internal market) that could derive a right from EC law to move and reside in the territory of another Member State. In addition, the Court has shown a tendency of

'Citizenship of the Union and Nationality of Member States' (1995) 32 *CMLRev* 487; B. Kunoy, 'A Union of national citizens: the origins of the Court's lack of *avant-gardisme* in the *Chen* case' (2006) 43 *CMLRev* 179.

40. *See* N. Reich, *supra* n. 38; B. Wilkinson, 'Towards European Citizenship? Nationality, Discrimination and Free Movement of Workers in the European Union' (1995) 1 *EPL* 417.

41. C. Lyons, 'A Voyage around Article 8: An Historical and Comparative Evaluation of the Fate of European Union Citizenship' (1997) 17 *YEL* 135, 138.

examining and deciding cases based on the fundamental freedoms provisions of the Treaty, using the citizenship provisions only as a last resort thus attributing to them a merely residual status.[42] As a result of this tendency, it took the Court five whole years to decide its first case relying, exclusively, on one of the citizenship provisions,[43] thus leaving, until quite recently, the real potential of this new status unexplored.

The formal introduction of the status of Union citizenship by the Treaty of Maastricht also brought with it a question which is of much interest to the central theme of the book: whether the introduction of this new status has necessitated a change of approach towards the question of the permissibility of reverse discrimination.

This question firstly arose in *Uecker and Jacquet*,[44] where the third-country national wives of German nationals working in Germany, sought to rely on EC law, and in particular the free movement of workers provisions, to obtain employment rights in that country. The Court found that the situation of the applicants was purely internal to Germany as their husbands had not exercised their freedom to move and work in other Member States and, consequently, a right could not be derived from EC law.

Nonetheless, the question of whether the status of citizenship had affected the view that reverse discrimination is a permissible difference in treatment in EC law, could not be avoided by the ECJ this time. The national court, apparently being of the view that reverse discrimination is no longer appropriate in a Citizens' Europe, made a reference for a preliminary ruling to the ECJ asking, inter alia, whether

> [T]he fundamental principles of a Community moving towards European Union still permit a rule of national law which is incompatible with Community law because it is in breach of Article 48(2) [now 39(2)] of the Treaty to continue to be applied by a Member State against its own nationals and their spouses from non-member countries.[45]

The Court in reply to that question stated:

> In that regard, it must be noted that citizenship of the Union, established by Article [17] of the EC Treaty, is not intended to extend the scope ratione

42. *Criminal proceedings against Skanavi and Chryssanthakopoulos*, Case No. C-193/94 [1996] ECR I-929, para. 22; *Stöber and Pereira v. Bundesanstalt Für Arbeit*, Joined Cases C-4/95 and C-5/95 [1997] ECR I-511; *Criminal proceedings against Calfa*, Case No. C-348/96 [1999] ECR I-11, para. 30. This approach is, also, evident in some of the more recent cases of the Court, *see*, among others, *Ministre de l'Intérieur v. Oteiza Olazabal*, Case No. C-100/01 [2002] ECR I-10981, para. 26; *Stylianakis v. Elliniko Dimosio*, Case No. C-92/01 [2003] ECR I-1291, paras 18-20; *Office national de l'emploi v. Ioannidis*, Case No. C-258/04 [2005] ECR I-8275. For an explanation of this approach *see* H. Toner, 'Judicial Interpretation of European Union Citizenship: Transformation or Consolidation?' (2000) 7 *MJ* 158, 172-173.
43. This was *Martínez Sala v. Freistaat Bayern*, Case No. C-85/96 [1998] ECR I-269.
44. *Uecker & Jacquet v. Land Nordrhein-Westfalen*, Joined Cases C-64/96 and C-65/96 [1997] ECR I-3171 – annotated by D.M. Weber, (1998) 35 *CMLRev* 1437.
45. *Uecker & Jacquet, supra* n. 44, para. 22.

> materiae of the Treaty also to internal situations which have no link with Community law . . . Any discrimination which nationals of a Member State may suffer under the law of that State falls within the scope of that law and must therefore be dealt with within the framework of the internal legal system of that State.[46]

The Court has repeated the above pronouncement in its latest case-law.[47] Accordingly, the formal position of the Court is still that the introduction of the status of citizenship of the Union has had no effect, whatsoever, on the reverse discrimination conundrum. According to the Court, instances of reverse discrimination still fall outside the scope of EC law[48] and thus cannot be remedied at EC level. The Court has washed its hands of such cases and has nonchalantly pointed out that the solution to the problem of reverse discrimination – if it is indeed a problem – lies with national legislatures or courts.

V BROADENING THE SCOPE OF APPLICATION OF COMMUNITY LAW: THE COURT'S NEW AIM OF DEVELOPING A MEANINGFUL NOTION OF UNION CITIZENSHIP

A meaningful notion of citizenship is one which attaches to *all* citizens of a State a core of rights (human rights, political rights, as well as certain social rights), a minimum set of entitlements that are necessary in order to enable a citizen to develop as a human being in such a way as to be able, in his or her turn, to contribute to the development of the society of the State as a whole. Therefore, if the EU had been aiming, through the provisions on citizenship, to create a meaningful status of citizen of the Union, the above preconditions should also be satisfied, that is, a number of specific minimum rights should be made available to *all* Union citizens without making any *unjustifiable* distinctions.

Advocate General Ruiz-Jarabo Colomer in his Opinion in the *Shingara* case appears to have been of the view that, by constitutionalizing the status of citizenship of the Union, the drafters of the Maastricht Treaty were, indeed, aiming at

46. *Ibid.*, para. 23.
47. *See Garcia Avello v. État belge*, Case No. C-148/02 [2003] ECR I-11613, para. 26 (annotated by T. Ackermann, (2007) 44 *CMLRev* 141); *Schempp v. Finanzamt München*, Case No. C-403/03 [2005] ECR I-6421, para. 20; *Tas-Hagen and Tas v. Raadskamer WUBO van de Pensioen- en Uitkeringsraad*, Case No. C-192/05 [2006] ECR I-10451, para. 23; *Government of the French Community and Walloon Government v. Flemish Government*, Case No. C-212/06, judgment of 1 Apr. 2008, not yet reported, para. 39; *Nerkowska v. Zaklad Ubezpieczeń Spolecznych Oddzial w Koszalinie*, Case No. C-499/06, judgment of 22 May 2008, not yet reported, para. 25. For an explanation of the position of the Court concerning the effect of citizenship on purely internal situations *see* J.D. Mather, 'The Court of Justice and the Union Citizen' (2005) 11 *ELJ* 722, 733-735.
48. *Metock and Others v. Minister for Justice, Equality and Law Reform*, Case No. C-127/08, judgment of 25 Jul. 2008, not yet reported, paras 77-78.

creating a meaningful citizenship status, and not one which is attached to the economic aims of the Treaty:

> The creation of citizenship of the Union, with the corollary . . . of freedom of movement for citizens throughout the territory of the Member States, represents a considerable qualitative step forward in that . . . it separates that freedom from its functional or instrumental elements (the link with an economic activity or attainment of the internal market) and raises it to the level of a genuinely independent right inherent in the political status of the citizens of the Union.[49]

Towards the end of the 1990s it was made clear by the Court that all citizens of the Union have the right to move freely between the Member States, irrespective of whether or not they are involved in an inter-state economic activity.[50] In addition, it has been held that all Union citizens have the (directly effective) right to reside in the territory of any of the Member States;[51] and that this right would be deprived of all 'useful effect' if a number of supplementary rights, such as family reunification rights, were not granted.[52]

Nonetheless, until quite recently, one could not argue with certainty that the view of Advocate General Ruiz-Jarabo Colomer was not merely a utopia; in other words, that the Community, indeed, intended through the introduction of the citizenship provisions to create a meaningful status of Union citizenship. This was because, in interpreting the citizenship provisions of the EC Treaty the Court of Justice had not – until very recently – expressly and clearly made available any EC rights (including free movement rights), to persons that did not contribute to the construction of the internal market in any way. In other words, in the various cases that were decided by the Court in the area of citizenship, there was always some kind of economic element present, deriving either from the fact that the Union citizen who was held to be entitled to a number of rights was economically self-sufficient (and, as was explained before, this meant that he or she could actually indirectly contribute to the attainment of the internal market);[53] or, from the fact

49. Para. 34 of the Opinion of Advocate General Ruiz-Jarabo Colomer in *The Queen v. Secretary of State for the Home Department ex parte Shingara and Radiom*, Joined Cases C-65/95 and C-111/95 [1997] ECR I-3343.

50. *See Wijsenbeek, supra* n. 27, which involved the inter-state movement of a Dutch MEP from the Netherlands to Strasbourg in order to be present in a plenary session of the European Parliament, and then back to the Netherlands.

51. *Baumbast and R v. Secretary of State for the Home Department*, Case No. C-413/99 [2002] ECR I-7091; *Commission v. Belgium*, Case No. C-408/03 [2006] 2 CMLR 41, para. 34.

52. *See*, for example, *Zhu and Chen v. Secretary of State for the Home Department*, Case No. C-200/02 [2004] ECR I-9925, para. 45. For an annotation of *Chen see* J.Y. Carlier, (2005) 42 *CMLRev* 1121. Family reunification rights have been extended to economically inactive persons by the 1990 Directives (*see* Art. 1 of the Directives, *supra* n. 20-22) as well as by the new Directive 2004/38 (*supra* n. 23).

53. *See*, for example, *Chen supra* n. 52; *Baumbast, supra* n. 51; *Grzelczyk v. Centre public d'aide sociale d'Ottignies-Louvain-la-Neuve*, Case No. C-184/99 [2001] ECR I-6193.

that the claimant had a status (e.g., tourist) which meant that he or she was actually contributing in some indirect way to the internal market.[54]

In this part of the chapter, I shall aim to illustrate that the Court of Justice, through its latest case-law, has proved that the Community is no longer a supranational organization having as its only aim the construction of an internal market. In particular, it will be seen that the most important Union citizenship rights have been extended by the Court to situations where this was in no way necessary for enabling a person to contribute to the establishment of the internal market. According to More, 'with the aid of market actors, Community institutions, and national courts, the Court developed layers of individual rights, linked to the exercise of market activity. Recent developments show however how – forty years on – some of these rights have started to grow free of any identifiable market roots'.[55]

As a result of that, it appears that the Community no longer views Member State nationals solely as factors of production contributing to the process of opening-up national markets. The Court's latest case-law illustrates that the Community has, now, a new aim that is equally important with its economic aim of creating an internal market: the development of a meaningful status of Union citizenship.

The Court's case-law through which we can trace the development of a notion of citizenship which is entirely detached from any economic elements, concerns the right to move freely and reside in the territory of a Member State other than that of a person's nationality, as well as the principle of non-discrimination on the grounds of nationality. And it is to the analysis of this case-law that we now turn.

A The Court's Case-Law where Rights have been Granted to Union Citizens who have not Contributed, even Indirectly, to the Process of Establishing an Internal Market

The first significant step towards the direction of extending EC rights to persons that have not contributed, in any way, to the economic aims of the Treaty, was made in the landmark case of *Martínez Sala*.[56] The case involved a Spanish national who, since the age of 12 (since 1968), was resident in Germany. In 1993, Martínez Sala gave birth to a child and applied for a child-raising allowance. The German authorities rejected her application on the ground that she was not in possession of a residence permit as required by the German legislation – a

54. *See*, for example, *Criminal proceedings against Bickel and Franz*, Case No. C-274/96 [1998] ECR I-7637.
55. G. More, 'The principle of Equal Treatment: From Market Unifier to Fundamental Right?', in *The Evolution of EU Law*, P. Craig and G. de Búrca (eds) (Oxford, OUP, 1999), p. 521.
56. *Supra* n. 43. For commentaries on the case *see* C. Tomuschat, (2000) 37 *CMLRev* 449; S. O'Leary, 'Putting Flesh on the Bones of European Union Citizenship' (1999) 24 *ELRev* 68; S. Fries and J. Shaw, 'Citizenship of the Union: First Steps in the European Court of Justice' (1998) 4 *EPL* 533; G. Gori, 'Union citizenship and equal treatment: A way of improving Community educational rights?' (1999) 21 *JSWFL* 405; A. Albors-Llorens, 'A broader construction of the EC Treaty provisions on citizenship?' (1998) *CLJ* 461.

requirement that did not have to be satisfied by German nationals. The Court stated at the outset that, the fact that the requirement of holding a residence permit was applied only in the case of non-nationals, amounted to discrimination on the grounds of nationality which would be prohibited by Article 12 EC (Article 18 TFEU) if it fell within the scope of EC law.

Therefore, the main issue of the case was whether the situation of Martínez Sala fell within the scope of EC law. The Court firstly recalled that the child-raising allowance had already been found in its previous case-law to fall within the material scope of Community law. The Court then went on to rule that since Martínez Sala was a national of a Member State lawfully residing in the territory of another (by virtue of the law of the latter State), she came within the scope *ratione personae* of Community law and, in particular, Article 17 EC (Article 20 TFEU). Accordingly, Article 12 EC (Article 18 TFEU) applied and thus Germany had to grant the child-raising allowance to Martínez Sala under the same conditions that were imposed on German nationals.

The result of the case is, indeed, revolutionary. Secondary legislation in the area of the free movement of persons grants a number of rights to migrant workers, *in order to enable them to further the Treaty's economic aims*. Under a traditional reading of such pieces of Community legislation, the right to a child-raising allowance would be granted to migrant workers, under the same terms that would be applied when granted to nationals of the host Member State, *as this would enable the migrant worker to move to the host State to work and thus contribute to the construction of the internal market*. However, now we are told that a right that has traditionally been granted to migrant workers merely in order to encourage them to take part in the process of creating a common market is extended to all Union citizens who reside lawfully in a State other than their State of nationality. In other words, it appears that there needs to be no longer a link between the scope *ratione materiae* and the scope *ratione personae* of the Treaty, for the principle of non-discrimination on the grounds of nationality to apply.[57] Once a Member State national finds himself or herself (lawfully) in the territory of another Member State, he or she must be treated in the same way as nationals of that State irrespective of whether this furthers, in any way, the economic aims of the Treaty.[58]

---

57. It should be noted that after *Martínez Sala*, the Court took the further step of not even requiring that the benefit or right claimed falls within the material scope of EC law. This further step was acknowledged by Advocate General Kokott in her Opinion in *Tas-Hagen and Tas, supra* n. 47, para. 33: 'Union citizens can assert their right to free movement even if the matter concerned or the benefit claimed is not governed by Community law'. It seems, now, that the mere exercise of one of the fundamental freedoms or the right to move and reside freely under Art. 18 EC (Art. 21 TFEU) suffices for a situation to fall within the scope of EC law, even though the benefit claimed does not fall within the material scope of EC law. *See*, for example, *Garcia Avello, supra* n. 47; *Schempp, supra* n. 47; and *Pusa v. Osuuspankkien Keskinäinen Vakuutusyhtiö*, Case No. C-224/02 [2004] ECR I-5763.
58. For an explanation *see* H. Toner, *supra* n. 42, 176-180.

With hindsight and, in particular, applying the Court's reasoning in the case of *My*,[59] it can be argued with certainty that Martínez Sala was not a direct contributor to the internal market as, the fact that she had moved to Germany at the age of 12 and thus had spent her entire working life in the host State, meant that she was not a 'worker' within the meaning of Article 39 EC (Article 45 TFEU).[60] More importantly for our purposes, the facts of the case did not involve an indirect contribution to the internal market either, since the fact that Martínez Sala had had recourse to the German social assistance system meant,[61] precisely, that she was not economically self-sufficient within the meaning of the Residency Directives. Therefore, *Martínez Sala* has justifiably been considered to be a revolutionary case since the Court's judgment in that case made it emphatically clear that the right to be treated equally with the host Member State's nationals can be granted to a Union citizen who does not contribute, in any way, to the economic aims of the Treaty.[62]

Martínez Sala found unequivocal confirmation in the Court's subsequent case-law. And as will be seen, in its ensuing case-law the Court, going one step further, even held that the right derived from EC law to *reside* in the territory of another Member State is not only granted to economically self-sufficient persons (i.e., once and only if a person satisfies the self-sufficiency requirements) but is a right available to all Union citizens, irrespective of whether they contribute, either directly or indirectly, to the economic aims of the Treaty.

But before moving on with the case-law where the above developments took place, it would be useful to provide a brief explanation of the Court's traditional stance on the question of whether an economically inactive Union citizen derives from EC law the right to reside in the territory of another Member State. Under the provisions of the 1990 Residence Directives, the right of residence in the territory of another Member State had been granted only once and if the self-sufficiency requirements were satisfied. This meant that a person who had acquired a right to reside in another Member State under one of the Directives would *automatically* lose it if he or she had recourse to the social assistance system of the host Member State. Therefore, Community law has traditionally refused to extend residency

59. *My v. Office national des pensions*, Case No. C-293/03 [2004] ECR I-12013, paras 39-43. In its judgment the Court stressed that a Member State national who had moved to another Member State at the age of nine and thus *had spent his entire working life* in the host Member State, was in a situation purely internal to the host State and thus could not rely on the free movement of workers provisions.

60. Note that, in any event, Martínez Sala had not been in paid employment since 1989 and definitely up until the time of her application for the child-raising allowance in 1993. During that period, she received social assistance from the German authorities. *See* para. 13 of the judgment.

61. *See* the previous footnote.

62. C. Jacqueson, 'Union citizenship and the Court of Justice: something new under the sun? Towards social citizenship' (2002) 27 *ELRev* 260, 267 and 273. *See* also H. Toner, *supra* n. 42, 176-180; G. Davies, *Nationality Discrimination in the European Internal Market* (The Hague, Kluwer Law International, 2003), pp. 192-193; S. O'Leary, *supra* note 56, 77-78; C. Tomuschat, *supra* n. 56, 456-457; S. Fries and J. Shaw, *supra* n. 56, 539.

rights to Union citizens who were unable to contribute, either directly or indirectly, to the Community's aim of attaining the internal market.[63]

Nonetheless, the position seems to have changed during the last few years. An important catalyst to this direction has been the Court's pronouncement in *Baumbast*[64] that Article 18 EC (Article 21 TFEU) is a directly effective provision. This has been hugely important because Article 18 EC, as a directly effective provision, grants to *all* Union citizens a right to move and reside in the territory of another Member State.[65] In order for a citizen to take advantage of that right, he or she must no longer, *first*, prove that he or she satisfies the self-sufficiency requirements provided in secondary legislation. Those requirements are no longer exhaustive conditions to be satisfied *before* a right of residence is granted, but are limitations to this right, or more accurately, criteria to be used for determining whether a Member State can limit the right of residence granted by the Treaty to a Union citizen.[66] More significantly, the Court has held that, as limitations to a fundamental provision of the Treaty, the self-sufficiency requirements must now be interpreted restrictively and in accordance with the general principles of Community law, in particular, the principle of proportionality which requires Member States to take into account the particular situation of the person in question in making their assessment.[67]

Grzelczyk[68] – a case pre-dating the Court's pronouncement in *Baumbast* that Article 18 EC (Article 21 TFEU) is directly effective – was the first case which showed that the EC is moving to a new phase regarding the entitlement of indigents to a right to reside in the territory of another Member State. Grzelczyk was a French national who went to Belgium to study at University and applied, in the final year of his studies, for the minimex (a minimum subsistence allowance). His application was rejected on the ground that a non-Belgian would only be entitled to the minimex if he was a migrant worker. The Court found that a Belgian student in the same

63. For an explanation of the traditional application of the Residence Directives requirements in relation to social rights *see* S. O'Leary, *supra* n. 4, pp. 126-145.
64. *Supra* n. 51. This has been recently affirmed in *Commission v. Netherlands*, Case No. C-50/06 [2007] ECR I-4384, paras 32-33. For an explanation *see* P. Craig and G. de Búrca, *EU Law: Text, Cases and Materials* (4th edn, Oxford, OUP, 2008), pp. 850-855. For a view that Art. 18 EC (Art. 21 TFEU), as such, is not directly effective *see* paras 119-126 of the Opinion of Advocate General Mengozzi in *Minister voor Vreemdelingenzaken en Integratie v. Eind*, Case No. C-291/05, judgment of 11 Dec. 2007, not yet reported.
65. For further explanation *see* R.C.A. White, 'Free movement, equal treatment, and citizenship of the Union' (2005) 54 *ICLQ* 885, 888.
66. *See* M. Dougan, 'The Constitutional dimension to the case law on Union citizenship' (2006) 31 *ELRev* 613, 615.
67. For comments *see* M. Dougan and E. Spaventa, 'Educating Rudy and the (non-)English Patient: A double-bill on residency rights under Article 18 EC' (2003) 28 *ELRev* 699, 706. *See* also O. Golynker, 'Partial migration in the EU after the *Baumbast* case: bringing social and legal perspectives together' (2004) 15 *KCLJ* 367.
68. *Grzelczyk, supra* n. 53 – annotated by A. Iliopoulou and H. Toner, (2002) 39 *CMLRev* 609. *See* also D. Martin, 'A big Step forward for Union Citizens, but a Step Backwards for Legal Coherence' (2002) 4 *EJML* 136.

position as Mr Grzelczyk would be entitled to the minimex, without having to prove that he was a worker. Accordingly, there was clearly discrimination on the grounds of nationality.[69]

The Court, after recalling *Martínez Sala* according to which a national of a Member State *lawfully resident* in the territory of another Member State must be treated equally with that Member State's nationals, had to consider whether Mr Grzelczyk *continued* to be lawfully resident in Belgium, *notwithstanding the fact that he had had recourse to the social assistance system of the host Member State.* With regard to that issue, the Court repeated the well-established principle that a Member State may withdraw or refuse to extend the residence permit of an economically inactive person who has had recourse to its social assistance system.[70]

What, however, is important for our purposes is the fact that the Court has provided an 'audacious interpretation'[71] of the Student Residence Directive and, in paragraph 43 of its judgment, pointed out that the withdrawal and non-renewal of a residence permit by the host Member State, may in no case[72]

> [B]ecome the *automatic* consequence of a student who is a national of another Member State having recourse to the host Member State's social assistance system.

This, according to the Court, was because the Residence Directives accepted

> [A] certain degree of financial solidarity between nationals of a host Member State and nationals of other Member States, *particularly if the difficulties which a beneficiary of the right of residence encounters are temporary.*[73]

Therefore, the host State must not automatically remove the right of a Union citizen to reside within its territory but must consider the specific circumstances of the case and must only withdraw a residence permit when a national of another Member State imposes an *unreasonable* burden on its social assistance system.[74]

Hence, the Court concluded that a person in Mr Grzelczyk's position could maintain the right to reside in Belgium which he derived from EC law, even if he had had recourse to the social assistance system of that Member State. Going even further, the Court had no hesitation in holding that a person such as Mr Grzelczyk, who is lawfully resident in the territory of another Member State, is entitled to social assistance benefits under the same conditions as the nationals of the host State *for the period that he is considered to be lawfully resident in that State* (in other words, until he becomes an unreasonable burden on the social assistance system of that State). The refusal of the host State to grant the same social

69. *Grzelczyk, supra* n. 53, para. 29.
70. *Ibid.*, para. 42. This principle was also mentioned in *Trojani v. Centre public d'aide sociale de Bruxelles*, Case No. C-456/02 [2004] ECR I-7573, para. 45; *Bidar, infra*, n. 83, para. 47.
71. A. Iliopoulou and H. Toner, *supra* n. 68, 613.
72. *Grzelczyk, supra* n. 53, para. 43 (emphasis added).
73. *Ibid.*, para. 44 (emphasis added).
74. *Ibid.*, para. 44.

assistance benefits to nationals of other Member States who are lawfully resident in its territory, amounts to discrimination on the grounds of nationality and is contrary to Article 12 of the EC Treaty (Article 18 TFEU).

The specific facts of *Grzelczyk* involved the possibility that the applicant had been a person who had made some contribution, albeit indirect, to the completion of the internal market.[75] In addition, there was the issue that Grzelczyk was a student and since the wording of Directive 93/96 was slightly different, in some respects, from that of the other Residence Directives, the Court might have intended the effect of its judgment in that case to be confined to cases involving students.[76]

That *Grzelczyk* was not a case confined to its own specific facts but a case which established a general principle that would be endorsed by the Court in its subsequent rulings, was made clear in *Trojani*.[77] In that case the Court dealt, once again, with an application for the minimex, but this time not by a student but by a French national who moved to Belgium as an economically inactive person. What is important for our purposes is the fact that the Court in its judgment repeated the general principle established in *Grzelczyk* in a case which did not involve a university student:

> It should be added that it remains open to the host Member State to take the view that a national of another Member State who has recourse to social assistance no longer fulfils the conditions of his right of residence. In such a case the host Member State may, within the limits imposed by Community law, take a measure to remove him. *However, recourse to the social assistance system by a citizen of the Union may not automatically entail such a measure.*[78]

Therefore, in *Trojani* the Court made it clear that recourse to the social assistance system of the host Member State by an economically inactive Union citizen does not entitle that State, *automatically*, to refuse or withdraw the right of residence of that person. In that case the Court of Justice clarified that a Union citizen who does not in any way contribute to the completion of the internal market has a right to reside (at least temporarily) in the territory of another Member State.[79]

75. By being a part-time worker whose work had not been merely 'marginal and ancillary' as he was able to support himself for three years through his proceeds – *see* the Opinion of Advocate General Alber in *Grzelczyk, ibid.*; and by being a student in higher education in the host Member State.
76. *See* O. Golynker, *supra* n. 67, 385. For an explanation of why students present a smaller danger to the social assistance system of the host Member State *see Commission v. Italy*, Case No. C-424/98 [2000] ECR-4001, para. 45 and para. 28 of the Opinion of Advocate General Ruiz-Jarabo Colomer in that case.
77. *Trojani supra* n. 70. This was also more recently affirmed in an Art. 226 EC (Art. 258 TFEU) action brought by the Commission against Belgium – *see Commission v. Belgium (Breach of Community legislation on the right of residence of citizens of the Union)*, Case No. C-408/03 [2006] ECR I-2647, paras 67-69.
78. *Trojani, supra* n. 70, para. 45, emphasis added. *See*, also, *Commission v. Belgium, supra* n. 77, para. 45.
79. This is reflected in Art. 6(1) of Directive 2004/38, *supra* n. 23.

Furthermore, as long as a Union citizen continues to be entitled to reside in the territory of another Member State, Community law *requires* the host State to grant social assistance benefits to that person *under exactly the same conditions* as it grants them to its own nationals.[80] The broad reasoning adopted in *Grzelczyk* was not confined to the situation of students (who, after all, are indirect contributors to the internal market).[81]

It follows that in order for a person to be entitled to the rights of residence and non-discrimination in the territory of a Member State other than that of their nationality, that person needs no longer further, in any way, the Community's economic aims.[82] Nonetheless, the right to reside in the territory of another Member State and be treated equally in matters of social assistance with the host Member State's nationals seems to be quite limited, in that a person continues to be lawfully resident in the host State by virtue of EC law, only as long as he or she is not an *unreasonable* burden on the social assistance system of the host Member State. In that way, the Court has managed to balance the need, on the one hand, of Union citizens resident in another Member State to be treated equally with the host Member State's nationals, with the need, on the other, of Member States to maintain a viable social assistance system.

In the recent case of *Bidar*[83] the Court affirmed the main principle derived from *Grzelczyk* and *Trojani* whilst at the same time it provided a further refinement of that principle. In particular, the Court confirmed that Union citizens can retain the EC right to reside in the territory of the host Member State even though they have recourse to public funds, but only until they become an 'unreasonable' burden on the social assistance system of that State (i.e., this can only be a temporary situation); however, it was further explained that Union citizens who have established a 'link'[84] with the society of the host Member State by being integrated into

80. For an excellent explanation of this (albeit one provided before the Court's judgment in *Trojani*), *see* C. Jacqueson *supra* n. 62, 273-276.

81. The results of *Grzelczyk* and *Trojani* have been incorporated in Art. 14 of Directive 2004/38, *supra* n. 23.

82. N. Foster, 'Family and welfare rights in Europe: the impact of recent European Court of Justice decisions in the area of the free movement of persons' (2003) 25 *JSWFL* 291, 295.

83. *R (ex parte Bidar) v. London Borough of Ealing and Secretary of State for Education and Skills*, Case No. C-209/03 [2005] ECR I-2119 – annotated by C. Barnard, (2005) 42 *CMLRev* 1465. *See* also A. Tryfonidou, 'Redefining the notion of belonging in a Citizens' Europe: *The Queen (on the application of Dany Bidar) v. London Borough of Ealing & Secretary of State for Education and Skills*' (2005) 12 *IJEL* 217.

84. For the importance attached to a 'link' with the society of the State in which a benefit is claimed *see*, also, *D'Hoop v. Office national de l'emploi*, Case No. C-224/98 [2002] ECR I-6191, para. 38; *Collins v. Secretary of State for Work and Pensions*, Case No. C-138/02 [2004] ECR I-2703, para. 47; *Tas-Hagen, supra* n. 47, para. 34; *Geven v. Land Nordrhein-Westfalen*, Case No. C-213/05 [2007] ECR I-6347, paras 23-25; *Hartmann v. Freistaat Bayern*, Case No. C-212/05 [2007] ECR I-6303, paras 33-36; *Morgan v. Bezirksregierung Köln; Bucher v. Landrat des Kreises Düren*, Joined Cases C-11 and 12/06, judgment of 23 Oct. 2007, not yet reported, para. 43; paras 47-54 of the Opinion of Advocate General Kokott in *Wood v. Fonds de garantie des victims des actes de terrorisme et d'autres infractions*, Case No. C-164/07, judgment of 5 Jun. 2008, not yet reported.

that society (e.g., by living in that State for a number of years) cannot, under any circumstances, be considered to pose an unreasonable burden on the social assistance system of that State, even if their need to have recourse to public funds is not merely temporary.

Dany Bidar was a French national who, in 1998, moved to the United Kingdom to live with his grandmother and complete his secondary education. After three years of living in London, Bidar enrolled at University College London (UCL) in order to study Economics. He applied for a loan granted by the London Borough of Ealing to students of higher education, in order to enable them to cover their maintenance costs. The loan was made under very beneficial terms and thus could be seen as a form of social assistance. The London Borough of Ealing refused to grant the loan to Bidar, on the ground that he did not satisfy the requirement of being settled in England (i.e., three-year residence prior to application without, at that time, being a student of secondary education). Bidar claimed that the refusal amounted to a breach of EC law and the national court before which the case was brought, made a reference for a preliminary ruling to the ECJ.

The first issue that was examined by the Court was whether *Bidar* was lawfully resident in the territory of the United Kingdom. If yes, he would be entitled to the adjunct right of non-discrimination on the grounds of nationality in respect of social assistance benefits. In response to that issue, the Court held that

> [A] national of a Member State who, like the claimant in the main proceedings, lives in another Member State where he pursues and completes his secondary education, without it being objected that he does not have sufficient resources or sickness insurance, enjoys a right of residence on the basis of Article 18 EC and Directive 90/364.[85]

As regards the further question of whether Bidar had lost this right of residence by reason of the fact that he had had recourse to the social assistance system of the United Kingdom, the Court confined its reply to merely pointing out the following:

> In a context such as that of the main proceedings where the right of residence of the applicant for assistance is not contested, the assertion, made by some of the governments which have submitted observations, that Community law allows a Member State to take the view that a national of another Member State who has recourse to social assistance no longer fulfils the conditions of his right of residence and if appropriate to take measures, within the limits imposed by Community law, for the removal of that national . . . is moreover immaterial.[86]

It is true that Bidar, until the beginning of his university studies in 2001, was self-sufficient and never had recourse to the United Kingdom social assistance system. Accordingly, there was no issue of not satisfying the requirements of the 1990 Directives. Nevertheless, the fact that Bidar applied for a maintenance grant for his

---

85. *Bidar, supra* n. 83, para. 36.
86. *Ibid.*, para. 47.

university studies in 2001, points exactly to the fact that from that time onwards, he was no longer self-sufficient within the meaning of the Residence Directives, as he in fact did exactly what, under the Directives, removes the right of residence from a person: he had recourse to the social assistance system of a Member State. Yet, the Court does not seem to consider that that fact alone could suffice for depriving Bidar of his right to reside in the United Kingdom.

In its judgment, the Court seems to have accepted that a person in the position of Bidar, an economically inactive Union citizen, should be entitled to a right to reside in the host Member State under EC law, notwithstanding the fact that he does not satisfy the self-sufficiency requirements provided in secondary legislation. This is a pure confirmation of *Grzelczyk* and *Trojani*. In those cases, however, it was also highlighted that an economically inactive Union citizen can have recourse to the social assistance system of the host State only temporarily; if recourse to the social assistance system is prolonged, then the citizen becomes an unreasonable burden on that system and he or she loses the right of residence in the host State. Yet, in *Bidar*, the Court nowhere in its judgment mentioned the possibility that the claimant could at some point pose an unreasonable burden on the social assistance system of the host State. The fact that Bidar could demonstrate a sufficient degree of integration into the society of the host State (by being resident there for three years), seems to have made all the difference, since it is implicit in the Court's judgment that persons who can show a link with the host State can never be considered to pose an unreasonable burden on its public finances, even if their recourse to the social assistance system is not merely temporary.[87] Therefore, economically inactive citizens who are sufficiently integrated into the society of the host Member State can retain the EC right to reside in the host State and the latter cannot remove them from its territory even if they need to have recourse to its social assistance system on a long-term basis. Not only that but, again, in a circular manner, the host Member State is required by EC law to grant to those Union citizens social assistance under the same conditions that it makes it available to its own nationals.

The four cases analyzed above show that some of the most important citizenship rights (the right to reside in the territory of another Member State and the right to non-discrimination on the grounds of nationality), have been held to be available

87. *See* paras 56 and 57 of Bidar (*ibid.*): 'it is permissible for a Member State to ensure that the grant of social assistance benefits to nationals of other Member States does not become an unreasonable burden which could have consequences for the overall level of assistance which may be granted by that State' and thus, it is 'legitimate for a Member State to grant such assistance only to students who have demonstrated a certain degree of integration into the society of that State'. This is reflected, also, in the 2004 Directive which grants a permanent right of residence in the host State (which, should be highlighted, is not subject to any conditions including any self-sufficiency requirements) to Union citizens who complete 5 years of residence in the host State. *See* Art. 16 of Directive 2004/38, *supra* n. 23. *See*, also, F.G. Jacobs, 'Citizenship of the European Union – A Legal Analysis' (2007) 13 *ELJ* 591, 596.

to persons that in no way contribute to the economic aims of the Treaty that is, persons who neither fall within one of the categories of traditional economic actor nor are they capable of contributing, indirectly, to the internal market since they are not economically self-sufficient.[88]

The above analysis illustrates that the EC is no longer a supranational organization of purely economic aims. Some of the most important citizenship rights have been extended by the ECJ to Union citizens that have in no way contributed to the internal market.[89] Since the second half of the 1980s, the scope of EC law has been extended to cover a number of non-economic aims[90] and, following that trend, the Court of Justice in its case-law seems to have (implicitly) added to the Community's aims the creation of a meaningful status of citizenship through which Member State nationals are no longer merely seen as factors of production to be used in the process of attaining an internal market. Therefore, Union citizenship has at last become 'the fundamental status of nationals of the Member States',[91] this meaning that Member State nationals are first and foremost Union citizens, and thus that status is no longer, in practical terms, attached to Member State nationals only once and if a contribution to the internal market can be demonstrated.[92] According to Advocate General Mazák

> [T]he concept of Union citizenship, as developed by the case-law of the Court, marks a process of emancipation of Community rights from their economic paradigm.[93]

In the next, final, part of the chapter, it will be argued that this re-orientation of the Court's objectives, from a dominant narrow aim of constructing a common market, to the addition of a wider aim of developing a meaningful notion of citizenship of the Union, has important implications for the issue of reverse discrimination.[94]

---

88. *See* P. Craig and G. de Búrca, *supra* n. 64, pp. 858-866.
89. S. Besson and A. Utzinger, 'Introduction: Future Challenges of European Citizenship – Facing a Wide-Open Pandora's Box' (2007) 13 *ELJ* 573, 578-580.
90. N. Nic Shuibhne, 'Free movement of persons and the wholly internal rule: Time to move on?' (2002) 39 *CMLRev* 731. For some examples of case-law where it appears that the aims of the Community are no longer merely economic or strictly related to its internal market objectives *see Mangold v. Helm*, Case No. C-144/04 [2005] ECR I-9981, para. 75 (prohibition of age discrimination); *Bidar, supra* n. 83, paras 39-41 (education); *P v. S and Cornwall County Council*, Case No. C-13/94 [1996] ECR I-2143, paras 19-22 (principle of equality on the grounds of sex).
91. Para. 31 of *Grzelczyk, supra* n. 53.
92. For a view that the Community is no longer merely concerned with the free movement of factors of production and undistorted competition *see* E. Spaventa, 'From *Gebhard* to *Carpenter*: Towards a (non)-economic European Constitution' (2004) 41 *CMLRev* 743, 772.
93. Para. 54 of the Opinion of Advocate General Mazák in *Förster v. IB-Groep*, Case C-158/07, judgment of 18 November 2008, not yet reported.
94. *See* S. Besson and A. Utzinger, *supra* n. 89, 583; Editorial Comment: 'Two-speed European Citizenship? Can the Lisbon Treaty help close the gap?' (2008) 45 *CMLRev* 1, 3, 4 and 11.

VI IS REVERSE DISCRIMINATION, NOW, A FORM OF A DIFFERENCE IN TREATMENT PROHIBITED BY EC LAW?

The principle of equality is one of the general principles that must be respected in EC law and thus any situation that falls within the general scope of Community law must not involve a violation of that principle. The Court of Justice has embraced the Aristotelian notion of equality, according to which discrimination is defined as treating differently situations which are identical, or treating in the same way situations which are different. Accordingly, in order to decide whether reverse discrimination is a difference in treatment that is prohibited under EC law, we need to determine whether persons who are reversely discriminated against are in a similar position with persons who enjoy the protection of EC law; and, if yes, whether there is, indeed, differential treatment between these two categories of persons that is not justified.

Although an orthodox assessment of the question as to whether a difference in treatment violates the Community principle of equality would start by enquiring whether the situation under scrutiny falls within the scope of EC law, the complexities of reverse discrimination require us to approach the matter by following a reverse order. Consequently, we shall commence our enquiry by examining whether the two categories of persons that are differentiated as a result of the existence of reverse discrimination are similarly situated; once this is answered in the affirmative, we will move on with the question of whether this difference in treatment is justified;[95] and, finally, the more difficult task of determining whether reverse discrimination is a difference in treatment that now falls within the scope of EC law shall be undertaken.[96]

A Reverse Discrimination as a Difference in Treatment based on Whether a Person has Contributed to the Establishment of the Internal Market

The first preliminary issue that has to be clarified is on what ground this difference in treatment between Union citizens (i.e., reverse discrimination), is based. To that effect, it should simply be recalled that in Chapter 1 of the book, it was explained

95. *Eman and Sevinger v. College van burgemeester en wethouders van Den Haag*, Case No. C-300/04 [2006] ECR I-8055, para. 57; *Royal Scholten Honig v. IBAP*, Joined cases 103 and 145/77 [1978] ECR 2037, paras 26-27; *EARL de Kerlast v. Union régionale de coopératives agricoles (Unicopa) and Coopérative du Trieux*, Case No. C-15/95 [1997] ECR I-1961, para. 35.
96. It appears that the scope of application of the general principle of equality is somewhat broader than the scope of application of Art. 12 EC (Art. 18 TFEU), the former covering any difference in treatment that impedes the achievement of one of the objectives of the Treaty, whilst the latter prohibiting discrimination on the grounds of nationality 'within the scope of application of this Treaty' (para. 63 of the Opinion of Advocate General Poiares Maduro in *Carbonati Apuani Srl v. Comune di Carrara*, Case No. C-72/03 [2004] ECR I-8027).

that reverse discrimination is a difference in treatment based on the fact that a person has not contributed to the construction of the internal market: it is a difference in treatment which emerges as a result of the fact that the scope of EC law has traditionally been delimited in such as way as to include only persons that have contributed to the Community's aim of attaining an internal market. Therefore, reverse discrimination is a difference in treatment between two categories of persons: a) persons who can show a contribution to the internal market (the 'favoured' ones) and b) persons who are unable to point to any link with the internal market (the 'reversely discriminated' ones).

B ARE PERSONS WHO CAN SHOW A CONTRIBUTION TO THE INTERNAL MARKET AND PERSONS WHO ARE UNABLE TO SHOW SUCH A CONTRIBUTION, SIMILARLY SITUATED FOR THE PURPOSES OF COMMUNITY LAW?

Traditionally, the Community legal system did not consider persons who had contributed to the internal market by exercising one of the fundamental freedoms, to be similarly situated with persons who had not exercised an economic activity in an inter-state context. Since the way of delimiting the scope of application of the Community legal system was based on the need to ensure that EC law applies only to situations where this is necessary in order to enable the internal market to be established, the only persons that had a position in that system were those that were serving that objective.

However, this seems to be no longer the case. Through its latest case-law on citizenship, the Court has brought economically inactive persons to the same position with economically active ones as regards the bestowal of certain basic rights. This convergence is important for two reasons. Firstly, it confirms what was suggested in the previous section of the chapter: that the EC is, at last, entirely freed from its purely economic shackles and the creation of a meaningful status of citizenship appears to be one of the new, non-economic, aims of the Treaty. Secondly, the fact that economically active and economically inactive persons are treated in the same way shows that those persons are, now, considered to be similarly situated for the purposes of Community law.

The first right that has been extended to economically inactive persons is the right to non-discrimination on the grounds of nationality of persons lawfully resident in a Member State other than their State of nationality. In the context of the free movement of economically active persons, there has been, since the early years of the Community's existence, a strict prohibition of discrimination on the grounds of nationality.[97] More specifically, and as was seen in section III of the chapter, migrant workers and self-employed persons have always been entitled to be treated equally with the host State's nationals in respect of all matters falling

97. *See*, for example, *Commission v. France (Code de Travail Maritime)*, Case No. 167/73 [1974] ECR 359.

within the scope of EC law.[98] As explained in the previous section of the chapter, the Court in 1998 in *Martínez Sala* held that a *Union citizen* lawfully resident in the territory of another Member State (irrespective of whether or not he or she is involved in an inter-state economic activity) comes within the scope *ratione personae* of the provisions of the Treaty on Union citizenship and, by virtue of Article 17(2) EC (Article 20(2) TFEU), is entitled to the right provided under Article 12 EC (Article 18 TFEU) not to suffer discrimination on the grounds of nationality as regards matters falling within the material scope of the Treaty.[99]

Subsequently, the right of persons contributing to the internal market to be treated equally with nationals of the host State with respect to the availability of *certain* (non-burdensome) advantages was extended to all Union citizens who had exercised their freedom to move to another Member State, even for a limited period of time. In *Cowan*,[100] the Court held that a British tourist who was assaulted outside a metro station in Paris was entitled, by virtue of Article 49 EC (Article 56 TFEU) as a recipient of services, to financial compensation for his injuries under a French compensation scheme for victims of crime under the same conditions as French nationals. That the right to non-discrimination as regards the grant of certain advantages is also available to persons who do not contribute to the internal market was established, quite recently, in the case of *Bickel and Franz*,[101] where the Court held that the right of Union citizens to move freely to another Member State would be enhanced if they were granted, in equal terms with that State's nationals, the right of having their court proceedings conducted in their mother tongue.

Shortly after the case of *Bickel and Franz*, the Court in *Wijsenbeek*[102] extended the (broader) prohibition on the imposition of any obstacles to the free movement of persons, to cover the situation of all Union citizens irrespective of economic status.[103]

---

98. This right was enshrined in secondary legislation and the case-law of the Court – *see*, for example, *Württembergische Milchverwertung-Südmilch AG v. Salvatore Ugliola*, Case No. 15/69 [1969] ECR 363.
99. For an explanation of the convergence on the position of economically active and economically inactive Member State nationals, as regards the right not to be discriminated against in the host Member State *see* A.P. Van der Mei, *supra* n. 23, pp. 48-50.
100. *Cowan, supra* n. 6. For a very recent similar ruling, though one involving a Member State national who moved *permanently* to the host State and thus the free movement of workers and self-employed persons were relevant (i.e., Arts 39 and 43 EC [Arts 45 and 49 TFEU] – on the facts, it was not clear which of these mutually exclusive provisions was applicable since the referring court had not provided sufficient information) *see Wood, supra* n. 84.
101. *Bickel and Franz, supra* n. 54. It could be suggested that this case involved indirect contributors to the internal market since one of the claimants was a tourist and the other was employed in his Member State of origin as a lorry driver (and thus must have been economically self-sufficient). Nonetheless, the above specific circumstances do not seem to have weighed in the Court's judgment since its wording refers to 'Union citizens' in general.
102. *Supra* n. 27.
103. This prohibition entails, also, any restrictions imposed by the home State to the exit of a Union citizen from its territory – *see Ministerul Administratiei si Internelor – Directia Generală de Paşsapoarte Bucureşti v. Jipa*, Case No. C-33/07, judgment of 10 Jul. 2008, not yet reported,

However, what about the right to move and reside freely within the territory of another Member State? Is this, also, available to Union citizens who do not contribute to the economic aims of the Treaty, *in the same way* as it is available to persons involved in the construction of the internal market? Moreover, does this right entail, also, the same adjunct right to be granted social assistance benefits, in case the migrant citizen falls on hard times?

In the context of the fundamental freedoms, the Court had early on realized that for a Member State national to be able to exercise his or her right to move to another Member State in the process of exercising an economic activity, that person had to be granted a right of residence under the Treaty. Hence, the fundamental freedoms provisions were interpreted as granting to the worker the right to reside in the territory of the host Member State[104] since, otherwise, the move to another State in order to work permanently would not be practically feasible. We saw in the previous section of the chapter that very recently, the Court of Justice in the *Baumbast* case extended the availability of the right of residence to economically inactive Union citizens by making it clear that they have a directly effective right of residence in the territory of Member States other than that of their nationality – albeit one that is subject to limitations and conditions.

Yet, the convergence on the position between Union citizens who contribute to the internal market and Union citizens who do not, as regards the right to reside and receive social assistance in the host Member State, has only gradually been achieved, through the trilogy of cases that were analyzed in the previous section: *Grzelczyk, Trojani*, and *Bidar*.

Before explaining how the abovementioned convergence has been reached, a brief explanation of the requirements of EC law as regards the provision (or refusal) of social assistance by a Member State to migrant Member State nationals, should be provided. It is well-known that there are a number of areas of Member State competence which are considered particularly interlinked with their sovereignty and, accordingly, EC law applies only in a marginal way, by merely requiring that the exercise of Member State competence in those areas does not come into conflict with the aims of the Treaty.[105] One such area has traditionally been that of social security and welfare/social assistance benefits.[106] Member States are free to organize their social assistance systems in accordance with their traditions and priorities and, as a result of that, major differences have occurred between Member

para. 18. For an article examining the development of the application of a non-discriminatory, obstacles-based approach, to all Treaty provisions governing the right of Member State nationals (whether economically active or economically inactive) to move and reside within the territory of the Member States *see* H. Toner, 'Non-discriminatory Obstacles to the Exercise of Treaty Rights – Articles 39, 43, 49 and 18 EC' (2004) *YEL* 275.

104. *Royer*, Case No. 48/75 [1976] ECR 497, para. 31.
105. *See*, for instance, Art. 137 EC (Art. 153 TFEU) (social policy); Arts 149-150 EC (Arts 165-166 TFEU) (education); Art. 152 EC (Art. 168 TFEU) (public health).
106. *See* Art. 42 EC (Art. 48 TFEU) and Art. 137(1)(c) EC (Art. 153(1)(c) TFEU) read together with Art. 137(4) EC (Art. 153(4) TFEU). *See* A. P. Van der Mei, *supra* n. 23, pp. 61-67; C. Tomuschat, case-note on *Martínez Sala, supra* n. 56, 454.

States with regard to the benefits granted under those schemes.[107] On account of those divergences in social assistance provision and, more specifically, in order to avoid the danger of 'benefit tourism', the Member States have, since the early years of the Community's existence, considered that each State should be obliged to provide social assistance only to persons who have had strong links with it, persons who belonged to its society and thus had a sufficient degree of solidarity between them.[108]

In the case of migrant workers and the self-employed, the Court seems to have considered that strong links with the host Member State existed, since such persons had moved to the host State in order to work there permanently and make that State their new home. Therefore, the host Member State would become the State responsible to provide for them, in case they fell on hard times.[109] This was established in *Kempf*.[110] In that case, the Court of Justice held that a German music teacher who worked part-time in the Netherlands could still be considered a 'worker' within the meaning of Article 39 EC (Article 45 TFEU), despite the fact that his part-time work did not provide him with the minimum resources necessary for subsistence and as a result of that, had recourse to the social assistance system of the host Member State. The fact that despite his recourse to the social assistance system, he was still considered to be a 'worker' within the meaning of Article 39 EC, meant that the host State could not require him to leave its territory, save under the Treaty derogations provided in Article 39(3); and not only that but, in a circular manner, the host Member State would be obliged, under EC law, to provide him with the minimum means of subsistence for as long as he was in need.

It seems that the rationale behind the Court's 'liberal' approach in such cases is that Member State nationals who move to another Member State to work permanently, are sufficiently integrated into its society and have a sufficient degree of solidarity with the nationals of that State. A more practical argument which seems to have weighed in the Court's reasoning back in the 1980s is that, in the case of economically active persons, there is no danger of a heavy burden being imposed on the social assistance system of the host State, as in the great majority of cases migrant workers can provide for themselves through their remunerated activities – it is only exceptionally that Member State nationals who qualify as 'workers' within the meaning of Article 39 EC (Article 45 TFEU), will need to have recourse to public funds.[111]

---

107. For an explanation *see* S. O'Leary, *supra* n. 4, pp. 126-129.
108. For an explanation *see* M. Dougan and E. Spaventa, ' "Wish You Weren't Here..." New Models of Social Solidarity in the European Union', in *Social Welfare and EU Law*, E. Spaventa and M. Dougan (eds) (Oxford, Hart, 2005), pp. 184-187. For a detailed discussion of the notion of solidarity and its relationship with Union citizenship *see* A. Somek, 'Solidarity decomposed: being and time in European citizenship' (2007) 32 *ELRev* 787.
109. For further explanation *see* M. Dougan and E. Spaventa, *supra* n. 108, pp. 189-190.
110. *Supra* n. 9.
111. R.C.A. White, 'Residence, Benefit Entitlement and Community Law' (2005) 12 *JSSL* 10, 13; A.P. Van der Mei, *supra* n. 23, pp. 115 and 126.

We saw in the previous section of the chapter that the Court in *Bidar* ruled that economically inactive Union citizens who are sufficiently integrated into the society of the host State, can retain their EC right to reside within the territory of that State, even if they have recourse to social assistance, and even if this is not done only temporarily. Therefore, in the same way as in the context of migrant workers, now, the host State cannot remove from its territory economically inactive Union citizens who can show a link with that society, merely because they have recourse to social assistance. Similarly, and again like in the context of migrant workers, economically inactive Union citizens who are sufficiently integrated into the host State can apply for the grant of social assistance and – as seen in *Bidar* – this can be on a long-term basis since Union citizens who are deemed to belong to the society of the host State can never be considered to pose an unreasonable burden on the social assistance system of that State. Conversely, following the Court's judgments in *Grzelczyck* and *Trojani*, it appears that economically inactive Union citizens who cannot demonstrate a link with the society of the host State are only entitled to a limited number of social assistance benefits and merely for a limited period of time; and as soon as they impose an unreasonable burden on the social assistance system of the host State, the latter can require them to leave its territory.[112]

This differentiation concerning rights-entitlement, depending on a person's integration into the society of a Member State, is equally applicable in the case of economically active persons. This is reflected, for instance, in the recognition of only a semi-status of job-seekers, who have always been considered entitled to only a limited number of rights – including limited rights to social assistance – apparently because they are not integrated into the society of the host State;[113] as opposed to 'workers' who are considered to be entitled to a wide spectrum of social assistance benefits and for an unlimited duration (i.e., not only temporarily), due to

112. For an explanation of this distinction depending on the Union citizen's integration into the society of the host State *see* M. Dougan and E. Spaventa, *supra* n. 108; C. Barnard, *supra* n. 38, pp. 413-420; R.C.A. White, 'Citizenship of the Union, governance, and equality' (2006) 29 *Fordham Int'l LJ* 790, 806-811; C. Barnard, 'EU Citizenship and the principle of Solidarity', in *Social Welfare and EU Law*, E. Spaventa and M. Dougan (eds) (Oxford, Hart, 2005), pp. 165-175; C. Barnard, 'Of students and babies' (2005) 64 *CLJ* 560, 563; Y. Borgmann-Prebil, 'The rule of reason in European citizenship' (2008) 14 *ELJ* 328, 344.

113. S. O'Leary, 'The principle of Equal Treatment on grounds of nationality in Article 6 EC: A lucrative source of rights for Member State nationals?', in *The principle of Equal Treatment in EC law*, A. Dashwood and S. O'Leary (eds) (London, Sweet & Maxwell, 1997), p. 114. In *The Queen v. Immigration Appeal Tribunal, ex parte Antonissen*, Case No. C-292/89 [1991] ECR I-745 and *Centre public d'aide sociale de Courcelles v. Lebon*, Case No. 316/85 [1987] ECR 2811 the Court held that job-seekers are only entitled to be treated equally with the nationals of the host State as regards 'access' to employment. As regards the grant of social assistance benefits, the Court in *Collins supra* n. 84 (paras 26-33) went one step further and, relying on the citizenship provisions of the Treaty, noted that job-seekers (as Union citizens) are entitled to be treated equally with the nationals of the host State as regards the grant of social assistance benefits (such as a job-seeker's allowance), *however*, the host State is justified in limiting the availability of such benefits only to job-seekers who are 'habitually resident' in the host State and thus can show a sufficient link with the employment market of the host State. For an explanation *see* M. Dougan, *supra* n. 24, 93-100.

the fact that they are presumed to be integrated in the host State by virtue of their (intended) long-term residence there.[114]

Accordingly, the position with regards to the availability of social assistance benefits and the right of residence seems to be as follows: Union citizens (*whether economically active or not*) who are sufficiently integrated into the host State are entitled to have recourse to the social assistance system of the host Member State in the same way as nationals of that State, and the host State cannot rely on that fact alone in order to deprive them of their right of residence derived from EC law. Conversely, Union citizens (*whether economically active or not)* who are not sufficiently integrated into the society of the host State are only entitled to have recourse to the social assistance system of the host State for a limited period of time and the host State is entitled to remove them from its territory when they become an unreasonable burden on that system.[115]

Therefore, it appears that the exercise of a cross-border economic activity is not any more of any importance in the eyes of the Court when making EC rights available to Member State nationals. A Union citizen comes within the scope of EC law and is entitled to exactly the same rights, whether he exercises a cross-border economic activity or not. Accordingly, the question of whether there has been a contribution to the internal market is no longer important in deciding whether a right provided by EC law should be made available to a particular Union citizen.

The conclusion reached through the analysis followed in this part of the chapter (i.e., of a convergence on the position of economically active and economically inactive Union citizens) could even lead us to the argument that the situation that now exists, under which there are different Treaty provisions governing the position of Member State nationals (i.e., the fundamental freedoms provisions,

114. It should be noted that social advantages which do not seem to be particularly burdensome for the public finances of the Member States (*see* for example the rights in *Bickel and Franz, supra* n. 54 and *Cristini supra* n. 10) or which are not in any way connected with a notion of contribution on the part of the recipients (*see* for example *Cowan, supra* n. 6) should still be enjoyed by all Union citizens who are in the host Member State even temporarily. It is only with regard to some social assistance/social security benefits such as welfare benefits which have traditionally been considered as particularly burdensome for Member States or as implying a notion of prior contribution, that the notion of integration into the society of the host Member State comes into play before they can become available – *see Lenoir v. Caisse d'allocations familiales des Alpes-Maritimes*, Case No. 313/86 [1988] ECR 5391. For an explanation of this distinction *see* M. Dougan and E. Spaventa, *supra* n. 67, 709; G. Davies, 'The High Water Point of Free Movement of Persons: Ending Benefit Tourism and Rescuing Welfare' (2004) 26 *JSWFL* 211, 214-215; M. Dougan, *supra* n. 24, 122-125, 127. For an explanation of a similar distinction made in the United States *see* A.P. Van der Mei, *supra* note 23, pp. 99-105.

115. For an excellent explanation of the EC right of residence and entitlement to benefits in the territory of the host Member State *see* R.C.A. White, *supra* n. 111. *See* also G. Davies, 'Higher education, equal access, and residence conditions: Does EU Law allow Member States to charge higher fees to students not previously resident?' (2005) 12 *MJ* 227, 229-231; Ch. 3 ('Minimum subsistence benefits') of A.P. Van der Mei, *supra* n. 23; R.C.A. White, *supra* n. 65, 894-901. For a criticism of the Court's approach in these cases *see* K. Hailbronner, 'Union Citizenship and Access to social benefits' (2005) 42 *CMLRev* 1245.

on the one hand, and the citizenship provisions on the other) should no longer be maintained;[116] a vast topic which would appropriately form the basis of another extensive study and therefore will not be further discussed in this work.

C Is Reverse Discrimination a Justified difference in Treatment between Persons Similarly Situated?

In the previous subsection, we concluded that Union citizens who have contributed to the completion of the internal market and Union citizens who have not appear, now, to be considered similarly situated for the purposes of EC law. Therefore, it seems that, to a great extent, Community law no longer differentiates between Union citizens depending on whether they contribute to the internal market objectives of the Treaty. Reverse discrimination, however, comes as an antithesis of the above conclusion since it is exactly a difference in treatment concerning the availability of rights under EC law between persons that, on the one hand, have contributed to the internal market, and persons, on the other, that cannot point to such a contribution.

Thus, the question that must now be answered is whether reverse discrimination is a *justified* difference in treatment between Union citizens who are economically active in an inter-state context and Union citizens who do not fall within the scope of application of one of the fundamental freedoms.

According to Cannizzaro, 'Community measures necessary for the achievement of the objectives of the Treaty, may legitimately discriminate between individuals and establish a particular group characterized by the fact of being addressees of a special set of norms . . . the discrimination between beneficiaries of Community norms and individuals excluded from the treatment afforded by them must conform to a criterion of reasonableness implicit in the scope of the Treaty'.[117] Traditionally, this criterion of reasonableness has been the need to promote the economic aims of the Community, as a supranational organization of limited scope and defined *economic* aims, whilst respecting the sovereignty of the Member States. Accordingly, reverse discrimination could traditionally be considered a difference in treatment justified by the need to use a reasonable criterion in order to differentiate between persons falling within the scope of EC law and persons falling outside it.

However, having in mind the fact that Community law no longer includes within its scope *only* situations that further its core aim of constructing an internal

---

116. Davies has noted that 'there is currently a strong convergence of principles between all the areas of free movement and it would be quite feasible in the near future to do away with all categories of mover other than citizens' – *see* G. Davies, *supra* n. 114, 220; *see* also G. Davies, *supra* n. 62, Ch. 10. Davies has noted that specific, broader, rights for economic actors were 'indeed on their last legs' – G. Davies, *supra* n. 62, p. 195. *See*, also, S. O'Leary *supra* n. 4, pp. 66-67.
117. E. Cannizzaro, 'Producing "Reverse Discrimination" through the exercise of EC competences' (1997) 17 *YEL* 29, 41-42.

market but has granted its protection to Union citizens by virtue of the fact that they are migrant Union citizens (and not as a result of their contribution to its economic aims), it is really questionable whether a difference in treatment between Union citizens, depending on whether they have contributed to the completion of the internal market, is still justified by the need of Community law to delimit its scope in such a way as to include only situations that further its aims.

In light of the fact that the Court in its case-law has extended the scope of EC law to include persons that have not contributed at all to the construction of the internal market and thus its scope, in respect of certain rights, has been extended in such a way as to include economically inactive persons, there seems to be no point in maintaining a difference in treatment between economically inactive and economically active persons, with regard to other rights that the Court has not yet had the opportunity to rule on their extension to the former. The delimitation of the scope of EC law in such a way as to include only persons contributing to the internal market appears to be no longer *reasonable*. Accordingly, and unless justified on a ground other than the need to confine the scope of EC law to situations that further the Community's aims, reverse discrimination is no longer a justified difference in treatment and thus should no longer be permissible in the EC legal system.[118]

Therefore, the next question that has to be answered is whether unjustified instances of reverse discrimination can now fall within the scope of EC law.

D Is Reverse Discrimination a form of Discrimination Prohibited by EC Law?

In order to reach a conclusion on this issue, I will firstly explain how the delimitation of the scope of the principles of equality and non-discrimination has been affected by the metamorphosis of the Community, from an organization of purely economic aims to one which values its citizens *qua* citizens and aims at creating a meaningful status of Union citizen. Based on the conclusions of that analysis, I will thereafter examine whether reverse discrimination is, now, a violation of the principle of non-discrimination as protected in the context of Community law.

1 The Development of the Scope of the Community Principles of Equality and Non-discrimination on the Grounds of Nationality

It is well-known that since the early 1970s, an unwritten bill of rights has been read by the Court of Justice into Community law and, according to Mancini, this is

118. *See* also N. Nic Shuibhne, 'The European Union and Fundamental Rights: Well in Spirit but Considerably Rumpled in Body?', in *Convergence and Divergence in European Public Law*, P. Beaumont, C. Lyons and N. Walker (eds) (Oxford, Hart, 2002), p. 188; R.C.A. White, 'A fresh look at reverse discrimination?' (1993) 18 *ELRev* 527, 532.

'indeed the most striking contribution the Court has made to the development of a constitution for Europe'.[119] And yet, this bill of rights has not gone far enough as a bastion of the human rights of Member State nationals. In particular, it only applies to situations which fall within the (traditionally drawn) scope of EC law that is, where there is an effect on the *economic* aims of the Treaty.[120] Indeed, it is not entirely coincidental that it is by and large the economic rights of Member State nationals that have been protected in the case-law of the Court,[121] and not the usual civil rights which form the major part of the European Court of Human Rights' 'daily diet'. To this it is certainly necessary to add that even in cases where the protection of human rights has been used in the Court's reasoning, this has only been done instrumentally,[122] in order to enable a Member State national to exercise a right which in some way furthers the economic objectives of the Treaty.[123]

119. F. Mancini, *supra* n. 7, 611. For literature dealing with the development of human rights protection in the EU *see* F.G. Jacobs, 'Human rights in the European Union: the role of the Court of Justice' (2001) 26 *ELRev* 331; N. Neuwahl, 'The Treaty on European Union: A Step Forward in the Protection of Human Rights?', in *The European Union and Human Rights*, N. A. Neuwahl and A. Rosas (eds) (The Hague, Kluwer Law International, 1995); K. Lenaerts, 'Respect for fundamental rights as a constitutional principle of the European Union' (2000) 6 *CJEL* 1; A. Von Bogdandy, 'The European Union as a human rights organization? Human rights and the core of the European Union' (2000) 37 *CMLRev* 1307; K. Lenaerts, 'Fundamental Rights in the European Union' (2000) 25 *ELRev* 575; B. de Witte, 'The Past and Future Role of the European Court of Justice in the Protection of Human Rights', in *The EU and Human Rights*, P. Alston (ed.) (Oxford, OUP, 1999).

120. *See Demirel v. Stadt Schwäbisch Gmünd*, Case No. 12/86 [1987] ECR 3719, para. 28; *The Society for the Protection of Unborn Children Ireland Ltd v. Grogan*, Case No. C-159/90 [1991] ECR I-4685, paras 30-31; *Vereinigte Familiapress Zeitungsverlags-und vertriebs GmbH v. Heinrich Bauer Verlag*, Case No. C-368/95 [1997] ECR I-3689; *ERT v. Dimotiki Etairia Pliroforissis and others*, Case No. C-260/89 [1991] ECR I-2925; *Wachauf v. Germany*, Case No. 5/88 [1989] ECR 2609. According to O'Leary, 'In an ideal world the protection of fundamental rights and citizenship rights would be inspired by the objective of protecting the individual. However, the Community's protection of fundamental rights is complicated by the fact that there are still limits on when it may substitute the competence of Member States in this field, given that the transfer of competences between them is "within limited fields" ' – *see* S. O'Leary, 'The Relationship between Community Citizenship and the Protection of Fundamental Rights in Community Law' (1995) 32 *CMLRev* 519, 535.

121. *Hauer v. Land Rheinland-Pfalz*, Case No. 44/79 [1979] ECR 3727; *Nold KG v. Commission*, Case No. 4/73 [1974] ECR 491; *International Handelsgesellschaft mbH v. Einfuhr- und Vorratsstelle für Getreide und Futtermittel*, Case No. 11/70 [1970] ECR 1125.

122. J. Coppel and A. O'Neill, 'The European Court of Justice: taking rights seriously?' (1992) 12 *LS* 227. For a different view and a critique of the views of Coppel and O'Neill *see* J.H.H. Weiler and N.J.S. Lockhart, ' "Taking rights seriously" seriously: the European Court and its fundamental rights jurisprudence – Part I' (1995) 32 *CMLRev* 51 and J.H.H. Weiler and N.J.S. Lockhart, ' "Taking rights seriously" seriously: the European Court and its fundamental rights jurisprudence – Part II' (1995) 32 *CMLRev* 579.

123. It seems that the fact that the Charter of Fundamental Rights of the European Union, OJ C 303/1, 2007, will become binding once the Treaty of Lisbon comes into force (*see* Art. 6(1) TEU, as amended by the Lisbon Treaty), will not change this position. Art. 51 of the Charter merely implements the case-law of the Court as regards the scope of application of EC human rights protection. In fact, the Charter may even have a more limited scope of application than the current scope of application of the EC human rights protection, as developed by the Court.

That human rights have traditionally been protected under EC law only in furtherance of its economic aims – and, in particular, mainly as part of the overall construction of a common market – is also evident from the fact that the purely internal rule has been held to apply even when persons have sought to rely on the fundamental rights protected under EC law. It has been well-established, therefore, that Member State nationals can only rely on the human rights protected under EC law if they have moved to another Member State and this move has contributed to the aims of the Treaty.[124] In the case of *Kremzow*,[125] the Court held that it had no jurisdiction to give interpretative guidance to the national court to determine whether the national legislation in question was in conformity with the fundamental rights protected under EC law, because the facts from which the question referred arose were purely internal to Austria.

Since the early years of the Community's existence, the principle of equality has been considered to be one of the general principles of Community law.[126] Nonetheless, like the fundamental rights protected under Community law, this principle has been traditionally protected only as long as this was necessary in order to further the economic aims of the EC Treaty. Therefore, the purely internal rule has also been applied when delimiting the scope of this principle.[127] The basis of the principle was, accordingly, an economic one.[128] As a result of that, a Member State national could, until very recently, only rely on the right to be treated equally with other persons similarly situated, where this would further one of the economic aims of the Treaty.[129] Since the core aim of the Community was, until recently, the construction of the internal market, any difference in treatment not

For a discussion of this possibility *see* A. Tryfonidou, 'Family reunification rights of (migrant) Union citizens: Towards a liberal approach' (2009) 15 *ELJ* (forthcoming).

124. A.G. Toth, *supra* n. 33, pp. 497-499; H.U.J. d'Oliveira, 'Is Reverse discrimination still permissible under the Single European Act?', in *Forty years on: The Evolution of Postwar Private International Law in Europe: symposium in celebration of the 40th anniversary of the Centre of Foreign Law and Private International Law, University of Amsterdam, on 27 October 1998* (The Hague, Kluwer Law International, 1990), pp. 81-82.
125. *Kremzow v. Republic Österreich*, Case No. C-299/95 [1997] ECR I-2629. For a more recent case confirming this *see Criminal proceedings against Vajnai*, Case No. C-328/04 [2005] ECR I-8577, paras 12-13.
126. *Ruckdeschel & Diamalt*, Joined Cases 117/76 and 16/77 [1977] ECR 1769, para. 7; *Allué and Coonan v. Università degli studi di Venezia*, Case No. 33/88 [1989] ECR 1591, para. 11. For an explanation of the Community principle of equality *see* T. Tridimas, 'The application of the Principle of Equality to Community Measures' and G. de Búrca, 'The Role of Equality in European Community Law', in *The Principle of Equal Treatment in EC law*, A. Dashwood and S. O'Leary (eds) (London, Sweet and Maxwell, 1997).
127. A. Lengauer, 'The New General Principle of Non-Discrimination in the EC Treaty as Amended by the Treaty of Amsterdam' (1998) 3 *ARIEL* 369, 382; M. Poiares Maduro, 'Striking the Elusive Balance Between Economic Freedom and Social Rights in the EU', in *The EU and Human Rights*, P. Alston (ed.) (Oxford, OUP, 1999), pp. 455-456; R.C.A. White, *Workers, Establishment and Services in the European Union* (Oxford, OUP, 2004), p. 58.
128. *See* J. Steiner *supra* n. 12, p. 40.
129. G. Barrett, 'Re-examining the Concept and Principle of Equality in EC Law' (2003) 22 *YEL* 117, 136-144.

impeding the above objective was considered to fall outside the scope of EC law and, thus, Member State nationals who remained confined within their own Member State and did not contribute in any way to the establishment of the internal market were unable to rely on the Community principle of equality.

However, the introduction of the status of Union citizenship seems to have created a new impetus for the extension of the scope of application of EC fundamental rights protection[130] and, in particular, the right to equality and non-discrimination on the grounds of nationality since it 'raises the expectation that citizens of the Union will enjoy equality, at least before Community law'.[131] This is reflected in the Court's latest case-law on citizenship, since the Court has 'cleansed' the right of Union citizens to be treated equally with the nationals of the host Member State, from any requirement as to a contribution to the economic aims of the Treaty.[132] As we saw in the previous section of the chapter, the principle of

---

130. Eeckhout has pointed out that the concept of EU citizenship, and its underlying rationale, will form a major force behind the conferral of fundamental rights on the moving European citizen. However, he very rightly goes one step further in his analysis and argues that if fundamental rights are conferred on the moving European citizen (i.e., any Member State national moving between Member States for whatever reason) then this, undoubtedly, will lead to the further question of the differentiation with regard to fundamental rights protection between moving European citizens and those who stay still: 'Why should only my neighbour, who happens to come from another Member State, have these rights and, perhaps more importantly, be able to set in motion the full European law machinery of direct effect, supremacy and preliminary reference so as to enforce them?'. Nonetheless, he made clear that since the EU cannot become a general human rights organization, some new way of delimiting the scope of fundamental rights protection granted by EU law should be found. *See* P. Eeckhout, 'The EU Charter of Fundamental Rights and the Federal Question' (2002) 39 *CMLRev* 945, 972. For a critique concerning the application of the traditional 'purely internal rule' to the fundamental rights protection granted by EC law *see* N. Nic Shuibhne, *supra* n. 118. Note, however, that the Court of Justice (implicitly) in one of its quite recent judgments did not follow its well-established principle that EC law requires Member States to respect fundamental (human) rights only when a situation falls within the scope of EC law. *See Secretary of State for the Home Department v. Akrich*, Case No. C-109/01 [2003] ECR 9607, para. 58. For comments on this *see* C. Schiltz, '*Akrich*: A Clear delimitation without limits' (2005) 12 *MJ* 241, 249-251. *See* also *Karner Industrie-Auktionen GmbH v. Troostwijk GmbH*, Case No. C-71/02 [2004] ECR I-3025 which, for this reason, has been characterized by Oliver and Enchelmaier as an anomaly (P. Oliver and S. Enchelmaier, 'Free movement of goods: Recent developments in the case law' (2007) 44 *CMLRev* 649, 660). For an argument that the Court of Justice in some of its case-law has decoupled human rights protection from the need to show a link with one of the economic aims of the Treaty *see* P. Craig and G. de Búrca, *EU Law: Text, Cases and Materials* (3rd edn, Oxford, OUP, 2003), pp. 364-365.
131. *See* para. 53 of the Opinion of Advocate General Jacobs in *Faccini Dori v. Recreb Srl*, Case No. C-91/92 [1994] ECR I-3325. Francis Jacobs, writing extra-judicially, has noted that the concept of citizenship might be deployed in the future so as to prohibit reverse discrimination – *see* F.G. Jacobs, *supra* n. 87, 598. *See* also G. Davies, 'Services, Citizenship and the Country of Origin Principle', *Mitchell Working Paper Series* 2/2007, available at <www.law.ed.ac.uk/file_download/series/29_servicescitizenshipandthecountryoforiginprinciple.pdf> (accessed on 8 Aug. 2008), 2.
132. For a very good explanation *see* R.C.A. White, 'The Citizen's Right to Free Movement' (2005) *EBLRev* 547, 552-555.

non-discrimination on the grounds of nationality has, already, been used in order to require Member States to grant the same treatment to nationals of other Member States residing in their territory, even where those migrant Union citizens were not contributing, either directly or indirectly, to the attainment of an internal market.[133] Reflecting on these developments, Mark Bell has rightly observed that 'the right to non-discrimination on grounds of EU nationality seems to be in a process of transition from a free movement right to a fundamental right'.[134]

Yet, this should not be taken to mean that the Community legal system now includes a general principle of equality *which applies in all circumstances*. The EC is, and will always be, a supranational organization of limited scope and aims and, accordingly, its general principles and rules should only apply to situations that fall within its scope. Therefore, reverse discrimination will be able to fall within the scope of the Community principle of equality only if it conflicts with one of the (broader) aims of the Community and thus comes within the general scope of EC law.

2 Is Reverse Discrimination a Violation of the Community Principle of Equality?

In the context of an organization of purely economic aims which viewed individuals merely as factors of production, it was not at all surprising that fundamental human rights and, more specifically, the principle of equality, were principally considered as tools for assisting the completion of the internal market and thus were available only to persons who contributed to that aim. And, going one step further, the fact that the principle of equality applied only in order to further the Community's economic aims and not so as to grant to all Union citizens, as human beings, a right to be treated equally with other Union citizens similarly situated, meant that reverse discrimination (being, exactly, a difference in treatment justified by the fact that some persons had not contributed to the aims of the Treaty) was not a violation of the fundamental principle of equality.[135] It was a difference in treatment which not only was justified by the fact that the Community was an economic organization of limited scope,[136] but also, a difference in treatment which could not be assessed for its compatibility with the Community principle of equality.

Nonetheless, as has been illustrated through the preceding analysis in this chapter, the latest cases on citizenship show that the Community is no longer

---

133. *See Martínez Sala, supra* n. 43; *Bidar, supra* n. 83; *Trojani, supra* n. 70.
134. M. Bell, *Anti-Discrimination Law and the European Union* (Oxford, OUP, 2002), p. 39.
135. According to G. de Búrca (*supra* n. 126, at p. 16), 'The fact that reverse discrimination is permissible can be explained if the rationale of the equal treatment requirement is, as it certainly has been interpreted in the past, to promote mobility, by removing hindrances to the free movement of workers from one Member State in coming to another Member State to work'.
136. *See* A. Evans, 'Union Citizenship and the Equality principle', in *A Citizens' Europe: In search of a new order*, A. Rosas and E. Antola (eds) (London, Sage, 1995), p. 95.

a supranational organization of purely economic objectives. As de Búrca has noted, '[t]he creation of a European common market is no longer the dominant constitutional core of the EU but stands alongside a commitment to a range of fundamental values which transcend purely market goals'.[137]

According to Advocate General Poiares Maduro in his Opinion in the *Carbonati Apuani* case,[138] one of the main aims of the Community, now, is that no discrimination of any kind should arise as a result of 'the application of its own rules'. This, according to the Advocate General, means that reverse discrimination now falls within the scope of EC law since it is a 'residual' situation from the point of view of Community law due to the fact that it emerges as a result of the application of EC law only to situations that further its economic aims.[139] A very similar position was recently advocated by Advocate General Sharpston in the *Flemish Government care insurance scheme* case.[140]

The fact that the Court may be sharing the view of the Advocates General above, becomes apparent from a careful reading of the ECJ's latest case-law on citizenship. In that case-law, it can be seen that Articles 17 and 18 EC (Articles 20 and 21 TFEU, respectively) only govern the situation of Union citizens who have exercised their right to move from one Member State to another,[141] or, more broadly, the situation of Union citizens who can point to a link with more than one Member State (e.g., by possessing the nationality of one Member State whilst being present in the territory of another) even though physical inter-state movement may have not been exercised.[142] In fact, both of the above requirements have

137. G. de Búrca, 'Human Rights: The Charter and Beyond' Jean Monnet Working Paper 10/01, at p. 7 available at <www.jeanmonnetprogram.org/papers/01/013601.rtf> (accessed on 8 Apr. 2008).
138. *Carbonati Apuani, supra* n. 96.
139. *See* paras 62-63 of the Opinion of Advocate General Poiares Maduro in *Carbonati Apuani, ibid.* According to Davies, 'Free movement is already having significant non-economic impacts, and as it affects welfare, family rights, and economic actors that are citizens rather than corporations, it can no longer be treated as exclusively economic policy. As occurs in domestic law-making and interpretation, economic rules must take account of their wider impact, and sometimes concede precedence to other, higher, norms.' – *see* G. Davies, *supra* n. 131, 20.
140. *See* paras 151-154 of the Opinion of Advocate General Sharpston in *Government of the French Community and Walloon Government v. Flemish Government, supra* n. 47.
141. *See Wijsenbeek, supra* n. 27, paras 18-23 and more recently, para. 46 of the Opinion of Advocate General Stix-Hackl in *Lyyski v. Universität Umeå*, Case No. C-40/05 [2007] ECR I-99. For some criticisms of this requirement *see* the Opinion of Advocate General in *Bickel and Franz, supra* n. 54 (in particular para. 23); N. Nic Shuibhne, *supra* n. 90, 757; H. Toner, *supra* n. 42, 170 and J.D. Mather, *supra* n. 47, 735, 739-740; P.J. Slot and M.K. Bulterman, 'Harmonization of legislation on migrating EU citizens and third country nationals: Towards a uniform evaluation framework?' (2006) 29 *Fordham Int'l LJ* 747, 758-759; J. Steiner, L. Woods and C. Twigg-Flesner, *EU Law* (9th edn, Oxford, OUP, 2006), pp. 512-513.
142. *Chen, supra* n. 52, para. 19 and *Garcia Avello, supra* n. 47, paras 26-28. Note that it appears from the Court's judgments in *Collins* (*supra* n. 84), *Chen* and *Garcia Avello* that *physical inter-state movement* is no longer necessary in order for a situation to fall within the scope of Art. 39 EC (Art. 45 TFEU) as well. For an explanation of this approach *see* P. Craig and G. de

been strenuously criticized by commentators for giving rise to reverse discrimination in situations which involve a Union citizen that does not satisfy either of them, without this difference in treatment being in any way justified (as used to be the case, until quite recently, with reverse discrimination arising as a result of the limited scope of the fundamental freedoms). And although a cursory reading of the Court's citizenship judgments where the need for a link with EC law in citizenship cases has been discussed, may give the impression that the *main* aim of *all* the citizenship provisions (i.e., not only Article 18 EC [Article 21 TFEU]) is to encourage Union citizens to move between Member States, nevertheless, I find it difficult to go along with this idea and I would like to suggest a different, more intellectually rigorous reading of the Court's judgments.

In my view, the fact that in its case-law on citizenship, the Court has extended the application of EC law to cover any difference in treatment suffered by a Union citizen who has exercised his or her free movement rights under Article 18 EC (Article 21 TFEU) or can point to a link with more than one Member State, can be explained by the fact that the Court has actually been striving to ensure that no discrimination between Union citizens arises as a consequence of them having taken part in the process of European integration under the rules of the Treaty. The fact that the encouragement of pure movement (i.e., not for an economic purpose) of Union citizens between Member States is not the *only* new aim of the Community, is, after all, immediately obvious from the fact that situations which do not involve *physical* movement from one Member State to another, are included within

Búrca, *supra* n. 64, pp. 855-858. For a criticism of this broader approach *see* A. Tryfonidou, '*Kunqian Catherine Zhu and Man Lavette Chen v. Secretary of State for the Home Department*: Further cracks in the "Great Wall" of the European Union?' (2005) 11 *EPL* 527, 536-541; B. Hofstotter, 'A cascade of rights, or who shall care for little Catherine? Some reflections on the Chen case' (2005) 30 *ELRev* 548, 551-553; A. Epiney, 'The Scope of Article 12 EC: Some Remarks on the Influence of European Citizenship' (2007) 13 *ELJ* 611, 616-617. This approach seems to have been accepted by the United Kingdom Court of Appeal in *W (China) and another v. Secretary of State for the Home Department*, [2006] All ER (D) 97 (Nov). For even more overreaching approaches *see Schempp, supra* n. 47 (paras 22-25), where the situation was found to fall within the scope of EC law even though the person relying on EC law and, in particular, on Art. 12 EC (Art. 18 TFEU), had not made use of his right of free movement provided in Art. 18 EC (Art. 21 TFEU) – the link with EC law was that the claimant paid maintenance to his ex-wife who was *resident in another Member State* and, because of that cross-border element, he was unable to deduct the maintenance sum from his taxable income (*see* also paras 14-15 of Advocate General Geelhoed in that case). And the Opinion of Advocate General Ruiz-Jarabo Colomer in *Baldinger v. Pensionsversicherungsanstalt der Arbeiter*, Case No. C-386/02 [2004] ECR I-8411. Advocate General Sharpston in para. 144 of her Opinion in *Government of the French Community and Walloon Government v. Flemish Government, supra* n. 47, pointed out that 'the Court would . . . have to decide whether on a proper construction, the "right to move and reside freely within the territory of the Member States" in Article 18 EC means "freedom to move and *then* reside" (i.e., freedom to reside derives from/flows from prior exercise of the freedom to move) or whether it means "freedom *both* to move *and* to reside" (so that it is possible to exercise the freedom to reside/go on residing without first exercising the freedom to move between Member States)'.

the scope of EC law.[143] Therefore, adopting the words of Advocate General Poiares Maduro in an Opinion delivered in 2008,[144] the principle of equality

> [I]s no longer merely an instrument at the service of freedom of movement; it is at the heart of the concept of European citizenship.

Accordingly, in its case-law on citizenship, the Court firstly ruled that the citizenship provisions prohibit discrimination on the grounds of nationality exercised by the host Member State against nationals of other Member States who are present (either temporarily or permanently) in its territory.[145] This can be explained as part of the Court's aim of remedying any instances of discrimination arising as a result of the exercise of a right granted by EC law (in those cases, the right to move and reside freely in the territory of the host Member State), since it is exactly because EC law has given the right to those Union citizens to move to another Member State, that they are now in a position where they can be discriminated against on the grounds of nationality.

More recently, the Court of Justice has made it clear that the citizenship provisions prohibit, also, discrimination against 'free movers', that is, discrimination exercised by a Member State against some of its own nationals, by reason of the fact that they have exercised their right to move freely and reside in the territory

143. *See* the previous footnote. This is also implicit in some of the Court's judgments where the Court pointed out that 'The situations falling within the scope of Community law *include* those involving the exercise of the fundamental freedoms guaranteed by the Treaty, in particular those involving the freedom to move and reside within the territory of the Member States, as conferred by Article 18 EC' (para. 17 of *Pusa, supra* n. 57 (emphasis added)). *See* also para. 24 of *Garcia Avello, supra* n. 47, para. 23 of *Morgan and Bucher, supra* n. 84. It is also implicit in para. 24 of *D'Hoop supra* n. 84 where the Court expressly pointed out that 'the main proceedings do not concern the recognition of Community law rights allegedly acquired before the entry into force of the provisions on citizenship of the Union, but relate to an allegation of current discriminatory treatment of a citizen of the Union'. Therefore, *D'Hoop* should not be taken as a case where the Court found a link with EC law as a result of the fact that the discrimination exercised against Ms D'Hoop by her Member State of nationality would impede the main aim of Art. 18 EC (Art. 21 TFEU) (i.e., the exercise of inter-state movement), since, in any event, when Ms D'Hoop had exercised her right to move from one Member State to another, in the late 1980s, Art. 18 EC did not exist. Similarly, the facts in *Martinez Sala* did not involve, in any way, a possible impediment to the EC right to free movement between Member States; when the claimant in that case had moved from Spain to Germany in 1968, Spain was not a Member State of the EU and, in any event, it was long before the introduction of Art. 18 EC into the EC Treaty (this is further reflected in paras 60-61 of the Court's judgment in that case). *See*, also, *Nerkowska, supra* n. 47. One could, however, argue that in these cases the Court was not justified in including the alleged discrimination within the scope of EC law since it did not emerge as a result of the process of European integration. In the above cases the action which had brought the claimant to a position in which she could be discriminated against was not an action which was undertaken as part of the process of European integration.

144. Para. 18 of the Opinion of Advocate General Poiares Maduro in *Huber v. Bundesrepublik Deutschland*, Case C-524/06, not yet decided.

145. *See*, for example, *Bickel and Franz supra* n. 54; *Grzelczyk supra* n. 53; and *Bidar supra* n. 83.

of another Member State.[146] Similarly, in such cases the Court's dominant aim has not been to encourage inter-state movement but, in fact, to ensure that no discrimination arises as a result of the exercise of a right granted by EC law; in other words, as a result of the process of European integration.[147] As the Court has pointed out,

> Inasmuch as a citizen of the Union must be granted in all Member States the same treatment in law as that accorded to nationals of those Member States who find themselves in the same situation, it would be incompatible with the right to freedom of movement were a citizen to receive in the Member State of which he is a national treatment less favourable than he would enjoy if he had not availed himself of the opportunities offered by the EC Treaty in relation to freedom of movement.[148]

That the scope of EC law now includes any situations which involve the refusal to grant a right to a person *because* that person has relied on EC rules and taken part in the process of European integration, has recently been affirmed in the case of *Nerkowska*, where the Court stressed that

> [A] situation in which the exercise by Ms Nerkowska of a freedom accorded by Community law has an impact on her right to the payment of a benefit under national legislation cannot be considered to be a purely internal matter with no link to Community law.[149]

146. *Pusa supra* n. 57; *De Cuyper v. Office national de l'emploi*, Case No. C-406/04 [2006] ECR I-6947, para. 39; *Turpeinen*, Case No. C-520/04 [2006] ECR I-10685, paras 20-23; *Tas-Hagen supra* n. 47, paras 30-32; *Nerkowska, supra* n. 47, paras 31-33; *Schwarz v. Finanzamt Bergisch Gladbach*, Case No. C-76/05, judgment of 11 Sep. 2007, not yet reported, paras 88-93; *Morgan and Bucher, supra* n. 84, paras 25-26. This reasoning has also been applied in the context of the free movement of economically active persons – *see Commission v. Germany (psychotherapists)*, Case No. C-456/05, judgment of 6 Dec. 2007, not yet reported, paras 58-59.
147. In *Schempp, supra* n. 47, para. 25, the Court seems to have embraced this approach: 'since the exercise by Mr Schempp's former spouse of a right conferred by the Community legal order had an effect on his right to deduct in his Member State of residence, such a situation cannot be regarded as an internal situation with no connection with Community law'.
148. *Schwarz, supra* n. 146, para. 88; *Pusa, supra* n. 57, para. 18; *D'Hoop, supra* n. 84, para. 30.
149. *Nerkowska, supra* n. 47, para. 29. Quite interestingly, the Court in the *Eman and Sevinger* case in 2006 held that the Netherlands was in violation of the Community principle of equality by discriminating between Dutch nationals who were residing in Aruba and Dutch nationals who were residing in non-EU countries (*see, supra* n. 95, paras 56-60, especially para. 58). The case involved the right to vote in European Parliament elections. I find it questionable whether this instance of discrimination by a Member State against some of its own nationals (i.e., Netherlands nationals resident in Aruba) should be found to fall within the scope of EC law. Clearly, this was not a case involving an impediment to inter-state movement. Moreover, it does not seem that the discrimination arose *directly* from the process of European integration. True, the claimants were seeking to obtain the right to vote in *European* Parliament elections. However, it was entirely left to the Member States to determine the 'persons entitled to vote and to stand for election' (*supra* n. 95, para. 45) and it therefore seems that the inequality of treatment resulting as a result of the application of the Dutch rules on the issue was too remote from EC law and its operation. Therefore, this is one case where it

Following the above conclusions, the Court should now rule that, since reverse discrimination is a form of a difference in treatment that arises as a result of the process of European integration, and in particular, as a result of the limited scope of application of EC law, it now falls within the scope of Community law. The fact that reverse discrimination is a problem which is caused or contributed to by the realization of EC market integration and by the form of governance selected for the EU,[150] means that it is all the more necessary for the EU to provide a solution.

Moreover, perhaps, in the interests of certainty, it would be best if the principle of equality between Union citizens would now be enshrined in the EC Treaty. Consequently, just as the EC Treaty was reformed by the Treaty of Amsterdam to include as one of the Community's tasks in Article 2[151] the promotion of equality between men and women and has also introduced into the EC Treaty a new Article 3(2) which states that in all the activities referred to in Article 3(1),[152] the Community shall aim to eliminate inequalities and to promote equality between men and women, in the same way, Articles 2 and 3 of the EC Treaty should be reformed again to include as one of the Community's aims, equality between all Union citizens similarly situated. In this way, whenever a case of reverse discrimination is brought before the ECJ, EC law will require that difference in treatment to be remedied, unless, of course, a legitimate reason for the contested difference in treatment will be provided. Moreover, it would be necessary for the Court of Justice to rule that the (new) Treaty provisions enshrining the principle of equality before the law are directly effective so that national courts, as enforcers of Community law, will also be able to remedy any instances of reverse discrimination.

---

seems that the Court overstepped the boundaries of the scope of application of the Community principle of equality.

150. N. Nic Shuibhne *supra* n. 118, p. 184.
151. Following the coming into force of the Lisbon Treaty (*supra* n. 3) this provision will be repealed and, in substance, replaced by the new Art. 3 TEU. The aim of promoting equality between women and men will be provided in Art. 3(3) TEU.
152. Following the coming into force of the Lisbon Treaty, *ibid.*, Art. 3(1) EC will be repealed and, in substance, replaced by Arts 3 to 6 TFEU. The current Art. 3(2) EC will be renumbered as Art. 8 TFEU.

Chapter 5

Reverse Discrimination and EC Trade: An Incongruity in a Genuine Internal Market

I INTRODUCTION

In the previous chapter of the book, it was explained how the recent developments in the context of Union citizenship have increasingly questioned the well-established view that reverse discrimination is a difference in treatment between Union citizens that falls outside the scope of EC law. The present chapter will revolve around similar axes (i.e., recent developments in EC law), but in this context the central theme will be the evolution of the internal market and how, following its completion, the issue of the permissibility of reverse discrimination in the area of EC trade has been affected. Adopting an approach similar to that followed in Chapter 4, the two main questions that this chapter aims to answer are whether reverse discrimination against products the situation of which falls outside the scope of the free movement provisions is, still, a permissible difference in treatment that escapes the ambit of EC law; and, if not, how reverse discrimination in this area can, now, be brought within the scope of Community law.

Chapter 5 will begin with a very brief explanation of the workings of the internal market during the early years of its existence, when the principal focus was placed on the construction and maintenance of a single market. It will be explained that during that phase – and until quite recently – reverse discrimination was a necessary evil of the system adopted for the establishment of the common market and an acceptable difference in treatment, not inhibiting the opening-up of national frontiers. However, following the (formal) completion of the internal market in 1993, the focus seems to be on the proper functioning of the newly-constructed market – an objective that had remained, to a large extent, dormant until the early 1990s. This, it will be argued, has had as a result that unjustified[1] instances of reverse discrimination are now contrary to the aims of the Community, as they amount to a violation of the principle of undistorted competition which must be respected in a properly-functioning market. And since reverse discrimination arises as a side-effect of the construction of the common market, it falls within the scope of EC law and – where appropriate – should be remedied at EC level, either judicially or legislatively.

Of course, again, it should be borne in mind that not all instances of reverse discrimination are problematic. As explained in Chapter 1, the important question in determining whether a specific case involving reverse discrimination is problematic from the point of view of Community law, is whether products that are in a purely internal situation are in a similar position with products the situation of which falls within the scope of the fundamental freedoms. If so, then the reverse discrimination in that case actually amounts to discrimination and, therefore, the analysis that will follow in this chapter will be relevant. If not, then the differential treatment that is contested does not amount to discrimination and, therefore, is not problematic from the point of view of Community law.

One caveat should precede the main analysis in this chapter. This chapter will not deal with the application of the internal market provisions to situations of reverse discrimination suffered by persons as factors of production. Although the same problems (i.e., competitive disadvantage) faced by traders that fall outside the scope of the free movement provisions, can be encountered by persons as factors of production, nevertheless, this chapter will only deal with products, since the issue of the compatibility with EC law of reverse discrimination suffered by persons who do not fall within the scope of the fundamental freedoms provisions, was dealt with in the previous chapter.

The provisions governing the free movement of *persons* in the process of the construction of the internal market are Articles 39 (workers), 43 (establishment) and 49 (services) EC (respectively, Articles 45, 49 and 56 TFEU), but the latter only as long as it involves *persons* moving between Member States to receive or provide services. However, it is well-known that Article 49 EC applies also to transactions that in no way involve Member State nationals crossing State frontiers, as long as the *service itself* moves between Member States.[2] Such services resemble goods, they are marketable commodities, and the term 'products' includes them as well as goods. Therefore, a similar approach to market regulation as that

1. In the next chapter, it will be explained that the doctrine of mandatory requirements should be made available to Member States for justifying any instances of reverse discrimination that fall within the scope of EC law. Thus, if such instances of reverse discrimination can be justified on a (valid) ground other than the desire to grant EC rights only to traders that have contributed to the economic aims of the Treaty, then the Member State which resorts to such differential treatment can continue doing so.
2. *See*, for example, *Canal Satélite Digital SL v. Administracíon General del Estato*, Case No. C-390/99 [2002] ECR I-607; *Alpine Investments BV v. Minister van Financiën*, Case No. C-384/93 [1995] ECR I-1141; *Commission v. Germany (Insurance Services)*, Case No. 205/84 [1986] ECR 3755.

followed in the context of goods should be followed when regulating such services.[3] In fact, such services are attaining increasing importance and, according to O'Keeffe and Bavasso, '[i]n the future Article 49 will be less about the movement of persons and more about the provision of services'.[4] This chapter will mainly refer to the free movement of goods since the law in this area has been much more developed, however, it should continuously be borne in mind that the arguments and suggestions that will be made, will be equally applicable to situations involving services as products.

II REVERSE DISCRIMINATION AS AN INDISPENSABLE FEATURE IN THE PROCESS OF ESTABLISHING AN INTERNAL MARKET

As we saw in Chapter 1 of the book, following the establishment of the ECSC its Member States attempted to include further areas in the process of European integration. Hence, in the early 1950s, a Treaty on political and defence cooperation was signed. However, as a result of the fact that the areas which formed the subject matter of this new Treaty were much more sensitive than the common administration of the coal and steel resources of the Ruhr and Saar regions (the objective of the ECSC), the Treaty failed to be ratified. This was the first blow inflicted on European integration sending a strong message that it was too early for integration to expand into areas which were central to the sovereignty of the participating States. This meant that the step that would follow would have to be very carefully planned since another failed attempt might mean the shelving of the plans for further European integration. As a result of that, the six States that signed the Treaty of Paris in 1951, decided in 1955 in Messina in Italy to move on with another, less ambitious, Treaty the main aim of which would be economic integration and, in particular, the creation of a common market – the EEC Treaty.

The first and most important step for the creation of a common market would be the opening-up of national markets and the free movement of products. The free movement of products, and in particular the free movement of goods, would be achieved by the establishment of a customs union (Articles 23-25 EC [Articles 28-30 TFEU]) on the one hand, and the abolition of quantitative restrictions and MEQRs on imports and exports of goods (Articles 28-30 EC [Articles 34-36 TFEU]), on the other. Since the customs union was completed without any difficulties in July 1968, the burden subsequently fell on the abolition of quantitative restrictions and MEQRs. The driving seat in the process of making the prohibition

3. L. Woods, *Free Movement of Goods and Services within the European Community* (Aldershot, Ashgate, 2004), pp. 163-164.
4. D. O'Keeffe and A. Bavasso, 'Four freedoms, one market and national competence: In search of a dividing line', in *Liber Amicorum in Honour of Lord Slynn of Hadley: Judicial Review in European Union Law*, D. O'Keeffe and A. Bavasso (eds) (The Hague, Kluwer Law International, 2000), p. 556.

on quantitative restrictions and MEQRs effective was taken by the Court of Justice which, as we saw in Chapter 3, gave a very broad interpretation to the term 'MEQRs' in *Dassonville*.[5] And although much was hinted at in the *Dassonville* case, the Court went much further in its judgment in the landmark case of *Cassis de Dijon*[6] which clarified that Article 28 EC catches both distinctly and indistinctly applicable rules, and which established the principle of mutual recognition[7] that, in the years to follow, would form the bedrock in the process of establishing the common market.

The Court's case-law in the 1970s and early 1980s had as a result that the basis for the construction of the common market would be a system with elements of both centralization and decentralization,[8] the main characteristics of which are negative harmonization, the country of origin and mutual recognition principles, competition among rules,[9] and minimum positive harmonization. The main advantage of this system is that it is not overly intrusive with national regulatory autonomy. This is because, under this system, different Member States can have different rules for manufacturing products in their own territory, and such rules can be applied as long as this will not inhibit the free movement of goods from one Member State to another. Under the principle of mutual recognition, whenever a product is lawfully produced and put on the market of a Member State, it must be accepted into the territory of another Member State, even though it may not comply with the exact requirements imposed by the latter on its own products. It is only in cases that the application of national rules is not, in reality, neutral in its effects upon entrepreneurs competing within the same national market and, in particular, when there is discrimination against traders engaged in inter-state trade that the EC must intervene. Hence, each Member State can continue imposing its own requirements as to how goods should be produced in its own territory and no common, harmonized, regulations are needed. Under this system, harmonization is used for

---

5. *Procureur du Roi v. Dassonville*, Case No. 8/74 [1974] ECR 837.
6. *Rewe-Zentrale AG v. Bundesmonopolverwaltung für Branntwein*, Case No. 120/78 [1979] ECR 649.
7. For an excellent, extensive, analysis of the principle of mutual recognition *see* K. Armstrong, 'Mutual Recognition', in *The Law of the Single European Market: Unpacking the premises*, C. Barnard and J. Scott (eds) (Oxford, Hart, 2002).
8. For an explanation of the centralized and decentralized systems adopted for the construction of the internal market *see* C. Barnard, *The Substantive Law of the EU: The Four Freedoms* (Oxford, OUP, 2007), pp. 17-23. For an excellent analysis of the advantages and disadvantages of both *see* J. Snell, 'Who's Got the Power? Free Movement and Allocation of Competences in EC Law' (2003) 22 *YEL* 323, 331-337.
9. For literature on the notion of a system of competition among rules *see* C. Barnard and S. Deakin, 'Market Access and Regulatory Competition', in *The Law of the Single European Market: Unpacking the Premises*, C. Barnard and J. Scott (eds) (Oxford, Hart, 2002); A. Ogus, 'Competition between national legal systems: A contribution of economic analysis to comparative law' (1999) 48 *ICLQ* 405; J.M. Sun and J. Pelkmans, 'Regulatory Competition in the Single Market' (1995) 33 *JCMS* 67; N. Reich, 'Competition between legal orders: A new paradigm of EC law?' (1992) 29 *CMLRev* 861; H. Søndergaard Birkmose, 'Regulatory Competition and the European Harmonization Process' (2006) *EBLRev* 1075.

establishing (mostly minimum) standards that always have to be followed and, usually once followed, will enable goods to move freely between Member States.

One of the most significant features of this mixed system for the establishment of the internal market is the purely internal rule. The rule reflects the core ideology of the system, that is, that Member States should be left free to regulate any situations where this does not give rise to an impediment to the free movement of products. By regulating (or, more often, deregulating) only the position of products that move between Member States, whilst leaving Member States entirely free to regulate trade in products that remain confined within their own territory, the Community has managed to balance its main aim of creating an internal market, with the need to respect the regulatory competences of the Member States when the latter do not interfere with the Community's aims. States should remain free to regulate the production and marketing of goods in their territory according to national preferences and values, as long as the regulatory diversity which emerges does not impede inter-state trade. This diversity allows regulatory competition to flourish and thus gives leeway to the Member States to experiment for the best regulatory package.

As we have already seen, the application of the purely internal rule often has as a side-effect the emergence of reverse discrimination. In the area of trade, the main problem caused by reverse discrimination is not, like in the area of persons, that different rules apply to different people, this causing injustice in areas often not closely related to inter-state trade. Rather, as observed in the Chapter 1, the main problem in this area is that traders who are the victims of reverse discrimination may suffer a competitive disadvantage[10] when competing with traders that can take advantage of the Treaty provisions on the free movement of goods and services.[11]

---

10. M. Poiares Maduro, 'The Scope of European Remedies: The Case of Purely Internal Situations and Reverse Discrimination', in *The Future of European Remedies*, C. Kilpatrick, T. Novitz and P. Skidmore (eds) (Oxford, Hart, 2000), p. 133; W. Kerber, 'Interjurisdictional Competition within the European Union' (2000) 23 *Fordham Int'l LJ* S217, S241. For a brief explanation of the economic consequences of reverse discrimination in the context of trade *see* H.C. Von Heydebrand u.d. Lasa, 'Free movement of foodstuffs, consumer protection and food standards in the European Community: has the Court of Justice got it wrong?' (1991) 16 *ELRev* 391, 411. Note that the very same problem is also present in the area of the free movement of economically active persons. A very good analysis of this was offered by S. Weatherill, in his case note on *Bosman*, (1996) 33 *CMLRev* 991, 1019-1026.
11. Some commentators also consider the danger of a regulatory race to the bottom as another potential problem arising from situations of reverse discrimination. It is submitted that Member States, faced with a possible massive exit from their companies as a result of the problems caused by reverse discrimination, may lower their higher standards imposed only on domestic goods and either adopt also for internal situations the minimum standard imposed by EC law for inter-state situations, or even, impose no standards at all – *see*, for example, S. Enchelmaier, 'The Awkward Selling of a Good Idea, or a Traditionalist Interpretation of *Keck*' (2003) 22 *YEL* 249, 279; D. Welch, 'From "Euro Beer" to "Newcastle Brown", A Review of European Community Action to Dismantle Divergent "Food" Laws' (1983) 22 *JCMS* 47, 67. For an explanation of this problem *see* C. Barnard, 'Social dumping and the race to the bottom: some lessons for the European Union from Delaware?' (2000) 25 *ELRev* 57; L. Conant, *Justice contained: Law and Politics in the European Union* (Ithaca NY, Cornell University Press,

As a result of reverse discrimination, products that fall within the scope of EC law may have a competitive advantage not linked to their own merit. At the same time, producers/traders in purely internal situations may suffer a competitive disadvantage, without this being a result of their own choice.[12]

The problem with reverse discrimination is that products produced in different Member States will compete in one and the same market (the domestic market of the products found to be in a purely internal situation) under different conditions, this being a result of the limited scope of the prohibitions imposed by the Treaty or the limited scope of application of EC secondary legislation. If, for instance, the Treaty required that a national measure which was restrictive of trade and was not justified should not be applied, *both* to goods imported from other Member States and to goods confined within the territory of the host State, different conditions of competition would not prevail *in the same market.*

However, the Court has always ruled that reverse discrimination is not a prohibited form of differential treatment under EC law. And, despite the negative economic repercussions that the emergence of reverse discrimination may have for traders operating solely within their domestic market, until not long ago, one could not but agree with the Court: reverse discrimination does not impede the establishment of the internal market which, until quite recently, has been the main aim of the Community. This will be explained in more detail in the following paragraphs.

The principle of equality in EC law has *traditionally* been used *solely* as a vehicle through which to proceed to further economic integration and thus 'its socio-economic function [has] not [been] to ensure fairness but to protect the comparative advantage' of goods involved in inter-state trade, in order to enable the internal market to be established.[13] Likewise, the sole aim of the prohibitions on quantitative restrictions on imports and exports (Articles 28 and 29 EC [Articles 34 and 35 TFEU]) and customs duties (Articles 23-25 [Articles 28-30 TFEU]) has

---

2002), p. 2. However, the possibility that this problem may arise in practice has been rejected by many commentators, mainly due to the fact that Member States may prefer to maintain their higher national standards, the latter being guarantees of goods of superior quality and, thus, a fine reputation – *see*, among others, F.W. Scharpf, 'Introduction: the Problem-solving Capacity of Multi-level Governance' (1997) 2 *JEPP* 520; R. Van den Bergh, 'Subsidiarity as an Economic Demarcation Principle and the Emergence of European Private Law' (1998) 5 *MJ* 129, 136-139; S. Woolcock, 'Competition among rules in the Single European market', in *International Regulatory Competition and Coordination*, W. Bratton, J. McCahery, S. Picciotto and C. Scott (eds) (Oxford, Clarendon Press, 1996), pp. 317-319.

12. It should be noted, however, that some firms may prefer to comply with stricter standards when manufacturing their goods because this will have as a result a competitive advantage when competing with goods made according to lower standards. This mostly occurs with goods that quality is an important part of them.
13. D. Chalmers, 'The Single Market: From Prima Donna to Journeyman', in *New Legal Dynamics of European Union*, J. Shaw and G. More (eds) (Oxford, Clarendon Press, 1995), p. 65. *See* also M. Poiares Maduro, *supra* n. 10, pp. 121-123; D. Chalmers, 'Repackaging the Internal Market – The Ramifications of the *Keck* Judgment' (1994) 17 *ELRev* 385, 397. This, after all, is also evident from the Court's judgments on reverse discrimination as seen in Ch. 2 (*see*, for example, paras 7-9 of *Criminal proceedings against Mathot*, Case No. 98/86 [1987] ECR 809).

been to ensure that intra-Community trade is not hindered, that the free movement of goods between Member States is facilitated. And, since a necessary precondition for the establishment of an internal market through the free movement of, inter alia, goods has been the removal of any Member State measures which discriminate against goods originating in other Member States, the fundamental freedoms provisions have been interpreted, from the beginning of the Community's existence, as including a prohibition of such discrimination.[14]

Accordingly, Member States are not free to apply a different, less favourable, trading regime to products coming from other Member States and marketed in their markets. The reason for this is that in such a case, imported products will be in a competitive disadvantage *and*, more importantly, this competitive disadvantage will deter traders from importing products from other Member States, thus imposing an obstacle to the construction of the internal market. If there was no deterrent effect on the inter-state movement of products as a result of this difference in treatment, this form of discrimination would not fall within the scope of EC law. It is only because it conflicts with the main aim of the Community (i.e., the establishment of the internal market) that discrimination on the grounds of nationality has been considered to amount to a violation of the fundamental freedoms provisions.

Conversely, reverse discrimination is a difference in treatment which does not result in the creation of an impediment to the inter-state movement of products. In fact, it would not be an exaggeration to say that reverse discrimination may actually be utilized as a tool in the process of establishing an internal market, since it may have as an effect an increase in cross-border trade by facilitating the marketing of imported products to the detriment of domestic ones. Unlike discrimination on the ground of the place of manufacture or of previous marketing of products, reverse discrimination usually does not partition the market along national lines but, on the contrary, facilitates the more rapid removal of inter-state frontiers and the de-crystallization of national habits.[15]

Accordingly, in an era when the sole aim of the EC was the construction of the internal market, and in particular the removal of inter-state frontiers,[16] reverse discrimination should not be considered a difference in treatment prohibited

---

14. As Gareth Davies has pointed out, goods, services and capital have no nationality as such, and thus, it is discrimination on the grounds of origin of goods/services/capital that is contrary to the aim of the free movement provisions. However, as explained by the same author, '[i]n an attempt to compare, and unite, them with free movement of persons, within a common conceptual framework' the term 'nationality' discrimination is used 'as a convenient shorthand for discrimination on the basis of origin'. *See* G. Davies, *Nationality Discrimination in the European Internal Market* (The Hague, Kluwer Law International, 2003), p. 60.
15. The Court's concern about the crystallization of consumer habits is evident in *Commission v. Germany (Beer)*, Case No. 178/84 [1987] ECR 1227; *Commission v. UK (tax arrangements for wine)*, Case No. 170/78 [1983] ECR 2265, para. 8.
16. According to Vogelaar, 'The initial period of the Community was characterized by a striving towards liberalization. Achieving the four freedoms (the free movement of goods, of persons, of services and of capital) was the foremost consideration'. *See* T. Vogelaar, 'The approximation of the laws of Member States under the Treaty of Rome' (1975) 12 *CMLRev* 211, 216.

under EC law. In other words, since reverse discrimination does not have a negative impact on the, until recently, principal aim of the Community, namely the conversion of national markets into integrated cross-border markets, it was – until quite recently – rightly excluded from the scope of application of EC law.

III THE SCOPE OF APPLICATION OF THE INTERNAL MARKET PROVISIONS OF THE TREATY

Before proceeding with the main analysis in the chapter, it would be wise to explain that the Treaty provisions governing the internal market policy of the Community can be divided into two 'groups'.

The first group includes provisions the *sole* aim of which is the establishment of an internal market by the removal of obstacles to the inter-state movement of goods and services. Such provisions are Articles 28-29 EC (Articles 34-35 TFEU) prohibiting the imposition of quantitative restrictions and MEQRs on the (inter-state) import and export of goods; Articles 23-25 EC (Articles 28-30 TFEU) prohibiting the imposition of customs duties and CEEs on goods by reason of the fact that they cross a frontier; and, as regards services as products, Article 49 EC (Article 56 TFEU) which prohibits any restrictions on the transnational movement of services.

The second group of provisions comprises Treaty Articles that have a twofold objective: to establish an internal market *and* to ensure that the internal market functions properly. Obvious candidates for inclusion within this group are Article 95 EC (Article 114 TFEU) and the older Article 94 EC (Article 115 TFEU), which give competence to the Community to make legislation which has as its object the establishment and/or functioning of the internal market. In this chapter it will also be suggested that a combination of Treaty Articles (Article 14(2) EC [Article 26(2) TFEU] read in conjunction with some of the paragraphs of Article 3 EC[17]) can be used in order to ensure that the internal market is a market that functions properly.

IV FROM THE CONSTRUCTION OF THE COMMON MARKET TO THE FUNCTIONING OF THE INTERNAL MARKET: REAPPRAISING THE PRIORITIES OF COMMUNITY TRADE

The establishment of an internal market is a never-ending process.[18] In the context of the Community in particular, at no point in time will it be possible to say that the

17. Following the coming into force of the Lisbon Treaty (Treaty of Lisbon amending the Treaty on European Union and the Treaty establishing the European Community, OJ C 306/1, 2007) this provision will be repealed and, in substance, replaced by Arts 3 to 6 TFEU.
18. K. Mortelmans, 'The Common Market, the Internal Market and the Single Market, What's in a market?' (1998) 35 *CMLRev* 101, 102; K. Armstrong and S. Bulmer, *The governance of the*

internal market has been totally accomplished and that no further steps to that direction are needed.[19] This is evident from the fact that, on the one hand, an internal market for certain goods or services still exists in only a rudimentary state and, on the other, that Member States, especially in periods of recession, continuously devise new ways for erecting barriers to the free movement of products.[20] Accordingly, the removal of obstacles to the free movement of products – being a pre-condition for the existence of an internal market – has always been, and will continue to be, one of the most important aims of the Community.

However, it is also a well-known fact that the Community's internal market, itself, is evolutionary in nature and, as it evolves, the order of priorities of action change correspondingly, directing the limited resources of the Community to the areas that are mostly needed.[21] Since the fundamental principles for ensuring the free movement of products between Member States have, to a satisfactory extent, been pronounced through landmark decisions of the Court of Justice and, thus, national courts can now easily remove any remaining obstacles without having recourse to the Court of Justice, the majority of the Court's resources should now be utilized for promoting other aims for which more work needs to be done at Community level. At the same time, since the internal market was formally completed in 1993 and fewer obstacles to the free movement of products exist following the vast amount of legislation made in accordance with the '1992 project' (and legislation which has been passed at the same pace following that date), it seems that the resources of the legislature can, also, be used for achieving other, more urgent, aims relating to the internal market.

The question that follows, therefore, is on what aim should, now, the Community redirect its resources?

A common market is much more than a market where goods and services can move freely between different Member States. Even though in order to create a single market, the first and most urgent step that has to be taken is to remove State frontiers, nevertheless, this cannot be the sole aim forever. A single market resembling a domestic market regulated by a State for the benefit of its own citizens,

---

Single European Market (Manchester, Manchester University Press, 1998), p. 14; P. Craig and G. de Búrca, *EU Law: Text, Cases and Materials* (Oxford, OUP, 2008), p. 613. *See* also the Commission's Internal Market Scoreboard 11 (November 2002), available at <ec.europa.eu/internal_market/score/docs/score11/score11-text_en.pdf> (*see* p. 4 of the report) (accessed on 6 Jul. 2008).

19. This is why the Treaty provisions that aim at the construction of the internal market (e.g. prohibitions on measures which impose obstacles to the free movement of goods (e.g. Art. 28 EC) [Art. 34 TFEU]) and the provisions for drafting legislation aiming, inter alia, at the construction of the common market (e.g., Art. 95 EC [Art. 114 TFEU])) are still in force and are still frequently used. *See* J. Steiner, L. Woods and C. Twigg-Flesner, *Textbook on EU Law* (Oxford, OUP, 2006), p. 6.
20. *See* B.T. Hanson, 'What happened to fortress Europe? External trade policy liberalization in the European Union' (1998) 52 *International Organization*, 55, 56.
21. G. Close, 'Harmonization of laws: use or abuse of the powers under the EEC Treaty?' (1978) 3 *ELRev* 461, 480; K. Armstrong and S. Bulmer, *supra* n. 18, p. 14.

should include broader issues within its remit.[22] Once a market is constructed (i.e., the free movement of products and factors of production is achieved to a sufficient extent), the next step is to ensure that this market is also a market that functions properly; that it is a market that operates in such a way as to benefit producers, traders and consumers within its boundaries, and its products are able to compete effectively on world markets.[23] According to Advocate General Geelhoed in the *British American Tobacco* case:

> With the advancement of the establishment of the internal market, as evidenced by decreasing frequency of obstacles in the way of cross-border trade between Member States . . . the emphasis will be increasingly placed on the functioning of the internal market. Genuine market unity requires more than simply the abolition of obstacles at borders.[24]

Therefore, the focus of the Community's activity in the area of the internal market is no longer placed on the removal of inter-state frontiers but on ensuring the proper functioning of that market.[25] The importance attained by the aim of ensuring that the internal market is, also, a properly-functioning market is reflected in the changes provided in the Treaty of Lisbon which, once it comes into force, will replace the current Article 14(1) EC which merely refers to the aim of *establishing* an internal market,[26] with Article 26(1) TFEU, which will provide: 'The Union shall adopt measures with the aim of establishing *or ensuring the functioning* of the internal market, in accordance with the relevant provisions of the Treaties'.[27]

---

22. L. Woods, *supra* n. 3, p. 9.
23. Advocate General Jacobs in his Opinion in *Netherlands v. Parliament (Biotechnology case)*, Case No. C-377/98 [2001] ECR I-7079, para. 50, suggests that the object of improving the competitive position of European undertakings on the world market underlies the entire internal market programme.
24. *See* para. 148 of the Opinion of Advocate General Geelhoed in *The Queen v. Secretary of State for Health, ex parte British American Tobacco (Investments) Ltd and others*, Case No. C-491/01 [2002] ECR I-11453.
25. *See* J. Snell and M. Andenas, 'Exploring the Outer Limits: Restrictions on the Free Movement of Goods and Services', in *Services and Free Movement in EU Law*, M. Andenas and W.H. Roth (eds) (Oxford, OUP, 2003), p. 102; J.H.H. Weiler, 'The Constitution of the Common Market Place: Text and Context in the Evolution of the Free Movement of Goods', in *The Evolution of EU Law*, P. Craig and G. de Búrca (eds) (Oxford, OUP, 1999), p. 371; N. Bernard, 'Flexibility in the European Single Market', in *The Law of the Single European Market: Unpacking the Premises*, C. Barnard and J. Scott (eds) (Hart, Oxford, 2002), p. 115; D. Chalmers, 'Environmental protection and the Single Market: An unsustainable development. Does the EC Treaty need a title on the environment?' (1995) 1 *LIEI* 65, 89; S. Weatherill, 'New Strategies for managing the EC's internal market' (2000) 53 *CLP* 595.
26. Article 14(1) EC provides: 'The Community shall adopt measures with the aim of progressively establishing the internal market over a period expiring on 31 December 1992, in accordance with the provisions of this Article and of Articles 15, 26, 47(2), 49, 80, 93 and 95 and without prejudice to other provisions of this Treaty'.
27. Emphasis added.

But what do the terms 'establishment' and 'functioning' of the internal market signify?[28]

Davies explains the meaning of the phrase 'establishment of the common market' as follows: '[T]the establishment of the common (or internal) market refers to the removal of barriers to free movement. This is the stuff of the case-law. Discrimination, product rules, and so on, are things which may affect the establishment of the market'.[29] It is obvious that Articles 28-30 EC (Articles 34-36 TFEU) and Article 49 EC (Article 56 TFEU) (as well as the provisions on the free movement of persons) are the main instruments to be used for achieving the aim of establishing an internal market. Of course, whenever the Treaty prohibitions prove insufficient for removing obstacles to the free movement of products, legislation can be passed at EC level in order to ensure that those obstacles are removed.[30]

Conversely – again according to Davies – '[t]he *functioning* of the internal market is a slightly broader concept, and includes national laws which do not directly inhibit free movement, but may "distort" competition'.[31] In a more recent article, the same commentator appears to be complementing his above statement by also including within the notion of a properly-functioning market, further principles: '[T]he internal market is a market with values... It is not just an area without frontiers, which would be a jungle of the harshest form of competition. It is an area in which frontiers are removed "in accordance" with other aims and goals, that is to say in a safe, clean and fair way'.[32]

I am fully expousing the above view. A market that functions well is a market that not only gives equal opportunities to all players by ensuring equal conditions of competition, but is also a clean and safe market. It is a market in which not only is trade increased and enhanced, but a market that promotes trade only if this is in line with other equally important values such as the protection of public health, consumer protection, the protection of the environment, and undistorted competition.[33] If products that are, for example, dangerous to human health or inappropriate for consumers are allowed to move and be marketed freely, it seems unlikely

28. Note that the Court and the Community legislature do not draw a clear distinction between the two terms, an observation made by Advocate General Geelhoed in his Opinion in the *British American Tobacco* case, *supra* n. 24 (*see* n. 73 of the Opinion).
29. G. Davies, *EU Internal Market Law* (2nd edn, London, Cavendish, 2003), p. 147.
30. For an excellent explanation *see* para. 103 of the Opinion of Advocate General Geelhoed in *British American Tobacco, supra* n. 24.
31. *See* G. Davies, *supra* n. 29, p. 147.
32. G. Davies, 'Can selling arrangements be harmonized' (2005) 30 *ELRev* 371, 380 and 385. *See* also P. Craig, 'The Evolution of the Single Market', in *The Law of the Single European Market: Unpacking the Premises*, C. Barnard and J. Scott (eds) (Oxford, Hart, 2002), pp. 37-40.
33. S. Weatherill, *supra* n. 25, 602; M. Poiares Maduro, 'Reforming the Market or the State? Article 30 and the European Constitution: Economic Freedom and Political Rights' (1997) 3 *ELJ* 55, 70; C. Gulmann, 'The Single European Act – Some Remarks from a Danish perspective' (1987) 24 *CMLRev* 31, 34-35; C. Barnard, *supra* n. 8, pp. 23-24; R. Barents, 'The Internal Market Unlimited: Some observations on the legal basis of Community legislation' (1993) 30 *CMLRev* 85, 104.

that the market in question will be able to exist for long – Member States will close down their borders, again, in order to ensure that the goods marketed in their markets are safe; and goods produced in the common market in question will not be marketable in other world markets which pay particular attention to the safety of the consumer and the protection of public health. Since the 1990s, '[t]he internal market is conceptualized in more holistic terms, to include not only economic integration, but also consumer safety, social rights, labour policy, and the environment.'[34]

In the following section of the chapter I will explain that the importance attained by the aim of maintaining a properly-functioning market, has had an effect on the delimitation of the scope of application of the internal market provisions. In particular, I will explain how the measures adopted by the EC legislature under Article 95 EC (Article 114 TFEU), already reflect to a great extent the modern conceptualization of the internal market, as an area not only without internal frontiers, but also a market that does not overvalue trade to the expense of other non-trade principles.

V THE USE OF ARTICLE 95 EC IN THE PROCESS OF ENSURING THAT THE INTERNAL MARKET IS FUNCTIONING PROPERLY

The SEA is mostly known as the Treaty which established a deadline for the completion of the internal market. That, following the completion of the internal market, the emphasis would be placed on maintaining a properly-functioning market is reflected in that same Treaty, since the new legal basis it introduced into the EC Treaty – Article 95 EC (Article 114 TFEU)[35] – gave competence to the Community to make legislation approximating national laws when this is necessary for the establishment *and functioning* of the internal market.[36]

---

34. P. Craig and G. De Búrca, *supra* n. 18, p. 632. Following the coming into force of the Lisbon Treaty (*supra* n. 17), this will be reflected in a number of provisions in the TFEU, for example, Art. 9 TFEU ('In defining and implementing its policies and actions, the Union shall take into account requirements linked to the promotion of a high level of employment, the guarantee of adequate social protection, the fight against social exclusion, and a high level of education, training and protection of human health'). *See*, also, Art. 11 TFEU which corresponds to the current Art. 6 EC (environmental protection); Art. 12 TFEU which contains the principle currently provided in Art. 153(2) EC (consumer protection); and Art. 168(1) TFEU which contains the principle currently provided in Art. 152(1) EC (human health).
35. Note, of course, that the EC legislature has had competence to draft legislation necessary both for the establishment and the functioning of the internal market since the beginning of the Community's existence (*see* Art. 94 EC [Art. 115 TFEU]). However, since the main concern of the Community during the 1970s and 1980s was to establish an internal market, the part of Art. 94 EC giving competence to the EC legislature to ensure that the internal market (which, at the time was far from complete) was functioning properly, remained, to a large extent, dormant.
36. Note that Art. 95 EC (Art. 114 TFEU) can only be used as a basis for measures establishing and ensuring the proper functioning of a market in goods and *services as products*. This is because

The Court of Justice has repeatedly interpreted Article 95 EC (Article 114 TFEU) as requiring the EC legislature to draft measures which genuinely contribute to the removal of obstacles to movement[37] (corresponding to the need to *establish* a market) or appreciable distortions of competition[38] (corresponding to the need to ensure that the internal market is functioning properly). In the words of Advocate General Geelhoed,

> It is through the complementary application of Article 95 EC, on the one hand, and of Articles 28 EC to 30 EC, on the other, that an internal market is established. This, however, still does not provide any guarantee that the market thus established can also function as a common market. Additional harmonisation measures will frequently be needed for that end. The Community legislature has acknowledged this problem and has provided a second component to the competence under Article 95 EC: the power based on Article 95 EC extends *ratione materiae* to harmonisation measures concerning, not the establishment, but the functioning of the internal market.[39]

Since the aim of establishing an internal market has, to a large extent, been attained, it would seem that Article 95 EC (Article 114 TFEU) will now be mostly used for ensuring that the common market is functioning properly. And since the EC legislature has competence to make legislation under Article 95 EC whenever there is a distortion on the proper functioning of the single market, such competence should arise where there are appreciable distortions of competition (as already accepted explicitly by the Court), or where there is a danger that other non-economic values that are immensely important for a market to function smoothly will not be appropriately respected.[40] Indeed, Article 95 EC itself

---

Art. 95(2) (Art. 114(2) TFEU) expressly provides that the Community legislature does not have competence to draft legislation based on Art. 95 EC in the area of the free movement of persons.

37. *Spain v. Council*, Case No. C-350/92 [1995] ECR I-1985, para. 33; *Germany v. Parliament and Council (Tobacco Advertising I)*, Case No. C-376/98 [2000] ECR I-8419, para. 84; *British American Tobacco, supra* n. 24; *Arnold André GmbH & Co. KG v. Landrat des Kreises Herford*, Case No. C-434/02 [2004] ECR I-11825, para. 34; *The Queen on the application of Swedish Match AB and Swedish Match UK Ltd v. Secretary of State for Health*, Case No. C-210/03 [2004] ECR I-11893, para. 33; *Alliance for Natural Health and Others*, Joined Cases C-154/04 and C-155/04 [2005] ECR I-6451, para. 32; *UK v. Parliament and Council (Smoke flavourings)*, Case No. C-66/04 [2005] ECR I-10553, para. 41; *Germany v. Council*, Case No. C-359/92 [1994] ECR I-3681, para. 22.
38. *Commission v. Council (titanium dioxide)*, Case No. C-300/89 [1991] ECR I-2867, para. 15; *Tobacco Advertising I* case, *supra* n. 37, para. 106; *Spain v. Council, supra* n. 37, para. 32; para. 80 of the Opinion of Advocate General Léger in *Germany v. Parliament and Council* (*Tobacco Advertising II*), Case No. C-380/03 [2006] ECR I-11573.
39. Para. 147 of the Opinion of Advocate General Geelhoed in the *British American Tobacco* case, *supra* n. 24.
40. For a similar argument *see* S. Weatherill, 'The Commission's Options for Developing EC Consumer Protection and Contract Law: Assessing the Constitutional Basis' (2002) 13 *EBLRev* 497, 512-513. This argument was also made (but for Art. 94 EC [Art. 115 TFEU] since Art. 95 EC [Art. 114 TFEU] did not exist at the time) in older literature – *see* D. Welch, *supra* n. 11, 49 and 58; G. Close, *supra* n. 21, 473-478. For an excellent discussion of whether non-market

requires that legislation passed in order to achieve the aim of the construction or the proper functioning of the internal market should respect principles such as the protection of the environment, consumer protection and the protection of human health (see Article 95(3) EC [Article 114(3) TFEU]).[41]

Nevertheless, the preceding conclusion should not be taken at face value – further refinement is required. This is because, if everything that had to do with important values that must be respected in a properly-functioning market was held to fall within the scope of EC law, then the Community would, once more, be confronted with the much-dreaded problem of competence creep: the EC acting when it has no competence to do so, contrary to the principle of attributed competence provided in Article 5(1) EC.[42,43] In other words, if any issue that had to do with, say, the protection of public health or the need to protect consumers was considered to fall within the scope of EC law, then this would transform the system adopted for the regulation of the internal market, from a system which is mixed, with elements of both centralization and decentralization, to a totally centralized one, this flying in the face of the principles of attributed competence and (assuming that in some instances the EC has competence) subsidiarity.[44]

---

considerations are taken into account by the Community institutions when promulgating legislation based on the internal market legal bases *see* B. de Witte, 'Non-market values in internal market legislation', in *Regulating the Internal Market*, N. Nic Shuibhne (ed.) (Cheltenham, Northampton, Edward Elgar, 2006).

41. For an analysis *see* S. Weatherill, 'Why Harmonize?', in *European Union Law for the Twenty-First Century: Rethinking the New Legal Order*, Volume 2, T. Tridimas and P. Nebbia (eds) (Oxford, Hart, 2004), pp. 16-17; S. Weatherill, 'Pre-emption, Harmonization and the Distribution of Competence to Regulate the Internal Market', in *The Law of the Single European Market: Unpacking the Premises*, C. Barnard and J. Scott (eds) (Oxford, Hart, 2002), pp. 53-56; R. Dehousse, '1992 and beyond: the institutional dimension of the internal market programme' (1989) *LIEI* 109, 118-119; S. Weatherill, 'Current developments, European Law, Free movement of goods' (2006) 55 *ICLQ* 457, 464-465; S. Weatherill, 'Supply of and demand for internal market regulation: strategies, preferences and interpretation', in *Regulating the Internal Market*, N. Nic Shuibhne (ed.) (Cheltenham, Northampton, Edward Elgar, 2006), pp. 52-54.
42. Following the coming into force of the Lisbon Treaty (*supra* n. 17), this provision will be replaced, in substance, by the new Art. 5(2) TEU.
43. For literature concerned with the problem of competence creep *see* S. Weatherill, 'Better Competence Monitoring' (2005) 30 *ELRev* 23; S. Weatherill, 'Harmonization: How Much, How Little?' (2005) *EBLRev* 533; S. Weatherill, 'Why Harmonize?', *supra* n. 41; S. Weatherill, 'Competence Creep and Competence Control' (2004) 23 *YEL* 1; G. Davies, 'Subsidiarity: the wrong idea, in the wrong place, at the wrong time' (2006) 43 *CMLRev* 63; A. Knook, 'The Court, the Charter, and the vertical division of powers in the European Union' (2005) 42 *CMLRev* 367; S. Douglas-Scott, *Constitutional Law of the European Union* (London, Longman, 2002), Ch. 4; M.A. Pollack, 'The End of Creeping Competence? EU Policy-Making Since Maastricht' (2000) 38 *JCMS* 519; A. Dashwood, 'The Limits of European Community Powers' (1996) 21 *ELRev* 113; S. Weatherill, *Law and Integration in the European Union* (Oxford, Clarendon Press, 1995), Ch. 2; S. Crosby, 'The Single Market and the Rule of Law' (1991) 16 *ELRev* 451.
44. N. Bernard, 'The Future of European Economic Law in the light of the principle of subsidiarity' (1996) 33 *CMLRev* 633, 640-642.

Therefore, a limiting principle seems to be necessary for determining the instances that the EC legislature has competence to take action for ensuring that the interests that must be respected in a properly-functioning market are protected. This is obvious, after all, from the fact that the Court, itself, has stated expressly that Article 95 EC (Article 114 TFEU) does not give the Community a general power of market regulation.[45]

Accordingly, in order for a situation involving an effect on one of the values necessary for a market to function properly (including the principle of undistorted competition) to fall within the scope of EC law, the situation must arise or have arisen, as a side-effect of the construction of the internal market:

> [T]he competence under Article 95 (Article 114 TFEU) must be justified by shortcomings in the internal market itself.[46]

Thus, apart from measures that present an obstacle to the free movement of goods, now any situation which involves a (substantially) negative impact on the functioning of the internal market which arises as a result of the process of constructing the internal market should be considered to fall within the scope of EC law. And the Community legislature can act in order to protect those values, either by including within the provisions of legislation removing obstacles to inter-state movement, the need to respect those values (thus achieving the right balance through one single piece of legislation); or by passing legislation solely for remedying the side-effects of the process of establishing the internal market, once they become apparent.

Hence, the Community legislature

> [N]ot only has to create the conditions for an internal market in products, but also has to guarantee that the products that appear on this market do not harm other public interests such as health, safety, environmental protection and consumer protection.[47]

This, broader, approach used in determining whether the Community legislature has competence to make legislation in a specific area, is also mirrored in paragraph 5 of the Opinion of Advocate General Poiares Maduro in the *Marks & Spencer* case:

> [L]egislative harmonisation may have the objective of facilitating the exercise of the freedoms of movement but it may also serve to correct the distortions resulting from the exercise of those freedoms.[48]

---

45. Para. 83 of the *Tobacco Advertising I* case, *supra* n. 37.
46. Para. 65 of the Joined Opinion of Advocate General Geelhoed in *Arnold André, supra* n. 37 and *Swedish Match, supra* n. 37.
47. Para. 76 of the Joined Opinion of Advocate General Geelhoed in *Arnold André, supra* n. 37; and *Swedish Match, supra* n. 37.
48. *Marks & Spencer plc v. David Halsey (HM Inspector of Taxes)*, Case No. C-446/03 [2005] ECR I-10837. *See* also S. Weatherill, *Cases and Materials on EU Law* (8th edn, Oxford, OUP, 2007), pp. 289-290.

A careful reading of the internal market provisions of the Treaty supports the above arguments. Article 14(2) EC (Article 26(2) TFEU) provides that '[t]he internal market shall comprise an area without internal frontiers in which the free movement of goods, persons, services and capital *is ensured in accordance with the provisions of this Treaty*'.[49] The italicized words should be taken to mean that, not only does Article 14 EC (Article 26 TFEU) require the establishment of an internal market through the removal of State frontiers, but that the process of establishing the internal market must be in accordance with the provisions of the EC Treaty. Therefore, the removal of obstacles to the free movement of products and factors of production must not be done in a way that will conflict with one of the other aims or tasks of the EC. The removal of inter-state frontiers must be done in such a way as to ensure, inter alia, that the newly-constructed market functions properly and that it operates in a way that does not jeopardize the protection of other principles which are equally important with the aim of establishing an internal market.

Accordingly, under Article 95 EC (Article 114 TFEU) read in the light of Article 14(2) EC (Article 26(2) TFEU) in conjunction with Articles 3(1)(t) (consumer protection), 3(1)(g) (undistorted competition), 3(1)(p) (public health)[50] and 6 EC (Article 11 TFEU) (environmental protection), the EC has competence to

49. Emphasis added.
50. Following the coming into force of the Lisbon Treaty, *supra* n. 17, Art. 3 EC will be repealed and, in substance, replaced by Arts 3 to 6 TFEU. In particular, consumer protection will be found in Art. 4(2)(f) TFEU and the protection of public health in Art. 6(a) TFEU. As is well-known, the maintenance of a system 'ensuring that competition in the internal market is not distorted' is, currently, under Art. 3(1)(g) EC, one of the means to achieve the Community's objectives as laid down in Art. 2 EC and thus is not, as such, one of the Community's objectives. If and when the Lisbon Treaty comes into force, the maintenance of a system of undistorted competition will continue not to be a Union objective under the (new) Art. 3 TEU, whereas the establishment of an internal market will be one of the Union's objectives, under the (new) Art. 3(3) TEU. However, this does not mean that the maintenance of a system of undistorted competition will not be important, once and if the Treaty of Lisbon comes into force. Quite the contrary. The Protocol on the Internal Market and Competition which will be annexed to the TFEU and TEU following the coming into force of the Treaty of Lisbon, provides that 'the internal market as set out in Art. 3 of the Treaty on European Union includes a system ensuring that competition is not distorted' and that the Union shall, if necessary, take action under the provisions of the Treaties, including Art. 352 TFEU (which is the current Art. 308 EC, as will be renumbered following the Treaty of Lisbon coming into force) to ensure that the internal market includes a system of undistorted competition. It should be noted that according to Art. 51 TEU (as will be amended by the Treaty of Lisbon), the Protocols and Annexes to the TEU and TFEU shall form an integral part of those Treaties and, thus, will have the same legal validity. For an explanation *see* E. Szyszczak and A. Cygan, *Understanding EU Law* (2nd edn, London, Sweet & Maxwell, 2008), p. 211. For an article criticizing the removal (by the Treaty of Lisbon) of the mention to the need to maintain a system of undistorted competition from the first provisions of the Treaties, *see* A. Riley, 'The EU Reform Treaty & the Competition Protocol: Undermining EC Competition Law', CEPS Policy brief No. 142, September 2007, available at <shop.ceps.eu/BookDetail.php?item_id=1541> (accessed on 7 Jul. 2008). For a discussion of the complementarity between EC competition law and internal market law (which will formally be reflected in the Treaties once the Treaty of Lisbon comes into force) *see* E. Szyszczak, *The regulation of the State in competitive markets in the EU* (Oxford, Hart, 2007), pp. 29-38.

make legislation to ensure that the internal market functions in a safe, healthy, fair and environmentally-friendly way.[51] And notwithstanding the fact that the Court has not delivered a judgment which *expressly* endorses the above approach, there are numerous instances where the EC legislature has adopted this approach[52] and the Court, in its turn, has sanctioned it. It is to examples of this that we now turn.

In the *Tobacco Advertising I* case[53] the Court of Justice held that Directive 98/43 (the 'Tobacco Advertising Directive')[54] which prohibited all advertising of tobacco products and did not include a market access clause for those products that complied with its minimum requirements,[55] was not validly based on Article 95 EC (Article 114 TFEU) because, in reality, it was a disguised public health measure.[56] It has been considered that the Court was right in its reasoning and, in particular, in the result it reached through its judgment.[57] According to the Court, since the Directive did not include a market access clause which would require Member States to accept within their territory press products that complied with its provisions (even though they might not comply with the host State's stricter requirements that the Directive allowed the Member States to impose), it did not contribute to the construction of the internal market – in other words, the Directive was not necessary for removing obstacles to the free movement of products.[58]

51. This line of reasoning is also implicit in para. 14 of the Court's judgment in *Titanium Dioxide, supra* n. 38.
52. Though, without basing the legislative measure on all of the above provisions, but only on Art. 95 EC (Art. 114 TFEU).
53. *Supra* n. 37 – annotated by J. Usher, (2001) 38 *CMLRev* 1519. There is a wealth of literature discussing the Court's judgment in *Tobacco Advertising I*. *See*, among others, T. K. Hervey, 'Up in smoke? Community (anti) tobacco law and policy' (2001) 26 *ELRev* 101; Editorial Comment: 'Taking (the limits of) competences seriously' (2000) 37 *CMLRev* 1301; S. Crosby, 'The new Tobacco Control Directive: an illiberal and illegal disdain for the law' (2002) 27 *ELRev* 177; S. Khanna, 'The defeat of the European Tobacco Advertising Directive: A Blow for Health' (2001) 20 *YEL* 113.
54. 98/43 (EC) Directive on the approximation of the laws, regulations and administrative provisions of the Member States relating to the advertising and sponsorship of tobacco products, OJ L 213/9, 1998.
55. Paras 101-104 of *Tobacco Advertising I, supra* n. 37.
56. Note that the Treaty does not give competence to the EC to legislate in the area of health protection. Health protection is a 'flanking policy': EC legislation can (and must) take into account health concerns, but must not be solely drafted as a health protection measure (*see* Art. 152(4)(c) EC [Art. 168(5) TFEU – note that a different and broader wording is used]). For an excellent article on the EC's competence in the area of public health *see* T. K. Hervey, 'Community and national competence in health after *Tobacco Advertising*' (2001) 38 *CMLRev* 1421.
57. *See*, for example, Editorial Comment *supra* n. 53, 1305; J. Usher, *supra* n. 53, 1543; S. Crosby, *supra* n. 53, 178-180.
58. The Court also mentioned this expressly in two of its subsequent judgments: *Germany v. Parliament and Council* (*Tobacco Advertising II*), *supra* n. 38, para. 73 and *British American Tobacco, supra* n. 24, para. 74. In the *British American Tobacco* case, the validity of 2001/37 (EC) Directive on the approximation of the laws, regulations and administrative provisions of the Member States concerning the manufacture, presentation and sale of tobacco products (OJ L 194/26, 2001) was contested. It was argued, inter alia, that it was wrongly based on Art. 95 EC (Art. 114 TFEU). The Court explained that the Directive was necessary for removing obstacles

Therefore, the Directive could only be able to be based on Article 95 EC (Article 114 TFEU) if such piece of secondary legislation was necessary for remedying any side-effects the construction of the internal market might have on the protection of non-economic interests and, in particular, the protection of public health. However, this was also not satisfied since, although the Directive would contribute to the protection of public health, the damaging effects of tobacco on public health were in no way connected to the removal of obstacles to the free movement of goods and the construction of the internal market, that is, those effects did not come about as a side-effect of the establishment of the internal market. The advertising of tobacco products predates the establishment of the internal market, and the increase in the use of tobacco products due to effective advertising can in no way be connected to the opening-up of national frontiers.[59]

The opposite result was reached in two more recent 'Tobacco' cases where the Court confirmed the legality of Directive 2001/37.[60] The contested measure, inter alia, prohibits Member States from placing on the market tobacco for oral use ('snus'), the only exception being Sweden, since snus is a traditional form of tobacco in that country. The Court in the *Arnold André*[61] and *Swedish Match*[62] cases stressed that the prohibition imposed by the Directive was necessary for removing obstacles to the free movement of snus arising as a result of the heterogeneous development of the conditions of marketing of tobacco products for oral use in the various Member States.[63]

I would like to argue that the aim of the Community legislature when drafting the Directive was different. In my view, it is unlikely that the Directive will, in any

---

to the inter-state movement of tobacco products (i.e., the construction of an internal market in tobacco products) – *see* paras 64-75. Unlike the Directive that was contested in the *Tobacco Advertising I* case, Directive 2001/37 'contains a provision, Article 13(1), which guarantees the free movement of products which comply with its requirements. By forbidding the Member States to prevent, on grounds relating to the matters harmonised by the Directive, the import, sale or consumption of tobacco products which do comply, that provision gives the Directive its full effect in relation to its object of improving the conditions for the functioning of the internal market' (*see* para. 74 of the judgment). Similarly, in *Tobacco Advertising II* (annotated by M. Ludwigs, (2007) 44 *CMLRev* 1159) the contested Directive contributed to the process of constructing an internal market in advertising media (press, radio and internet) since it prohibited all tobacco advertising in those media *and* included a 'market access' clause which *required* Member States to accept within their markets those media which complied with the Directive. Therefore, although there was a total ban on advertising and, thus, a negative impact on the free movement of tobacco products and advertising services, nevertheless, the Directive, at the same time, contributed to the process of establishing an internal market since it removed obstacles to the free movement of advertising media.

59. For a similar argument *see* G. Davies, *supra* n. 32, 380. For further comments *see* G.G. Howells, 'Federalism in USA and EC – The Scope for Harmonized Legislative Activity Compared' (2002) 5 *ERPL* 601, 605.
60. *Supra* n. 58.
61. *Supra* n. 37.
62. *Supra* n. 37.
63. *Arnold André, supra* n. 37, paras 38-42; *Swedish Match, supra* n. 37, paras 37-41.

way, remove any obstacles to the free movement of goods.[64] First, it imposes a total prohibition on the placing on the market of tobacco for oral use – therefore, how can it be said that it promotes the free movement of such tobacco when it totally prohibits its marketing? Moreover, snus is not a substance that is used in the manufacture of other products and thus its prohibition would not ensure that other related primary products can move freely between Member States, if their manufacture is guaranteed to be free from snus.[65]

Hence, the only possibility that remains is that the Directive was necessary for ensuring that the internal market is functioning properly. Snus is a traditional product in Sweden and it is submitted that only the Swedes are accustomed to its use. Therefore, the opening-up of national frontiers and the free movement of this product from Sweden to other Member States would have as a result that a *new* tobacco product would be imported into the markets of other States[66] – a product which seems to be particularly attractive to young people.[67] Accordingly, the removal of inter-state frontiers appears to be capable of jeopardizing the protection of public health since it would enable the free movement of a product that is harmful to human health, which would otherwise have stayed confined within the market of a single State (Sweden). Consequently, although the EC legislature adopted the right action by drafting the above Directive, nevertheless, the real reason behind the adoption of the contested legislation was not the one that was alleged by its drafters (i.e., establishment of the internal market) but, rather, to ensure the proper functioning of the internal market.

Legislation has, also, been drafted by the Community institutions to remedy distortions of competition arising as a result of the process of establishing the internal market, especially since such distortions are increasingly considered to be an anomaly in a properly-functioning market.[68] Just as the competition law provisions are not only concerned with agreements that divide the internal market along national lines, but also with the maintenance of the internal market as an arena of undistorted competition now, as well, (some of) the internal market provisions are concerned with both, the construction of the internal market and its maintenance as an area without internal frontiers which respects, inter alia, the principle of undistorted competition.

---

64. For another commentator advocating this view *see* S. de Vries, *Tensions within the Internal Market: The Functioning of the Internal Market and the Development of Horizontal and Flanking Policies* (Groningen, Europa Law Publishing, 2006), p. 270.
65. For an explanation of how, in certain cases, a total ban on the marketing of a product may, at the same time, contribute to the internal market and thus have a 'constructive' as opposed to an 'obstructive' effect on the internal market *see* M. Ludwigs, *supra* n. 58, 1170.
66. Note that the fact that snus is a product that is new in all Member States apart from Sweden is continuously repeated throughout the judgments, showing the importance that the Court has attached to this factor.
67. Paras 47 and 64-66 of *Arnold André, supra* n. 37; paras 49 and 66-67 of *Swedish Match, supra* n. 37.
68. Para. 11 of the Advocate General's Opinion in *Les Assurances du Crédit SA and Compagnie Belge d'Assurance Crédit SA v. Council and Commission*, Case No. C-63/89 [1991] ECR I-1799.

However, how is competition in the internal market distorted as a result of the operation of the internal market?

It is undoubtedly trite to state that breaking down national frontiers injects an unprecedented amount of competition into previously protected markets. The opening-up of national borders means that there will be competition among products and factors of production that otherwise would not have taken place.[69] The fact that different States have different laws (and thus products may have to comply with different requirements) means that there may be a distortion of competition, since products competing in the same market (which would not compete, had national borders not been removed), will have been subject to different regulatory regimes.

Therefore, measures at EC level may be necessary to compensate for this. These measures can either be taken by the EC legislature (through legislation under Article 95 EC [Article 114 TFEU])[70] or by the Court of Justice which will admit such situations within the scope of EC law.[71]

An example of legislation promulgated with the aim of removing appreciable distortions of competition that had arisen as a result of the construction of the internal market was Directive 89/428.[72] The Directive laid down 'procedures

---

69. W. Kerber, *supra* n. 10, S220.
70. According to Davies, 'the risk of unfairness which arises when companies are forced to compete without there being a level regulatory playing field is caused by the removal of obstacles to movement . . . measures necessary for the establishment and functioning of the market – Art. 95 – include measures necessary for it to function fairly. Hence distortions of competition resulting from free trade may be harmonized away.' – *see* G. Davies, *supra* n. 32, 379-380. *See* also G.G. Howells, *supra* n. 59, 615-616.
71. An early example of the Community's concern to remedy any distortions of competition arising as a result of the construction of the common market is Art. 141 EC (Art. 157 TFEU) which, according to the Court in *Defrenne v. Sabena*, Case No. 43/75 [1976] ECR 455, pursues a double (economic and social) aim. According to para. 9 of the Court's judgment, the economic aim of Art. 141 EC is 'to avoid a situation in which undertakings established in States which have actually implemented the principle of equal pay suffer a competitive disadvantage in intra-Community competition as compared with undertakings established in States which have not yet eliminated discrimination against women workers as regards pay'. Had the common market not been constructed, there would not be an issue of a competitive disadvantage suffered by some undertakings when competing with undertakings from Member States with different laws. For a more recent case where the aim of preventing the emergence of competitive distortions between undertakings was taken into account by the Court in its judgment *see Laval un Partneri Ltd v. Svenska Byggnadsarbetareförbundet and others*, Case No. C-341/05, judgment of 18 Dec. 2007, not yet reported, paras 73-75. The same concern has also more recently been noted (though not, merely, with regard to competitive distortions) by Advocate General Poiares Maduro who has noted that '[a]lthough the Treaty establishes the common market, it does not turn a blind eye to the workers who are adversely affected by its negative traits' (para. 59 of the Opinion of Advocate General Poiares Maduro in *The International Transport Workers' Federation and The Finnish Seamen's Union v. Viking Line ABP and OÜ Viking Line Eesti*, Case No. C-438/05, judgment of 11 Dec. 2007, not yet reported).
72. 89/428 (EEC) Directive on procedures for harmonizing the programmes for the reduction and eventual elimination of pollution caused by waste from the titanium dioxide industry, OJ L201/56, 1989.

for harmonizing the programmes for the reduction and eventual elimination of pollution from existing industrial establishments and is intended to improve the conditions of competition in the titanium dioxide industry'.

This Directive was adopted on the basis of Article 175 EC (Article 192 TFEU). However, the Court of Justice in the *Titanium Dioxide* case[73] held that the Directive should be annulled since it was based on the wrong legal basis – rather than basing it on Article 175 EC, the EC legislature should use Article 95 EC (Article 114 TFEU) as a legal basis.[74]

In reaching the above conclusion the Court firstly pointed out that the Directive

> [I]s concerned, indissociably, with both the protection of the environment and the elimination of disparities in conditions of competition.[75]

This was due to the fact that by

> [I]mposing obligations concerning the treatment of waste from the titanium dioxide production process, the directive conduces, at the same time, to the reduction of pollution and to the establishment of greater uniformity of production conditions and therefore of conditions of competition, since the national rules on the treatment of waste which the directive seeks to harmonise have an impact on production costs in the titanium dioxide industry.[76]

In other words, since Member States have traditionally imposed different rules on the treatment of waste from the titanium dioxide industries, this resulting in different production costs, and since the opening-up of national frontiers meant that those industries would now have to compete within the same market, the resultant distortion of competition came about as a result of the opening-up of inter-state frontiers. Had State frontiers not been removed, then industries complying with different rules and incurring different costs would not have to compete within the same market.[77]

---

73. *Supra* n. 38.
74. In fact, following the annulment of Directive 89/428 and in order to fill-in the void left by the annulment of that instrument, the Council drafted 92/112 (EEC) Directive on procedures for harmonizing the programmes for the reduction and eventual elimination of pollution caused by waste from the titanium dioxide industry, OJ L 409/11, 1992. The legal basis of this new measure was, of course, Art. 95 EC (Art. 114 TFEU).
75. *Titanium Dioxide, supra* n. 38, para. 13.
76. *Ibid.*, para. 12.
77. Note that in accordance with the principle of subsidiarity (*see* N. Bernard, *supra* n. 44, 642-644), it is only where there is an *appreciable* distortion of competition that the Community legislature should be held to have competence to make legislation to remedy this (*see* the case-law cited in n. 38). The mere fact that different requirements are imposed on different producers depending on their country of establishment does not suffice for bringing a situation within the scope of EC law. This would, in the end, amount to the EC having competence over all issues as 'any government measure in the economic or social sphere – from rates of corporate taxation to the school-leaving age – is liable to have some impact on the competitive position of business in the country in question, as compared with businesses elsewhere in the Community'

The above analysis illustrates that the dynamic process of dismantling barriers to the free movement of goods has sometimes been matched by Community legislation remedying the negative side-effects that have arisen as a result of that process and which are considered to be inhibiting the important aim of ensuring that the internal market is functioning smoothly. In the next section of the chapter, I will demonstrate how negative effects on the protection of important interests that must be safeguarded in a properly-functioning market, can also be remedied judicially, through the use of a combination of EC Treaty Articles.

VI THE USE OF TREATY PROVISIONS FOR PROHIBITING NATIONAL MEASURES THAT JEOPARDIZE THE PROPER FUNCTIONING OF THE INTERNAL MARKET

Since the early years of the Community's existence, both the EC legislature and the judiciary have worked together in order to achieve the Community's tasks. Especially in the process of establishing the internal market, there has always been an interplay between negative and positive harmonization. At different phases of the evolution of the internal market, either of these methods of harmonization prevailed, reflecting the Community's various priorities at the time. As explained above, in order to ensure that the internal market is functioning properly, the EC can (where appropriate) make legislation under Article 95 EC (Article 114 TFEU) for remedying any negative impact the construction of the internal market may have on other important principles and policies.

However, it is well-known that the resources of any legislature (either of a supranational organization such as the EU, or of a State) are limited. Moreover, making legislation at EC level for remedying all instances where the proper functioning of the market is jeopardized will, in the long run, lead to a totally centralized system which, undoubtedly, will cause the vehement objection of the Member States and will amount to a violation of the principle of subsidiarity. Therefore, not all instances where a central body must intervene in order to remedy a side-effect of the construction of the internal market can be undertaken by the Community legislature. Consequently, a way must be found for removing national measures which, as a result of the process of European economic integration, now have an appreciably negative impact on the proper functioning of the single market.

Clearly, the free movement provisions of the Treaty cannot be used for the above purpose. As already explained in the beginning of this chapter, Articles 28-30, 23-25 and 49 EC (Articles 34-36, 28-30 and 56 TFEU) are only concerned with the establishment and maintenance of the internal market by ensuring that State frontiers remain open and products move freely within the internal market.

Nonetheless, I would like to argue that a combination of Treaty provisions can be used for striking down any national measures which, as a result of the operation

---

(*see* A. Dashwood, *supra* n. 43). This is also stressed by the Court in para. 107 of the *Tobacco Advertising I* case, *supra* n. 37.

of the internal market and the application of EC law, may negatively affect the functioning of the market. To this effect, a similar analysis to that used with regard to Article 95 EC (Article 114 TFEU) will be provided. Article 14(2) EC (Article 26(2) TFEU) provides that the free movement of products and factors of production is ensured in accordance with the provisions of the Treaty. Therefore, whenever the inter-state movement of products/factors of production has a negative impact on one of the non-trade principles valued in the Community such as the protection of public health, or consumer and environmental protection, this situation is contrary to Article 14(2) EC read in conjunction with one of the provisions which provide that those principles should be respected/promoted in the internal market.

However, how can Member States be held liable for a breach of EC law (in this instance, Article 14(2) EC [Article 26(2) TFEU] in conjunction with one of the other Articles), since, clearly, the construction and maintenance of a properly-functioning market is a task of the Community? The answer lies in Article 10 EC[78] which, inter alia, provides: 'Member States . . . shall abstain from any measure which could jeopardize the attainment of the objectives of this Treaty'. In the context of the free movement provisions, Article 10 EC has already been used by the Court for finding that Member States are liable for failing to take measures to prevent private persons from impeding the achievement of the objective of Article 28 EC (Article 34 TFEU).[79] Therefore, whenever the removal of inter-state frontiers and, in particular, the free movement of products, has as a result that the application of a national measure will have a sufficiently negative impact on one of the principles that must be respected under the EC Treaty, that Member State must be found to be in violation of Articles 14(2) EC, 10 EC and the relevant Treaty Article, and the contested national measure must be struck down.

VII REVERSE DISCRIMINATION AND THE PRINCIPLE OF UNDISTORTED COMPETITION IN A PROPERLY-FUNCTIONING MARKET

It is true that since the beginning of the Community's existence, (some) measures that were considered to be giving rise to distortions of competition, were held to be in violation of EC law and, in particular, Article 28 EC (Article 34 TFEU). As I explained in section II of the chapter, discrimination on the grounds of the place of manufacture of goods or the previous marketing of a product, has been prohibited by EC law, not because it gives rise to competitive distortions but *only* because those distortions of competition *also* inhibit the free movement of products. I also explained that it was absolutely right to prohibit, initially, only those instances of

78. If and when the Treaty of Lisbon, *supra* n. 17, comes into force, Art. 10 EC will be repealed and replaced, in substance, by Art. 4, para. 3, TEU (as will be amended).
79. *See Schmidberger v. Austria*, Case No. C-112/00 [2003] ECR I-5659; *Commission v. France (Strawberries)*, Case No. C-265/95 [1997] ECR I-6959.

competitive distortions since, until quite recently, the main (and urgent) aim of the Treaty was the establishment of the internal market. Therefore, it was only measures which inhibited the free movement of products that should be struck down; only measures that conflicted with the Community's central aim of establishing a single market.

Prior to the completion of the internal market, the maintenance of a system of undistorted competition was not, as such, an independent aim of the Community's internal market provisions. Nevertheless, as has been repeated throughout the chapter, following the (formal) completion of the single market project, the focus has been placed on the aim of maintaining a properly-functioning market. And, as already explained, the principle of undistorted competition is clearly one of the principles that have to be respected in a properly-functioning market. Therefore, a system of undistorted competition must now be safeguarded for its own sake, and not only in order to enable the free movement of factors and fruits of production to take place. This is due to the fact that, in a properly-functioning market, equal opportunities must be given to all economic players and an effective system of competition must be put in place[80] since there is an inherent belief that the latter is an indispensable part of a system where there is an increase in the quantity and quality of output, whilst prices reflect the 'true' value of the products. Hence, a parallelism can be drawn with the approach followed in EC competition law, as, according to Mortelmans, 'since the completion of the internal market, the emphasis of competition law lies less on the establishment of the Common Market and more on prohibiting restrictions of competition within the internal market'.[81]

The preceding analysis begs the question of where the above conclusion leaves us with the issue of reverse discrimination. As already explained, the main problem with reverse discrimination is that it distorts competition in the internal market. Traders the situation of which falls outside the scope of EC law because their products are marketed in their own Member State, may have to comply with a different trading regime than the one applicable to traders whose products cross inter-state frontiers. Yet, the mere existence of different rules for the production or marketing of products in different Member States is not, in itself, sufficient for ruling that a situation is contrary to Community law.[82] The problem with reverse discrimination is that products that comply with different rules have to

80. *See Procureur du Roi v. Lagauche*, Joined Cases C-46/90 and C-93/91 [1993] ECR I-5267, p. 5331 (para. 44); *RTT v. GB-Inno-BM*, Case No. 18/88 [1991] ECR I-5941, para. 25; *France v. Commission*, Case No. 202/88 [1991] ECR I-1223, para. 51.
81. K. Mortelmans, 'Towards Convergence in the application of the rules on free movement and on competition?' (2001) 38 *CMLRev* 613, 631. *See* also L. Gormley, 'The internal market: history and evolution', in *Regulating the Internal Market*, N. Nic Shuibhne (ed.) (Cheltenham, Northampton, Edward Elgar, 2006), p. 25.
82. This is 'harmonization discrimination' which the Court of Justice has clearly held not to be prohibited by EC law: *Smit Transport BV v. Commissie Grensoverschrijdend Beroepsgoederenvervoer*, Case No. 126/82 [1983] ECR 73, para. 27; *Kenny v. Insurance Officer*, Case No. 1/78 1978] ECR 1489, para. 18; *Walt-Wilhelm et al v. Bundeskartellamt*, Case No. 14/68 [1969] ECR 1, para. 13.

compete within *the same market* (the market of the Member State where the reversely discriminated products originate). This inequality of treatment appears to be improper in a properly-functioning market not because it is unfair but, more significantly, because it does not enable the market to function properly. As one commentator has put it, 'reverse discrimination accepts an inequality which is anathema to a genuine internal market'.[83]

However, does reverse discrimination fall within the scope of EC law? Or, more specifically, is reverse discrimination a difference in treatment between traders that arises as a result of the process of the construction of the internal market?

In many instances, the answer to the above questions is clearly a positive one – in other words, whenever reverse discrimination arises as a result of the limited scope of application of EC law, it is a form of differential treatment that falls within the scope of Community law. This occurs, mainly, in two instances. Firstly, it is a cardinal principle of EC law that the Treaty rules on free movement govern only the situation of products that are involved in inter-state trade. Therefore, national legislation which is restrictive of trade and is applicable to both imported and domestic products becomes inapplicable, *as a result of the operation of EC law* (e.g., following a judgment of the ECJ or a national court applying EC law), only to imported products, whilst it continues being applicable to traders whose situation is a purely internal one.[84] Secondly, the limited scope of application of pieces of partial[85] or minimum[86] harmonization (these applying only to products that fall within the scope of EC law), allows national legislatures to maintain a stricter trading regime for their domestic products, this, obviously, leading to the emergence of reverse discrimination. Therefore, reverse discrimination is, often, a side-effect of the establishment of the internal market and thus may fall within the scope of Community law.[87]

---

83. M.A. Jarvis, *The application of EC Law by National Courts: The Free Movement of Goods* (Oxford, Clarendon Press, 1998), p. 154.
84. *See*, for instance, *Drei Glocken GmbH and Gertraud Kritzinger v. USL Centro-Sud and Provincia autonoma di Bolzano*, Case No. 407/85 [1988] ECR 4233.
85. For an excellent explanation *see* the Opinion of Advocate General Tesauro in the *Les Assurances du Crédit* case, *supra* n. 68.
86. For an explanation of how reverse discrimination arises as a result of the implementation of minimum harmonization measures *see* Ch. 2 of the book.
87. Note, of course, that it is not only in the context of the internal market that any distortions of competition arising as a result of the process of European integration have been considered to fall within the scope of EC law. In a much older case (*Bussone v. Ministro dell'agricoltura e foreste*, Case No. 31/78 [1978] ECR 2429) the Court held that the common organization of the market for eggs in the Community, in accordance with which the Community authorized Member States to entrust exclusively to their public authorities the supervision of the preparation and distribution of bands and labels for eggs, required that the consideration paid in respect of that supervision does not exceed the real costs of the supervisory system in question. In Italy, the consideration paid for these services exceeded their real costs. The Court noted that this would be 'incompatible with the objectives of the common organization of the market as it would affect the competitiveness of Italian producers and would distort the "common rules on competition".' (para. 23).

It should be noted that there are certain instances where a Member State treats its own products more restrictively than products coming from other Member States, even though this does not come about as a result of the application of EC law (e.g., as a result of a judgment of the Court of Justice requiring national legislation to become inapplicable *only in situations falling within the scope of EC law*). An example of such a situation of reverse discrimination is the factual background to *Mathot*,[88] where Belgian legislation applied a more restrictive legal regime to domestic butter than to imported butter and this did not come about as a result of a judgment requiring Belgium to comply with its obligations under EC law. Therefore, it could be argued that such instances of reverse discrimination should be excluded from the scope of EC law. One could, however, argue that these instances of reverse discrimination should, also, fall within the scope of EC law since they *indirectly* arise as a result of the existence of EC rules. In other words, and if we take, again, *Mathot* as an example, it could be said that Belgium laid down a different legal regime for imported products in order to comply *ex ante* with its obligations under Article 28 EC (Article 34 TFEU).

One of the available solutions to the problem of reverse discrimination is, of course, positive harmonization having as its legal basis Article 95 EC (Article 114 TFEU) and which is *specifically* aimed at remedying reverse discrimination.[89] However, as will be explained in Chapter 6, this possible solution presents the important disadvantage that the EC will be making legislation that is explicitly targeted at purely internal situations (i.e., EC legislation that extends the application of EC rules to products confined within their State of origin), something which is almost certainly likely to cause the fervent objection of the Member States. Moreover, this solution goes against important principles that have always been valued in the European internal market, such as the principle of subsidiarity; competition among rules which promotes experimentation and innovation; as well as the fact that the overall responsibility for regulating national markets should rest with the Member States.

Reverse discrimination in the area of trade can, naturally, also be remedied judicially. As can be deduced from the conclusions derived from previous parts of this chapter, reverse discrimination is contrary to Article 14(2) read in conjunction with Article 3(1)(g) EC.[90] In particular, national legislation which remains applicable only to domestic products as a result of the partial application of the prohibitions imposed by the EC Treaty, should now be held to be a violation of Article 14(2) EC read in conjunction with Articles 10 and 3(1)(g) EC, if it appreciably distorts competition and cannot be justified on an acceptable ground.[91] In the next

88. *Supra* n. 13.
89. A similar view appears to have been advocated G. Davies, *supra* n. 29, pp. 154-155.
90. Or, once the Treaty of Lisbon (*supra* n. 17) comes into force, Art. 26(2) TFEU read in conjunction with the Protocol on the Internal Market and Competition which, according to Art. 51 TEU (as will be amended by the Treaty of Lisbon), has the same legal validity as the Treaties.
91. Jarvis includes in his book a number of judgments of French courts where reverse discrimination was held to be prohibited *under EC law* because it was found to be contrary to the principle of undistorted competition, as provided in Art. 3(1)(g) EC – *see* M.A. Jarvis, *supra* n. 83, 159-162

chapter, however, it will be seen that this solution also has significant disadvantages and thus extensive use of it would be inappropriate.

In the next section of this chapter, it will be argued that in some of its quite recent case-law the Court seems to have been aiming to prevent the emergence of reverse discrimination, most probably having realized that this difference in treatment is, now, an EC problem. More specifically, it will be explained that the Court of Justice in its latest case-law appears to be including within the scope of application of EC secondary legislation or EC Treaty provisions situations which, on their face, appear to be purely internal ones. This, it will be suggested, conceals a desire on the part of the Court to avoid the emergence of reverse discrimination, that is, it could be seen as an *ex ante* judicial solution to the problem of reverse discrimination. And it is an explanation of this that we now turn.

VIII PREVENTING THE EMERGENCE OF REVERSE DISCRIMINATION IN A PROPERLY-FUNCTIONING MARKET

It should be recalled that in Chapter 3 it was explained that the Court of Justice appears to have been applying a revised linking factor test in some of its recent case-law in the area of the free movement of products. The main question under this test is whether the application of the contested national measure has a substantial impact on inter-state trade – a requirement which can be satisfied, even where the contested measure is applied to products confined within the territory of a single Member State. Since, as explained in this chapter, an effect on inter-state trade can now be felt either where a situation involves the application of a measure that gives rise to an obstacle to the free movement of products, or, where it affects the proper functioning of the internal market (as the aim of the Community's internal market policy now is to ensure that a *properly-functioning internal market* is established and maintained), the revised linking factor test can be satisfied when either of the above can be proved.

However, it is important to bear in mind that, as already explained in section III of this chapter, not all provisions of the Treaty have both of the above objectives, that is, the establishment *and* the proper functioning of the internal market. Accordingly, care should be taken to make sure that the revised linking factor test is deemed to be satisfied by reason of the fact that a situation has an effect on the *functioning* of the internal market, only if the applicable provision of EC law has as its aim to ensure that the internal market functions properly.

---

and 167-168. Another commentator has been of the view that the distortions of competition that arise as a result of reverse discrimination are contrary to the prohibition of discrimination on the grounds of nationality under Art. 12 EC (Art. 18 TFEU) – *see* G. Davies, 'Services, Citizenship and the Country of Origin Principle', *Mitchell Working Paper Series* 2/2007, available at <law.ed.ac.uk/file_download/series/29_servicescitizenshipandthecountryoforiginprinciple.pdf> (accessed on 8 Aug. 2008), pp. 8-11.

The aim of this part of the chapter is to explain how the overall approach of the Court in its recent case-law in the area of purely internal situations, has been affected by the evolution of the internal market. Some of the cases where the Court appears to have applied the revised test in delimiting the scope of the free movement of goods provisions – the customs duties case-law – and the scope of secondary legislation based on Article 95 EC (Article 114 TFEU), will be examined and analyzed on a deeper level, to show how this revised linking factor test is capable of reflecting and including within the scope of EC law the broader concerns that must be safeguarded in a properly-functioning market. In particular, the revised linking factor test now seems to be enabling the Court of Justice (or national courts) to prevent the emergence of reverse discrimination, since reverse discrimination (with the resultant competitive distortions) is contrary to the important aim of ensuring that the internal market is functioning properly and, thus, has an effect on inter-state trade. Accordingly, when examining whether secondary legislation (based on Article 95 EC [Article 114 TFEU]) or a Treaty provision which has, inter alia, as its aim to ensure that the internal market functions properly should be applicable to a specific situation, the revised linking factor test can be satisfied even where there is no effect whatsoever on the free movement of products (or factors of production), as long as the situation involves a measure the application of which has a substantial effect on the proper functioning of the internal market.

A Delimiting the Scope of Application of EC Legislation in Accordance with the Aim of Preventing the Emergence of Reverse Discrimination

Through its provisions aimed at establishing an internal market, the Community is merely concerned with promoting the free *movement* of products and factors of production, and thus, for a situation to fall within the scope of those provisions, an effect on such movement must be shown. This is why, both the traditional and the revised linking factor tests used in delimiting the scope of the free movement provisions pay so much attention to inter-state movement – the latter to a detrimental impact (either actual or potential) on such movement, the former to *both* the existence and a detrimental impact on such movement. O'Keeffe and Bavasso have pointed out that 'in the free movement provisions, the circulation of the activity or of products is the value protected by the set of rules' and, in the case of those provisions, 'the freedom of circulation is the very means to attain' the objective of creating a common market. Accordingly, in the context of the free movement provisions, 'the presence of a cross-border element is not merely a jurisdictional aspect but also a substantive requirement; it is the value which is protected by the rule'.[92]

92. *Supra* n. 4, p. 554.

However, the aim of ensuring that the internal market is functioning properly is not so much (if at all) attached to free movement. An effect on the proper functioning of the internal market can arise even from a situation where a (national or EC) measure applies to products or factors of production that are confined, in every respect, within the territory of a single Member State and there is no effect whatsoever on the free movement of any products or factors of production. This can be seen in some of the Court's recent case-law on the scope of application of legislative measures the legal basis of which is Article 95 EC (Article 114 TFEU).

In *Rechnungshof v. Österreichischer Rundfunk*,[93] at issue was the compatibility with Community law and in particular, Directive 95/46,[94] of Austrian legislation which required entities which are subject to control by the Austrian Court of Audit, to inform the latter about the proceeds of those persons whose annual salaries are higher than a certain level. Once that information was received by the Court of Audit, the latter would publish it in a report. One of the preliminary issues that arose before the Court of Justice, was whether the situation was purely internal to Austria, since the dispute concerned the compatibility with EC law (and, in particular, Directive 95/46) of the above Austrian legislation when applied to information about Austrian employees of Austrian bodies in Austria. The Court of Justice, contrary to the suggestion of the Advocate General, held that the situation fell within the scope of EC law and, in particular, the scope of the 1995 Directive. It reasoned as follows:

> [R]ecourse to Article 100a [now Article 95] of the Treaty as legal basis does not presuppose the existence of an actual link with free movement between Member States in every situation referred to by the measure founded on that basis. As the Court has previously held . . . to justify recourse to Article 100a of the Treaty as the legal basis, what matters is that the measure adopted on that basis must actually be intended to improve the conditions for the establishment and functioning of the internal market. In the present case, that fundamental attribute was never in dispute before the Court with respect to the provisions of Directive 95/46, in particular those in the light of which the national court raises the question of the compatibility of the national legislation in question with Community law.
>
> In those circumstances, the applicability of Directive 95/46 cannot depend on whether the specific situations at issue in the main proceedings have a sufficient link with the exercise of the fundamental freedoms guaranteed by the Treaty, in particular, in those cases, the freedom of movement of workers. A contrary interpretation could make the limits of the field of

93. *Rechnungshof v. Österreichischer Rundfunk*, Case No. C-465/00 [2003] ECR I-4989, annotated by C.D. Classen, (2004) 41 *CMLRev* 1377.

94. 95/46 (EC) Directive on the protection of individuals with regard to the processing of personal data and on the free movement of such data, OJ L 281/31, 1995. The aim of the Directive is to ensure that the opening-up of national frontiers and the need arising as a result of the construction of the internal market to ensure the free movement of information, will not have a negative impact on the protection of fundamental human rights (*see* Recital 3 of the Directive).

application of the directive particularly unsure and uncertain, which would be contrary to its essential objective of approximating the laws, regulations and administrative provisions of the Member States in order to eliminate obstacles to the functioning of the internal market deriving precisely from disparities between national legislations.[95]

This reasoning was confirmed soon afterwards in the *Lindqvist* case[96] and more recently in *Germany v. Parliament and Council* (*Tobacco Advertising II*).[97]

The Court has been criticized for its judgment in *Rechnungshof*. Classen views that judgment as 'particularly disappointing', especially in the light of, inter alia, the original *Tobacco Advertising* judgment.[98] According to that commentator, who notes that the Court's approach in *Rechnungshof* is similar to the approach followed in cases such as *Carpenter*, '[c]ertainly it proves the increasing interest of the ECJ in human rights questions, but this does not exonerate the Court from the obligation to examine the applicability of Community law'.[99] Similarly, Knook points out that the outcome of the case 'reveals a remarkable situation'[100] and, together with the Court's judgment in *Lindqvist* illustrates that, 'when the legality of the Directive is not disputed . . . the Court has no choice but to apply it, thereby extending its fundamental rights review of Member State measures'.[101]

In my view, in *Rechnungshof, Lindqvist* and, more recently in a different context, the *Tobacco Advertising II* case, the Court confirmed that whenever there can be an effect on the smooth functioning of the internal market, EC law (whether primary or secondary) applies, notwithstanding the fact that the factual background to a situation does not involve an effect on the inter-state movement of products or factors of production. Whenever a situation appears to fall within the scope of a piece of secondary legislation by involving an effect on inter-state trade,

95. *Supra* n. 93, paras 41-42. It could be argued that the Court's reasoning in these paragraphs resembles its reasoning in its recent customs duties case-law analyzed in section III(B)(1) of Ch. 3, according to which when it is impossible to determine which situations involve goods that have crossed inter-state borders and thus fall within the scope of EC law, the customs duties provisions of the Treaty should apply in all situations involving national legislation imposing customs duties on all goods entering a region of a Member State (whether those goods come from another Member State, or from another region of the same Member State).
96. *Criminal proceedings against Lindqvist*, Case No. C-101/01 [2003] ECR I-12971. In that case, the facts were even more far removed from (inter-state) trade: they concerned the publication by a woman on the internet of personal data in relation to a number of people working with her on a *voluntary* basis in a parish of the Swedish Protestant Church – activities which, according to the Court were 'essentially not economic but charitable and religious' (para. 39 of the judgment). For another case where the same approach was followed, though in the context of determining the scope of the Brussels Convention of 1968 on Jurisdiction and Enforcement of Judgments in Civil and Commercial Matters *see Owusu v. N. B. Jackson, trading as 'Villa Holidays Bal-Inn Villas' and others*, Case No. C-281/02 [2005] ECR I-1383.
97. *Supra* n. 38, para. 80.
98. C.D. Classen, *supra* n. 93, 1382.
99. *Ibid.*
100. *Supra* n. 43, 389.
101. *Ibid.*, 390-391.

that legislation should govern the situation, even though an effect on the inter-state *movement* of products or factors of production is not involved. However, in order to be able to compromise the above three judgments with the need to confine the application of legislation made under Article 95 EC (Article 114 TFEU) to situations where there is actually an effect on inter-state trade, further refinement of the Court's reasoning should be offered.

The Court's reasoning should not be taken to mean that all legislation (validly) based on Article 95 EC (Article 114 TFEU), applies always to situations that do not involve cross-border movement, as has been suggested by Knook above. Rather, in order to rule that legislation passed under Article 95 EC should apply in a situation not involving an impediment to inter-state movement, an actual or potential effect on the proper functioning of the internal market must be established.

Although the Court does not mention this in any part of its judgments, I would like to argue that in situations such as those in *Rechnungshof* and *Lindqvist*, a negative impact on the protection of fundamental rights (in particular, the right to privacy) might arise as a result of the partial application of the said Directive.[102] If, for example, a Member State does not impede in any way the free movement of information when this is necessary to respect the right to privacy of individuals, a citizen of that Member State in a purely internal situation claiming that the circulation of information concerning his or her person would violate his or her right to privacy, would not have any remedy under EC law. More importantly, he or she would be in a worse position than that of a person from another Member State coming to that State, since the latter would have a remedy by relying on Directive 95/46. This, obviously, is an instance of reverse discrimination regarding the availability of fundamental human rights protection. And it would be an instance of reverse discrimination arising as a result of the limited scope of application of EC law – the limited scope of application of a piece of secondary legislation.

Similarly, in the *Tobacco Advertising II* judgment, the Court held that Article 3 of Directive 2003/33[103] imposes a prohibition as regards tobacco advertising also on press products that are not involved in inter-state trade. Obviously, in this instance as well, the Court was eager to avoid the emergence of reverse

---

102. The Court seems, rightly, to have recognized that EC law should provide a remedy for any negative impact on the protection of human rights that might arise as a result of the process of European integration – *see* N. Nic Shuibhne, 'The European Union and Fundamental Rights: Well in spirit but considerably rumpled in body?', in *Convergence and Divergence in European Public law*, P. Beaumont, C. Lyons and N. Walker (eds) (Oxford, Hart, 2002), p. 184. For example, in the *T. Port* case, the Court held that the Union has a duty to protect human rights 'when the transition to the common organisation of the market infringes certain traders' fundamental rights protected by Community law' (*see T. Port GmbH & Co. KG v. Bundesanstalt für Landwirtschaft und Ernährung*, Case No. C-68/95 [1996] ECR I-6065, para. 40). The Community legislature seems to have taken steps towards the same direction this being obvious, after all, from the Directive the scope of application of which was examined in *Rechnungshof* and *Lindqvist* (*see* n. 94).

103. 2003/33 (EC) Directive on the approximation of the laws, regulations and administrative provisions of the Member States relating to the advertising and sponsorship of tobacco products, OJ L 152/16, 2003.

discrimination, by making it clear that the contested legislation was not a minimum harmonization measure which applied only to regulate the situation of press products involved in inter-state trade. Therefore, all press products that comply with the requirements of the contested legislation by not including advertising of tobacco products (even products that have never crossed and are not intended to cross any State frontiers), should be able to be marketed on the market of any of the Member States of the EC. Further restrictions cannot be imposed by Member States on their own press products that are not involved in inter-state trade.

Accordingly, following the Court's judgments in the above three cases, one would find it difficult to resist reaching the conclusion that the ECJ may now actually be diffidently moving towards a situation where many pieces of EC secondary legislation will be interpreted as applying to products (or, sometimes, even persons) that have not taken part in the process of establishing an internal market. The reason for this is that the Community's focus, now, is on ensuring that the newly-constructed market is a market that functions properly. Accordingly, legislation that is drafted at EC level in order to remove obstacles to the free movement of goods and services and/or ensure the proper functioning of the internal market, should not lead to a situation which jeopardizes the proper functioning of the internal market by giving rise to the emergence of reverse discrimination. It seems that the Community legislature will continue drafting legislation at EC level under Article 95 EC (Article 114 TFEU) for regulating the production and marketing of products and, where necessary, the Court of Justice will interpret that legislation in such a way as to avoid the emergence of reverse discrimination. In other words, the Court will read EC legislation as covering purely internal situations, when this will be necessary for avoiding the emergence of unjustifiable instances of reverse discrimination. In fact, this may also have been the intent of the Community legislature when making legislation since, according to Poiares Maduro (writing before his appointment as an Advocate General), '[i]n reality, Directives allowing States to impose higher requirements on their nationals (and thus creating reverse discrimination) are an exception. The rule is normally that the requirements apply to both imported and domestic products with those conforming to those requirements benefiting from a market access clause'.[104] It remains to be

104. M. Poiares Maduro, *We the Court: The European Court of Justice and the European Economic Constitution* (Hart, Oxford, 1998), p. 135. For an example of secondary legislation which may apply, partly, to purely internal situations and in this way reverse discrimination will not emerge *see* Ch. III ('Freedom of establishment for providers') of 2006/123 (EC) Directive on services in the internal market, OJ L 376/36, 2006. For an excellent discussion of the issue of whether Ch. III of the Services Directive is intended to apply not merely to cross-border but also to purely internal situations *see* C. Barnard, 'Unravelling the Services Directive' (2008) 45 *CMLRev* 323, 351-352. *See* also, G. Davies, *supra* n. 91, 241-243, who is of the view that not only the Chapter on Establishment, but also the Chapter on administrative simplification may be interpreted as applying to purely internal situations. It appears from p. 30 of the Commission's Handbook on Implementation of the Services Directive that Ch. III of the Directive also applies to purely internal situations: '[Chapter III] covers both the situation where a service provider seeks to establish in another Member State and the situation where a provider seeks to establish in his own Member State' (the Handbook is available at

seen whether the Community legislature, following the example set by the Court of Justice, will itself make it clear in its future legislative measures that – where appropriate – they should be held to apply even in situations that do not involve an effect on the establishment of the internal market, if this is necessary in order to prevent the emergence of reverse discrimination.

B Avoiding the Emergence of Reverse Discrimination in the Area of Customs Duties

As seen in Chapter 3, the area of customs duties is the first one where the Court departed from its traditional approach towards finding a link with EC law. Two cases in the 1990s and two in the following decade, illustrate that the Court, at least in this area, is no longer attaching importance to whether the goods that are involved in a case have crossed inter-state frontiers in order for the Treaty Articles on customs duties to apply – the sole requirement is that there is an effect on inter-state trade. An explanation of the factual background to (some of) these cases was provided in Chapter 3 of the book, therefore, in this chapter the aim will merely be to provide a deeper analysis, an analysis which has been largely inspired by the excellent Opinion of Advocate General Léger in the case of *Jersey Potatoes*.[105]

In *Lancry*,[106] the French overseas department (a region of France) imposed customs duties *on all goods entering that region* (i.e., both goods coming from metropolitan France and goods coming from other Member States). In *Carbonati Apuani*,[107] the Italian municipality of Carrara levied a tax on all marble exported from that municipality, *whether destined for other parts of Italy or for another Member State*. *Simitzi v. Kos*[108] involved the imposition of customs duties on goods moving between a group of islands (the Dodecanese) and *other parts of Greece or other Member States*. The question in each case was whether the Treaty prohibition on the imposition of customs duties should *also* apply to the imposition of dues on goods moving between parts of the same Member State (i.e., where

---

<ec.europa.eu/internal_market/services/services-dir/proposal_en.htm#handbook> (accessed on 3 Sep. 2008)). Of course, it is not made clear by the Handbook, whether the situation of a service provider seeking to establish in his or her own Member State is only covered when a cross-border element is present in the case that is, if the person returns to his or her own Member State after being in another Member State where he obtained a qualification which he or she wants to use there. This would amount to a mere consolidation of the Court's case-law and thus not a departure from the purely internal rule. It seems that we will have to wait for further clarification of this issue from the Court's jurisprudence.

105. *Jersey Produce Marketing Organisation Ltd v. States of Jersey and Jersey Potato Export Marketing Board*, Case No. C-293/02 [2005] ECR I-9543.
106. *Lancry SA v. Direction Générale des Douanes*, Joined Cases C-363/93, C-407/93, C-409/93 and C-411/93 [1994] ECR I-3957.
107. *Carbonati Apuani Srl v. Comune di Carrara*, Case No. C-72/03 [2004] ECR I-8027.
108. *Simitzi v. Kos*, Joined Cases C-485/93 and C-486/93 [1995] ECR I-2655.

goods did not cross an inter-state frontier). The Court gave an affirmative answer to this question, and supported its decision by saying that

> [S]ince the very principle of a customs union covers all trade in goods ... it requires the free movement of goods generally as opposed to inter-state trade alone, to be ensured within the Union.[109]

The immediate response to these rulings was that they abolished the purely internal rule, at least in the area of customs duties. The wording used by the Court in its judgments seems to imply that the prohibitions on the imposition of customs duties on goods, no longer merely aim at ensuring the free movement of goods *between Member States* but also 'the free movement of goods generally'. According to that view, in order for Articles 23-25 EC (Articles 28-30 TFEU) to bite, it is now sufficient that dues are imposed on goods that merely move within one and the same Member State – the only thing that has to be proved, therefore, is the physical movement of goods (whereto, or wherefrom, seems no longer to make any difference).

However, very recently, Advocate General Léger[110] offered an intellectually more rigorous explanation of the Court's reasoning in the above three cases. In his Opinion in the *Jersey Potatoes* case, Advocate General Léger explained that the Court, in the customs duties cases, did not purely and simply hold that the purely internal rule was entirely abolished in the area of customs duties. Rather, the reason that the Court in the above three cases held that the imposition of customs duties in situations which involved goods crossing intra-state frontiers was in violation of Article 25 EC (Article 30 TFEU), was that the (partial) application of the Treaty Articles on customs duties only to goods that had crossed inter-state frontiers, would have given rise to a situation of reverse discrimination. This was because, the non-applicability of the customs duties provisions to situations involving goods moving within one and the same Member State would mean that such goods would continue being subject to the payment of customs duties, whereas goods moving between Member States would not. Obviously, this difference in treatment would lead the former to incur extra costs which would make them less attractive when competing in the market of their own Member State with the latter.

The fact that the Court's judgments in *Lancry, Simitzi* and *Carbonati Apuani* are consistent with the above explanation is also evident from the very recent judgment of the Court in the case of *Jersey Potatoes*,[111] an analysis of which was provided in Chapter 3 of the book. It should be recalled that the issue in that case was whether legislation which applied to goods (potatoes) that would

---

109. *Lancry, supra* n. 106, para. 29; *Carbonati Apuani, supra* n. 107, para. 22.

110. *See* the Opinion of Advocate General Léger in *Jersey Potatoes, supra* n. 105. Note that this view is also implicit in the Opinion of Advocate General Poiares Maduro in the *Carbonati Apuani* case (*supra* n. 107) where he argued that goods in purely internal situations may suffer reverse discrimination as a result of the partial application of Community law, and thus such situations must be remedied under EC law.

111. *Supra* n. 105.

be 'exported' from one region (Jersey) of a Member State to another region of that same State (United Kingdom), was contrary to Articles 23-25 and 29 EC (Articles 28-30 and 35 TFEU). It should also be recalled that that legislation, unlike the measures contested in *Lancry, Simitzi* and *Carbonati Apuani*, applied *only* to movements of potatoes within one the same Member State (and, not, to potatoes sent from Jersey directly to other Member States). Accordingly, in this case, unlike the above-mentioned cases, reverse discrimination would not emerge following a finding that the customs duties provisions did not apply to prohibit the imposition of dues on goods that were in a purely internal situation. The Court in its judgment found that the impugned legislation amounted to a violation of the above provisions since, given the specific situation of the Jersey market in potatoes, it was virtually certain that a portion of the potatoes sent to the United Kingdom would be re-exported to other Member States, and thus any restrictive impact the contested legislation might have on the *movement* of potatoes within the United Kingdom, would (almost definitely) also be felt by those Jersey potatoes that would be re-exported to other Member States through the United Kingdom.[112]

I would like to argue that the Court of Justice in *Jersey Potatoes* did not simply ignore Advocate General Léger's suggestion, according to which the legislation in question did not fall within the scope of EC law since no reverse discrimination would arise as a result of the limited application of EC law. Although the Court admitted that the facts of the case did not involve inter-state movement at first sight, nevertheless, the Court in its judgment seems to be struggling to find that the application of the legislation to goods moving from Jersey to the United Kingdom would, nevertheless, have an effect on inter-state trade. In this case the effect would be on the *inter-state movement* of goods (from Jersey to other Member States via the United Kingdom) as opposed to a finding of a negative impact on the functioning of the common market in the form of a distortion of competition as a result of the existence of reverse discrimination.

And I would like to suggest that, on the specific facts of the case, the Court adopted the correct reasoning. Since it was virtually certain that the further movement to other Member States of, at least, some of the potatoes would materialize, the Court was right in accepting that the application of the impugned legislation only to potatoes destined for other parts of the United Kingdom, in fact also had an effect on inter-state trade. However, unlike its reasoning in the previous customs duties cases the Court, here, required an effect on the *inter-state movement* of (at least some of the) goods to be proved – something which was not necessary in *Lancry-Simitzi-Carbonati Apuani*, since the effect on inter-state trade, in those cases, would come as a result of a negative impact on the proper functioning of the internal market.

Therefore, it seems that in *Lancry, Simitzi* and *Carbonati Apuani* the Court was of the view that, since the *partial* striking down of the contested legislation would have as a result the emergence of reverse discrimination, there would be an

112. *See* paras 113-115 of the Opinion of Advocate General Léger in *Jersey Potatoes, ibid.*

effect on inter-state trade, and thus the legislation should be held inapplicable in its entirety, in order to prevent this negative impact on the proper functioning of the internal market from arising.[113]

Although in the above cases the Court seems to be mistakenly using one of the provisions of the Treaty which has as its aim to prevent the imposition of *obstacles* on the transnational movement of goods (Article 25 EC [Article 30 TFEU]) in order to prohibit reverse discrimination (which is a difference in treatment that does not conflict with the aim of that provision), nevertheless, it has definitely made a positive step towards the resolution of the problem of reverse discrimination in the European internal market. The same approach as that followed in the area of customs duties, should also be followed in other instances where reverse discrimination, with the resultant competitive distortions, may emerge as a result of the limited application of EC law; however, the following Treaty provisions should (solely) be used: Articles 14(2) and 3(1)(g) EC.[114]

IX 'SPONTANEOUS HARMONIZATION': AN ALTERNATIVE SOLUTION TO THE PROBLEM OF REVERSE DISCRIMINATION

As already explained, reverse discrimination is caused by the fact that Member State laws usually impose different obligations or grant different entitlements to traders or persons that fall within their scope, than the obligations that are imposed on, or entitlements that are granted to, traders or persons that fall within the scope of EC law. Accordingly, reverse discrimination is a side-effect of the existence of different laws at different levels which govern very similar situations, the dividing line being the scope of application of each legal system.

---

113. Advocate General Poiares Maduro in his Opinion in the *Carbonati Apuani* case (*supra* n. 107) suggested the following solution: Arts 23-25 EC (Arts 28-30 TFEU) should be concerned only with customs duties imposed on goods by reason of the fact that they cross a transnational frontier. Conversely, customs duties imposed on goods moving between two parts of the same Member State (i.e., goods in purely internal situations) should be allowed only if they are compatible with the general principles of Community law, and in particular the principle of non-discrimination, since such goods are in a situation which is 'residual' from the point of view of Community law. Goods in purely internal situations may suffer reverse discrimination *as a result of the partial application of Community law to the national legislation at issue* and thus in those instances the general Community principle of equality may require the non-imposition of such dues on domestic goods moving between regions of the same Member State. For further explanation of the Advocate General's Opinion *see* A. Tryfonidou, '*Carbonati Apuani Srl v. Comune di Carrara:* Should we reverse "reverse discrimination"?' (2005) 16 *KCLJ* 373, 379-381.

114. Following the coming into force of the Lisbon Treaty, *supra* n. 17, the provisions that will appropriately be used will be Art. 26(2) TFEU and the Protocol on the Internal Market and Competition.

In the analysis provided in this chapter, two kinds of solutions for the resolution of the reverse discrimination conundrum in the area of EC trade have been suggested.

On the one hand, it has been suggested that reverse discrimination in the area of EC trade can be corrected judicially, by the use of a combination of Treaty Articles in order to strike down any national measures the continued application of which to national products gives rise to reverse discrimination. Moreover, it has been observed that a similar – but *ex ante* – solution has also been resorted to (diffidently) by the Court of Justice which in some of its case-law has delimited the scope of EC legislation or Treaty provisions in such a way as to prevent the emergence of reverse discrimination. These 'solutions', however, can only be used on a case-by-case basis, and only once and if a case involving (either actually or potentially) reverse discrimination is brought before a court of law.

On the other hand, it has been argued that the Community legislature can act, where appropriate, by using Article 95 EC (Article 114 TFEU) specifically in order to prevent the emergence – or remedy instances – of reverse discrimination. In this way, the internal market would be transformed into an area primarily characterized by legal homogeneity. Since a genuine internal market is a market in which an undistorted system of competition is maintained, it cannot be accepted that the conditions of production and marketing of goods and services should perpetually differ, depending on the Member State in which a company chooses to manufacture its products. Hence, according to some,[115] legislation should be increasingly adopted at EC level in order to level the playing field between products manufactured in different Member States and thus achieve a genuine internal market. More specifically, in the mid-1980s, Advocate General Mischo in his Opinion in the *Edah* case argued that the appropriate solution to the problem of reverse discrimination is positive harmonization:

> Reverse discrimination is clearly impossible in the long run within a true common market, which must of necessity be based on the principle of equal treatment. Such discrimination must be eliminated by the means of the harmonization of legislation.[116]

However, this move away from a system of competition between legal orders and towards a system of legal homogeneity, presents its own problems and, most importantly, it is questionable whether it is not contrary to the principle of subsidiarity which has attained increasing importance since 1993 (i.e., the date of the formal completion of the internal market). Hence although, in theory, making legislation at EC level can be a solution to the problem of reverse discrimination in the area of EC trade, nevertheless, it is my contention that it is unlikely that Article 95 EC (Article 114 TFEU) will be *specifically* used to remedy instances of reverse discrimination.

---

115. *See* D. Chalmers, *supra* n. 25, 67.
116. *Nederlandse Bakkerij Stichting and Others v. Edah BV*, Joined cases 80 and 159/85 [1986] ECR 3359, p. 3375.

In this part of the chapter I would like to argue that the same result, that is, legal homogeneity, can be achieved (and perhaps, to a certain extent, has actually been achieved) through a more 'diplomatic' route. In particular, I will argue that in the long run, many instances of reverse discrimination in the area of EC trade will be remedied automatically, as a result of the increased emergence of 'spontaneous harmonization'[117] which will result from the constant and increased contact of the legal systems and markets of the different Member States.[118] This indirect solution to the problem of reverse discrimination has the important advantage that it is a solution which will not cause the vehement objection of the Member States, since legal homogeneity will not be imposed 'from above' but will actually be a voluntary action on the part of the Member States which will be adapting their legal systems in such a way as to conform to their obligations as Member States of the EU, whilst enabling their domestic traders to effectively compete with other traders in the internal market.

The emergence of 'spontaneous harmonization' has already been achieved, to a certain extent, through the combined application of some of the principles (principle of mutual recognition) and instruments (Directive 83/189, Decision 3052/95) used for the construction of the internal market and this trend will increasingly emerge in the future. I would like to argue that the correct use of those instruments and principles will lead to a situation whereby national legal rules will no longer have to be partially struck down by a court in order to protect one of the fundamental freedoms: Member State laws will be consistent with the fundamental freedoms provisions from their inception and since, for practical reasons, Member States, will, in the majority of cases, draft a single piece of legislation for both, internal and inter-state situations, reverse discrimination will be eliminated as a result of the application of the same rules to both internal and inter-state situations. It is to the explanation of these principles and instruments that we now turn.

It should be recalled that in the early 1980s, due to the difficulties faced with the legislative process at EC level, great emphasis was placed on the removal of inter-state frontiers through the use of negative harmonization. It has already been explained that the ECJ was very active during that period in order to fill the void left by an inactive legislature. However, it was soon made clear that reactive control by a Court through striking down national measures that were contrary to EC law, was not an effective method that would be sufficient for removing all

117. For an explanation of spontaneous harmonization *see* S. de Vries, *supra* n. 64, p. 252.

118. Competition law is one area where 'spontaneous harmonization' has taken place. *See* K. Mortelmans, *supra* n. 81, 631-632; de Vries, *supra* n. 64, p. 252; D. O'Keeffe and A. Bavasso, *supra* n. 4, p. 544. *See* also para. 24 of the Opinion of Advocate General Kokott in *Confederación Española de Empresarios de Estaciones de Servicio v. Compañía Española de Petróleos SA*, Case No. C-217/05 [2006] ECR I-11987. Another area where 'spontaneous harmonization' has emerged is that of State liability formulated by the ECJ in *Francovich and Others*, Joined Cases C-6/90 and C-9/90 [1991] ECR I-5357. For an explanation of this *see* M.P.F. Granger, 'National applications of *Francovich* and the construction of a European administrative ius commune' (2007) 32 *ELRev* 157, 188-189.

obstacles to the free movement of, inter alia, goods. And since prevention is always better than cure, the Community institutions came up with a solution that has proved to be extremely successful – Directive 83/189,[119] which has now been replaced by Directive 98/34 which provides a system of *ex ante* control of national legislative measures.[120]

Like its predecessor, Directive 98/34 protects, by means of preventive control, the free movement of goods.[121] It requires all Member States to communicate to the Commission all draft technical regulations[122] for products that fall within the scope of the Directive and suspend the adoption of such technical regulations for specified periods of time. During the standstill period, the Commission can examine the compatibility of those technical regulations with EC law prior to their adoption in national law and, where appropriate, the Commission and/or the other Member States may make suggestions for alterations in order to make them compatible with EC law and prevent the erection of new barriers to interstate trade.

Accordingly, as a result of their obligations under Directive 98/34, the national legislatures seem to be no longer entirely free when drafting legislation,[123] but have to bring to light their proposed legislative measures and, as far as possible, incorporate in their final legislative drafts any suggestions made by the Commission or other Member States.

---

119. 83/189 (EEC) Directive laying down a procedure for the provision of information in the field of technical standards and regulations, OJ L 109/8, 1983, as amended by 88/182 (EEC) Directive amending Directive 83/189 laying down a procedure of information in the field of technical standards and regulations, OJ L 81/75, 1988 and 94/10 (EC) Directive materially amending for the second time Directive 83/189 laying down a procedure for the provision of information in the field of technical standards and regulations, OJ L 100/30, 1994. For an authoritative analysis of the Directive *see* S. Weatherill, 'Compulsory notification of draft technical regulations: the contribution of Directive 83/189 to the management of the internal market' (1996) 16 *YEL* 129. *See* also L. Gormley, 'Some reflections on the internal market and free movement of goods' (1989) 1 *LIEI* 9, 13-14.
120. 98/34 (EC) Directive laying down a procedure for the provision of information in the field of technical standards and regulations and on rules on Information Society services, OJ L 204/37, 1998 (as amended by 98/48 (EC) Directive amending Directive 98/34 laying down a procedure for the provision of information in the field of technical standards and regulations, OJ L 217/18, 1998).
121. *CIA Security International SA v. Signalson SA and Securitel SPRL*, Case No. C-194/94 [1996] ECR I-2201, para. 40; *Criminal proceedings against Lindberg*, Case No. C-267/03 [2005] ECR I-3247, para. 48; *Criminal proceedings against Lemmens*, Case No. C-226/97 [1998] ECR I-3711, para. 32; *Colim NV v. Bigg's Continent Noord NV*, Case No. C-33/97 [1999] ECR I-3175, para. 22.
122. For an explanation of the term 'draft technical regulations' *see*, among others, *Sapod Audic v. Eco-Emballages SA*, Case No. C-159/00 [2002] ECR I-5031; *Bic Benelux SA v. Belgian State*, Case No. C-13/96 [1997] ECR I-1753; *Criminal proceedings against Van der Burg*, Case No. C-278/99 [2001] ECR I-2015; *Commission v. Italy*, Case No. C-289/94 [1996] ECR I-4405.
123. For an excellent explanation of how European law affects the national legislative process, in particular through notification and standstill requirements, *see* J.H. Jans, 'National legislative autonomy? The procedural constraints of European law' (1998) 25 *LIEI* 25.

The fact that failure to observe the notification and standstill requirements of Directive 98/34 constitutes a substantial procedural defect such as to render the national technical regulations relied upon in a case before a national court inapplicable to individuals – as was recognized by the ECJ in the *CIA* judgment[124] – means that the national court which hears the case must decline to apply the national measure that has not been notified and thus that measure cannot be enforced against third parties. What is more, when there is a failure by a Member State to respect the notification and standstill requirements, it seems possible that individuals may be able to bring an action for damages under the *Francovich*[125] principle to claim compensation from that State if they can show that the three conditions laid down in *Francovich* are fulfilled.[126] Of course, the Commission can also bring proceedings under Article 226 EC (Article 258 TFEU) for failure to fulfil obligations if a Member State fails to notify a draft technical regulation that falls within the scope of the Directive. In this way the Community institutions, and in particular the Court of Justice, make sure that the provisions of Directive 98/34 are not side-stepped by national legislatures that are eager to avoid their obligations under EC law and protect their domestic products – only Member State laws that comply with EC law and which have been drafted in compliance with the procedure of Directive 98/34, can be applied by national courts.

Through the notification procedure under Directive 98/34, the Commission may also be able to ensure better respect of the mutual recognition principle. Dehousse has pointed out that the process under Directive 98/34 (then Directive 83/189) – a 'transparency process' – is very important since 'Member States are more likely to give legal value to the principle of mutual recognition if they are aware of the legal requirements and of the procedures existing in other Member States'.[127] The principle of mutual recognition – like Directive 98/34 – ensures that Member States are not entirely free in fields which are not regulated at Community

124. *CIA, supra* n. 121. *See* also *Sapod Audic, supra* n. 122; *Unilever Italia SpA v. Central Food Spa*, Case No. C-443/98 [2000] ECR I-7535 (breach of obligation to observe periods of postponement) [note, however, that some qualification to this principle was placed by the Court in *Lemmens, supra* n. 121]. For an explanation of the implications of the Court's enhancement of the judicial protection of rights to trade in the European internal market through its ruling in *CIA see* S. Weatherill, 'A case study in judicial activism in the 1990s: the status before national courts of measures wrongfully un-notified to the Commission', in *Liber Amicorum in Honour of Lord Slynn of Hadley: Judicial Review in European Union Law*, D. O'Keeffe and A. Bavasso (eds) (The Hague, Kluwer Law International, 2000). Note that the Commission seems to have held this view since the early days of life of the Directive: *see* Commission communication concerning the non-respect of certain provisions of Council Directive 83/189 (EEC) of 28 Mar. 1983 laying down a procedure for the provision of information in the field of technical standards and regulations, OJ C 245/4, 1986. For a more recent case confirming that this principle applies, also, to Directive 98/34 *see Lidl Italia Srl v. Comune di Stradella*, Case No. C-303/04 [2005] ECR I-7865, para. 23.
125. *Supra* n. 118.
126. *See* J.H. Jans, *supra* n. 123, 52.
127. R. Dehousse, *supra* n. 41, 115.

level.[128] In a number of cases, the Court has held that Member States which do not cater in their laws for products which have been lawfully manufactured and/or marketed in another Member State but which do not comply with the exact requirements imposed by that State's legislation, are in violation of Article 28 EC (Article 34 TFEU). In other words, Member States must make provision for mutual recognition in their laws, in order to comply with the requirements of Article 28 EC.[129]

The impressive contribution that Directive 83/189 (and, now, Directive 98/34) has made to the prevention of the emergence of new obstacles to the free movement of goods[130] has been recognized by the Community legislature which, in 1995, drafted Decision 3052/95.[131] This piece of Community legislation is very similar, in effect, to Directive 83/189 (and, now, Directive 98/34) since it requires Member States that take steps to prevent the free movement or placing on the market of a particular model or type of product lawfully produced or marketed in another Member State, to notify the Commission accordingly.[132]

It is obvious that the principles and instruments mentioned above facilitate (and, in fact, require) a constructive dialogue between the Member States and the Community, on the one hand, and between Member States among themselves, on the other. Accordingly, through the interaction between Member State legislatures and the Commission in order to ensure that legislation drafted at Member State level will not conflict with EC law, emerges a new reality in law-making. Law-making at Member State level appears to be increasingly affected by EC law. Since

---

128. *Ibid.*, 114-115.
129. *Commission v. France (foie gras)*, Case No. C-184/96 [1998] ECR I-6197. *See* also *Commission v. Spain*, Case No. C-358/01 [2003] ECR I-13145. For an explanation *see* C. Barnard, *supra* n. 8, pp. 589-590. Note, however, that the principle of mutual recognition allows Member States to subject to prior authorization certain products in order to establish equivalence of protection of certain non-trade principles, provided that a number of conditions are complied with and provided that the requirement of authorization is justified on one of the public interest grounds set out in Art. 30 EC (Art. 36 TFEU) or by an imperative requirement. *See Commission v. France*, Case No. C-24/00 [2004] ECR I-1277; *Commission v. Italy*, Case No. C-270/02 [2004] ECR I-1559; *Greenham v. Abel*, Case No. C-95/01 [2004] ECR I-1333. For an annotation of these three judgments *see* M.A. Jarvis, (2004) 41 *CMLRev* 1395. *See* also *Commission v. Denmark*, Case No. C-192/01 [2003] ECR I-9693.
130. Note that in the context of freedom of establishment for providers of services, Art. 15(7) of the Services Directive (*supra* n. 104) includes a communication mechanism similar to the one provided under Directive 98/34, though the Services Directive does not include a standstill clause. It should be noted that the Directive does not include a similar mechanism for services and this has been considered an omission (*see* Editorial Comment: 'The services directive proposal: Striking a balance between the promotion of the internal market and preserving the European social model?' (2006) 43 *CMLRev* 307, 311).
131. 3052/95 (EC) Decision establishing a procedure for the exchange of information on national measures derogating from the principle of the free movement of goods within the Community, OJ L 321/1, 1995.
132. For case-law on this *see*, among others, *Commission v. Portugal*, Case No. C-432/03 [2005] ECR I-9665; *Radiosistemi Srl v. Prefetto di Genova*, Joined Cases C-388/00 and C-429/00 [2002] ECR I-5845; *Commission v. France*, Case No. C-23/99 [2000] ECR I-7653.

Member States can no longer 'take a strictly national point of view when drawing up technical and commercial regulations'[133] and since '[t]he proper functioning of the common market demands that each Member State also give consideration to the legitimate requirements of the other Member States',[134] law-making at national level has now been metamorphosed to a broader process that not only has to take into account the balancing of aims and principles that has to take place at Member State level, but also includes a broader dimension: the need to balance the aims and principles of national governments whilst taking into account the obligations of Member States deriving from EC law.

However, this brings us to the question of how reverse discrimination can be remedied through the above process. The answer lies in the fact that in practical terms, it is highly unlikely that Member States will make two pieces of legislation for each product or category of products, the application of each depending on whether the affected product is imported or domestic; though, of course, exceptions can arise in instances where a Member State feels particularly strongly about a specific product (e.g., traditional products such as pasta in Italy or beer in Germany) and the application of its own traditional rules for the regulation of such products to *imported* products would be contrary to EC law.

What I would like to point out is that, when a Member State could draft legislation without having to inform the Community institutions and/or the other Member States about its exact provisions, it was easy for Member States to make legislation that would be contrary to EC law by imposing an obstacle to the free movement of goods. Such legislation would only subsequently be partially struck down if and when a Member State national or a firm would bring an action before a national court relying on the fact that the contested legislation was in breach of EC law; or, when the Commission was informed of its existence provided, of course, that it would decide to pursue the matter further through an action under Article 226 EC (Article 258 TFEU).

In these instances, reverse discrimination would emerge as such national legislation would be held by the national court or the ECJ to be inapplicable only to imported goods. However since, now, the Community requires that Member States must comply with EC law when drafting national legislation – and, more importantly, ensures that this is so through, inter alia, the application of Directive 98/34 and the direct effect given to its provisions through the *CIA* judgment – Member States will no longer be able to make legislation which, when applied to imported goods, will be contrary to EC law. And since, as already explained, in the great majority of cases Member States will not consider it worthwhile to set-up a different trading regime for imported and domestic products and may even be totally opposed to the emergence of reverse discrimination against domestic products, reverse discrimination will be automatically remedied in this way.

---

133. *See* First biennial report on the application of the principle of mutual recognition in product and services markets, SEC (1999) 1106, not published in the Official Journal.
134. Communication from the Commission concerning the consequences of the judgment given by the Court of Justice on 20 Feb. 1979 in case 120/78 ('Cassis de Dijon'), OJ C 256/2, 1980.

X CONCLUSION

The clear conclusion at which we can arrive following the analysis provided in this chapter, is that reverse discrimination is no longer acceptable in the European internal market. At a time when the main (and only) aim of the Community was the construction of the internal market, reverse discrimination was considered a necessary evil of the system adopted for the attainment of that aim. Nevertheless, following the completion of the internal market and the increasing importance attached to the aim of ensuring that the market is one that functions properly, reverse discrimination suffered in cases where traders involved in cross-border trade and traders that are in a purely internal situation are similarly situated, is a form of differential treatment that comes into conflict with the broader aims of the Community in the context of its policy on the internal market. If unjustified, it is a form of discrimination which comes into conflict with the main aim of maintaining a properly functioning market since it gives rise to a distortion of the conditions of competition.

Accordingly, any unjustified instances of reverse discrimination should now be remedied at EC level, either through legislative action under Article 95 EC (Article 114 TFEU) or through the judicial application of a combination of Treaty Articles (14(2), 10 and 3(1)(g) EC)[135] striking down national measures the continued application of which gives rise to (unjustifiable instances of) reverse discrimination. The Court of Justice in its recent case-law seems (implicitly) to be concerned with the problem of reverse discrimination and through its rulings seeks to prevent its emergence. However, as explained in the last part of the chapter, in pragmatic terms, reverse discrimination in the area of trade may – in the majority of cases – actually be remedied automatically as a result of the increased emergence of 'spontaneous harmonization'. Therefore, the possible EC solutions to the problem of reveres discrimination in the area of EC trade proposed in this chapter, would be left for more difficult instances of reverse discrimination and, in particular, for instances of reverse discrimination that arise as a result of legislation that has already existed in the legal systems of Member States for quite a long time and perhaps even before the birth of the Community.

---

135. For the situation after the coming into force of the Treaty of Lisbon, *see* n. 50.

Chapter 6

Conclusion

The theme of this book has been the problem of reverse discrimination in EC law. In particular, the main aim of this study has been to illustrate that reverse discrimination is not any more an acceptable difference in treatment that falls outside the scope of EC law. To this effect, two developments that have taken place in the EC during the 1990s[1] have been extensively analyzed, illustrating that the EC is a supranational organization that is no longer concerned merely with the construction and maintenance of the internal market. It has been concluded that those developments have tilted the balance against reverse discrimination and have created a new reality for the Community which, as a result, will sooner or later have to provide a solution to the problem of reverse discrimination.

This chapter includes a summary of the basic conclusions that have been reached through the analysis provided in the book. This is followed by a brief description of the solutions which are available for the resolution of the reverse discrimination conundrum and their advantages and disadvantages. It should be noted, however, that the different available solutions are only very briefly examined in the course of this study. This is because the question that was aimed to be answered through this work has been *whether* reverse discrimination is still a difference in treatment that falls outside the scope of EC law. *How* the problem of reverse discrimination should actually be remedied, is a different question that can only be answered once and if it is proved and accepted that reverse discrimination is a problem that falls within the scope of application of EC law.

1. The institution of the status of citizenship and the formal completion of the internal market.

I CONCLUSIONS

It should be recalled that the main question of the study has been whether, viewed against the background of the post-Maastricht developments, reverse discrimination should, now, be considered to be a difference in treatment which falls within the scope of EC law. This question was answered through the analysis provided in Part II of the book (Chapters 4 and 5).

In Chapter 1 of the book, the problem of reverse discrimination together with its cause, the purely internal rule, were presented. There was, also, an explanation of the 'linking factor test' implicitly applied by the Court for determining whether a situation falls within the scope of the fundamental freedoms provisions. In Chapter 2 the traditional approach of the Court towards the application of that test was presented. An explanation of the problems arising from this approach was also provided. It was seen that the two major problems are: (a) the failure, in certain instances, to reflect the economic realities of a case, by excluding from the scope of EC law situations which have a sufficient connection with the aims of the fundamental freedoms provisions; and, (b) the fact that under this approach, the negative effects (i.e., reverse discrimination) that the application of the purely internal rule has in situations which do not involve a negative impact on the sole aim of the fundamental freedoms are ignored, this having been justified, until recently, by the fact that the sole aim of the Community – until the early 1990s – was the construction of an internal market. Chapter 3 had as its aim to present the different ('new') approaches to the application of the linking factor test, which have been followed by the Court in some of its recent case-law. It was argued that these approaches appear to be a subtle confirmation of the fact that the Court now recognizes the problems caused from the application of its traditional approach to purely internal situations. The new approach followed in some of the Court's case-law in the context of the free movement of goods and services appears to have been a response to one of the problems of the traditional approach (i.e., the failure to reflect economic reality). The Court, also, seems to have been implicitly working for the resolution of the second problem (i.e., reverse discrimination), by including within the scope of the free movement of (economically active) persons provisions as many situations as possible – even situations which only include a very artificial link with the economic aim of those provisions. It was concluded, however, that making it overly easy for a situation to fall within the scope of the fundamental freedoms provisions merely scratches the surface of the problem and, in fact, causes more problems than it solves. Since the only aim of the free movement of (economically active) persons provisions is to build a common market in labour, any situations which do not involve a negative impact on the achievement of this aim should not be included within the scope of these provisions. And since reverse discrimination does not impede in any way the attainment of this objective it should not be held to be a difference in treatment that is contrary to the fundamental freedoms provisions. Therefore, some other way has to be found for including instances of reverse discrimination within the scope of EC law.

The aim of Part II of the book was to illustrate that even though reverse discrimination rightly continues to be considered a difference in treatment that falls outside the scope of the fundamental freedoms provisions, other principles/ provisions of Community law can be employed for prohibiting this form of differential treatment, where appropriate. In fact, two major developments that have taken place in the EC during the 1990s now make it imperative for the EC to provide a solution to this problem. Chapters 4 and 5 of the book dealt with each of these developments.

The main question in Chapter 4 was whether the introduction of the status of citizenship of the Union, and the development of this status through the Court's jurisprudence, have had any implications for the view according to which reverse discrimination falls outside the scope of EC law. It was explained that, until very recently, the EC was still mainly – if not solely – an *economic* organization of limited scope and aims and thus a difference in treatment based on a person's contribution to the internal market was justified by the need to confine the scope of application of Community law to situations where this would be necessary for the attainment of its economic aims. However, following the introduction of the status of Union citizenship and, in particular, as a result of the Court's latest judgments in the area of citizenship, Community rights have been extended to economically inactive Union citizens who cannot point in any way to a link with the economic aims of the Treaty. Accordingly, it seems that the status of Union citizenship is not merely symbolic but a status through which Member State nationals have attained importance in the Community legal order as citizens (and not, merely, as factors of production). Since the latest case-law of the Court has brought economically active and economically inactive persons to the same position under EC law and, thus, a person's contribution to the completion of the internal market seems to bear little importance in relation to the question of whether a person should enjoy a number of rights under Community law, reverse discrimination is no longer a justified difference in treatment, unless the differentiation made is based on a (valid) ground other than the desire to grant EC rights only to persons who contribute to the economic aims of the Treaty. This difference in treatment falls within the scope of EC law since it is a 'residual situation' from the point of view of the Community, as it arises as a side-effect of the process of European integration. Hence, since one of the aims of the Community, now, is to prevent the emergence of any unjustified difference in treatment as a result of the process of European integration, reverse discrimination may amount to a violation of the Community principle of equality.

In Chapter 5, the question was whether reverse discrimination against producers/traders the situation of which is purely internal to a Member State is, still, a difference in treatment which is not prohibited by EC law. It was explained that until quite recently and because the principal focus of the internal market provisions of the Treaty was the construction of the internal market, reverse discrimination was a necessary evil of the system adopted for the creation of a common market and an acceptable difference in treatment since it does not inhibit the opening-up of national frontiers. However, following the (formal) completion of the internal market in 1992, the focus of the Community's internal market policy has been placed on the proper functioning of the newly-constructed market. This has had as a result that reverse discrimination may now, in certain instances, be considered a difference in treatment contrary to the aims of the Treaty, since it amounts to a violation of the principle of undistorted competition which must be respected in a properly functioning market. Since reverse discrimination arises as a side-effect of the construction of the internal market, it is a problem which emerges as a result of the process of European integration and thus falls within the scope of EC law.

Therefore, through the analysis provided in this study, it has been concluded that the main question of the study can be answered in the affirmative. In particular, viewed against the background of the post-Maastricht developments, reverse discrimination can, now, be considered to be a difference in treatment which falls within the scope of EC law as a result of the fact that it may have a negative impact on the achievement of the (now broader) objectives of the Community.

II WHICH INSTANCES OF REVERSE DISCRIMINATION MUST BE REMEDIED?

Before moving on with the available solutions to the reverse discrimination conundrum, it should be highlighted that it is my view that not all instances of reverse discrimination are problematic from the point of view of Community law. Therefore, a line must be drawn between situations of reverse discrimination that are, indeed, problematic and must be remedied as a matter of EC law; and situations of reverse discrimination which are, in reality, instances of differential treatment of different situations and which thus do not amount to discrimination. For this purpose, in cases involving reverse discrimination, the important question should be whether, in the relevant area in question, situations that fall within the scope of the fundamental freedoms provisions are similar to situations that are purely internal to a Member State and, therefore, must be treated in the same way. It should be noted that such a distinction between problematic instances of reverse discrimination and instances of reverse discrimination that do not, in reality, amount to discrimination, has not been made earlier in the book, since I did not wish to add an extra layer of perplexity to the analysis.

As explained in Chapter 1, reverse discrimination firstly emerged as a side-effect of the Community's desire to bring persons and traders taking part in the process of European economic integration to the same position as persons and traders whose economic activities were confined within the territory of a single Member State, so that the exercise of the fundamental freedoms would not be deterred. In such instances, reverse discrimination was merely a difference in treatment that emerged as a result of the Community having recourse to 'positive action' in order to achieve substantive equality – in order to compensate persons/traders taking part in the process of European economic integration for disadvantages they would have suffered as a result of exercising one of the fundamental freedoms. Obviously, such instances of reverse discrimination are not problematic since, in reality, they do not lead to the emergence of differential treatment of similar situations. The situation of persons/traders that suffer a disadvantage *as a result of having exercised one of the fundamental freedoms* is not similar to the situation of persons who are in a purely internal situation and do not suffer such a disadvantage. Hence, one could even go one step further and argue that, strictly speaking, such forms of differential treatment should not even be defined as 'reverse *discrimination*'.[2] The situations only become similar once the persons/traders who fall within the scope of EC law are given the more favourable treatment that they are entitled under EC law in order to be compensated for the disadvantages arising from their exercise of one of the fundamental freedoms.

Nonetheless, reverse discrimination becomes problematic when it emerges as a result of the overcompensation of a disadvantage; or when it involves the provision of more favourable treatment in situations where no disadvantage would have been suffered as a result of exercising one of the fundamental freedoms. In these instances, the two situations – that is, the purely internal situation and the situation falling within the scope of EC law – are similar and the Community merely rewards persons/traders who have exercised one of the fundamental freedoms. In such instances of reverse discrimination, extra rights are granted to persons/traders whose situations fall within the scope of EC law and, therefore, they are not merely brought to the same position as persons/traders who are in a purely internal situation but are, in fact, treated more beneficially. It is these instances of reverse discrimination that are problematic from the point of view of Community law and for which a solution must be provided.

A better understanding of these two different 'categories' of reverse discrimination can be gained through the use of practical examples both in the context of the free movement of persons and in the area of EC trade.

Starting with the area of persons, the paradigmatic situation of reverse discrimination which amounts, in reality, to merely a form of positive action leading to substantive equality, is that suffered in instances having to do with occupational/educational qualifications. In Chapter 2, we saw the case of *Aubertin*.[3] The Court in its judgment held that Community law does not preclude national rules whereby a Member State requires its own nationals who have received their training in that State to hold a diploma in order to operate a hairdressing salon, whilst permitting

2. According to Sundberg-Weitman, 'It is probably that, where a state or an undertaking gives special favours to immigrants, there will in most cases be no "discrimination" in lack of "comparability". Normally, such favours aim at equality in fact' – B. Sundberg-Weitman, *Discrimination on Grounds of Nationality: Free Movement of Workers and Freedom of Establishment under the EEC Treaty* (Amsterdam, New York, Oxford, North-Holland Publishing Company, 1977), p. 115.
3. *Criminal proceedings against Aubertin and others*, Joined Cases C-29/94, C-30/94, C-31/94, C-32/94, C-33/94, C-34/94 and C-35/94 [1995] ECR I-301.

hairdressers who are nationals of other Member States to operate a hairdressing salon without holding such a diploma, provided they have pursued that occupation in another Member State for a number of years. The Community, recognizing that it is most probable that nationals of other Member States will not possess the exact qualifications required by the host State, has required States to accept in their labour market nationals of other Member States (or, even, their own nationals) who have exercised an occupation in the territory of another Member State for a number of years and thus appear to possess adequate knowledge for the performance of that occupation, even though they do not possess the exact qualifications required for its own nationals. Those persons have already complied with the requirements of their Member State of origin for the performance of that activity and, therefore, any requirements imposed by the host State on them as regards qualifications are additional – in other words, if the host State is given the right to regulate their situation, then they will suffer a double burden and thus will probably be deterred from exercising one of the fundamental freedoms. In such instances, the Community requires the host State to apply different requirements to nationals of other Member States than those imposed on its own nationals, since these two categories of persons are not similarly situated in terms of regulation: nationals of other Member States have already complied with one set of regulations, whereas nationals of the host State will only be regulated by the host Member State. Therefore, such instances of reverse discrimination should not be considered as amounting to discrimination.

On the other hand, certain instances of reverse discrimination appear to amount to a differential treatment of similar situations since the more favourable treatment afforded to persons who fall within the scope of EC law is not necessary for compensating a disadvantage that they would have suffered as a result of exercising one of the fundamental freedoms. These instances of reverse discrimination are the ones that should be targeted for resolution. An example of such an instance of reverse discrimination is the one that was challenged in *Hurd v. Jones*,[4] again seen in Chapter 2. It should be recalled that in that case it was held that the United Kingdom was not in violation of Article 12 EC (Article 18 TFEU) read in conjunction with Article 39 EC (Article 45 TFEU) when it subjected to income tax both the basic salary paid by the United Kingdom to British teachers in the European School in Britain and the 'European supplement' paid to them by the European School, whilst the 'European supplement' of nationals of other Member States who worked in the same school was not subject to British income tax. Since, according to the Court, the situation of the former was a purely internal one, this difference in treatment fell outside the scope of EC law. As can be deduced from the facts of the case,[5] teachers who were not British nationals and who worked in the European school situated in Britain, would not have already had to pay income tax on their 'European supplement' in their State of origin. Therefore,

4. *Hurd v. Jones (Her Majesty's Inspector of Taxes)*, Case No. 44/84 [1986] ECR 29.
5. *Ibid.*, paras 9-10.

the requirement that nationals of other Member States would be exempted from national income tax as regards their 'European supplement' over-compensated those persons who had exercised one of the fundamental freedoms. If they were already subject to such taxation in their State of origin, the exemption would be necessary to bring them to the same position as British nationals who were in a purely internal situation, since the latter would only be taxed once as regards their 'European supplement' – by exempting nationals of other Member States working in Britain from income tax as regards the 'European supplement' it would have been ensured that they would not suffer a double burden, since they would only be taxed once (in their State of origin). However, since no such taxation was imposed by their State of nationality and thus they had not, already, once paid such a tax in their home State, they were in a similar situation to that of British nationals and, thus, the two categories of workers should be treated in the same way. Therefore, through the exercise of this instance of reverse discrimination, nationals of other Member States were treated better than British nationals, even though their situations were similar. Such instances of reverse discrimination should be considered as amounting to discrimination.

The area of family reunification rights provides an excellent example of an area where instances of reverse discrimination that used to be acceptable because they achieved substantive equality, have now been transformed to unacceptable instances of reverse discrimination that must be targeted for resolution.

As explained, traditionally the Community legislature and the judiciary have made family reunification rights available, merely in order to encourage economic actors to migrate to other Member States in furtherance of the Community's economic objectives. The grant of EC family reunification rights was merely a form of 'positive action' aiming at bringing migrant economic actors to the same position as non-migrants, as regards the right to live with close family members. Therefore, for instance, the right given to a man, moving from his Member State of origin (*where he lived with his wife*) to another Member State in order to work, to be accompanied in the latter by his wife, brought him to the same position as persons who were in a purely internal situation and who thus enjoyed their family life undisturbed since they had not changed their State of residence and work. Under the Court's traditional family reunification rights case-law, it was only in situations where the movement of the worker *would result* in the loss of the right to live with his family members – *which was already enjoyed in the State from which he moved* and which was still enjoyed by persons in purely internal situations – that family reunification rights were granted by EC law. Hence, any instances which involved reverse discrimination as a result of the grant of EC family reunification rights to migrant Member State nationals whilst such rights were denied to persons in purely internal situations could, in fact, be described merely as instances of positive action necessary for enabling persons to exercise one of the fundamental freedoms. In such instances of reverse discrimination, the Community was merely compensating migrant workers for a right (the right to enjoy family life) that would be lost *as a result of the exercise of one of the fundamental freedoms.*

However, in cases like *Carpenter*,[6] *Jia*[7] and *Eind*[8] (seen in Chapter 3) where the grant of family reunification rights was not necessary for enabling a Member State national to *continue* living the family life he or she lived before exercising one of the fundamental freedoms, we no longer have, merely, a form of (permissible) 'positive action'. Rather, the extra rights given to some Member State nationals just because they are lucky enough to be able to point to a link with EC law (even an entirely artificial one!), transforms this form of 'positive action' to blatant discrimination.[9] And this form of (reverse) discrimination is no longer suffered by persons because they have not contributed to the economic aims of the Treaty – something which could, to a certain extent, form a valid justification; but by persons who just happen to be unable to point to a (even artificial) link with EC law.

In the area of EC trade, also, two different kinds of situations involving reverse discrimination can be distinguished.

Firstly, we have situations involving the application of rules regarding the production requirements with which products must comply. An example of such a rule is the rule challenged in *Drei Glocken*[10] which required pasta (whether imported or domestic) that was to be marketed in Italy to be produced solely from durum wheat. In this situation, imported goods and domestic goods should not be considered to be in a similar position, from a regulatory point of view. This is because imported goods had, already, had to comply with the production requirements of their own State, whereas domestic goods would *only* be regulated by the Italian rules on the production of pasta. Therefore, although the contested legislation treated, on its face, domestic and imported goods in the same way, nevertheless, it gave rise to discrimination *against imported goods*, since it imposed on them a double regulatory burden. This is why the Court in that case held that EC law required the Italian rules not to be applied, but only as regards imported pasta. Accordingly, as regards the application of rules regulating the production conditions of products, domestic and imported goods do not appear to be similarly situated and, therefore, the State of production of the domestic goods should remain free to treat them differently than imported goods, since the latter have *already* been *lawfully* produced in the territory of another Member State.

6. *Carpenter v. Secretary of State for the Home Department*, Case No. C-60/00 [2002] ECR 6279.
7. *Jia v. Migrationsverket*, Case No. C-1/05 [2007] ECR I-1
8. *Minister voor Vreemdelingenzaken en Integratie v. R. N. G. Eind*, Case No. C-291/05, judgment of 11 Dec. 2007, not yet reported.
9. In the context of the bestowal of family reunification rights, it is possible for the migrant to be over-compensated, because the EC provisions requiring the grant of family reunification rights do not require merely the removal of discrimination on the grounds of nationality (this, for example, is the case with Art. 7 of 1612/68 (EEC) Regulation on freedom of movement for workers within the Community, OJ L 257/2, 1968) as regards the grant of such rights, but, require the grant of family reunification rights in all cases involving a migrant Union citizen whose situation falls within the scope of EC law (irrespective of whether such rights are enjoyed under the national law of the host State).
10. *Drei Glocken GmbH and Gertraud Kritzinger v. USL Centro-Sud and Provincia autonoma di Bolzano*, Case No. 407/85 [1988] ECR 4233.

Therefore, in such situations it is unlikely that reverse discrimination will be considered to be a form of a difference in treatment that is in violation of EC law.

On the other hand, the position is different as regards marketing rules. If we take as an example the rules that were found to be in violation of Article 28 EC (Article 34 TFEU) in *Franzén*[11] (rules which, inter alia, required wholesalers of alcoholic drinks to obtain a 'wholesale licence' in order to be able to market such drinks), it can be seen that goods that were in a cross-border situation and goods that were in a purely internal situation were in a similar position: here, there was no issue of some of them already complying with a different trading regime, this resulting in the imposition of a double regulatory burden. Domestic and imported alcoholic drinks were in a comparable situation since the sale of both was subject to the holding of a 'wholesale licence' *and*, obviously, imported beverages had not, already, complied with a similar rule in their home State (their State of production). The result of the case (i.e., the non-applicability of the contested restrictive rules *only* to imported alcoholic beverages) would lead to the emergence of reverse discrimination and since, in this situation, the two categories of products are in the same position as regards the imposition of *marketing* rules – both have to be regulated by the State in the territory of which they are marketed – this instance of reverse discrimination amounts to a difference in treatment which, if unjustified, will be considered to amount to discrimination.

III POSSIBLE SOLUTIONS TO THE REVERSE DISCRIMINATION CONUNDRUM: THE WAY FORWARD

A National Level

1 Spontaneous Harmonization

As was seen in Chapters 3 and 5, 'spontaneous harmonization' is one of the most popular solutions for the reverse discrimination conundrum that can be provided at national level.

'Spontaneous harmonization' emerges when national legislators determine that it is advantageous to amend their laws and bring them into line with the laws of other States or, in case a State is a member of a supranational organization, with the laws of that organization. In other words, it is a form of harmonization that emerges as a result of the own volition of the legislator, as opposed to being imposed by others (and this is why it is also called 'voluntary harmonization').

The Court of Justice has repeatedly hinted in its case-law that reverse discrimination is a problem that does not concern the EC; and that it should be the Member States that will provide a remedy by, inter alia, trading up to Community

11. *Criminal proceedings against Franzén*, Case No. C-189/95 [1997] ECR I-5909.

standards. Therefore, the Court has traditionally viewed 'spontaneous harmonization' as the most appropriate solution to the problem of reverse discrimination.

In the last main section of Chapter 3, I briefly mentioned the *Dzodzi* case,[12] where the Court replied to a question referred for a preliminary ruling that emerged from facts that were purely internal to a Member State (Belgium). The need to provide an interpretation of Community law in such a case arose from the fact that Belgian law required that Belgian workers who were in a purely internal situation be given the same rights of family reunification as were given, by virtue of EC law, to nationals of other Member States who worked in Belgium. Clearly, this was a form of 'spontaneous harmonization' since, in order to prevent the emergence of reverse discrimination in the context of family reunification rights, the Belgian legislature extended to Belgian nationals in purely internal situations, the protection bestowed by EC law on migrant workers.

The case of Belgium is not an isolated example. Many other Member States have brought some of their laws into line with EC rules when this was not required by EC law, in order to prevent the emergence of reverse discrimination. And as seen in the previous chapter, this trend will increasingly emerge in the future, especially in the area of trade, as a result of the constant interaction between the national legislators and the Commission, through communication mechanisms such as that provided under Directive 98/34,[13] as well as through the actual process of completing and maintaining a genuine internal market.

The main advantage of 'spontaneous harmonization' is that it leads to the *voluntary* alignment of the laws of the different Member States with Community rules. In other words, it is a form of harmonization that is not imposed 'from above' and thus Member States cannot complain that the Community institutions are driving the Community towards an internal market that is wholly centralized, that is, to a market where the values of cultural diversity and experimentation (the latter being achieved through the process of competition among rules) are replaced by complete uniformity. Moreover, it is only when the emergence of reverse discrimination is absolutely irreconcilable with the proper functioning of their markets, that Member States resort to 'spontaneous harmonization', thus leaving instances of reverse discrimination which are necessary for the maintenance of, say, the good reputation of their traditional products, untouched.

Although 'spontaneous harmonization' is one of the ways available to Member States for effectively dealing with the problem of reverse discrimination, in my view, it cannot appropriately be considered a 'solution'. It is merely a random way of removing the most disturbing instances of reverse discrimination. And not only that, but one could even move one step further and argue that 'spontaneous harmonization' gives rise to further instances of inequality since, as a result of this process, there is no longer merely a difference in treatment between persons who

12. *Dzodzi v. Belgian State*, Joined Cases 297/88 and 197/89 [1990], ECR I-3763.
13. 98/34 (EC) Directive laying down a procedure for the provision of information in the field of technical standards and regulations and on rules on Information Society services, OJ L 204/37, 1998.

fall within the scope of EC law and persons that are not entitled to EC law protection as a result of the fact that they have not contributed to the internal market; as a result of 'spontaneous harmonization', now, there is also a difference in treatment between persons who happen to be nationals of a Member State that has resorted to the method of 'spontaneous harmonization', and persons who are nationals of a Member State which has preferred to continue applying its more restrictive laws in purely internal situations.

2 The (national) Constitutional Principle of Equality

In Chapter 3 of the book, it was also briefly mentioned that in some Member States, such as Italy, Austria and France, the national courts have ruled that reverse discrimination is a difference in treatment that is prohibited by the Constitutional principle of equality.

This way of dealing with instances of reverse discrimination (i.e., by ruling that it is contrary to the Constitutional principle of equality of a Member State) has, again, the advantage that it is a 'solution' imposed 'from below' and, thus, cannot lead to objections on the part of the Member States. Nonetheless, like 'spontaneous harmonization', it suffers from the major disadvantage that it may be the cause of a different kind of inequality, arising from the fact that even if most of the Member States have a constitutionally enshrined principle of equality, nevertheless, not all Member State courts have ruled that reverse discrimination actually amounts to a violation of that principle.

Accordingly, although the application of the national principle of equality can, indeed, remove instances of reverse discrimination in some Member States, nonetheless, it cannot be considered a 'solution' within the proper meaning of the term: some Member State nationals will continue to be the victims of reverse discrimination, merely because they happen to be nationals of a Member State which either does not protect the principle of equality in its constitution, or the courts of law of that State have not ruled that reverse discrimination amounts to a violation of that principle.

B EC Level

1 Positive Harmonization

In Chapter 5 of the book, it was concluded that one of the available solutions for the reverse discrimination conundrum in the area of EC trade is the making of legislation by the Community using as a legal basis Article 95 EC (Article 114 TFEU), specifically in order to remedy instances of reverse discrimination. In particular, it was argued that as the Community legislature has already passed legislation based on Article 95 EC to correct deficiencies in the protection of public health or the maintenance of a system of undistorted competition arising as a result of the completion of the internal market, in the same way, legislation *could* be drafted for ensuring the proper functioning of the market by removing (appreciable) distortions of competition resulting from the emergence of reverse discrimination.

This, however, seems to be the solution less likely to be adopted – or, if adopted at all, it will only be in extremely hard cases of reverse discrimination, which persist despite the efforts of all interested parties to remove them. This is due to the fact that it appears somewhat improbable that the Community legislature will resort to positive harmonization, specifically in order to remedy instances of reverse discrimination; or, if we view things from the other side, that Member States will happily accept such an unwarranted intrusion into their regulatory powers. The idea of making legislation that is explicitly targeted at purely internal situations (i.e., EC legislation that extends the application of EC rules to products confined within their State of origin), seems to be on a collision course with the whole philosophy of the EC, according to which the overall responsibility for regulating national markets lies with the Member States. In addition, there are many areas in which the Community has no competence to act by making legislation (for instance, ethical issues having to do with abortion, reproduction, alcohol consumption), even though the scope of application of EC law may extend to cover a situation falling within that area of law.[14] The application of Community law in that context may have as an effect that the national laws regulating the area in question must become inapplicable in situations falling within the scope of EC law. Obviously, in such instances reverse discrimination may emerge, since the contested national rule only becomes inapplicable to situations falling within the scope of EC law. And because the Community legislature does not have the competence to act in the area in question, such instances of reverse discrimination will not be remediable by having recourse to positive harmonization.

The Community legislature can contribute to the resolution of the reverse discrimination conundrum by adopting a more subtle course of action. When the Community legislature has recourse to positive harmonization in order to lay down the standards that must be satisfied by products which *circulate* within the internal market, it also provides an *indirect* solution to the problem of reverse discrimination. This is due to the fact that, most instances of reverse discrimination are involuntary: Member States merely continue to apply their laws to their own products after those laws have been held – by virtue of application of EC law – to be inapplicable to imported products. It is only very seldom that Member States *specifically* make legislation which imposes stricter requirements only on their own products, the national legislatures themselves being aware of the negative repercussions that reverse discrimination may have for the competitiveness of their own products – in the words of Davies, this is 'pure national regulatory masochism'![15] Therefore, under normal circumstances, Member States are eager to remove any instances of reverse discrimination.

14. See n. 21 in Ch. 1.
15. G. Davies, *Nationality Discrimination in the European Internal Market* (The Hague, Kluwer Law International, 2003), p. 136.

Accordingly, if rules for the production and marketing of specific products are laid down by the Community itself, and those rules have to be implemented into the national legal systems by Member State legislatures, it is highly unlikely that the latter will make (or retain) two pieces of legislation laying down rules for the production or marketing of specific products, one applying to products involved in inter-state trade (as required by the Community legislation), and the other applying to purely internal situations. This, in effect, means that reverse discrimination will hardly ever be suffered by products which remain confined within their own Member State but which are of a kind for which – if they fell within the scope of EC law – EC rules would apply; the national legislatures will, most probably, *voluntarily* apply the same rules to situations that fall within the scope of national law.

Accordingly, whenever the Community legislature regulates the conditions for production and marketing of certain products, Member States will have to incorporate those standards in their national laws (unless, of course, the legislation is in the form of a Regulation). And, for the reasons explained in the immediately preceding paragraph, it is highly probable that the national legislation that will be made for incorporating those standards in national law will be held to apply *both* to situations that involve inter-state trade *and* to purely internal situations.

In this way, reverse discrimination against products that fall within a category for which standards have been provided by the Community (EC law, however, requiring those standards to be imposed only on inter-state situations) will no longer emerge, this being another instance of 'spontaneous harmonization' the seeds of which in this instance, however, are sown by the actions of the Community legislature. It should be remembered, nonetheless, that this (indirect) solution can only be used *in tandem* with the other solutions, especially since it is well-known that the principle of subsidiarity calls for a restraint on the part of the Community legislature which should use its powers only where 'the objectives of the proposed action cannot be sufficiently achieved by the Member States'.[16]

2 Negative Harmonization

In Chapter 5, it was seen that it is not only the Community legislature that can contribute to the resolution of the reverse discrimination conundrum. In that chapter, it was suggested that reverse discrimination in the area of EC trade will be able to be ruled contrary to EC law and thus remedied through the use of a number of Treaty Articles. In particular, it was suggested that since reverse discrimination causes competitive distortions which conflict with the Community's task of maintaining a system ensuring that competition in the internal market is not distorted (Article 3(1)(g) EC);[17] and since, according to Article 14(2) EC (Article 26(2)

16. *See* Art. 5(2) EC. With the coming into force of the Treaty of Lisbon (Treaty of Lisbon amending the Treaty on European Union and the Treaty establishing the European Community, OJ C 306/1, 2007), Art. 5(2) EC will be replaced, in substance, by Art. 5, para. 3, TEU.
17. For the situation after the Treaty of Lisbon comes into force *see* n. 50 in Ch. 5.

TFEU), the internal market is an area without internal frontiers where the free movement of products and factors of production is ensured in accordance with the provisions of the Treaty; any national rules the continued application of which – following a judgment of the ECJ – gives rise to reverse discrimination, should be held to be in breach of Articles 3(1)(g) and 14(2) EC read in conjunction with Article 10 EC.[18,19]

Clearly, the ECJ will be able to require Member States to remedy such instances of reverse discrimination, when cases are brought before it under the Article 226 EC (Article 258 TFEU) procedure. However, like in most other instances, only if the direct effect of those provisions is accepted, will it be possible for most instances of reverse discrimination to be remedied, since it is the victims of reverse discrimination (traders and companies in purely internal situations) that will mostly be interested in remedying those competitive distortions. Therefore, the Court of Justice should deliver a ruling of principle holding that instances of reverse discrimination against products in purely internal situations, are prohibited by Articles 10, 14(2) and 3(1)(g) EC; and, that those provisions are directly effective and so traders in all Member States can rely on them before their national courts in order to require their own Member State to refrain from applying stricter rules to traders in purely internal situations.

Judicial solutions will most likely be used for remedying (or preventing the emergence of) instances of reverse discrimination that persist, despite the adoption of positive harmonization measures by the Community legislature and despite the increased resort to 'spontaneous harmonization' by Member States. And, in practical terms, the judicial solution explained in the immediately preceding paragraphs will mostly be used for remedying instances of reverse discrimination that arise as a result of *maintaining* national rules that impose stricter requirements on national products, this form of reverse discrimination usually arising as a result of a previous judicial ruling according to which a national rule should be *partially* struck down because it inhibits the process of establishing the internal market.

The above solutions will be used in instances where traders in purely internal situations suffer a competitive disadvantage as a result of reverse discrimination, that is, they are solutions that will largely be used for remedying the negative implications of reverse discrimination in the context of EC trade.

---

18. With the coming into force of the Treaty of Lisbon (*supra* n. 16), Art. 10 EC will be replaced, in substance, by Art. 4, para. 3, TEU.
19. In Ch. 5 of the book it was also suggested that the Court of Justice in some of its recent case-law in the area of customs duties and in the context of interpreting secondary legislation adopted under Art. 95 EC (Art. 114 TFEU), has resorted to another kind of *ex ante* judicial solution. More specifically, it was seen that the Court has delimited the scope of EC Treaty provisions or of secondary EC legislation in such a way as to include situations that did not involve an impediment to the inter-state movement of products or factors of production, most probably in order to avoid the reverse discrimination that would emerge if it interpreted those provisions/pieces of legislation as excluding those situations from their scope. Whether the Court of Justice will resort to this solution more often in the future, remains to be seen.

As we saw in Chapter 4 of the book, Union citizens who are not contributing to the process of establishing an internal market and remain confined within their State of origin, are also the victims of reverse discrimination. In this instance, the problem is clearly one of unfair treatment. In Chapter 4, it was concluded that reverse discrimination suffered by Union citizens that fall outside the scope of the fundamental freedoms provisions can, now, amount to a violation of the Community principle of equality which, following the latest case-law of the Court on citizenship, appears to include within its scope any situation that involves an (unjustified) inequality which arises as a side-effect of the process of European integration. Relying largely on the Opinion of Advocate General Poiares Maduro in the *Carbonati Apuani* case,[20] it was explained that reverse discrimination – being a 'residual' situation from the point of view of Community law – should now be considered an unjustified difference in treatment that is contrary to the Community principle of equality.

Therefore, when a case involving a situation of reverse discrimination is brought before the Court of Justice, the latter will be able to rule that the contested measure which imposes stricter requirements on persons that are in a purely internal situation, is contrary to EC law because it violates the Community principle of equality.[21] If any differentiation regarding the persons that will be entitled to EC rights will have to be made – especially in areas far removed from inter-state trade – this will have to be based on a ground other than the contribution that a person has made to the construction of the internal market. More importantly, however, the Community principle of equality should be held to be directly effective, so that Union citizens who are nationals of Member States that do not prohibit reverse discrimination through their own constitutional principle of equality, will be provided with this remedy by EC law.

The various judicial solutions proposed above carry with them the usual problems that arise in instances of 'negative' rulings, that is, rulings which strike down national measures for being in violation of EC law. It is well-known that in such instances, the fact that the Court merely has the power to remove a national measure *without replacing it with another rule*, results in the creation of a regulatory void. However, in the specific context of purely internal situations, this problem is exacerbated by the fact that a body of unelected judges *imposes* a common low standard (the lower standard applicable in situations falling within the scope of the fundamental freedoms), even in situations that have traditionally been considered to fall within the realm of the national (democratically elected) legislator. Moreover, examining the potential problems of the above judicial solutions from the angle of the EC, the danger lurks that through an *extensive* use of them, the long-cherished values of competition among rules, experimentation and cultural diversity will be abandoned, giving their place to common low European

20. *Carbonati Apuani Srl v. Comune di Carrara*, Case No. C-72/03 [2004] ECR I-8027.
21. It has been suggested that, for the sake of clarity, the EC Treaty should be amended in such a way as to include equality between Union citizens as one of the tasks and aims of the Community.

standards, or, in some – even worse – instances, to complete deregulation. However, the regulatory void problem can be remedied by the Community legislature which, where necessary, can fill-in the void left by making legislation laying down EC rules for the area in question and, in such situations, the piece of secondary legislation will, most probably, take the form of total harmonization.

A final point that should be made is that, even if certain instances of reverse discrimination are found to fall – prima facie – within the scope of EC law, this does not mean that the national measures which give rise to their emergence should be struck down automatically. More specifically, such measures will only have to be struck down if they are not justified by a legitimate reason. In other words, what it is suggested here is that the doctrine of mandatory requirements should be extended and be available to Member State governments also in reverse discrimination cases, enabling them to argue that in certain cases, they are justified in treating their nationals/products more strictly than they treat nationals of other Member States/imported products. For instance, in the context of EC trade, the mandatory requirements of consumer protection, environmental protection as well as a justification based on the need to maintain the good name and quality of traditional products[22] are obvious candidates for inclusion in this mandatory requirements (non-exhaustive) list, whilst the imposition of stricter marketing rules on domestic goods will be more difficult to justify. For example, it cannot plausibly be argued that consumer protection requires Member States to impose (only) on domestic producers strict rules as regards the regulation of advertising, whilst importers of similar products remain entirely free to choose the method for advertising their products.

It is obvious that there are a number of possibilities for the resolution of the reverse discrimination conundrum in the EC. Solutions are available at both, Member State and EC level, as well as through judicial action and via legislative means. It is clear that the use of one single solution is not appropriate since all solutions have both advantages and disadvantages. Therefore, it is my contention that the best way out of this problem is to utilize all of the available solutions. In fact, since the EC is a dynamic supranational organization and since the approach of different Member States towards the EU changes through time, at least to a certain extent, it is obvious that the extent of the use of each of the above solutions will change over time, in accordance with the trends that are present in the EC, as well as the positions of the Member States.

However, one thing is certain: reverse discrimination is, indeed, a problem that falls within the scope of EC law. Therefore, even though most Member State legal systems provide, in most instances, their own solutions to this problem, some 'hard cases' persist, and thus the EC should fill the gaps that remain in the protection from reverse discrimination.

---

22. This is similar to the 'imperative reason of public interest' relied on by the Netherlands in *Alpine Investments BV v. Minister van Financiën*, Case No. C-384/93 [1995] ECR I-1141, paras 41-44 ('to safeguard the reputation of the Netherlands financial markets and to protect the investing public').

List of References

I. BOOKS AND BOOK CHAPTERS

Albors-Llorens, A., *EC Competition Law and Policy* (Cullompton, Willan Publishing, 2002)

Armstrong, K. and S. Bulmer, *The Governance of the Single European Market* (Manchester, Manchester University Press, 1998)

Armstrong, K., 'Mutual Recognition', in *The Law of the Single European Market: Unpacking the premises*, C. Barnard and J. Scott (eds) (Oxford, Hart, 2002)

Arnull, A., *The General Principles of EEC Law and the Individual* (London, Leicester, Leicester University Press, 1990)

Arnull, A., *The European Union and Its Court of Justice* (Oxford, OUP, 1999)

Arnull, A. (ed.), *Wyatt and Dashwood's European Union Law* (4th edn, London, Sweet & Maxwell, 2000)

Bamforth, N., M. Malik and C. O'Cinneide, *Discrimination Law: Theory and Context* (London, Sweet & Maxwell, 2008)

Barnard, C. and S. Deakin, 'Market Access and Regulatory Competition', in *The Law of the Single European Market: Unpacking the premises*, C. Barnard and J. Scott (eds) (Oxford, Hart, 2002)

Barnard, C., *The Substantive Law of the EU: The Four Freedoms* (Oxford, OUP, 2004)

Barnard, C., *The Substantive Law of the EU: The Four Freedoms* (2nd edn, Oxford, OUP, 2007)

Barnard, C., 'EU Citizenship and the Principle of Solidarity', in *Social Welfare and EU Law*, E. Spaventa and M. Dougan (eds) (Oxford, Hart, 2005)

Bell, M., *Anti-Discrimination Law and the European Union* (Oxford, OUP, 2002)

Bernard, N., 'Flexibility in the European Single Market', in *The Law of the Single European Market: Unpacking the Premises*, C. Barnard and J. Scott (eds) (Oxford, Hart, 2002)

Chalmers, D., 'The Single Market: From Prima Donna to Journeyman', in *New Legal Dynamics of European Union*, J. Shaw and G. More (eds) (Oxford, Clarendon Press, 1995)

Conant, L., *Justice Contained: Law and Politics in the European Union* (Ithaca NY, Cornell University Press, 2002)

Craig, P., 'The Evolution of the Single Market', in *The Law of the Single European Market: Unpacking the Premises*, C. Barnard and J. Scott (eds) (Oxford, Hart, 2002)

Craig, P. and G. de Búrca, *EU Law: Text, Cases and Materials* (3rd edn, Oxford, OUP, 2003)

Craig, P. and G. de Búrca, *EU Law: Text, Cases and Materials* (4th edn, Oxford, OUP, 2008)

Davies, G., *Nationality Discrimination in the European Internal Market* (The Hague, Kluwer Law International, 2003)

Davies, G., *EU Internal Market Law* (2nd edn, London, Cavendish, 2003)

De Búrca, G., 'The Role of Equality in European Community Law', in *The Principle of Equal Treatment in EC law*, A. Dashwood and S. O'Leary (eds) (London, Sweet and Maxwell, 1997)

De Vries, S., *Tensions within the Internal Market: The Functioning of the Internal Market and the Development of Horizontal and Flanking Policies* (Groningen, Europa Law Publishing, 2006)

De Witte, B., 'The Past and Future Role of the European Court of Justice in the Protection of Human Rights', in *The EU and Human Rights*, P. Alston (ed.) (Oxford, OUP, 1999)

De Witte, B., 'Non-market Values in Internal Market Legislation', in *Regulating the Internal Market*, N. Nic Shuibhne (ed.) (Edward Elgar, Cheltenham, Northampton, 2006).

D'Oliveira, H.U.J., 'Is Reverse Discrimination Still Permissible under the Single European Act?', in *Forty Years On: The Evolution of Postwar Private International Law in Europe: Symposium in Celebration of the 40th Anniversary of the Centre of Foreign Law and Private International Law, University of Amsterdam, on 27 October 1998* (The Hague, Kluwer Law International, 1990)

D'Oliveira, H.U.J., 'European Citizenship: Its Meaning, Its Potential', in *Europe after Maastricht: An ever closer Union*, R. Dehousse (ed.) (Munich, Beck, 1994)

Dougan, M. and E. Spaventa, ''Wish You Weren't Here ...'' New Models of Social Solidarity in the European Union', in *Social Welfare and EU Law*, E. Spaventa and M. Dougan (eds) (Oxford, Hart, 2005)

Douglas-Scott, S., *Constitutional law of the European Union* (London, Longman, 2002)

Evans, A., 'Union Citizenship and the Equality principle', in *A Citizens' Europe: In Search of a New Order*, A. Rosas and E. Antola (eds) (London, Sage, 1995)

Evans, A., *A Textbook on EU Law* (Oxford, Hart, 1998)

Everson, M., 'The Legacy of the Market Citizen', in *New Legal Dynamics of European Integration*, J. Shaw and G. More (eds) (Oxford, Clarendon Press, 1995)

Gormley, L., 'The Internal Market: History and Evolution', in *Regulating the Internal Market*, N. Nic Shuibhne (ed.) (Edward Elgar, Cheltenham, Northampton, 2006)

Goyder, D., *EC Competition Law* (4th edn, Oxford, OUP, 2003)

Hervey, T.K., 'Migrant Workers and Their Families in the European Union: The Pervasive Market Ideology of Community Law', in *New Legal Dynamics of European Union*, J. Shaw and G. More (eds) (Oxford, Clarendon Press, 1995)

Ingoldsy, B., 'Free Movement – A Department of Justice Perspective', in *The Free Movement of Workers Within the European Union*, N. Hyland (ed.) (ICEL, 1999)

Jarvis, M.A., *The Application of EC Law by National Courts: The Free Movement of Goods* (Oxford, Clarendon Press, 1998)

Jones, A. and B. Sufrin, *EC Competition Law: Texts, Cases and Materials* (2nd edn, Oxford, OUP, 2004)

Korah, V., *An Introductory Guide to EC Competition Law and Practice* (8th edn, Oxford, Hart, 2004)

Lane, R., *EC Competition Law* (Harlow, Longman: Pearson Education, 2000)

Lyons, C., 'Citizenship in the Constitution of the European Union: Rhetoric or Reality?', in *Constitutionalism, Democracy and Sovereignty: American and European Perspectives*, R. Bellamy (ed.) (Aldershot, Avebury, 1996)

Lyons, C., 'The Limits of European Union Citizenship', in *The European Union and Its Order: The Legal Theory of European Integration*, Z. Bańkowski and A. Scott (eds) (Oxford, Blackwell, 2000)

Marias, E., 'From Market Citizen to Union Citizen', in *European Citizenship*, E. Marias (ed.) (Maastricht, EIPA, 1994)

Martin, D. and E. Guild, *Free Movement of Persons in the European Union* (London, Edinburgh, Butterworths, 1996)

More, G., 'The Principle of Equal Treatment: From Market Unifier to Fundamental Right?', in *The Evolution of EU Law*, P. Craig and G. de Búrca (eds) (Oxford, OUP, 1999)

Neuwahl, N.A., 'The Treaty on European Union: A Step Forward in the Protection of Human Rights?', in *The European Union and Human Rights*, N.A. Neuwahl and A. Rosas (eds) (The Hague, Kluwer Law International, 1995)

Nic Shuibhne, N., 'The European Union and Fundamental Rights: Well in Spirit but Considerably Rumpled in Body?', in *Convergence and Divergence in*

European Public Law, P. Beaumont, C. Lyons and N. Walker (eds) (Oxford, Hart, 2002)

O'Keeffe, D., 'Trends in the Free Movement of Persons within the European Communities', in *Human Rights and Constitutional Law: Essays in Honour of Brian Walsh*, J. O'Reilly (ed.) (Dublin, The Round Hall Press, 1992)

O'Keeffe, D., 'Union Citizenship', in *Legal Issues of the Maastricht Treaty*, D. O'Keeffe and P. Twomey (eds) (London: Chancery/Wiley, 1994)

O'Keeffe D. and A. Bavasso, 'Four Freedoms, One Market and National Competence: In Search of a Dividing Line', in *Liber Amicorum in Honour of Lord Slynn of Hadley: Judicial Review in European Union Law*, D. O'Keeffe and A. Bavasso (eds) (The Hague, Kluwer Law International, 2000)

O'Leary, S., *The Evolving Concept of Community Citizenship: From the Free Movement of Persons to Union Citizenship* (The Hague, Kluwer Law International, 1996)

O'Leary, S., 'The Principle of Equal Treatment on Grounds of Nationality in Article 6 EC: A Lucrative Source of Rights for Member State nationals?', in *The Principle of Equal Treatment in EC Law*, A. Dashwood and S. O'Leary (eds) (London, Sweet & Maxwell, 1997)

Oliver, P., *Free Movement of Goods in the European Community* (4th edn, London, Sweet and Maxwell, 2003)

Plender, R., 'An Incipient Form of European Citizenship', in *European Law and the Individual*, F.G. Jacobs (ed.) (Amsterdam, North-Holland Publishing Company, 1976)

Poiares Maduro, M., *We the Court: The European Court of Justice and the European Economic Constitution* (Oxford, Hart, 1998)

Poiares Maduro, M., 'Striking the Elusive Balance between Economic Freedom and Social Rights in the EU', in *The EU and Human Rights*, P. Alston (ed.) (Oxford, OUP, 1999)

Poiares Maduro, M., 'The Scope of European Remedies: The Case of Purely Internal Situations and Reverse Discrimination', in *The Future of European Remedies*, C. Kilpatrick, T. Novitz and P. Skidmore (eds) (Oxford, Hart, 2000)

Sauter, W. and E. Vos, 'Harmonisation under Community Law: The Comitology Issue', in *Lawmaking in the European Union*, P. Craig and C. Harlow (eds) (The Hague, Kluwer Law International, 1998)

Snell, J., *Goods and Services in EC Law: A Study of the Relationship between the Freedoms* (Oxford, OUP, 2002)

Snell, J. and M. Andenas, 'Exploring the Outer Limits: Restrictions on the Free Movement of Goods and Services', in *Services and Free Movement in EU Law*, M. Andenas and W.H. Roth (eds) (Oxford, OUP, 2003)

Staples, H., *The Legal Status of Third Country Nationals Resident in the European Union* (The Hague, Kluwer Law International, 1999)

Steiner, J., L. Woods and C. Twigg-Flesner, *Textbook on EC Law* (8th edn, Oxford, OUP, 2003)
Steiner, J., L. Woods and C. Twigg-Flesner, *EU Law* (9th edn, Oxford, OUP, 2006)
Sundberg-Weitman, B., *Discrimination on Grounds of Nationality – Free Movement of Workers and Freedom of Establishment under the EEC Treaty* (Amsterdam, North-Holland Publishing Company, 1977)
Szyszczak, E., *The Regulation of the State in Competitive Markets in the EU* (Oxford, Hart, 2007)
Szyszczak, E. and A. Cygan, *Understanding EU Law* (2nd edn, London, Sweet & Maxwell, 2008)

Tridimas, T., 'The Application of the Principle of Equality to Community Measures', in *The Principle of Equal Treatment in EC Law*, A. Dashwood and S. O'Leary (eds) (London, Sweet & Maxwell, 1997)

Van der Mei, A.P., *Free Movement of Persons within the European Community: Cross-Border Access to Public Benefits* (Oxford, Hart, 2003)

Weatherill, S., *Law and Integration in the European Union* (Oxford, Clarendon Press, 1995)
Weatherill, S. and P. Beaumont, *EU Law* (3rd edn, London, Penguin, 1999)
Weatherill, S., 'A Case Study in Judicial Activism in the 1990s: The Status Before National Courts of Measures Wrongfully Un-notified to the Commission', in *Liber Amicorum in Honour of Lord Slynn of Hadley: Judicial Review in European Union Law*, D. O'Keeffe and A. Bavasso (eds) (The Hague, Kluwer Law International, 2000)
Weatherill, S., 'Pre-emption, Harmonization and the Distribution of Competence to Regulate the Internal Market', in *The Law of the Single European Market: Unpacking the Premises*, C. Barnard and J. Scott (eds) (Oxford, Hart, 2002)
Weatherill, S., 'Why Harmonize?', in *European Union Law for the Twenty-First Century: Rethinking the New Legal Order*, Volume 2, T. Tridimas and P. Nebbia (eds) (Oxford, Hart, 2004)
Weatherill, S., 'Supply of and Demand for Internal Market Regulation: Strategies, Preferences and Interpretation', in *Regulating the Internal Market*, N. Nic Shuibhne (ed.) (Edward Elgar, Cheltenham, Northampton, 2006)
Weatherill, S., *Cases and Materials on EU Law* (8th edn, Oxford, OUP, 2007)
Weiler, J.H.H., 'The Constitution of the Common Market Place: Text and Context in the Evolution of the Free Movement of Goods', in *The Evolution of EU Law*, P. Craig and C. de Búrca (eds) (Oxford, OUP, 1999)
Weiler, J.H.H., 'To be a European Citizen: Eros and Civilization', in *The Constitutions of Europe*, J.H.H. Weiler (ed.) (Cambridge, Cambridge University Press, 1999)
Weiss, F. and F. Wooldridge, *Free Movement of Persons within the European Community* (The Hague, Kluwer Law International, 2002)
Whish, R., *Competition Law* (5th edn, London, Butterworths, 2003)

White, R.C.A., *Workers, Establishment and Services in the European Union* (Oxford, OUP, 2004)

Woods, L., *Free Movement of Goods and Services within the European Community* (Aldershot, Ashgate, 2004)

Woolcock, S., 'Competition among Rules in the Single European market', in *International Regulatory Competition and Coordination*, W. Bratton, J. McCahery, S. Picciotto and C. Scott (eds) (Oxford, Clarendon Press, 1996)

Young, A. and H. Wallace, 'The Single Market: A New Approach to Policy', in *Policy-Making in the European Union*, H. Wallace and W. Wallace (eds) (Oxford, OUP, 2000)

II. ARTICLES AND ANNOTATIONS IN JOURNALS

Acierno, S., 'The Carpenter Judgment: Fundamental Rights and the Limits of the Community Legal Order' (2003) 28 ELRev 398

Ackermann, T., Annotation of Case C-148/02, *Garcia Avello v. État belge*, [2003] ECR I-11613, (2007) 44 CMLRev 141

Adinolfi, A., 'The Judicial application of Community law in Italy (1981 – 1997)' (1998) 35 CMLRev 1313

Albors-Llorens, A., 'A broader construction of the EC Treaty provisions on citizenship?' (1998) CLJ 461

Anderson, D., 'The admissibility of Preliminary References' (1994) 14 YEL 179

Barents, R., 'New Developments in measures having equivalent effect' (1981) 18 CMLRev 271

Barents, R., 'The Internal Market Unlimited: Some observations on the legal basis of Community legislation' (1993) 30 CMLRev 85

Barnard, C., and E. Sharpston, 'The changing face of article 177 references' (1997) 34 CMLRev 1113

Barnard, C., 'Social dumping and the race to the bottom: some lessons for the European Union from Delaware?' (2000) 25 ELRev 57

Barnard, C., 'Fitting the remaining pieces into the goods and persons jigsaw' (2001) 26 ELRev 35

Barnard, C., Annotation of Case C-209/03, *R (ex parte Bidar) v. London Borough of Ealing and Secretary of State for Education and Skills*, [2005] ECR I-2119, (2005) 42 CMLRev 1465

Barnard, C., 'Of students and babies' (2005) 64 CLJ 560

Barnard, C., 'Unravelling the Services Directive' (2008) 45 CMLRev 323

Barrett, G., 'Family matters: European Community law and third-country family members' (2003) 40 CMLRev 369

Barrett, G., 'Re-examining the Concept and Principle of Equality in EC Law' (2003) 22 YEL 117

Bernard, N., 'Discrimination and Free Movement in EC Law' (1996) 45 ICLQ 82

Bernard, N., 'The Future of European Economic Law in the light of the principle of subsidiarity' (1996) 33 CMLRev 633

Besson, S. and A. Utzinger, 'Introduction: Future Challenges of European Citizenship – Facing a Wide-Open Pandora's Box' (2007) 13 ELJ 573

Betlem, G., Annotation of Case C-28/95, *Leur-Bloem*, [1997] ECR I-4161, (1999) 36 CMLRev 1656

Biondi, A., 'In and Out of the Internal Market' (1999/2000) YEL 469

Borgmann-Prebil, Y., 'The rule of reason in European citizenship' (2008) 14 ELJ 328

Bravo-Ferrer Delgado, M. and N. La Casta Muñoa, Annotation of Joined Cases 297/88 and 197/89, *Dzodzi v. Belgian State*, [1990] ECR I-3763, (1992) 29 CMLRev 152

Cannizzaro, E., 'Producing "Reverse Discrimination" through the exercise of EC competences' (1997) 17 YEL 29

Carlier, J.Y., Annotation of Case C-200/02, *Kunqian Catherine Zhu and Man Lavette Chen v. Secretary of State for the Home Department*, [2004] ECR I-9925, (2005) 42 CMLRev 1121

Castro Oliveira, A., 'Workers and other persons: step-by-step from movement to citizenship – Case-law 1995-2001' (2002) 39 CMLRev 77

Chalmers, D., 'Free Movement of goods within the European Community: An unhealthy addiction to Scotch Whisky?' (1993) 42 ICLQ 269

Chalmers, D., 'Repackaging the Internal Market – The Ramifications of the *Keck* Judgment' (1994) 17 ELRev 385

Chalmers, D., 'Environmental protection and the Single Market: An unsustainable development. Does the EC Treaty need a title on the environment?' (1995) 1 LIEI 65

Classen, C.D., Annotation of C-465/00, *Rechnungshof v. Österreichischer Rundfunk*, [2003] ECR I-4989, (2004) 41 CMLRev 1377

Closa, C., 'The Concept of Citizenship in the Treaty on European Union' (1992) 29 CMLRev 1137

Closa, C., 'Citizenship of the Union and Nationality of Member States' (1995) 32 CMLRev 487

Close, G., 'Harmonization of laws: use or abuse of the powers under the EEC Treaty?' (1978) 3 ELRev 461

Connor, T., 'Accentuating the positive: the "selling arrangement", the first decade and beyond' (2005) 54 ICLQ 127

Coppel, J. and A. O'Neill, 'The European Court of Justice: taking rights seriously?' (1992) 12 LS 227

Crosby, S., 'The Single Market and the Rule of Law' (1991) 16 ELRev 451

Crosby, S., 'The new Tobacco Control Directive: an illiberal and illegal disdain for the law' (2002) 27 ELRev 177

Currall, J., 'Some Aspects of the Relation between Articles 30-36 and Article 100 of the EEC Treaty, with a Closer Look at Optional Harmonisation' (1984) 4 YEL 169

Daniele, L., 'Non-discriminatory restrictions to the free movement of persons' (1997) 22 ELRev 191
Dashwood, A., 'The Limits of European Community Powers' (1996) 21 ELRev 113
Dashwood, A., 'Non-Discriminatory trade restrictions after *Keck*' (2002) CLJ 35
Davies, G., 'The High Water Point of Free Movement of Persons: Ending Benefit Tourism and Rescuing Welfare' (2004) 26 JSWFL 211
Davies, G., 'Higher education, equal access, and residence conditions: Does EU Law allow Member States to charge higher fees to students not previously resident?' (2005) 12 MJ 227
Davies, G., 'Can selling arrangements be harmonized' (2005) 30 ELRev 371
Davies, G., 'Subsidiarity: the wrong idea, in the wrong place, at the wrong time' (2006) 43 CMLRev 63
Dawes, A., 'Importing and exporting poor reasoning: worrying trends in relation to the case law on the free movement of goods' (2007) 8 GLJ 761
Dehousse, R., '1992 and beyond: the institutional dimension of the internal market programme' (1989) LIEI 109
Dougan, M., 'Minimum harmonization and the internal market' (2000) 37 CMLRev 853
Dougan, M., 'Free Movement: The work-seeker as Citizen' (2001) CYELS 93
Dougan, M. and E. Spaventa, 'Educating Rudy and the (non-)English Patient: A double-bill on residency rights under Article 18 EC' (2003) 28 ELRev 699
Dougan, M., 'The Constitutional dimension to the case law on Union citizenship' (2006) 31 ELRev 613
Durand, A., 'European Citizenship' (1979) 4 ELRev 3

Editorial Comment: 'Taking (the limits of) competences seriously' (2000) 37 CMLRev 1301
Editorial Comment: 'Freedoms unlimited? Reflections on Mary Carpenter v. Secretary of State' (2003) 40 CMLRev 537
Editorial Comment: 'The services directive proposal: Striking a balance between the promotion of the internal market and preserving the European social model?' (2006) 43 CMLRev 307
Editorial Comment: 'Two-speed European Citizenship? Can the Lisbon Treaty help close the gap?' (2008) 45 CMLRev 1
Eeckhout, P., 'The EU Charter of Fundamental Rights and the Federal Question' (2002) 39 CMLRev 945
Enchelmaier, S., 'The Awkward Selling of a Good Idea, or a Traditionalist Interpretation of *Keck*' (2003) 22 YEL 249
Epiney, A., 'The Scope of Article 12 EC: Some Remarks on the Influence of European Citizenship' (2007) 13 ELJ 611
Evans, A., 'European Citizenship' (1982) 45 MLR 497
Evans, A., 'European Citizenship: A Novel Concept in EEC Law' (1984) 32 AJCL 679

Flynn, L., 'Coming of Age: The free movement of capital case-law 1993-2002' (2002) 39 CMLRev 773

Foster, N., 'Family and welfare rights in Europe: the impact of recent European Court of Justice decisions in the area of the free movement of persons' (2003) 25 JSWFL 291

Fries, S. and J. Shaw, 'Citizenship of the Union: First Steps in the European Court of Justice' (1998) 4 EPL 533

Golynker, O., 'Partial migration in the EU after the *Baumbast* case: bringing social and legal perspectives together' (2004) 15 KCLJ 367

Gori, G., 'Union citizenship and equal treatment: A way of improving Community educational rights?' (1999) 21 JSWFL 405

Gormley, L., 'Some reflections on the internal market and free movement of goods' (1989) 1 LIEI 9

Gormley, L., 'Two years after *Keck*' (1996) 19 Fordham Int'l LJ 866

Gormley, L., 'Competition and Free Movement: Is the Internal Market the Same as a Common Market?' (2002) 13 EBLRev 517

Granger, M.P.F., 'National applications of *Francovich* and the construction of a European administrative ius commune' (2007) 32 ELRev 157

Greenwood, C., 'Nationality and the Limits of the Free movement of Persons in Community Law' (1987) 7 YEL 185

Gulmann, C., 'The Single European Act – Some Remarks from a Danish perspective' (1987) 24 CMLRev 31

Hailbronner, K., 'Union Citizenship and Access to social benefits' (2005) 42 CMLRev 1245

Hanson, B.T., 'What happened to fortress Europe? External trade policy liberalization in the European Union' (1998) 52 *International Organization* 55

Hatzopoulos, V., 'Recent Developments of the Case law of the ECJ in the field of services' (2000) 37 CMLRev 43

Hatzopoulos, V., 'A (more) social Europe: a political crossroad or a legal one-way? Dialogues between Luxembourg and Lisbon' (2006) 42 CMLRev 1599

Hatzopoulos, V. and T.U. Do, 'The case law of the ECJ concerning the free provision of services: 2000-2005' (2006) 43 CMLRev 923

Hervey, T.K., 'Community and national competence in health after *Tobacco Advertising*' (2001) 38 CMLRev 1421

Hervey, T.K., 'Up in smoke? Community (anti) tobacco law and policy' (2001) 26 ELRev 101

Hilson, C., 'Discrimination in Community free movement law' (1999) 24 ELRev 445

Hofstotter, B., 'A cascade of rights, or who shall care for little Catherine? Some reflections on the Chen case' (2005) 30 ELRev 548

Howells, G.G., 'Federalism in USA and EC – The Scope for Harmonized Legislative Activity Compared' (2002) 5 ERPL 601

Iliopoulou, A. and H. Toner, Annotation of Case C-184/99, *Grzelczyk v. Centre public d'aide sociale d'Ottignies-Louvain-la-Neuve*, [2001] ECR I-6193, (2002) 39 CMLRev 609

Jacobs, F.G., 'Human rights in the European Union: the role of the Court of Justice' (2001) 26 ELRev 331

Jacobs, F.G., 'Citizenship of the European Union – A Legal Analysis' (2007) 13 ELJ 591

Jacqueson, C., 'Union citizenship and the Court of Justice: something new under the sun? Towards social citizenship' (2002) 27 ELRev 260

Jans, J. H., 'National legislative autonomy? The procedural constraints of European law' (1998) 25 LIEI 25

Jarvis, M.A., Annotation of Cases C-24/00, *Commission v. France*, [2004] ECR I-1277; C-270/02, *Commission v. Italy*, [2004] ECR I-1559; C-95/01, *Greenham v. Abel*, [2004] ECR I-1333, (2004) 41 CMLRev 1395

Johnson, E. and D. O'Keeffe, 'From discrimination to obstacles to free movement: recent developments concerning the free movement of workers 1989-1994' (1994) 31 CMLRev 1313

Kaczorowska, A., 'Gourmet can have his *Keck* and eat it!' (2004) 10 ELJ 479

Kerber, W., 'Interjurisdictional Competition within the European Union' (2000) 23 Fordham Int'l LJ S217

Khanna, S., 'The defeat of the European Tobacco Advertising Directive: A Blow for Health' (2001) 20 YEL 113

Knook, A., 'The Court, the Charter, and the vertical division of powers in the European Union' (2005) 42 CMLRev 367

Kon, S.D., 'Aspects of Reverse Discrimination in Community Law' (1981) 6 ELRev 75

Kostakopoulou, D., 'Ideas, Norms and European Citizenship: Explaining Institutional Change' (2005) 68 MLR 233

Koutrakos, P., 'On groceries, alcohol and olive oil: More on free movement of goods after *Keck*' (2001) 26 ELRev 391

Kunoy, B., 'A Union of national citizens: the origins of the Court's lack of *avant-gardisme* in the *Chen* case' (2006) 43 CMLRev 179

Kurcz, B., 'Harmonisation by means of Directives – never-ending story?' (2001) EBLRev 287

Lane, R. and N. Nic Shuibhne, Annotation of Case C-281/98, *Angonese v. Cassa di Risparmio di Bolzano Spa* [2000] ECR I-4139, (2000) 37 CMLRev 1237

Lenaerts, K., 'Respect for fundamental rights as a constitutional principle of the European Union' (2000) 6 CJEL 1

Lenaerts, K., 'Fundamental Rights in the European Union' (2000) 25 ELRev 575

Lengauer, A.,'The New General Principle of Non-Discrimination in the EC Treaty as Amended by the Treaty of Amsterdam' (1998) 3 ARIEL 369

Ludwigs, M., Annotation of Case C-380/03, *Germany v. Parliament and Council* (Directive 2003/33) (*Tobacco Advertising II*), [2006] ECR I-11573, (2007) 44 CMLRev 1159
Lyons, C., 'A Voyage around Article 8: An Historical and Comparative Evaluation of the Fate of European Union Citizenship' (1997) 17 YEL 135

Mancini, F., 'The making of a Constitution for Europe' (1989) 26 CMLRev 595
Martin, D., 'A big Step forward for Union Citizens, but a Step Backwards for Legal Coherence' (2002) 4 EJML 136
Mather, J.D., 'The Court of Justice and the Union Citizen' (2005) 11 ELJ 722
Moore, S., 'Re-visiting the limits of Article 30 EEC' (1994) 19 ELRev 195
Mortelmans, K., 'Article 30 of the EEC Treaty and legislation relating to market circumstances; Time to consider a new definition?' (1991) 28 CMLRev 115
Mortelmans, K., 'The Common Market, the Internal Market and the Single Market, What's in a Market?' (1998) 35 CMLRev 101
Mortelmans, K., 'Towards convergence in the application of the rules on free movement and on competition?' (2001) 38 CMLRev 613

Nic Shuibhne, N., 'Free movement of persons and the wholly internal rule: Time to move on?' (2002) 39 CMLRev 731
Nic Shuibhne, N., 'The Free Movement of Goods and Article 28 EC: An evolving Framework' (2002) 27 ELRev 408

Ogus, A., 'Competition between national legal systems: A contribution of economic analysis to comparative law' (1999) 48 ICLQ 405
O'Keeffe, D., 'Equal Rights for Migrants: the Concept of Social Advantages in Article 7(2), Regulation 1612/68' (1985) 5 YEL 93
O'Keeffe, D., 'Reflections on European Union Citizenship' (1996) 49 CLP 347
O'Keeffe, D., 'Is the spirit of Article 177 under attack? Preliminary references and admissibility' (1998) 23 ELRev 509
O'Keeffe, D. and M. Horspool, 'European Citizenship and the Free Movement of Persons' (1996) 31 *The Irish Jurist* 145
O'Keeffe, D. and P. Osborne, 'The European Court Scores a Goal' (1996) IJCLLIR 111
O'Leary, S., 'Nationality Law and Community Citizenship: A Tale of Two Uneasy Bedfellows' (1992) 12 YEL 353
O'Leary, S., 'The Relationship between Community Citizenship and the Protection of Fundamental Rights in Community Law' (1995) 32 CMLRev 519
O'Leary, S., 'Putting Flesh on the Bones of European Union Citizenship' (1999) 24 ELRev 68
Oliver, P., 'Non-Community nationals and the Treaty of Rome' (1985) YEL 57
Oliver, P., 'Some further reflections on the scope of Articles 28-30' (1999) 36 CMLRev 783

Oliver, P. and W.H. Roth, 'The internal market and the four freedoms' (2004) 41 CMLRev 407

Oliver, P. and S. Enchelmaier, 'Free movement of goods: Recent developments in the case law' (2007) 44 CMLRev 649

Peebles, G., ' "A very Eden of the Innate Rights of Man"? A Marxist Look at the European Union Treaties and Case Law' (1997) 22 *Law and Social Inquiry* 581

Pescatore, P., 'Some critical remarks on the "Single European Act" ' (1987) 24 CMLRev 11

Pickup, D.M.W., 'Reverse Discrimination and Freedom of Movement for workers' (1986) 23 CMLRev 135

Poiares Maduro, M., '*Keck*: The end? The beginning of the end? Or just the end of the beginning?' (1994) 1 IJEL 30

Poiares Maduro, M., 'Reforming the Market or the State? Article 30 and the European Constitution: Economic Freedom and Political Rights' (1997) 3 ELJ 55

Poiares Maduro, M., 'The Saga of Article 30 EC Treaty: To Be Continued' (1998) 5 MJ 298

Poiares Maduro, M., 'Harmony and Dissonance in Free Movement' (2001) 4 CYELS 315

Pollack, M.A., 'The End of Creeping Competence? EU Policy-Making Since Maastricht' (2000) 38 JCMS 519

Prete, L., 'Of Motorcycle Trailers and Personal Watercrafts: the Battle over *Keck*' (2008) 35 LIEI 133

Reich, N., 'Competition between legal orders: A New paradigm of EC law?' (1992) 29 CMLRev 861

Reich, N., 'The November Revolution of the European Court of Justice: Keck, Meng and Audi revisited' (1994) 31 CMLRev 459

Reich, N., 'A European Constitution for Citizens: Reflections on the Rethinking of Union and Community Law' (1997) 3 ELJ 131

Reich, N., 'Europe's Economic Constitution, or: A New Look at Keck' (1999) 19 OJLS 337

Reich, N., 'Union Citizenship – Metaphor or Source of Rights?' (2001) 7 ELJ 4

Ritter, C., 'Purely Internal situations, reverse discrimination, Guimont, Dzodzi and Article 234' (2006) 31 ELRev 690

Scharpf, F.W., 'Introduction: the Problem-solving Capacity of Multi-level Governance' (1997) 2 JEPP 520

Schiltz, C., '*Akrich*: A Clear delimitation without limits' (2005) 12 MJ 241

Shaw, J., 'The Interpretation of European Union Citizenship' (1998) 61 MLR 293

Slot, P.J., 'Harmonisation' (1996) 21 ELRev 378

Slot, P.J. and M.K. Bulterman, 'Harmonization of legislation on migrating EU citizens and third country nationals: Towards a uniform evaluation framework?' (2006) 29 Fordham Int'l LJ 747

Snell, J., 'Who's Got the Power? Free Movement and Allocation of Competences in EC Law' (2003) 22 YEL 323

Somek, A., 'Solidarity decomposed: being and time in European citizenship' (2007) 32 ELRev 787

Søndergaard Birkmose, H., 'Regulatory Competition and the European Harmonization Process' (2006) EBLRev 1075

Spaventa, E., Annotation of Case C-254/98, *Schutzverband gegen unlauteren Wettbewerb v. TK-Heimdienst Sass GmbH*, [2000] ECR I-151, (2000) 37 CMLRev 1265

Spaventa, E., 'From *Gebhard* to *Carpenter*: Towards a (non)-economic European Constitution' (2004) 41 CMLRev 743

Stanley, P., Annotation of Case C-107/94, *Asscher v. Staatssecretaris van Financiën*, [1996] ECR I-3089, (1997) 34 CMLRev 713

Steiner, J., 'The Right to Welfare: Equality and Equity under Community Law' (1985) 10 ELRev 21

Steiner, J., 'Drawing the line: Uses and abuses of Article 30 EEC' (1992) 29 CMLRev 749

Straetmans, G., Annotation of Case C-6/01, *Anomar v. Estado português*, [2003] ECR I-8621, (2004) 41 CMLRev 1409

Sun, J.M. and J. Pelkmans, 'Regulatory Competition in the Single Market' (1995) 33 JCMS 67

Tesauro, G., 'The Community's internal market in the light of the recent case-law of the Court of Justice' (1995) YEL 1

Tomuschat, C., Annotation of Case C-85/96, *Martínez Sala v. Freistaat Bayern*, [1998] ECR I-2691, (2000) 37 CMLRev 449

Toner, H., 'Judicial Interpretation of European Union Citizenship: Transformation or Consolidation?' (2000) 7 MJ 158

Toner, H., Annotation of Case C-60/00, *Carpenter v. Secretary of State for the Home Department*, [2002] ECR 6279, (2003) 5 EJML 163

Toner, H., 'Non-discriminatory Obstacles to the Exercise of Treaty Rights – Articles 39, 43, 49 and 18 EC' (2004) YEL 275

Toth, A.G., 'The European Union and Human Rights: The way forward' (1997) 34 CMLRev 491

Tryfonidou, A., '*Mary Carpenter v. Secretary of State for the Home Department*: The beginning of a new era in the European Union?' (2003) 14 KCLJ 81

Tryfonidou, A., '*Carbonati Apuani Srl v. Comune di Carrara*: Should we reverse "reverse discrimination"?' (2005) 16 KCLJ 373

Tryfonidou, A., 'Redefining the notion of belonging in a Citizens' Europe: *The Queen (on the application of Dany Bidar) v. London Borough of Ealing & Secretary of State for Education and Skills*' (2005) 12 IJEL 217

Tryfonidou, A., '*Kunqian Catherine Zhu and Man Lavette Chen v. Secretary of State for the Home Department*: Further cracks in the "Great Wall" of the European Union?' (2005) 11 EPL 527

Tryfonidou, A., Annotation of Case C-293/02, *Jersey Produce Marketing Organization Ltd v. States of Jersey and Jersey Potato Export Marketing Board*, [2005] ECR I-9543, (2006) 43 CMLRev 1727

Tryfonidou, A., 'Was *Keck* a half-baked solution after all?' (2007) 34 LIEI 167

Tryfonidou, A., '*Jia* or "*Carpenter* II": The edge of reason' (2007) 32 ELRev 908

Tryfonidou, A., 'Reverse discrimination in purely internal situations: an incongruity in a Citizens' Europe' (2008) 35 LIEI 43

Tryfonidou, A., 'Family reunification rights of (migrant) Union citizens: Towards a liberal approach' (2009) 15 ELJ (forthcoming)

Usher, J., Annotation of Case C-376/98, *Germany v. Parliament and Council (Tobacco Advertising I)*, [2000] ECR I-8419, (2001) 38 CMLRev 1519

Van den Bergh, R.,'Subsidiarity as an Economic Demarcation Principle and the Emergence of European Private Law' (1998) 5 MJ 129

Van Rijn, T., 'A review of the case-law of the Court of Justice on Articles 30 to 36 EEC in 1986 and 1987' (1988) 25 CMLRev 593

Vogelaar, T., 'The approximation of the laws of Member States under the Treaty of Rome' (1975) 12 CMLRev 211

Von Bogdandy, A., 'The European Union as a human rights organization? Human rights and the core of the European Union' (2000) 37 CMLRev 1307

Von Heydebrand u.d. Lasa, H.C., 'Free movement of foodstuffs, consumer protection and food standards in the European Community: has the Court of Justice got it wrong?' (1991) 16 ELRev 391

Wagner, G., 'The Economics of Harmonization: the case of Contract law' (2002) 39 CMLRev 995

Watson, P., 'Free Movement of Workers: a one way ticket?' (1993) 22 ILJ 68

Weatherill, S., 'Regulating the Internal Market: Result orientation in the Court of Justice' (1994) 19 ELRev 55

Weatherill, S., 'Compulsory notification of draft technical regulations: the contribution of Directive 83/189 to the management of the internal market' (1996) 16 YEL 129

Weatherill, S., 'After *Keck*: Some Thoughts on How to Clarify the Clarification?' (1996) 33 CMLRev 885

Weatherill, S., Annotation of Case C-415/93, *Union Royal Belge des Société de Football Association ASBL & others v. Bosman*, [1995] ECR I-4921, (1996) 33 CMLRev 991

Weatherill, S., 'New Strategies for managing the EC's internal market' (2000) 53 CLP 595

Weatherill, S., 'The Commission's Options for Developing EC Consumer Protection and Contract Law: Assessing the Constitutional Basis' (2002) 13 EBLRev 497

Weatherill, S., 'Competence Creep and Competence Control' (2004) 23 YEL 1
Weatherill, S., 'Better Competence Monitoring' (2005) 30 ELRev 23
Weatherill, S., 'Harmonization: How Much, How Little?' (2005) EBLRev 533
Weatherill, S., 'Current Developments, European law, Free movement of goods' (2006) 55 ICLQ 457
Weber, D.M., Annotation of Case C-64/96, *Land Nordrhein-Westfalen v. Uecker and Jacquet*, [1997] ECR I-3171, (1998) 35 CMLRev 1437
Weiler J.H.H. and N.J.S. Lockhart, ''Taking rights seriously'' seriously: the European Court and its fundamental rights jurisprudence – Part I' (1995) 32 CMLRev 51
Weiler J.H.H. and N.J.S. Lockhart, ' ''Taking rights seriously'' seriously: the European Court and its fundamental rights jurisprudence – Part II' (1995) 32 CMLRev 579
Welch, D., 'From ''Euro Beer'' to ''Newcastle Brown'', A Review of European Community Action to Dismantle Divergent ''Food'' Laws' (1983) 22 JCMS 47
White, E., 'In search of the limits to Article 30 of the EEC Treaty' (1989) 26 CMLRev 235
White, R.C.A., 'A fresh look at reverse discrimination?' (1993) 18 ELRev 527
White, R.C.A., 'Conflicting competences: free movement rules and immigration laws' (2004) 29 ELRev 385
White, R.C.A., 'Free movement, equal treatment, and citizenship of the Union' (2005) 54 ICLQ 885
White, R.C.A., 'Residence, Benefit Entitlement and Community Law' (2005) 12 JSSL 10
White, R.C.A., 'The Citizen's Right to Free Movement' (2005) EBLRev 547
White, R.C.A., 'Citizenship of the Union, governance, and equality' (2006) 29 Fordham Int'l LJ 790
Wilkinson, B., 'Towards European Citizenship? Nationality, Discrimination and Free Movement of Workers in the European Union' (1995) 1 EPL 417
Wilsher, D., 'Does Keck discrimination make any sense? An assessment of the non-discrimination principle within the European Single Market' (2008) 33 ELRev 3
Wyatt, D., 'Social security benefits and discrimination by a Member State against its own nationals' (1978) 3 ELRev 488

III. ARTICLES AND DOCUMENTS ON WEBSITES

Commission's Handbook on Implementation of the Services Directive available at <ec.europa.eu/internal_market/services/services-dir/proposal_en.htm#handbook>

Davies, G, 'Services, Citizenship and the Country of Origin Principle', *Mitchell Working Paper Series* 2/2007, available at <www.law.ed.ac.uk/file_download/series/29_servicescitizenshipandthecountryoforiginprinciple.pdf>

De Búrca, G, 'Human Rights: The Charter and Beyond' Jean Monnet Working Paper 10/01 available at <jeanmonnetprogram.org/papers/01/013601.rtf>

'Denmark, immigration and the EU: Hoist by its own policy', published in *The Economist*, 14 August 2008, available at <www.economist.com/world/europe/displaystory.cfm?story_id=11921278&fsrc=RSS>

Kaleda, S.L, 'Extension of the preliminary rulings procedure outside the scope of Community law: "The Dzodzi line of cases" ', European Integration online Papers (EIoP), Vol. 4, No. 11, October 19, 2000 available at <eiop.or.at/eiop/texte/2000-011a.htm>

Riley, A, 'The EU Reform Treaty & the Competition Protocol: Undermining EC Competition Law', CEPS Policy brief No. 142, September 2007, available at <shop.ceps.eu/BookDetail.php?item_id=1541>

Table of Cases and Secondary Legislation

I. TABLE OF CASES

a) EUROPEAN COURT OF JUSTICE

Abrahamsson and Anderson v. Fogelqvist, Case No. C-407/98 [2000] ECR I-5539
Administration des Douanes et Droits Indirects v. Legros and Others, Case No. C-163/90 [1992] ECR I-4625
A.J. van Pommeren-Bourgondiën v. Raad van Bestuur van de Sociale verzekeringsbank, Case No. C-227/03 [2005] ECR I-6101
Alfa Vita Vassilopoulos AE v. Elliniko Dimosio and Nomarkhiaki Aftodiikisi Ioanninon, Joined Cases C-158/04 and C-159/04 [2006] ECR I-8135
Alliance for Natural Health and Others, Joined Cases C-154/04 and C-155/04 [2005] ECR I-6451
Allué and Coonan v. Università degli studi di Venezia, Case No. 33/88 [1989] ECR 1591
Alpine Investments BV v. Minister van Financiën, Case No. C-384/93 [1995] ECR I-1141
ANAV v. Comune di Bari and AMTAB Servizio Spa, Case No. C-410/04 [2006] ECR I-3303
Andersen og Jensen ApS v. Skatteministeriet, Case No. C-43/00 [2002] ECR I-379
Angonese v. Cassa di Risparmio di Bolzano Spa, Case No. C-281/98 [2000] ECR I-4139
Anomar v. Estado português, Case No. C-6/01 [2003] ECR I-8621
A-Punkt Schmuckhandel v. Schmidt, Case No. C-441/04 [2006] ECR I-2093
ARD v. PRO Sieben Media, Case No. C-6/98 [1999] ECR I-7599

ARGE Gewässerschutz v. Bundesministerium für Land- und Forstwirtschaft, Case No. C-94/99 [2000] ECR I-11037
Arnold André GmbH & Co. KG v. Landrat des Kreises Herford, Case No. C-434/02 [2004] ECR I-11825
Aslanidou v. Ypourgos Ygeias & Pronoias, Case No. C-142/04 [2005] ECR I-7181
ASM Brescia SpA v. Comune di Rodengo Saiano, Case No. C-347/06, judgment of 17 July 2008, not yet reported
Asscher v. Staatssecretaris van Financiën, Case No. C-107/94 [1996] ECR I-3089
Association des Centres disributeurs Édouard Leclerc and others v. SARL 'Au blé vert' and others, Case No. 229/83 [1985] ECR 1
Auer v. Ministère Public (No. 2), Case No. 271/82 [1983] ECR 2727

Bagnasco and Others v. Banca Popolare di Novara soc. Coop. arl. (BNP) and Cassa di Risparmio di Genova e Imperia SpA (Carige), Joined Cases C-215/96 and C-216/96 [1999] ECR I-135
Baldinger v. Pensionsversicherungsanstalt der Arbeiter, Case No. C-386/02 [2004] ECR I-8411
BASF AG v. Prasident des Deutschen Patentamts, Case No. C-44/98 [1999] ECR I-6269
Baumbast and R v. Secretary of State for the Home Department, Case C-413/99 [2002] ECR I-7091
Béguelin Import v. SAGL Import-Export and Others, Case No. 22/71 [1971] ECR 949
Belgapom v. ITM and Vocarex, Case No. C-36/94 [1995] ECR I-2647
Belgium v. Spain, Case No. C-388/95 [2000] ECR I-3121
Berliner Kindl Brauerei AG v. Andreas Siepert, Case No. C-208/98 [2000] ECR I-1741
BIAO v. Finanzamt für Großunternehmen in Hamburg, Case No. C-306/99 [2003] ECR I-1
Bic Benelux SA v. Belgian State, Case No. C-13/96 [1997] ECR I-1753
Blaizot v. University of Liège and Others, Case No. 24/86 [1988] ECR 379
BNIC v. Clair, Case No. 123/83 [1985] ECR 391
Bond van Adverteerders v. Netherlands, Case No. 352/85 [1988] ECR 2085
Broekmeulen v. Huisarts Registratie Commissie, Case No. 246/80 [1981] ECR 2311
Bussone v. Ministro dell'agricoltura e foreste, Case No. 31/78 [1978] ECR 2429

Cadbury Schweppes plc & Cadbury Schweppes Overseas Ltd v. Commisioners of Inland Revenue, Case No. C-196/04 [2006] ECR I-7995
CaixaBank France v. Ministere de l'Economie, des Finances et de l'Industrie, Case No. C-442/02 [2004] ECR I-8961
Canal Satélite Digital SL v. Administracíon General del Estato, Case No. C-390/99 [2002] ECR I-607
Carbonati Apuani Srl v. Comune di Carrara, Case No. C-72/03 [2004] ECR I-8027

Carpenter v. Secretary of State for the Home Department, Case No. C-60/00 [2002] ECR 6279
Castelli v. ONPTS, Case No. 261/83 [1984] ECR 3199
C. Baars v. Inspecteur der Belastingdienst Particulieren/Ondernemingen Gorinchem, Case No. C-251/98 [2000] ECR I-2787
C. C. van de Bijl v. Staatssecretaris van Economische Zaken, Case No. 130/88 [1989] ECR 3039
Centre public d'aide sociale de Courcelles v. Lebon, Case No. 316/85 [1987] ECR 2811
Centro Europa 7 Srl v. Ministero delle Comunicazioni e Autorità per le garanzie nelle comunicazioni and Direzione generale per le concessioni e le autorizzazioni del Ministero delle Comunicazioni, Case No. C-380/05, judgment of 31 January 2008, not yet reported
Centro Servizi Spediporto Srl v. Spedizioni Marittima del Golfo Srl, Case No. C-96/94 [1995] ECR I-2883
Centros Ltd v. Erhvervs- og Selskabsstyrelsen, Case No. C-212/97 [1999] ECR I-1459
CIA Security International SA v. Signalson SA and Securitel SPRL, Case No. C-194/94 [1996] ECR I-2201
Cinéthèque SA and others v. Fédération nationale des cinemas français, Joined Cases 60 and 61/84 [1985] ECR 2605
Cipolla v. Portolese and *Macrino and Capodarte v. Meloni*, Joined Cases C-94/04 and C-202/04 [2006] ECR I-11421
Coenen v. Sociaal-Economische Raad, Case No. 39/75 [1975] ECR 1547
Colim NV v. Bigg's Continent Noord NV, Case No. C-33/97 [1999] ECR I-3175
Collins v. Secretary of State for Work and Pensions, Case No. C-138/02 [2004] ECR I-2703
Commission v. Belgium, Case No. C-278/94 [1996] ECR I-4307
Commission v. Belgium, Case No. C-408/03 [2006] 2 CMLR 41
Commission v. Council (titanium dioxide), Case No. C-300/89 [1991] ECR I-2867
Commission v. Denmark, Case No. C-192/01 [2003] ECR I-9693
Commission v. Denmark (motor vehicles), Case No. C-464/02 [2005] ECR I-7929
Commission v. France (Code de Travail Maritime), Case No. 167/73 [1974] ECR 359
Commission v. France, Case No. 152/78 [1980] ECR 2299
Commission v. France, Case No. 269/83 [1985] ECR 837
Commission v. France (tourist guides), Case No. C-154/89 [1991] ECR I-659
Commission v. France (Strawberries), Case No. C-265/95 [1997] ECR I-6959
Commission v. France (foie gras), Case No. C-184/96 [1998] ECR I-6197
Commission v. France, Case No. C-23/99 [2000] ECR I-7653
Commission v. France, Case No. C-24/00 [2004] ECR I-1277
Commission v. Germany (German Beer), Case No. 178/84 [1987] ECR 1227
Commission v. Germany (Insurance Services), Case No. 205/84 [1986] ECR 3755
Commission v. Germany (Label of origin and quality), Case No. C-325/00 [2002] ECR I-9977

Commission v. Germany (subsidy for the construction or purchase of a dwelling), Case No. C-152/05, judgment of 17 January 2008, not yet reported
Commission v. Germany (psychotherapists), Case No. C-456/05, judgment of 6 December 2007, not yet reported
Commission v. Greece (Greek Beer), Case No. 176/84 [1987] ECR 1193
Commission v. Greece (Baby milk), Case No. C-391/92 [1995] ECR I-1621
Commission v. Italy (subsidies for the purchase of national vehicles), Case No. 103/84 [1986] ECR 1759
Commission v. Italy, Case No. C-289/94 [1996] ECR I-4405
Commission v. Italy, Case No. C-35/96 [1998] ECR I-3851
Commission v. Italy, Case No. C-424/98 [2000] ECR-4001
Commission v. Italy (Chocolate), Case No. C-14/00 [2003] ECR I-513
Commission v. Italy, Case No. C-270/02 [2004] ECR I-1559
Commission v. Netherlands, Case No. C-50/06 [2007] ECR I-4384
Commission v. Portugal, Case No. C-432/03 [2005] ECR I-9665
Commission v. Spain, Case No. C-358/01 [2003] ECR I-13145
Commission v. UK (tax arrangements for wine), Case No. 170/78 [1983] ECR 2265
Commission v. UK (Indications of origin), Case No. 207/83 [1985] ECR 1201
Commission v. UK (Dim-Dip Headlights), Case No. 60/86 [1988] ECR 3921
Coname v. Comune di Cingia de' Botti, Case No. C-231/03 [2005] ECR I-7287
Confederación Española de Empresarios de Estaciones de Servicio v. Compañía Española de Petróleos SA, Case No. C-217/05 [2006] ECR I-11987
Conseil National de l'Ordre des Architects v. Dreessen, Case No. C-31/00 [2002] ECR I-663
Corsica Ferries Italia Srl v. Corpo dei Piloti del Porto di Genova, Case No. C-18/93 [1994] ECR I-1783
Cowan v. Le Trésor Public, Case No. 186/87 [1989] ECR 195
Criminal proceedings against Aubertin and others, Joined Cases C-29/94, C-30/94, C-31/94, C-32/94, C-33/94, C-34/94 and C-35/94 [1995] ECR I-301
Criminal proceedings against Bekaert, Case No. 204/87 [1988] ECR 209
Criminal proceedings against Bickel and Franz, Case No. C-274/96 [1998] ECR I-7637
Criminal proceedings against Bluhme, Case No. C-67/97 [1998] ECR I-8033
Criminal proceedings against Bouchoucha, Case No. C-61/89 [1990] ECR I-3551
Criminal proceedings against Burmanjer, Van Der Linden and De Jong, Case No. C-20/03 [2005] ECR I-4133
Criminal proceedings against Calfa, Case No. C-348/96 [1999] ECR I-11
Criminal proceedings against Franzén, Case No. C-189/95 [1997] ECR I -5909
Criminal proceedings against Keck and Mithouard, Joined Cases C-267/91 and C-268/91 [1993] ECR I-6097
Criminal proceedings against Lindqvist, Case No. C-101/01 [2003] ECR I-12971
Criminal proceedings against Nadin, Nadin-Lux SA and Durré, Joined Cases C-151/04 and C-152/04 [2005] ECR I-11203
Criminal proceedings against Niño and others, Joined Cases 54 and 91/88 and 14/89 [1990] ECR 3537

Criminal proceedings against Gervais et al., Case No. C-17/94 [1995] ECR I-4353
Criminal proceedings against Guimont, Case No. C-448/98 [2000] ECR I-10663
Criminal proceedings against Heinonen, Case No. C-394/97 [1999] ECR I-3599
Criminal proceedings against Ledoux, Case No. 127/86 [1988] ECR 3741
Criminal proceedings against Lemmens, Case No. C-226/97 [1998] ECR I-3711
Criminal proceedings against Lindberg, Case No. C-267/03 [2005] ECR I-3247
Criminal proceedings against Lopez Brea, Joined Cases C-330/90 and C-331/90 [1992] ECR I-323
Criminal proceedings against Mathot, Case No. 98/86 [1987] ECR 809
Criminal proceedings against Morais, Case No. C-60/91 [1992] ECR I-2085
Criminal proceedings against Prantl, Case No. 16/83 [1984] ECR 1299
Criminal proceedings against Peralta, Case No. C-379/92 [1994] ECR I-3453
Criminal proceedings against Pistre, Joined Cases C-321/94, C-322/94, C-323/94 and C-324/94 [1997] ECR I-2343
Criminal proceedings against Placanica, Palazzese and Sorricchio, Joined Cases C-338/04, C-359/04 and C-360/04 [2007] ECR I-1891
Criminal proceedings against Sanz de Lera, Joined Cases C-163, 165 and 250/94 [1995] ECR I-4821
Criminal proceedings against Skanavi and Chryssanthakopoulos, Case No. C-193/94 [1996] ECR I-929
Criminal proceedings against Tomatis and Fulchiron, Case No. C-384/89 [1991] ECR I-127
Criminal proceedings against Vajnai, Case No. C-328/04 [2005] ECR I-8577
Criminal proceedings against Van Buynder, Case No. C-152/94 [1995] ECR I-3981
Criminal proceedings against Van der Burg, Case No. C-278/99 [2001] ECR I-2015
Criminal proceedings against Van de Haar, Joined Cases 177 and 178/82 [1984] ECR 1797
Criminal proceedings against Van Lent, Case No. C-232/01 [2003] ECR I-11525
Criminal proceedings against Wijsenbeek, Case No. C-378/97 [1999] ECR I-6207

De Bobadilla v. Museo Nacional del Prado, Case No. C-234/97 [1999] ECR I-4773
De Cuyper v. Office national de l'emploi, Case No. C-406/04 [2006] ECR I-6947
Defrenne v. Sabena, Case No. 43/75 [1976] ECR 455
Deliège v. Ligue Francophone de Judi et Disciplines Associées ASBL, Joined Cases C-51/96 and C-191/97 [2000] ECR I-2549
Demirel v. Stadt Schwäbisch Gmünd, Case No. 12/86 [1987] ECR 3719
Deutscher Apothekerverband eV v. 0800 DocMorris NV and Jacques Waterval, Case No. C-322/01 [2003] ECR I-14887
D'Hoop v.Office national de l'emploi, Case No. C-224/98 [2002] ECR I-6191
DIP SpA et al. v. Comune di Bassano del Grappa et al, Joined Cases C-140/94, C-141/94 and C-142/94 [1995] ECR I-3527

Douwe Egberts NV v. Westrom Pharma NV and Christophe Souranis, carrying on business under the commercial name of 'Etablissements FICS' and Douwe Egberts NV v. FICS-World BVBA, Case No. C-239/02 [2004] ECR I-7007
Drei Glocken GmbH and Gertraud Kritzinger v. USL Centro-Sud and Provincia autonoma di Bolzano, Case No. 407/85 [1988] ECR 4233
Du Pont de Nemours Italiana SpA v. Unità sanitaria locale No 2 di Carrara, Case No. 21/88 [1990] ECR I-889
Dzodzi v. Belgian State, Joined Cases 297/88 and 197/89 [1990] ECR I-3763

EARL de Kerlast v. Union régionale de coopératives agricoles (Unicopa) and Coopérative du Trieux, Case No. C-15/95 [1997] ECR I-1961
ED Srl v. Italo Fenocchio, Case No. C-412/97 [1999] ECR I-3845
Emsland-Stärke GmbH v. Hauptzollamt Hamurg-Jonas, Case No. C-110/99 [2000] ECR I-11569
Eggers v. Freie Hansestadt Bremen, Case No. 13/78 [1978] ECR 1935
Eismann Alto Adige Srl v. Ufficio IVA di Bolzano, Case No. C-217/94 [1996] ECR I-5287
Eman and Sevinger v. College van burgemeester en wethouders van Den Haag, Case No. C-300/04 [2006] ECR I-8055
ERT v. Dimotiki Etairia Pliroforissis and others, Case No. C-260/89 [1991] ECR I-2925
Esso Española v. Comunidad Autónoma de Canarias, Case No. C-134/94 [1995] ECR I-4223
Etablissements Consten SA and Grundig-Verkaufs-GmbH v. Commission, Joined Cases 56 and 58/64 [1966] ECR 229
Établissements Delhaize Freres et Compagnie Le Lion SA v. Promalvin and AGE Bodegas Unidas, Case No. C-47/90 [1992] ECR I-3669

Faccini Dori v. Recreb Srl, Case No. C-91/92 [1994] ECR I-3325
Fascicolo and Others v. Regione Puglia and others, Joined Cases C-10/02 and C-11/02 [2004] ECR I-11107
Federconsorzi v. Azienda di Stato per gli Interventi nel Mercato Agricolo, Case No. C-88/91 [1992] ECR I-4035
Fidium Finanz AG v. Bundesanstalt für Finanzdienstleistungsaufsicht, Case No. C-452/04 [2006] ECR I-9521
Finanzamt Köln-Altstadt v. Schumacker, Case No. C-279/93 [1995] ECR I-225
Finanzamt Offenbach am Main-Land v. Keller Holding GmbH, Case No. C-471/04 [2006] ECR I-2107
Fiorini (neé Cristini) v. Société Nationale des Chemins de Fer Français, Case No. 32/75 [1975] ECR 1085
Forcheri v. Belgium, Case No. 152/82 [1983] ECR 2323
Förster v. IB-Groep, Case No. C-158/07, judgment of 18 November 2008, not yet reported.
Fournier v. Van Werven, Case No. C-73/89 [1992] ECR I-5621
France v. Commission, Case No. 202/88 [1991] ECR I-1223

France v. Commission, Case No. C-41/93 [1994] ECR I-1829
Francovich and Others, Joined Cases C-6/90 and C-9/90 [1991] ECR I-5357
Frascogna v. Caisse des Dépôts et consignations, Case No. 157/84 [1985] ECR 1739
Freskot AE v. Elliniko Dimosio, Case No. C-355/00 [2003] ECR I-5263
F.W.L. de Groot v. Staatssecretaris van Financiën, Case No. C-385/00 [2002] ECR I-11819

Garcia Avello v. État belge, Case No. C-148/02 [2003] ECR I-11613
Gaston Schul Douane-Expediteur BV v. Inspecteur der Invoerrechten en Accijnzen, Case No. 15/81 [1982] ECR 1409
GB-INNO-BM v. Confédération du commerce luxembourgeois, Case No. 362/88 [1990] ECR I-667
Gebhard v. Consiglio dell'Ordine degli Avvocato e Procuratori di Milano, Case No. C-55/94 [1995] ECR I-4165
Germany v. Council, Case No. C-359/92 [1994] ECR I-3681
Germany v. Parliament and Council (Tobacco Advertising I), Case No. C-376/98 [2000] ECR I-8419
Germany v. Parliament and Council (Directive 2003/33) (*Tobacco Advertising II*), Case No. C-380/03 [2006] ECR I-11573
Geurts and Vogten v. Administratie van de BTW, registratie en domeinen, Belgische Staat, Case No. C-464/05, judgment of 25 October 2007, not yet reported
Geven v. Land Nordrhein-Westfalen, Case No. C-213/05 [2007] ECR I-6347
Gilly v. Directeur des Services Fiscaux du Bas-Rhin, Case No. C-336/96 [1998] ECR I-2793
Giloy v. Hauptzollamt Frankfurt am Main-Ost, Case No. C-130/95 [1997] ECR I-4291
Gmurzynska-Bsher, Case No. C-231/89 [1990] ECR I-4003
Gøttrup-Klim e.a. Grovvareforeninger v. Dansk Landbrugs Grovvareselskab AmbA, Case No. C-250/92 [1994] ECR I-5641
Government of the French Community and Walloon Government v. Flemish Government, Case No. C-212/06, judgment of 1 April 2008, not yet reported
Graf v. Filzmoser Maschinenbau GmbH, Case No. C-190/98 [2000] ECR I-493
Gravier v. City of Liège, Case No. 293/83 [1985] ECR 593
Greenham v. Abel, Case No. C-95/01 [2004] ECR I-1333
Grzelczyk v. Centre public d'aide sociale d'Ottignies-Louvain-la-Neuve, Case No. C-184/99 [2001] ECR I-6193
Gullung v. Conseil de l'Ordre des Avocats, Case No. 292/86 [1988] ECR 111

Hartmann v. Freistaat Bayern, Case No. C-212/05 [2007] ECR I-6303
Hauer v. Land Rheinland-Pfalz, Case No. 44/79 [1979] ECR 3727
Heirs of M.E.A. van Hilten-van der Heijden v. Inspecteur van de Belastingdienst/Particulieren/Ondernemingen buitenland te Heerlen, Case No. C-513/03 [2006] ECR I-1957
Hendrix v. Raad van Bestuur van het Uitvoeringsinstituut Werknemersverzekeringen, Case No. C-287/05 [2007] ECR I-6909
Herrera v. Servicio Cántabro de Salud, Case No. C-466/04 [2006] ECR I-5341

Höfner and Elser v. Mactroton GmbH, Case No. C-41/90 [1991] ECR I-1979
Hönig v. Stadt Stockach, Case No. C-128/94 [1995] ECR I-3389
Huber v. Bundesrepublik Deutschland, Case No. C-524/06, not yet decided
Hugin Kassaregister AB and Hugin Cash Registers Ltd v. Commission, Case No. 22/78 [1979] ECR 1869
Hurd v. Jones (Her Majesty's Inspector of Taxes), Case No. 44/84 [1986] 2 CMLR 1

Ianelli & Volpi v. Meroni, Case No. 74/76 [1977] 2 CMLR 688
International Handelsgesellschaft mbH v. Einfuhr- und Vorratsstelle für Getreide und Futtermittel, Case No. 11/70 [1970] ECR 1125
Inzirillo v. Caisse d'allocations familiales de l'Arrondissement de Lyon, Case No. 63/76 [1976] ECR 2057
Iorio v. Azienda autonoma delle ferrovie dello Stato, Case No. 298/84 [1986] ECR 247
Istituto Chemioterapico Italiano S.p.A. and Commercial Solvents Corporation v. Commission, Joined Cases 6 and 7/73 [1974] ECR 223
ITC Innovative Technology Center GmbH v. Bundesagentur für Arbeit, Case No. C-208/05 [2007] ECR I-181

Jäger v. Finanzamt Kusel-Landstuhl, Case No. C-256/06, judgment of 17 January 2008, not yet reported
Jägerskiöld v. Gustafsson, Case No. C-97/98 [1999] ECR I-7319
Jersey Produce Marketing Organisation Ltd v. States of Jersey and Jersey Potato Export Marketing Board, Case No. C-293/02 [2005] ECR I-9543
Jia v. Migrationsverket, Case No. C-1/05 [2007] ECR I-1
Jongeneel Kaas BV and others v. The Netherlands and Stichting Centraal Orgaan Zuivelcontrole, Case No. 237/82 [1984] ECR 483

Kalanke v. Bremen, Case No. C-450/93 [1995] ECR I-3051
Kamer van Koophandel en Fabrieken voor Amsterdam v. Inspire Art, Case No. C-167/01 [2001] ECR I-10155
Kapasakalis, Skiathitis and Kougiagkas v. Greek State, Joined Cases C-225/95, C-226/95 and C-227/95 [1998] ECR I-4239
Karner Industrie-Auktionen GmbH v. Troostwijk GmbH, Case No. C-71/02 [2004] ECR I-3025
Kempf v. Staatsecretaris van Justitie, Case No. 139/85 [1986] ECR 1741
Kenny v. Insurance Officer, Case No. 1/78 [1978] ECR 1489
Khalil and others v. Bundesanstalt für Arbeit, Joined Cases C-95/99, C-96/99, C-97/99, C-98/99 and C-180/99 [2001] ECR I-7413
Kleinwort Benson Ltd v. City of Glasgow, Case No. C-346/92 [1995] ECR I-615
Knoors v. Secretary of State for Economic Affairs, Case No. 115/78 [1979] ECR 399
Kofisa Italia Srl v. Ministero delle Finanze, Case No. C-1/99 [2001] ECR I-207
Konstantinidis v. Stadt Altensteig-Standesamt, Case No. C-168/91 [1993] ECR I-1191

Konsumentombudsmannen (KO) v. De Agostini (Svenska) Förlag AB and TV-Shop I Sverige AB, Joined Cases C-34/95, C-35/95 and C-36/95 [1997] ECR I-3843
Konsumentombudsmannen v. Gourmet International Products AB (GIP), Case No. C-405/98 [2001] ECR I-1795
Koua Poirrez v. Caisse d'allocations familiales de la region parisienne, substituée par la Caisse d'allocations familiales de la Seine-Saint-Denis, Case No. C-206/91 [1992] ECR 6685
Kranemann v. Land Nordrhein-Westfalen, Case No. C-109/04 [2005] ECR I-2421
Krantz GmbH & Co. v. Ontvanger der Directe Belastingen and Netherlands, Case No. 69/88 [1990] ECR I-583
Kraus v. Land Baden-Württemberg, Case No. C-19/92 [1993] ECR I-1663
Kremzow v. Republic Österreich, Case No. C-299/95 [1997] ECR I-2629

Lancry SA v. Direction Générale des Douanes, Joined Cases C-363/93, C-407/93, C-409/93 and C-411/93 [1994] ECR I-3957
Land Nordrhein-Westfalen v. Uecker and Jacquet, Case No. C-64/96 [1997] ECR I-3171
Laval un Partneri Ltd v. Svenska Byggnadsarbetareförbundet and others, Case No. C-341/05, judgment of 18 December 2007, not yet reported
Lawrie-Blum v. Land Baden-Württemberg, Case No. 66/85 [1986] ECR 2121
Leclerc-Siplec v. TF1 Publicité, Case No. C-412/93 [1995] ECR I-179
Lenoir v. Caisse d'allocations familiales des Alpes-Maritimes, Case No. 313/86 [1988] ECR 5391
Les Assurances du Crédit SA and Compagnie Belge d'Assurance Crédit SA v. Council and Commission, Case No. C-63/89 [1991] ECR I-1799
Leur-Bloem v. Inspecteur der Belastingdienst/Ondernemingen Amsterdam 2, Case No. C-28/95 [1997] ECR I-4161
Levin v. Staatssecretaris van Justitie, Case No. 53/81 [1982] ECR 1035
Lidl Belgium GmbH & Co. KG v. Etablissementen Franz Colruyt NV, Case No. C-356/04 [2006] ECR I-08501
Lidl Italia Srl v. Comune di Stradella, Case No. C-303/04 [2005] ECR I-7865
Lucien Ortscheit GmbH v. Eurim-Pharm Arzneimittel GmbH, Case No. C-320/93 [1994] ECR I-5243
Luisi and Carbone v. Ministero del Tesoro, Joined Cases 286/82 and 26/83 [1984] ECR 377
Lyyski v. Universität Umeå, Case No. C-40/05 [2007] ECR I-99

Mangold v. Helm, Case No. C-144/04 [2005] ECR I-9981
Marks & Spencer plc v. David Halsey (HM Inspector of Taxes), Case No. C-446/03 [2005] ECR I-10837
Marschall v. Land Nordrhein-Westfalen, Case No. C-409/95 [1997] ECR I-6363
Martínez Sala v. Freistaat Bayern, Case No. C-85/96 [1998] ECR I-2691
Masgio v. Bundesknappschaft, Case No. C-10/90 [1991] ECR I-1119
Mattern and Cikotic v. Ministre du Travail et de l'Emploi, Case No. C-10/05 [2006] ECR I-3145

Mauri v. Ministero della Giustizia, Commissione per gli esami di avvocato presso la Corte d'appello di Milano, Case No. C-250/03 [2005] ECR I-1267
Metock and Others v. Minister for Justice, Equality and Law Reform, Case No. C-127/08 judgment of 25 July 2008, not yet reported
Micheletti v. Delegación del Gobierno en Cantabria, Case No. C-369/90 [1992] ECR I-4239
Michelin v. Commission, Case No. 322/81 [1983] ECR 3461
Middleburgh v. Chief Adjudication Officer, Case No. C-15/90 [1991] ECR I-4655
Miller International Schallplatten GmbH v. Commission, Case No. 19/77 [1978] ECR 131
Ministère Public v. Auer, Case No. 136/78 [1979] ECR 437
Ministère Public v. Gauchard, Case No. 20/87 [1987] ECR 4879
Ministère Public v. Verbrugge, Case No. 160/86 [1987] ECR 1783
Minister voor Vreemdelingenzaken en Integratie v. Eind, Case No. C-291/05, judgment of 11 December 2007, not yet reported
Ministerul Administrației și Internelor – Direcția Generală de Pașapoarte București v. Jipa, Case No. C-33/07, judgment of 10 July 2008, not yet reported
Ministre de l'Intérieur v. Oteiza Olazabal, Case No. C-100/01 [2002] ECR I-10981
Monsees v. Unabhängiger Verwaltungssenat für Kärnten, Case No. C-350/97 [1999] ECR I-2921
Morellato v. Comune di Padova, Case No. C-416/00 [2003] ECR I-9343
Morgan v. Bezirksregierung Köln; Bucher v. Landrat des Kreises Düren, Joined Cases C-11 and 12/06, judgment of 23 October 2007, not yet reported
Morson and Jhanjan v. Netherlands, Joined Cases 35 and 36/82 [1982] ECR 3723
Moser v. Land Baden-Württemberg, Case No. 180/83 [1984] ECR 2539
Mr and Mrs F. v. Belgian State, Case No. 7/75 [1975] ECR 679
Musique Diffusion Française and others v. Commission, Joined Cases 100-103/80 [1983] ECR 1825
Mutsch v. Ministère public, No. [1985] ECR 2681
My v. Office national des pensions, Case No. C-293/03 [2004] ECR I-12013

N v. Inspecteur van de Belastingdienst Oost/kantoor Almelo, Case No. C-470/04 [2006] ECR I-7409
Nerkowska v. Zaklad Ubezpieczen Spolecznych Oddzial w Koszalinie, Case No. C-499/06, judgment of 22 May 2008, not yet reported
Netherlands v. Parliament (Biotechnology case), Case No. C-377/98 [2001] ECR I-7079
Nederlandse Bakkerij Stichting and Others v. Edah BV, Joined Cases 80 and 159/85 [1986] ECR 3359
Nold KG v. Commission, Case No. 4/73 [1974] ECR 491

Office national de l'emploi v. Deak, [1985] ECR 1873
Office national de l'emploi v. Ioannidis, Case No. C-258/04 [2005] ECR I-8275
O'Flynn v. Adjudication Officer, Case No. C-237/94 [1996] ECR I-2617

Oosthoek's Uitgeversmaatschappij BV, Case No. 286/81 [1982] ECR 4575
Owusu v. N. B. Jackson, trading as 'Villa Holidays Bal-Inn Villas' and others, Case No. C-281/02 [2005] ECR I-1383

P v. S and Cornwall County Council, Case No. C-13/94 [1996] ECR I-2143
Parfums Christian Dior SA and Parfums Christian Dior BV v. Evora BV, Case No. C-337/95 [1997] ECR I-6013
Parking Brixen GmbH v. Gemeinde Brixen and Stadtwerke Brixen AG, Case No. C-458/03 [2005] ECR I-8612
P. B. Groenveld BV v. Produktschap voor Vee en Vlees, Case No. 15/79 [1979] ECR 3409
Peros v. Technico Epimelitirio Ellados, Case No. C-141/04 [2005] ECR I-7163
Petit v. Office National des Pensions, Case No. C-153/91 [1992] ECR I-4973
Phil Collins v. Imtrat Handelsgesellschaft mbH, Joined Cases C-92/92 and C-326/92 [1993] ECR I-5145
Polydor v. Harlequin, Case No. 270/80 [1982] ECR 329
Poseidon Chartering BV v. Marianne Zeeschip VOF and others, Case No. C-3/04 [2006] ECR I-2505
PreussenElektra AG v. Schleswag AG, Case No. C-379/98 [2001] ECR I-2099
Proceedings for a compulsory reconstruction against Smanor SA, Case No. 298/87 [1988] ECR 4489
Procureur de la République and Comité national de defense contre l'alcoolisme v. Waterkeyn and others, Joined Cases 314-316/81 and 83/82 [1982] ECR 4337
Procureur du Roi v. Dassonville, Case No. 8/74 [1974] ECR 837
Procureur du Roi v. Debauve and others, Case No. 52/79 [1980] ECR 833
Procureur du Roi v. Lagauche, Joined Cases C-46/90 and C-93/91 [1993] ECR I-5267
Procureur Général v. Rousseau, Case No. 168/86 [1987] ECR 995
Public Prosecutor v. Cognet, Case No. 355/85 [1986] ECR 3231
Pusa v. Osuuspankkien Keskinäinen Vakuutusyhtiö, Case No. C-224/02 [2004] ECR I-5763

R v. Saunders, Case No. 175/78 [1979] ECR 1129
R v. Minister of Agriculture, Fisheries and Food ex parte Compassion in World Farming, Case No. C-1/96 [1998] ECR I-1251
R v. Secretary of State for the Home Department, ex p. Kaur, Case No. C-192/99 [2001] ECR I-1237
R (ex parte Bidar) v. London Borough of Ealing and Secretary of State for Education and Skills, Case No. C-209/03 [2005] ECR I-2119
Radiosistemi Srl v. Prefetto di Genova, Joined Cases C-388/00 and C-429/00 [2002] ECR I-5845
Raulin v. Minister van Onderwijs en Wetenschappen, Case No. C-357/89 [1992] ECR I-1027
Rechnungshof v. Österreichischer Rundfunk, Case No. C-465/00 [2003] ECR I-4989

Reina v. Landeskreditbank Baden-Werttemberg, Case No. 65/81 [1982] ECR 33
Reisch and Others, Joined Cases C-515/99, C-519/99 to C-524/99 and C-526/99 to C-540/99 [2002] ECR I-2157
Remia BV v. Commission, Case No. 42/84 [1985] ECR 2545
Rewe-Zentrale AG v. Bundesmonopolverwaltung für Branntwein, Case No. 120/78 [1979] ECR 649
Reyners v. Belgium, Case No. 2/74 [1974] ECR 631
Rijksdienst voor Pensioenen v. Robert Engelbrecht, Case No. C-262/97 [2000] ECR I-7321
RI.SAN. Srl v. Comune di Ischia, Case No. C-108/98 [1999] ECR I-5219
Ritter-Coulais v. Finanzamt Germersheim, Case No. C-152/03 [2006] ECR I-1711
Roux v. Belgium, Case No. C-363/89 [1991] ECR I-273
Royal Scholten Honig v. IBAP, Joined Cases 103 and 145/77 [1978] ECR 2037
Royer, Case No. 48/75 [1976] ECR 497
RTT v. GB-Inno-BM, Case No. 18/88 [1991] ECR I-5941
Ruckdeschel & Diamalt, Joined Cases 117/76 and 16/77 [1977] ECR 1769

SA Brasserie de Haecht v. Consorts Wilkin-Janssen, Case No. 23/67 [1967] ECR 407
SA des grandes distilleries Peureux v. Directeur des Services fiscaux de la Haute-Saône et du territoire de Belfort, Case No. 86/78 [1979] ECR 897
Säger v. Dennemeyer & Co. Ltd, Case No. C-76/90 [1991] ECR I-4221
S. A. Krüger v. Directie van de rechtspersoonlijkheid bezittende Dienst Wegverkeer, Criminal proceedings against Hans van Lent, Case No. C-232/01 [2003] ECR I-11525 [2004] ECR I-1191
Salonia v. Poidomani and Baglieri, née Giglio, Case No. 126/80 [1981] ECR 1563
Salzmann, Case No. C-300/01 [2003] ECR I-4899
Sapod Audic v. Eco-Emballages SA, Case No. C-159/00 [2002] ECR I-5031
SARPP v. Chambre syndicale des raffineurs et conditionneurs de sucre de France and others, Case No. C-241/89 [1990] ECR I-4695
SC Belasco and others v. Commission, Case No. 246/86 [1989] ECR 2117
Schempp v. Finanzamt München, Case No. C-403/03 [2005] ECR I-6421
Schilling v. Finanzamt Nürnberg-Süd, Case No. C-209/01 [2003] ECR I-13389
Schmid v. Belgian State, Case No. C-310/91 [1993] ECR I-3011
Schmidberger v. Austria, Case No. C-112/00 [2003] ECR I-5659
Scholz v. Opera Universitaria di Cagliari and Cinzia Porcedda, Case No. C-419/92 [1994] ECR I-505
Schoonbroodt, Case No. C-247/97 [1998] ECR I-8095
Schutzverband gegen unlauteren Wettbewerb v. TK-Heimdienst Sass GmbH, Case No. C-254/98 [2000] ECR I-151
Schwarz v. Finanzamt Bergisch Gladbach, Case No. C-76/05, judgment of 11 September 2007, not yet reported
Scorpio Konzertproduktionen GmbH, Case No. C-290/04 [2006] ECR I-9461
Secretary of State for the Home Department v. Akrich, Case No. C-109/01 [2003] ECR 9607

Sehrer v. Bundesknappschaft, Case No. C-302/98 [2000] ECR I-4585
Servizi Ausiliari Dottori Commercialisti Srl v. Giuseppe Calafiori, Case No. C-451/03 [2006] ECR I-2941
Simitzi v. Dimos Kos, Joined Cases C-485/93 and C-486/93 [1995] ECR I-2655
Smit Transport BV v. Commissie Grensoverschrijdend Beroepsgoederenvervoer, Case No. 126/82 [1983] ECR 73
Società Italiana per l'Oleodotto Transalpino (SIOT) v. Ministero delle finanze, Ministero della marina mercantile, Circoscrizione doganale di Trieste and Ente autonomo del porto di Trieste, Case No. 266/81 [1983] ECR 731
Société Civile Agricole du Centre d'insémination de la Crespelle v. Coopérative D'Elevage et d'Insémination Artificielle du Département de la Mayenne, Case No. C-323/93 [1994] ECR I-5077
Société Générale Alsacienne de Banque SA v. Koestler, Case No. 15/78 [1978] ECR 1971
Société Technique Minière v. Maschinenbau Ulm, Case No. 56/65 [1966] ECR 235
Sodemare SA, Anni Azzuri Holdings SpA & Anni Azzuri Rezzato Srl v. Regione Lombardia, Case No. C-70/95 [1997] ECR I-3395
Spain v. Council, Case No. C-350/92 [1995] ECR I-1985
Staatssecretaris van Financiën v. Feron, Case No. C-170/03 [2005] ECR I-2299
State of Netherlands v. Reed, Case No. 59/85 [1986] ECR 1283
Steen v. Deutsche Bundespost, Case No. C-332/90 [1992] ECR I-341
Steen v. Deutsche Bundespost (No. 2), Case No. C-132/93 [1994] ECR I-2715
Steymann v. Staatsecretaris van Justitie, Case No. 196/87 [1988] ECR 6159
Stöber and Pereira v. Bundesanstalt Für Arbeit, Joined Cases C-4/95 and C-5/95 [1997] ECR I-511
Stoke-on-Trend and Norwich City Councils v. B & Q plc, Case No. C-169/91 [1992] ECR I-6635
Stylianakis v. Elliniko Dimosio, Case No. C-92/01 [2003] ECR I-1291
Svensson and Gustavsson v. Ministre du Logement et de l'Urbanisme, Case No. C-484/93 [1995] ECR I-3955
Syndesmos ton en Elladi Touristikon kai Taxidiotikon Grafeion v. Ypourgos Ergasias (SETTG), Case No. C-398/95 [1997] ECR I-3091

Tas-Hagen and Tas v. Raadskamer WUBO van de Pensioen- en Uitkeringsraad, Case No. C-192/05 [2006] ECR I-10451
Terhoeve v. Inspecteur van de Belastingdiens Particulieren/Ondernemingen Buitenland, Case No. C-18/95 [1999] ECR I-345
The International Transport Workers' Federation and The Finnish Seamen's Union v. Viking Line ABP and OÜ Viking Line Eesti, Case No. C-438/05, judgment of 11 December 2007, not yet reported
The Queen v. H.M. Treasury and Commissioners of Inland Revenue ex parte Daily Mail and General Trust plc, Case No. 81/87 [1988] ECR 5483
The Queen v. Immigration Appeal Tribunal, ex parte Antonissen, Case No. C-292/89 [1991] ECR I-745

The Queen v. Immigration Appeal Tribunal and Singh, ex parte Secretary of State for the Home Department, Case No. C-370/90 [1992] ECR I-4265

The Queen v. Secretary of State for Health, ex parte British American Tobacco (Investments) Ltd and others, Case No. C-491/01 [2002] ECR I-11453

The Queen v. Secretary of State for Health, ex parte Gallaher Ltd, Imperial Tobacco Ltd and Rothmans International Tobacco (UK) Ltd, Case No. C-11/92 [1993] ECR 3545

The Queen v. Secretary of State for the Home Department ex parte Shingara and Radiom, Joined Cases C-65/95 and C-111/95 [1997] ECR I-3343

The Queen on the application of Swedish Match AB and Swedish Match UK Ltd v. Secretary of State for Health, Case No. C-210/03 [2004] ECR I-11893

The Society for the Protection of Unborn Children Ireland Ltd v. Grogan, Case No. C-159/90 [1991] ECR I-4685

Thieffry v. Conseil de l'Ordre des Avocats à la Cour de Paris, Case No. 71/76 [1977] ECR 1199

Thomasdunger GmbH v. Oberfinanzdirektion Frankfurt am Main, Case No. 166/84 [1985] ECR 3001

Torfaen BV v. B & Q plc, Case No. 145/88 [1989] ECR 765

T. Port GmbH & Co. KG v. Bundesanstalt für Landwirtschaft und Ernährung, Case No. C-68/95 [1996] ECR I-6065

Tridon v. Fédération départementale des cahsseurs de l'Isère, Case No. C-510/99 [2001] ECR I-7777

Trojani v. Centre public d'aide sociale de Bruxelles, Case No. C-456/02 [2004] ECR I-7573

Turpeinen, Case No. C-520/04 [2006] ECR I-10685

TV10, Case No. C-23/93 [1994] ECR I-4795

UK v. Parliament and Council (Smoke flavourings), Case No. C-66/04 [2005] ECR I-10553

Unilever Italia SpA v. Central Food Spa, Case No. C-443/98 [2000] ECR I-7535

Union Royal Belge des Société de Football Association ASBL & others v. Bosman, Case No. C-415/93 [1995] ECR I-4921

United Pan-Europe Communications Belgium SA and others v. État belge, Case No. C-250/06, judgment of 13 December 2007, not yet reported

Urbing-Adam v. Administration de l'enregistrement et des domains, Case No. C-267/99 [2001] ECR I-7467

USSL No 47 di Biella, Case No. C-134/95 [1997] ECR I-195

Van Binsbergen v. Bestuur van de Bedrijfsvereniging voor de Metaalnijverheid, Case No. 33/74 [1974] ECR 1299

Vereeniging van Cementhandelaren v. Commission, Case No. 8/72 [1972] ECR 977

Vereinigte Familiapress Zeitungsverlags-und vertriebs GmbH v. Heinrich Bauer Verlag, Case No. C-368/95 [1997] ECR I-3689

Veronica Omroep Organisatie, Case No. C-148/91 [1993] ECR I-487

Viacom Outdoor Srl v. Giotto Immobilier SARL, Case No. C-134/03 [2005] ECR I-1167
Völk v. Vervaecke, Case No. 5/69 [1969] ECR 295

Wachauf v. Germany, Case No. 5/88 [1989] ECR 2609
Walt-Wilhelm et al v. Bundeskartellamt, Case No. 14/68 [1969] ECR 1
Werner v. Finanzamt Aachen-Innenstadt, Case No. C-112/91 [1993] ECR I-429
Wood v. Fonds de garantie des victims des actes de terrorisme et d'autres infractions, Case No. C-164/07, judgment of 5 June 2008, not yet reported
Württembergische Milchverwertung-Südmilch AG v. Salvatore Ugliola, Case No. 15/69 [1969] ECR 363

X and Y v. Riksskatteverket, Case No. C-436/00 [2002] ECR I-10829

Zaoui v. Cramif, Case No. 147/87 [1987] ECR 5511
Zhu and Chen v. Secretary of State for the Home Department, Case No. C-200/02 [2004] ECR I-9925

b) COURT OF FIRST INSTANCE

BPB Industries Plc and British Gypsum Ltd v. Commission, Case No. T-65/89 [1993] ECR II-389
Compagnie maritime belge transports SA and Compagnie maritime belge SA, Dafra-Lines A/S, Deutsche Afrika-Linien GmbH & Co. and Nedlloyd Lijnen BV v. Commission, Joined Cases T-24 to 26/93 and T-28/93 [1996] ECR II-1201
Publishers Association v. Commission, Case No. T-66/89 [1992] ECR II-1995
Tate & Lyle plc and others v. Commission, Joined Cases T-202/98, T-204/98 and T-207/98 [2001] ECR II-2035
Tréfilunion SA v. Commission, Case No. T-148/89 [1995] ECR II-1063

c) COMMISSION DECISIONS

Dutch Banks, Commission Decision 99/687 [2000] 4 CMLR 137
Eirpage, Commission Decision 91/562/EEC [1993] 4 CMLR 64
Italian Cast Glass, Commission Decision 80/1334/EEC [1982] 2 CMLR 61
Italian Flat Glass, Commission Decision 81/881/EEC [1982] 3 CMLR 366
Re Vacuum Interrupters Ltd, Commission Decision 77/160/EEC [1977] 1 CMLR D67

d) UK CASES

W (China) and another v. Secretary of State for the Home Department, [2006] All ER (D) 97 (Nov)

The Queen v. Secretary of State for the Home Department ex parte Muhammad Ayub, [1983] 3 CMLR 140

e) GERMAN CASES

Re Residence Permit for an Egyptian National, [1975] 2 CMLR 402

f) IRISH CASES

Wael Kweder v. Minister for Justice, [1996] IR 381

g) ITALIAN CASES

Decision 30 Dec. 1997, No 443, Riv dir Internaz (1998)

II. TABLE OF SECONDARY LEGISLATION

a) REGULATIONS

1612/68 (EEC) Regulation on freedom of movement for workers within the Community, OJ L 257/2, 1968

b) DIRECTIVES

70/50 (EEC) Directive on the abolition of measures which have an effect equivalent to quantitative restrictions on imports and are not covered by other provisions adopted in pursuance of the EEC Treaty, OJ L 13/29, 1970

73/148 (EEC) Directive on the abolition of restrictions on movement and residence within the Community for nationals of Member States with regard to establishment and the provision of services, OJ L 172/14, 1973

83/189 (EEC) Directive laying down a procedure for the provision of information in the field of technical standards and regulations, OJ L 109/8, 1983

88/182 (EEC) Directive amending Directive 83/189 (EEC) laying down a procedure of information in the field of technical standards and regulations, OJ L 81/75, 1988

89/48 (EEC) Directive on a general system for the recognition of higher education diplomas awarded on completion of professional education and training of at least three years' duration, OJ L 19/16, 1989

89/428 (EEC) Directive on procedures for harmonizing the programmes for the reduction and eventual elimination of pollution caused by waste from the titanium dioxide industry, OJ L 201/56, 1989

90/364 (EEC) Directive on the right of residence, OJ L 180/26, 1990

90/365 (EEC) Directive on the right of residence for employees and self-employed persons who have ceased their occupational activity, OJ L 180/28, 1990

92/112 (EEC) Directive on procedures for harmonizing the programmes for the reduction and eventual elimination of pollution caused by waste from the titanium dioxide industry, OJ L 409/11, 1992

93/96 (EEC) Directive on the right of residence for students, OJ L 317/59, 1993

94/10 (EC) Directive materially amending for the second time Directive 83/189 laying down a procedure for the provision of information in the field of technical standards and regulations, OJ L 100/30, 1994

95/46 (EC) Directive on the protection of individuals with regard to the processing of personal data and on the free movement of such data, OJ L 281/31, 1995

98/34 (EC) Directive laying down a procedure for the provision of information in the field of technical standards and regulations and on rules on Information Society services, OJ L 204/37, 1998

98/43 (EC) Directive on the approximation of the laws, regulations and administrative provisions of the Member States relating to the advertising and sponsorship of tobacco products, OJ L 213/9, 1998

98/48 (EC) Directive amending Directive 98/34 laying down a procedure for the provision of information in the field of technical standards and regulations, OJ L 217/18, 1998

2000/43 (EC) Directive implementing the principle of equal treatment between persons irrespective of racial or ethnic origin, OJ L 180/22, 2000

2000/78 (EC) Directive establishing a general framework for equal treatment in employment and occupation, OJ L 303/16, 2000

2001/37 (EC) Directive on the approximation of the laws, regulations and administrative provisions of the Member States concerning the manufacture, presentation and sale of tobacco products, OJ L 194/26, 2001

2003/33 (EC) Directive on the approximation of the laws, regulations and administrative provisions of the Member States relating to the advertising and sponsorship of tobacco products, OJ L 152/16, 2003

2003/86 (EC) Directive on the right to family reunification, OJ L 251/12, 2003

2004/38 (EC) Directive on the right of citizens of the Union and their family members to move and reside freely within the territory of the Member States, OJ L 158/77, 2004

2005/36 (EC) Directive on the recognition of professional qualifications, OJ L 255/22, 2005

2006/54 (EC) Directive on the implementation of the principle of equal opportunities and equal treatment of men and women in matters of employment and occupation (recast), OJ L 204/23, 2006

2006/123 (EC) Directive on services in the internal market, OJ L 376/36, 2006

c) DECISIONS

3052/95 (EC) Decision establishing a procedure for the exchange of information on national measures derogating from the principle of the free movement of goods within the Community, OJ L 321/1, 1995

III. OTHER DOCUMENTS

Communication from the Commission concerning the consequences of the judgment given by the Court of Justice on 20 February 1979 in case 120/78 ('Cassis de Dijon'), OJ C 256/2, 1980

Commission communication concerning the non-respect of certain provisions of Council Directive 83/189/EEC of 28 March 1983 laying down a procedure for the provision of information in the field of technical standards and regulations, OJ C 245/4, 1986

First biennial report on the application of the principle of mutual recognition in product and services markets, SEC (1999) 1106, not published in the Official Journal

Commission's 'Sixteenth Annual Report on Monitoring the Application of Community Law' COM (99) 301 final, OJ C 354/1, 1999

Commission's XXIXth Report on Competition Policy 1999, SEC (2000) 720 final, not published in the Official Journal

Commission's Internal Market Scoreboard 11 (November 2002), available at <www.ec.europa.eu/internal_market/score/docs/score11/score11-text_en.pdf>

Commission's Notice on the effect on trade concept contained in Articles 81 and 82 of the Treaty, OJ C 101/81, 2004

Table of Treaty Articles

European Community Treaty (EC Treaty)	Renumbering following the coming into force of the Treaty of Lisbon
Article 2	Repealed and, in substance, replaced by (the new) Article 3 TEU
Article 3(1)	Repealed and, in substance, replaced by Articles 3-6 TFEU
Article 3(2)	Article 8 TFEU
Article 5	Repealed and, in substance, replaced by (the new)Article 5 TEU
Article 6	Article 11 TFEU
Article 10	Repealed and, in substance, replaced by (the new) Article 4(3) TEU
Article 12	Article 18 TFEU
Article 14	Article 26 TFEU
Article 17	Article 20 TFEU
Article 18	Article 21 TFEU
Article 19	Article 22 TFEU
Article 20	Article 23 TFEU
Article 21	Article 24 TFEU
Article 23	Article 28 TFEU
Article 24	Article 29 TFEU
Article 25	Article 30 TFEU
Article 28	Article 34 TFEU
Article 29	Article 35 TFEU
Article 30	Article 36 TFEU

European Community Treaty (EC Treaty)	**Renumbering following the coming into force of the Treaty of Lisbon**
Article 39	Article 45 TFEU
Article 42	Article 48 TFEU
Article 43	Article 49 TFEU
Article 48	Article 54 TFEU
Article 49	Article 56 TFEU
Article 56	Article 63 TFEU
Article 81	Article 101 TFEU
Article 82	Article 102 TFEU
Article 87	Article 107 TFEU
Article 90	Article 110 TFEU
Article 94	Article 115 TFEU
Article 95	Article 114 TFEU
Article 137	Article 153 TFEU
Article 141	Article 157 TFEU
Article 149	Article 165 TFEU
Article 150	Article 166 TFEU
Article 152	Article 168 TFEU
Article 153	
– paragraphs 1, 3, 4 and 5	Article 169 TFEU
– paragraph 2	Article 12 TFEU
Article 175	Article 192 TFEU
Article 226	Article 258 TFEU
Article 234	Article 267 TFEU
Article 308	Article 352 TFEU

Charter of Fundamental Rights of the European Union

Article 51

Declaration on Nationality of a Member State appended to the TEU

Treaty Articles/Protocols that will come into force once the Treaty of Lisbon is ratified by all Member States and which do not have an equivalent in the current Treaties:

Article 6(1) TEU
Article 51 TEU
Article 9 TFEU

Protocol on the Internal Market and Competition Law

Index

EUMO – EUROPEAN MONOGRAPH SERIES

1. Lamm Betten (ed.), *The Future of European Social Policy* (1991), ISBN 9065445854, ISBN-13 9789065445858.
2. Annemarie Loman, Kamiel Mortelmans, Harry H.G. Post, Stewart Watson, *Culture and Common Law: Before and After Maastricht* (1992), ISBN 9065446389, ISBN-13 9789065446381.
3. John A.E. Vervaele, *Fraud against the Community: The Need for European Fraud Legislation* (1994), ISBN 9065446346, ISBN-13 9789065446343.
4. Philip Raworth, *The Legislative Process in the European Community* (1993), ISBN 9065446907, ISBN-13 9789065446909.
5. Jules Stuyck, *Financial and Monetary Integration in the European Economic Community* (1993), ISBN 9065447180.
6. Jules Stuyck, A.J. Vossestein (eds), *State Entrepreneurship, National Monopolies and European Community Law* (1993), ISBN 9065447733, ISBN-13 9789065447739.
7. Jules Stuyck, A. Looijestijn-Clearie (eds), *The European Economic Area EC-EFTA* (1994), ISBN 9065448152.
8. Rosita B. Bouterse, *Competition and Integration: What Goals Count?* (1995), ISBN 9065448160, ISBN-13 9789065448163.
9. René Barents, *The Agricultural Law of the EC: An Inquiry into the Administrative Law* (1994), ISBN 9065448675, ISBN-13 9789065448675.
10. Nicholas Emiliou, *Principles of Proportionality in European Law: A Comparative Study* (1996), ISBN 9041108661, ISBN-13 9789041108661.
11. Eivind Smith, *National Parliaments as Cornerstones of European Integration* (1996), ISBN 904110898X, ISBN-13 9789041108982.
12. Jan H. Jans, *European Environmental Law* (1996), ISBN 9041108777, ISBN-13 9789041108777.
13. Síofra O'Leary, *The Evolving Concept of Community Citizenship: From the Free Movement of Persons to Union Citizenship* (1997), ISBN 9041108785, ISBN-13 9789041108784.
14. Laurence W. Gormley (ed.), *Current and Future Perspectives on EC Competition Law* (1983), ISBN 904110691X, ISBN-13 9789041106919.
15. Simone White, *Protection of the Financial Interests of the European Communities: The Fight against Fraud and Corruption* (1998), ISBN 9041196471, ISBN-13 9789041196477.
16. Morten P. Broberg, *The European Commission's Jurisdiction to Scrutinize Mergers*, 3rd Edition (2006), ISBN 9041124748, ISBN-13 9789041124746.
17. Doris Hildebrand, *The Role of Economic Analysis in the EC Competition Rules: The European School*, 2nd Edition (2002), ISBN 9041117067, ISBN-13 9789041117069.
18. Christof R.A. Swaak, *European Community Law and the Automobile Industry* (1999), ISBN 9041111409, ISBN-13 9789041111401.

19. Dorthe Dahlgaard Dingel, *Public Procurement: A Harmonization of the National Judicial Review of the Application of European Community Law* (1999), ISBN 9041111611, ISBN-13 9789041111616.
20. John A.E. Vervaele (ed.), *Compliance and Enforcement of European Community Law* (1999), ISBN 9041111514, ISBN-13 9789041111517.
21. Martin Trybus, *European Defence Procurement Law: International and National Procurement Systems as Models for a Liberalized Defence Procurement Market in Europe* (1999), ISBN 9041111670, ISBN-13 9789041111678.
22. Helen Staples, *The Legal Status of Third Country Nationals Resident in the European Union* (1999), ISBN 9041112774, ISBN-13 9789041112774.
23. Damien Geradin (ed.), *The Liberalization of State Monopolies in the European Union and Beyond* (1999), ISBN 9041112642, ISBN-13 9789041112644.
24. Katja Heede, *European Ombudsman: Redress and Control at Union Level* (2000), ISBN 9041114130, ISBN-13 9789041114136.
25. Ulf Bernitz, Joakim Nergelius (eds), *General Principles of European Community Law* (2000), ISBN 9041114025, ISBN-13 9789041114020.
26. Michaela Drahos, *Convergence of Competition Laws and Policies in the European Community* (2002), ISBN 9041115625, ISBN-13 9789041115621.
27. Damien Geradin (ed.), *The Liberalization of Electricity and Natural Gas in the European Union* (2001), ISBN 9041115609, ISBN-13 9789041115607.
28. Gisella Gori, *Towards an EU Right to Education* (2001), ISBN 9041116702, ISBN-13 9789041116703.
29. Brendan P.G. Smith, *Constitution Building in the European Union* (2001), ISBN 9041116958, ISBN-13 9789041116956.
30. Friedl Weiss, Frank Wooldridge, *Free Movement of Persons within the European Community*, 2nd Edition (2007), ISBN 9041125450, ISBN-13 9789041125453.
31. Ingrid Boccardi, *Europe and Refugees: Towards an EU Asylum Policy* (2002), ISBN 9041117091, ISBN-13 9789041117090.
32. John A.E. Vervaele, André Klip (eds), *European Cooperation Between Tax, Customs and Judicial Authorities* (2001), ISBN 9041117474, ISBN-13 9789041117472.
33. Wouter P.J. Wils, *The Optimal Enforcement of EC Antitrust Law: Essays in Law and Economics* (2002), ISBN 9041117571, ISBN-13 9789041117571.
34. Damien Geradin (ed.), *The Liberalization of Postal Services in the European Union* (2002), ISBN 9041117806, ISBN-13 9789041117809.
35. Nick Bernard, *Multilevel Governance in the European Union* (2002), ISBN 9041118128, ISBN-13 9789041118127.
36. Jill Wakefield, *Judicial Protection through the Use of Article 288(2) EC* (2002), ISBN 9041118233, ISBN-13 9789041118233.
37. Sebastiaan Princen, *EU Regulation and Transatlantic Trade* (2002), ISBN 9041118713, ISBN-13 9789041118714.

38. Amaryllis Verhoeven, *The European Union in Search of a Democratic and Constitutional Theory* (2002), ISBN 9041118721.
39. Paul L.C. Torremans, *Cross Border Insolvencies in EU, English and Belgian Law* (2002), ISBN 9041118888, ISBN-13 9789041118882.
40. Malcolm Anderson, Joanna Apap (eds), *Police and Justice Cooperation and the New European Borders* (2002), ISBN 9041118934, ISBN-13 9789041118936.
41. Christin M. Forstinger, *Takeover Law in EU and USA: A Comparative Analysis* (2002), ISBN 9041119191, ISBN-13 9789041119193.
42. Antonio Bavasso, *Communications in EU Antitrust Law: Market Power and Public Interest* (2003), ISBN 9041119744, ISBN-13 9789041119742.
43. Fiona G. Wishlade, *Regional State Aid and Competition Policy in the European Union* (2003), ISBN 9041119752, ISBN-13 9789041119759.
44. Gareth Davies, *Nationality Discrimination in the European Internal Market* (2003), ISBN 9041119981, ISBN-13 9789041119988.
45. René Barents, *The Autonomy of Community Law* (2003), ISBN 9041122516, ISBN-13 9789041122513.
46. Gerhard Dannecker, Oswald Jansen (eds), *Competition Law Sanctioning in the European Union* (2004), ISBN 9041121005, ISBN-13 9789041121004.
47. Nauta Dutilh (ed.), *Dealing with Dominance: The Experience of National Competition Authorities* (2004), ISBN 9041122117, ISBN-13 9789041122117.
48. Stefaan van den Bogaert, *Practical Regulation of the Mobility of Sportsmen in the EU Post Bosman* (2005), ISBN 904112327X, ISBN-13 9789041123275.
49. Katalin Judit Cseres, *Competition Law and Consumer Protection* (2005), ISBN 9041123806, ISBN-13 9789041123800.
50. Philipp Kiiver, *The National Parliaments in the European Union: A Critical View on EU Constitution Building* (2006), ISBN 9041124527, ISBN-13 9789041124524.
51. Alexander Turk, *The Concept of Legislation in European Community Law* (2006), ISBN 9041124721, ISBN-13 9789041124722.
52. Dimitrios Sinaniotis, *The Interim Protection of Individuals before the European and National Courts* (2006), ISBN 9041124985, ISBN-13 9789041124982.
53. M. Holoubek, D. Damjanovic, M. Traimer (eds), *Regulating Content: The European Regulatory Framework for the Media and Related Creative Sectors* (2006), ISBN 9041125973, ISBN-13 9789041125972.
54. Anneli Albi, Jacques Ziller (eds), *The European Constitution and National Constitutions: Ratification and Beyond* (2006), ISBN 9041125248, ISBN-13 9789041125248.
55. Gustavo E. Luengo, *Regulation of Subsidies and State Aids in WTO and EC Law: Conflicts in International Trade Law* (2007), ISBN 9041125477, ISBN-13 9789041125477.

56. Eniko Horvath, *Mandating Identity: Citizenship, Kinship Laws and Plural Nationality in the European Union* (2007), ISBN 9041126627, ISBN-13 9789041126627.
57. Rass Holdgaard, *External Relations Law of the European Community: Legal Reasoning and Legal Discourses* (2007), ISBN 904112604X, ISBN-13 9789041126047.
58. Jill Wakefield, *The Right to Good Administration* (2007), ISBN 904112697X, ISBN-13 9789041126979.
59. Dimitry Kochenov, *EU Enlargement and the Failure of Conditionality: Pre-accession Conditionality in the Fields of Democracy and the Rule of Law* (2008), ISBN 9041126961, ISBN-13 9789041126962.
60. Despina Mavromati, *The Law of Payment Services in the EU: The EC Directive on Payment Services in the Internal Market* (2008), ISBN 9041127003, ISBN-13 9789041127006.
61. Anne Meuwese, *Impact Assessment in EU Lawmaking* (2008), ISBN-13 9789041127204.
62. Ulf Bernitz, Joakim Nergelius and Cecilia Cardner (eds.), *General Principles of EC Law in a Process of Development* (2008), ISBN-13 9789041127051.
63. Johan van de Gronden (ed.), *The EU and WTO Law on Services: Limits to the Realisation of General Interest policies within the Services Markets?* (2008), ISBN-13 9789041128096.
64. Alina Tryfonidou, *Reverse Discrimination in EC Law* (2009), ISBN-13 9789041127518.